TEACHERS' LIVES AND CAREERS

Issues in Education and Training Series: 3

Teachers' Lives and Careers

Edited By
Stephen J. Ball
and
Ivor F. Goodson

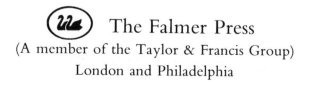 The Falmer Press
(A member of the Taylor & Francis Group)
London and Philadelphia

UK   The Falmer Press, Falmer House, Barcombe, Lewes, East Sussex, BN8 5DL

USA   The Falmer Press, Taylor & Francis Inc., 242 Cherry Street, Philadelphia, PA 19106-1906

First published in 1985

Library of Congress Cataloging in Publication Data

Main entry under title:

Teachers' lives and careers.

  (Issues in education and training series; 3)
  Selected papers from a conference held Sept. 1983 at St. Hilda's College, Oxford.
  Includes bibliographical references and index.
  1. Teaching—Vocational guidance—Great Britain—Congresses. I. Ball, Stephen J. II. Goodson, Ivor. III. Series.
LB1775.T417 1985   371.1'0023'41   85-4562
ISBN 1-85000-030-1
ISBN 1-85000-029-8 (pbk.)

Typeset in 10/12 Bembo by
Imago Publishing Ltd, Thame, Oxon

Jacket design by Leonard Williams

Printed in Great Britain by Taylor & Francis (Printers) Ltd, Basingstoke

Contents

Introduction

The papers in this volume are a selection from those given at the conference on 'Teachers' Lives and Teachers' Careers' at St Hilda's College, Oxford in September 1983. The editors are very grateful to the givers of other papers and participants at the conference whose contributions made the pulling together of a coherent collection from the proceedings so much easier. Colin Lacey, Martin Lawn, Margaret Bowen, Phil Carspecken and Henry Miller, Brian Davies and John Evans, Delscey Burns and Geoff Walford gave papers, and Bob Moon, Peter Woods, Sheila Riddell, Harry Osser, Peter Medway, Douglas Barnes, Bill Greer, Andy Hargreaves, Andrew Pollard and June Purvis also attended. This conference was one in a series that have been held at St Hilda's College over a number of years, bringing together educational researchers committed to ethnographic and interactionist methods for the study of educational institutions and processes. Collections of papers drawn from previous conferences have already been published *Teacher Strategies and Pupil Strategies* (Editor: Peter Woods, Croom Helm, 1980), *The Ethnography of Schooling* (Editor: Martyn Hammersley, Nafferton, 1983), *Curriculum Practice* (Editors: Martyn Hammersley and Andrew Hargreaves, Falmer Press, 1983), *Defining the Curriculum* (Editors: Ivor Goodson and Stephen Ball, Falmer Press, 1984).

Understanding Teachers: Concepts and Contexts

Stephen J. Ball and Ivor F. Goodson

I have arrived home for good at last. There will never again be a morning now when I shall say to myself here: 'Tomorrow the guillotine descends. Tomorrow I must return to London and to my job as a teacher'. Until I die, or until I am kept in bed by a serious illness, I shall be able every day after breakfast to come into this pleasant white and yellow room which is still called the 'drawing-room' both by me and Elsie just as it was by my parents before us and my grandparents before them; I shall be able to look through the large panes of the French window at the verandah and the lawn and the flint wall beneath the holly tree where on fine days an oblong of sunlight is reflected as now from one of the other windows of this house, or to sit out on the verandah in spring and autumn when the weather is neither too cool nor too warm; and every day I shall be free to write poetry. But in spite of my having retired from teaching more than a month ago I still can't easily believe that the life I have always wanted to live has become fully possible for me at last. I don't seem even to have convinced myself absolutely that I am not due back in London for the beginning of the Easter term. At nights I still dream fairly often that I am in school, though the type of nightmare I've had recently hasn't been quite as bad as the type I recurrently had during my years of teaching: then, long after I'd 'matured' as a teacher and did not have serious 'disciplinary' difficulties any more, I used to dream I was standing powerless in the middle of a crowd of boys who had got outrageously out of control; whereas during the past few weeks I've dreamt three or four times that I am hurriedly going up a concrete staircase to take a class I am disgracefully late for, and when I eventually reach the classroom I find there are no boys in it — or only a few, who drift out as soon as I begin to speak to them. Perhaps I must expect such lesser nightmares for a while yet after more than thirty years in a job which, however honourable and necessary it may be, cannot in present conditions be without heavy strain even for teachers far more capable than I ever was. Let me try to dissolve from my mind all disagreeable residues of my working years by remembering often how, as I walked out of the school building for the last time, I imagined myself arriving home here and saying to my mother and father: 'It has been a bad patch, but it's all finished with now'. I had forgotten for an instant that they were both dead and that this patch had covered more than half of my life so far, but my mood was the right one. Let me revive it. Those years are done with for ever and for ever, and I am free.

Edward Upward *No Home But the Struggle*,
London, Quartet Books, pp. 9–10.

The Political, Social and Economic Contexts of Teachers' Work

Any attempt to portray the contemporary situation of teachers' work and teachers' careers must inevitably begin by recognizing the changing context within which this work is undertaken and careers constructed. Changes in the financing of education, in the degree of political intervention into school matters, and in the views of and general level of esteem for teachers held within the public at large, have, and are having, profound effects upon the ways that teachers experience their jobs.

From the late 1960s we have moved from a situation of teacher shortage and apparently infinite possibilities for the expansion of educational provision to, in the 1980s, a situation of teacher unemployment and contraction in provision, with one or two exceptions, across the system as a whole.

> The contemporary situation in which teachers find themselves is one where there is an overall decline in demand for their services. At the same time there is increasing demand for control over the nature of their work by outside agencies. Both of these forces, therefore, point to a future in which the considerable freedom and independence in a variety of areas enjoyed by teachers is likely to be challenged. Moreover, this challenge will have important implications for the nature of the teaching profession and for the conditions of service under which teachers work. (Whiteside and Bernbaum, 1979)

Redundancy, redeployment and early retirement are real possibilities being faced by many established teachers as local authorities plan cuts in educational expenditure.[1] The number of teachers on temporary, fixed-term contracts is increasing (they are used, for example, in Liverpool, Hampshire and Solihull). In many cases these contracts include waiver clauses which dispense with rights to unfair dismissal protection. Probationary periods for Headteachers have been proposed by Keith Joseph (speech, 27 February, 1984), ancillary and clerical staff have been drastically cut, minority subjects (so-called) are disappearing entirely from some schools and at least one local authority has proposed the use of ability tests to select teachers for compulsory redundancy (*The Teacher*, 10 February 1984). For those new entrants who do obtain permanent posts the prospect is of a long period in a scale one post with little opportunity to move between schools. For those in mid-career also the chances of promotion will be few and far between.[2]

The whole conception of a career in teaching has been radically altered by these changes in conditions of work and employment but it is not only the objective, financial context that has changed drastically. There has also been a profound political and social shift in the status and public perception of teachers. Since the publication of the first collection of *Black Papers* in 1969, teachers have, from one direction or another, been under attack. They have been portrayed by commentators and critics from a variety of political persuasions as having failed to recognize or service the changing needs of society (the declining status of teachers is discussed in particular by Webb, in this volume).

For the Black Paper writers this failure is represented in three main themes which ran through their critiques of teachers. First, teachers have been overly influenced by progressive theories of education and the advocates of innovations like integration of subjects, mixed ability teaching, discovery learning methods. This has resulted in a neglect of the teaching of basic skills and a concomitant decline in standards of pupil achievement. And the attack on progressive methods was given further impetus by the research of Bennett (1976) which was reported as showing that formal teaching methods produced better pupil performance in tests of various kinds, although 'mixed' methods, used by experienced teachers appeared to be most successful of all. (The apparent clarity of Bennett's findings has however been clouded by subsequent statistical reworking).

Secondly, in a similar way liberal thinking by teachers and the use of child-centred methods were related to declining standards of discipline in schools and increases in pupil misbehaviour and classroom violence. Several horror stories in the newspapers, most recently the accounts of St. Saviour's in Toxteth, have fuelled the belief that schools have become dangerous places for both pupils and teachers (Denscombe, 1984). Lack of formal discipline also came to be identified with declining academic standards. Again widely publicised research gave support for this line of argument, the study *Fifteen Thousand Hours* (Rutter *et al.*, 1980) associated aspects of pupil performance with overall standards of discipline in schools and with the somewhat elusive notion of school 'ethos'.

Thirdly, the previous areas of criticism have in many instances been associated with accusations of the political bias and radical political motivations, of some teachers at least, who were involved with the introduction of more liberal or progressive methods and forms of education. Some progressive innovations were thereby labelled as attempts to politically indoctrinate pupils. (The assumption always being that existing forms of teaching were politically neutral.) Thus, in the early 1970s, even the normally sedate *Times* wrote of the need to tame 'the wild men of the classroom'. The primary focus of these concerns was provided in the case of William Tyndale Primary School which in 1976 became the subject of a public enquiry, when:

> an increasing number of parents (put) pressure on the school managers to modify the educational policies of the headmaster and certain members of his staff. The parents were dissatisfied with the mainly non-directive open-ended teaching methods pursued, with the attempt to modify the conven-

tional curriculum in the direction of pupils' independent choices and with the absence of traditional mechanisms for controlling pupils' behaviour. (Whiteside and Bernbaum, 1979, p. 103)

Significantly many of the initial criticisms levelled at the William Tyndale teachers came from two directions. On the one hand from a teacher in the school who maintained a correspondence with Rhodes Boyson (editor of the later *Black Papers*) and, on the other, members of the local Labour Party who used their contacts in County Hall and in the mass media to draw attention to what they saw as the ideologically motivated teaching methods employed in the school. The Tyndale affair focussed public attention on the accountability of teachers, and pointed to the increasing power of parental choice in a situation of falling rolls. In the subsequent public inquiry the view of the headmaster of William Tyndale that 'ultimately the teacher must decide how best to teach the children regardless of the views of the parents' was thoroughly rejected.

The claims of political bias in the schools have been continued in the 1980s, for example through allegations about teachers' sympathies for the CND. The mantle of the Black Papers has been taken on by the National Council for Academic Standards, the Centre for Policy Studies and the Social Affairs Unit. The involvement of the local Labour Party in the William Tyndale affair foreshadowed in certain respects the subsequent initiation by Prime Minister James Callaghan of the 'Great Education Debate'. In retrospect this may be seen both as the Labour Party's response to the apparent growth of public disillusion with the condition of education in Britain and as an attempt to wrest the political initiative in this area from the Conservative critics of the comprehensive school. Four main areas of concern were outlined in Callaghan's Ruskin College speech and the subsequent Green Paper issued by Secretary of State, Shirley Williams:

1   the need for clearer links between school and industry;
2   the need for greater public accountability of schools;
3   the need for a common curriculum in the secondary school;
4   the need for some kind of political education in schools.

It is the first two of these that made the greatest public impact and had the most significant consequences for teachers, and which have been picked up subsequently by Conservative governments. The general thesis underlying the Great Debate was that teachers had failed to adapt the school curriculum to, or prepare pupils for, the changing needs of British industry. The condemnation was fulsome:

Boys and girls are not sufficiently aware of the importance of industry to our society, and they are not taught much about it. In some schools the curriculum has been overloaded, so that the basic skills of literacy and numeracy, the building blocks of education, have been neglected. A small minority of schools have simply failed to provide an adequate education by modern standards. More frequently, schools have been over-ambitious . . . without making sure that teachers understood what they were teaching or whether it was appropriate to the pupils' capacities for the needs of their future employers. (DES, 1977)

In some senses teachers were being blamed for the economic recession. The human capital theory of education to which the Labour Party had comitted themselves in the 1960s (along with most other governments in the developed and less developed areas of the world) a theory which argued that increased educational participation would result in increased economic development, was apparently shown to be false.

One outcome of the debate was that attempts were made to make schools and teachers more responsive to and more accountable to the needs of industry and the personal concerns of parents. The force of the latter entered into law through the Education Act of 1981, which required schools to publish their examination results and gave parents the right to choose the school that they wished to send their children to. In other words, schools were to be subject to market forces. The weak would go to the wall.

The Great Education Debate, and the public chastisement of the teaching profession, together with the 'slack' in the system brought about by the onset of falling rolls (a result of declining birth rate) provided powerful legitimation for the financial cuts in education spending initiated by Labour and pursued with enthusiasm by the Conservative Government since 1979. We have already noted the objective consequences of these cuts for teachers' careers, the subjective consequences are evident in a marked decline in teacher morale. This was noted in Her Majesty's Inspectorate (HMI) Report on the effects on the education service in England of local authority expenditure policies 1980–81:

> In their visits to institutions the HMIs strong impression is of professional commitment and resourcefulness. Nevertheless there is evidence that teachers' morale has been adversely affected in many schools. Its weakening, if it became widespread, would pose a major problem in the efforts to maintain present standards, let alone an improvement. (DES, 1981, p. 13)

This decline marks both a loss of professional self-respect among teachers and a shift in public esteem for the teaching profession. Webb (in this volume describing a similar situation in the USA) reports that 'teachers we interviewed were aware of the flagging image in the community and were disturbed that the public didn't understand the problems teachers face or appreciate what they took to be the real accomplishments of public education'.

Alongside this very public process of 'teacher-bashing', and drawing legitimation from it, there has been a subtle and continuing process of state intervention into the conduct of schooling and teachers' classroom work. There has been a clear intention by both Labour and Conservative governments to stride into 'the secret garden of the curriculum'. This is evidenced in a whole variety of ways both direct and indirect. Since the mid-seventies, the HMI has become far more active than previously in initiating and engaging in debates about good practice, in particular through the publication of *Surveys, Matters for Discussion*, and, most recently, inspection reports. However, it must be said that the views of the HMI do not always coincide with those of the Secretary of State for Education. The current Secretary of State, Sir Keith Joseph, has been forthright in his own attempts to influence or intervene in educational practice. The White Paper on teacher training, *Teacher Quality*, is already having widespread impact on the organization of courses, it has reinforced the subject specialist basis of secondary training and effectively proscribed certain subjects, like sociology. In addition, the 1981 Education Act has given the Secretary of State powers to veto the public criteria for the latest versions of a common 16+ examination. He has made use of these powers to express his dissatisfaction with certain inclusions and omissions in several of the subject areas presented to him. Such strategies for intervention go beyond attempts to specify curricula content towards actually seeking to influence the *form* which the curriculum takes. This is most starkly evident in the recent activities of the Manpower Services Commission (MSC), which is not an agency of the Department of Education and Science (DES) but of the Department of Industry (DOI). In offering financial support to schools for vocational training schemes for 14 to 18 year olds the MSC may be staking a claim for the future to dictate aspects of the school curriculum. Generally, more and more of the financing of education is being centralized and more and more of this financing is being attached to specific schemes or payments which effectively remove the control from the school level, and thus away from teachers. (By 1985 the DES will be centrally administering £46 million intended for innovations and improvements in education; this is money withdrawn from the amount payable to local education authorities through the rate support grant).

Britain is moving steadily closer to a form of centralized control over the curriculum which would bring it into line with some of its European neighbours. It is important, however, to recognize that the feelings of loss and betrayal felt by British teachers make sense only within the almost unique fifty year period of relative autonomy granted to them by the withdrawal of the Board of Education from direct oversight of the school curriculum in the late 1920s. Previous attempts to wrest control of the curriculum away from the teachers, in the early 1960s for instance, met with stubborn and to a great extent successful resistance from the teacher unions. In the 1980s those same unions find themselves virtually powerless to resist claims from the present Secretary of State that are more fundamental and far reaching.

Researching the Teacher

Research into teaching and teachers' careers over the past two decades can be seen to have moved through several distinct phases which reflect the social, political and economic changes outlined above. In the 1960s teachers were shadowy figures on the educational landscape mainly known, or unknown, through large scale surveys (Cortis, 1975), or historical analyses of their position in society (Tropp, 1957), the key concept in apprehending the practice of teaching was that of role (Wilson, 1962). The relationship between teachers' work in the classroom and their 'products', the pupils, was rarely explored or analyzed. British educational researchers certainly never took up the concern with the measurement of educational efficiency which periodically swept through the United States (Callahan, 1962). Teachers were represented in aggregate through imprecise statistics or were viewed as individuals only as formal role incumbents mechanistically and unproblematically responding to the powerful expectations of their role set. Researchers were preoccupied with varieties of ways of explaining differences in school performances which involved 'blaming the pupils', forms of cultural deprivation and social pathology theories dominated.

At the end of the 1960s the dominance of these approaches was eroded when case-study researchers (notably Lacey, 1970 and Hargreaves, 1967) broke into the 'black box' of the school and began to examine the ways in which the school (in the person of its teachers) 'processed' pupils. Labelling and typification became key concepts in understanding the mechanisms via which teachers categorized and differentiated their pupils and thus channelled and imposed limits upon their careers at school and life chances beyond. Research thus shifted from 'blaming the pupil' to 'blaming the teacher' (Sharp and Green, 1975; Ball, 1981a; Woods, 1979). Teachers were implicated centrally not only in constructing differences in pupil performance but also in the maintenance and reproduction of gender stereotypes (Delamont, 1980). Hence the sympathies of the researchers lay primarily with the pupils, working class and female pupils in particular, who were the 'under dogs' in the classroom, teachers were the villains of the piece.

In the later seventies however, the research terrain shifted once again. Attention began to be directed to the constraints within which teachers work (neo-marxists in particular began to stress the field of determinants within which the teachers operated). Teachers were transformed from villains to 'victims' and, in some cases, 'dupes' of the system within which they were required to operate. As Riseborough (1983, p.8) puts it, in the structural marxist paradigm 'teachers and pupils become mere passive cyphers ideologically subjugated by factors outside themselves playing on and through them. That the demiurgic proclivities of teachers and pupils become denied for intentionality is *un*-intended because it is *super*-intended by the deep structures of captialism'. These marxist analysts tended to stress the societal and economic determinants of education and portray teachers as puppets of the capitalist state, helpless agents in the reproduction of the relations of production. In contrast, the interactionist perspective emphasized the more immediate problems involved in resolving the dual demands of instruction and control in the classroom. The limitations imposed by class size, class composition, classroom ecology and collegial and pupil expectation (Denscombe, 1980) were drawn together into a complex matrix of framing factors (Lundgren, 1972; Ball, 1981b; Evans, 1982). The teacher's essential problem was that of survival (Woods, 1979). The importance of socialization and the norms and values of subject sub-cultures (Lacey, 1977; Ball and Lacey, 1980; Goodson, 1983; 1984a; 1984b) were analyzed and added to the list of constraints. As the limitations inherent in both macro-marxist and interactionist approaches were recognized a more productive and dialectical conception of teachers' work has begun to emerge. The teacher is seen as involved in the development of creative, strategical responses to societal and situational constraints

(Hargreaves, 1977; and Pollard, 1982) or as resolving ever present dilemmas (Berlack and Berlack, 1982) through and within their interaction with pupils.

Alongside this recognition of the complexity of the teachers' task and the importance of the interplay between initiating and responsive acts in the classroom greater attention has been directed to teachers as human beings, as rounded social actors with their own problems and perspectives, making careers, struggling to achieve their ideals or just struggling to 'survive'. In several respects then teachers have themselves become 'under dogs', very much on the defensive in an education system which is contracting and where *accountability* is now being stressed over and against autonomy. The school must now be viewed also as a *teaching-processing* institution. Researchers have begun to focus on the careers (subjective and objective) of teachers (Lortie, 1975; Woods, 1981; Lyons, 1981) and to examine more closely their motivations, experiences and strategies as workers in the education system. Some analyses present a conception of teachers' careers in purely materialistic terms, teachers are seen as individual agents competing for personal advancement and promotion, as Lyons' (1981) work suggests, others trade on an 'idealist' view, seeing all teachers as altruistic missionaries, neither is adequate.

This volume is intended to contribute in a constructive way to the existing body of research on teachers' careers both in substantive terms providing data on neglected and under-researched aspects of teachers' work *and* by attempting some conceptual development, which may improve the ways in which we conceive of and understand careers in teaching. In particular, we are hoping to emphasize the need to view teachers' careers and teachers' work in relation to and in the context of their lives as a whole.

The Bureaucratization and Proletarianization of Teaching

Taken together recent changes in the context of teaching and alterations in the basis of teachers' conditions of employment and the ways that schools are organized have begun to affect the teachers' work experience. In particular, teaching in the comprehensive school has become more highly bureaucratized and stratified, compared with the smaller grammar and secondary modern schools.

> Even after falling rolls, today's average secondary school is twice the size of the grammar or secondary modern of twenty years ago, and organizational complexity is clearly related to size. In fact, complexity in terms of the number of combinations of internal organizational arrangements or in terms of the number of inevitable human interfaces, increases at both a faster rate and in greater proportion than the arithmetic increase in the overall number of pupils. However, the complexity is not solely a matter of size and logistics; catering for the comprehensive range of pupil abilities under the same roof brings with it considerable technical complexity with the sheer range of curriculum options, syllabuses and pastoral support policies that must be determined. (Morgan, Hall and MacKay, 1983, p. 11)

Comprehensive schools are denoted by a highly complex division of labour. Scale points which are allocated for posts of responsibility also create specialist positions and duties. Some duties which had previously been carried out by class tutors or class teachers are now separated off as the responsibility of specialists. This is particularly true in the case of pastoral care work; many schools now have sophisticated pastoral structures with year tutors and assistant year tutors, heads of school, community liaison officers etc. These specialist positions are now well supported and further institutionalized by a range of in-service and award bearing courses in colleges and universities. The result, increasing specialization and complexity is in turn increasing bureaucratization in school procedures — form-filling, record-keeping — and in teacher-pupil relations. Woods (1979), in his study of Lowfield secondary modern, distinguishes between teacher-bureaucrats and teacher-persons:

> The former are more bound by institutional forms and processes and more geared to the formal definition of the teacher role. They are more likely to show a high degree of rule consciousness, exert their authority, and foster formal and depersonalized relationships. They are categorized by pupils in this study as 'too strict', 'full of moans', 'won't laugh', 'treat you like kids'. Teacher persons capitalize on humour and togetherness. They are 'more natural', 'more like a friend than a teacher', 'have a laugh with you', 'talk to you like real people'. They are still in control of the institution, using it for their own ends. Teacher bureaucrats however, are governed by it. (p. 244)

As Weber (1968) points out:

> Bureaucracy develops the more perfectly the more it is 'dehumanized', the more completely it succeeds in eliminating from official business, love, hatred, and all purely personal, irrational and emotional elements which escape calculation. (p. 975)

If then pupils are now dealt with in an increasingly rational and impersonal fashion in school, this may equally well be the case for teachers. Certainly it can be argued that the perpetuation of a strongly classified subject-based curriculum contributes to bureaucratization in large schools.

> The knowledge is organized and distributed through a series of well-insulated subject hierarchies. Such a structure points to oligarchic control of the institution, through formal and informal meetings of heads of department with the head or principal of the institution. Thus, senior staff will have strong horizontal work relationships (that is, with their peers in other subject hierarchies) and strong vertical work relationships within their own department. However, junior staff are likely to have only vertical (within the subject hierarchy) allegiances and work relationships. (Bernstein, 1971, p. 61)

Another facet of the increased complexity of the organization and administration of large schools and a further manifestion of the oligarchic control referred to by Bernstein, is apparent in the phenomenon of the *senior management team*. These teams, normally made up of the Headteacher, Deputy Heads and Senior Teachers, are distinctly separate from the classroom teaching workforce of the school. (Although deputies normally have some teaching responsibilities). And it is in this area that most major policy discussions in schools are now held. The application of management terminology to school government is in itself significant.

The concept of management is drawn from the methods of organization, administration and control employed in industry and it contains a set of assumptions which derived from the work of F.W. 'Speedy' Taylor. Taylor argued that wherever possible planning should be separated from execution and should be the exclusive province of management. Work tasks should be carefully prescribed, and these prescriptions should lay down standards that will facilitate the precise measurement of work output. One of the fundamental tenets of this method is thus 'the increasing control over the work and the workforce ... concentrated in management hands' (Clegg and Dunkerley, 1980, p. 91). Indeed, Taylor advocated authoritarian methods of management, and was judged to have 'offered the most thorough dehumanization of work ever seen under capitalism' (Clegg and Dunkerley, 1980. p. 91). If not all the details of Taylor's scientific management are recognizable in our schools, the trends are unmistakeable. In recent years management training courses for incumbent or aspiring heads and deputies have proliferated; in 1983 the DES allocated six million pounds for this purpose, of which £350,000 has gone to the University of Bristol to establish a national education management centre. It may not be too far-fetched to relate this enthusiasm for the management training of school administrators to the increased level of intervention of the political centre in matters of school curriculum and the need to deal efficiently with technical and managerial problems thrown up by falling rolls and cuts in educational expenditure. It may be that management control over teachers' classroom work is extended much further in the near future as the introduction of graded testing allows for more direct and immediate forms of quality control. This is certainly the trend in the United States:

> Management ideology focussed sharply on measurable educational 'outputs' in relation to society 'inputs' by introducing educational schemes which fit the terminology of the ideology: competence based education (CBE), performance based education (PBE), competancy based teacher education (CBTE), behavioural objectives, mastery learning, learner verification, assessment systems (federal, state and local), and criterion-reference testing. (Wirth, 1983, p. 116)

And it is perhaps worth noting that a major factor in Japanese management styles that are beginning to be imported is the concept of 'total quality control'.

While in many respects there is nothing at all wrong with efficiency as an organizational goal, management itself is not simply a neutral administrative technology. It is one form of organizational control, based on executive control of labour, but not necessarily the only available one. Participative procedures are one alternative which few schools have attempted (Watts, 1977; Scrimshaw, 1975).

Salaman (1978) argues that the importance of management training courses lies in the way in which they influence the attitudes and motivation of their participants:

> The function of these courses is to adjust organizational members to organizational demands and realities; to encourage members to gain 'insight' into themselves, their colleagues and the organization (insight of a rather limited sort, usually); to inform members about the organization, and to develop new skills. They achieve insidious control. (p. 203)

Wallace, Miller and Ginsburg (1983) describe such effects at work in one local education authority (LEA) which they studied:

> ... the LEA increasingly followed the principles of hierarchical authority ... in their ideological rhetoric. Thus, heads were encouraged to see themselves in schools as managers and were required to 'manage' with appropriate authority. This could place heads and deputies (who were the mediators between County directives and staff complaints) at the point of conflict making them less able to deal effectively with teachers' problems.

Management theories are concerned primarily with organizing and controlling workers rather than dealing with them as people (Ball, 1984). Their application to a person-centred enterprise such as education is deeply problematic.

Objective and Subjective Careers in Teaching

It is against the background of factors outlined above that any contemporary research on teachers must be set. But it would be conceptually misleading either to assume that all teachers share the same subjective experiences of these factors or that concentration on the immediate contexts of teaching will provide an adequate framework for the analysis of such careers.

The concept of career must take into account both the objective and subjective aspects of the incumbent's experience. By definition individual careers are socially constructed and individually experienced over time. They are subjective trajectories through historical periods and at the same time contain their own organizing principles and distinct phases. However, there are important ways in which individual careers can be tied to wider political and economic events. In some cases particular historial 'moments' or periods assume special significance in the construction of or experience of a career. Three such 'moments' crop up regularly in this volume in the experiences and career perceptions of teachers quoted:

1 the economic depression of the 1930s and the stultifying effect that this had on the teaching profession and teachers' perspectives;
2 the period of educational expansion and progressive consensus in the mid-to-late 1960s and the diverse flowering of radical innovations that this allowed;

3   the current context of economic cuts and falling rolls which, as noted already, is inhibiting career development for new entrants and producing low morale in the profession as a whole.

The possibilities and constraints experienced in these periods seem to imprint themselves on the views and attitudes of the teachers involved and in the case of the first two at least, have long term implications for the career patterns and progress of those individuals. Over and above the impact of these external influences there are also ways in which work in teaching and teachers' careers are marked by and may be divided into a set of commonly understood stages linked to the process of ageing. This may be understood in particular in terms of teachers' changing relations with pupils and their conceptions of themselves in role. Life history and career history methods and longitudinal studies of entrants into teaching provide different ways of eliciting both these objective and subjective aspects of careers in teaching.

The first life histories were collected by anthropologists at the beginning of the century, notably in the form of autobiographies of American Indian chiefs. The major landmark in the development of sociological life histories came with the publication of Thomas and Znaniecki's (1921) pioneering study *The Polish Peasant in Europe and America*. From this point on life history methods were adopted as an important research device in the work being undertaken in the University of Chicago Sociology Department. With the arrival of Robert Park in the department in 1916 the life history method became established as a central part of the research apparatus employed by sociologists working there. A range of studies of city life completed under Park such as *The Gang, The Gold Coast and the Slum, The Hobo* and *The Ghetto* all employed the life history method. Life history studies reached their peak in the 1930s with publications such as Clifford Shaw's (1930) study of a mugger in *The Jackroller* and Edwin Sutherland's (1937) study of *The Professional Thief*.

Becker (1966) has since written about the decline of the life history method and develops some hypotheses as to why this has happened. But also in his essay he develops the arguments about life history by seeking to show why Shaw's study of *The Jackroller* is so exemplary. He notes that by:

> putting ourselves inside Stanley's (the Jackroller's) skin we can feel and become aware of the deep biases about such people that ordinarily permeate our thinking and shape the kind of problems we investigate. By truly entering into Stanley's life we can begin to see what we take for granted (and ought not to) in deciding our research — what kinds of assumptions about delinquents, slums and Poles are embedded in the way we set the questions we study. (p. 71)

More recently educational researchers have been exploring the possibilities of rehabilitating the life history method for their own work. Goodson (1981; 1983) has pursued this exhortation with some examples of how studies of the life history of key personnel can illuminate our understanding of curriculum change. In particular, he argued that most interactionist and ethnomethodolgical studies on schooling have generated a predominant but implausible model of the teacher 'largely interchangeable, subject to timeless problems and employing a variety of standard but apparently spontaneously developed strategies':

> Whilst not wishing to argue that teachers do not have important characteristics in common, we argue that there are important distinctions in attitude, performance and strategies which can be identified in different teachers in different times. To understand the degree of importance of these distinctions we have to reconnect our studies of schooling with investigations of personal biography and historical background: above all we are arguing for the reintegration of situational with biographical and historical analysis. Through such a reintegration we might move away from studies where the human actor is located and studied in a manner contrively divorced from the previous history of both the actor and the situation. (Goodson, 1981, p. 69)

This leads on to a number of investigative assumptions. First, that the teachers' previous career and life experience shapes their view of teaching and the way he or she sets about it. Secondly, that teachers' lives outside school, their latent identities and cultures, have an important impact on their work as teachers. This relates to 'central life interest' and commitments. And thirdly, that we must, following Bogdan and Taylor (1970), seek to locate the life history of the individual within 'the history of his time'. Clearly there are limits to this aspiration with regard to schooling. But life histories of schools, subjects and the teaching profession would provide vital contextual information.

Since these exhortations the move towards life history work in the study of schooling has been substantially strengthened by the methodological ammunition provided in the collection edited by Bertaux (1981). This has allowed researchers like Beynon (in this volume) to explore the use of life history methods in an ethnographic study. Beynon has studied 'Lower School', a large urban comprehensive in South Wales. The life history data was gathered over an eighteen month period of ethnographic fieldwork. In his summary Beynon points towards the potential for life history work 'filling in the gaps in our knowledge of schooling':

> More needs to be known about how, for example, teachers' lives outside classes influence their teaching and the crucial espisodes and watersheds that mark shifts in attitudes in their careers. Ethnographers are becoming more sensitive to the multi-dimensionality of teachers' (and pupils'/students') lives and are now less likely to treat them as unidimensional which has, to date, often been the case. Teachers are not . . . cardboard cut-outs: behind their teaching lies a range of motives and emotions . . . they are influenced by past, as well as contemporary, events and more attention should be paid to how critical incidents in an institution's history affect its teacers.

Such methods provide ways of opening up for study the sealed boxes within which teachers work and survive. They serve to identify aspects of common experience and to isolate some of those factors which separate and differentiate teachers; factors like age, subject, level of specialization (primary, secondary, sixth

Stephen J. Ball and Ivor F. Goodson

form etc.). These methods tap into the lived experiences of teachers in schools, their successes and failures, their relationships with 'the hierarchy', their conditions of work, their responses to change.

The paper by Sikes in this volume provides another example of the uses of career history data this time in revealing the process of ageing as it particularly and peculiarly affects teachers. In contrast with most other forms of employment teaching embodies within it the constant reflection of the ageing process, for while teachers get older pupils inevitably stay the same age.

In existing research on teaching it is the first phase of the teaching career and its attendant stresses that has received most attention. Apparently old teachers just fade away. However it is in the first few years of teaching that survival is most problematic. Research has tended to focus on both the newly qualified teachers' adaptation to the school in the broader organizational sense and the problems of achieving a working relationship with pupils in the classroom. In both cases there has been particular interest in the problems of and 'fate' of radical teachers. Attitudinal surveys have tended to stress the decline in radical orientation among newly qualified teachers once they are faced with the realities of teaching. Such changes are evidenced in Figure 1.

Figure 1   Four attitude scales plotted at T_1, T_2, and T_3 — Sussex PGCE

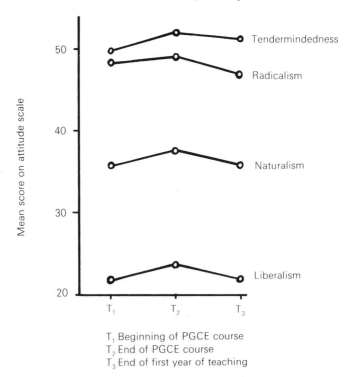

T_1 Beginning of PGCE course
T_2 End of PGCE course
T_3 End of first year of teaching

Source: Lacey 1977 p. 130.

14

On all four indicators there is a marked increase in scores from the beginning to the end of the PGCE course and a marked decline from the end of the PGCE course to the end of the first year of teaching. When questioned at the end of their first teaching year many of the respondents in this study described their reactions as representing a major change in their views (Lacey, 1977, p. 134). Both the responses of pupils and the power of collegiate expectations are implicated in bringing about these reorientations of attitude and belief. Indeed, in some cases overt pressures are placed upon the new entrant to conform to the institutional conventions and conceptions of 'good practice'.

> I found it difficult to talk to the other staff because I thought they all knew what a hash I was making of it. There was a lot of noise coming from my classroom and it shouldn't have been. This is partly because it is a new school designed for open-plan teaching, with no doors between the classrooms, and yet old-fashioned teaching methods are being used; and so anything that went on in my classroom I felt could be heard in the next classroom. We always knew when we'd been making a dreadful din — I had a very awkward teacher at one time next to me who used to come up when there was the slightest noise and say 'I can't hear myself talk down there, could you shut your class up?' and I couldn't always shut my class up, so it was creating rather an awful situation. She never showed me how to do it. I had some friendly tips, I suppose, but they seemed to take it terribly lightheartedly and make jokes about it. Perhaps they didn't really under-stand how badly I felt about it. But I think it was awkward for the teachers too, because they don't like to approach us and say 'Do you want some help? Can I help you?' They think they might be interfering. I really don't know why. Something to do with the professionalism ... you don't want to tell a teacher how to ... you don't want to admit your failures by approaching them. (Jean Musgrove, junior school teacher, quoted in Hannam *et al.* (1976, p. 141)).

However, adaptation is not necessarily always a simple one way process. Building on Becker's work Lacey (1977) has suggested a tripartite schema for analyzing the processes of adaptation involved in becoming a teacher. He says 'the school has now become the arena for competing pressures. On the one hand there is the need to become effective and accepted within the school; on the other hand the desire to make the school more like the place in which the teacher would like to teach' (p. 136). Lacey's three categories of adaptation are:

1 strategic compliance, in which the individual complies with the authority figure's definition of the situation and the constraints of the situation but retains private reservations about them. He is merely seen to be good.
2 Internalized adjustment, in which the individual complies with the con-straints and believes that the constraints of the situation are for the best. He really is good. (p. 72)
3 'Strategic redefinition of the situation' which 'implies that change is brought

about by individuals who do not possess the formal power to do so. They achieve change by causing or enabling those with formal power to change their interpretation of what is happening in the situation' (p. 73).

From this perspective the new entrant to teaching is to be seen not simply as a naive subject responding unthinkingly to outside pressures and constraints but rather, as Lacey indicates, as the initiator of 'action–idea systems that are innovative within situations and change them' (p. 72). This approach to the analysis of teachers' careers has been extended further by Woods (1981) who, using case studies of the careers of two 'radical' teachers, separates *pragmatic* from *paradigmatic* types of strategic orientation. The former combines partial redefinition with situational adjustment and the 'privatization' of educational problems; the latter allows for no compromise, and involves the undisguised pursuit of 'how teaching ought to be'. Tom, the teacher who represents the pragmatic orientation, was content to acquire power within the existing structures of school organization and was well aware of 'what is or is not possible in given circumstances'. He survived and to an extent flourished within the system, carving a niche for himself on the margins of his school where his personal views were tolerated and which made life, for him, tolerable. Dick, on the other hand, the paradigmatist, was frequently in open conflict with his superiors and indeed he appeared to court public confrontations. Rather than work within the structure of his schools he attempted to take them on head on and to reform them, he resigned from or was eased out of three schools in as many years and then left teaching altogether, unwilling to adapt his principles to the demands of the system.

Sikes' paper in this volume highlights the pressures towards accommodation and adaptation that the tyro faces in the early years of teaching. But, in different ways, Nias and Bennett (also in this volume) provide accounts of the ways in which initial idealism and 'deviant' identities can be maintained despite these pressures. Nias's primary teachers sought out, by moving school if necessary, like-minded teachers to reinforce their own strongly-held beliefs and conceptions of the work of teaching. Many carried with them a missionary commitment to teaching which was not necessarily dimmed by the passing of time although some did drop out, literally or figuratively, when faced with adverse circumstances or when unable to find reference group support for their particular self concept as teachers. Those who stayed employed impression management and forms of strategic compliance in order to get things done in their schools. Bennett's art teachers, working on the periphery of the school world, were granted 'normative licence' by their more orthodox colleagues, as well as maintaining a strong counter-cultural value system of their own.

Whatever the influence of colleagues on the new teacher it emerges from the studies reported here that the early days in the classroom contain, for virtually all teachers, periods of stress and moments of interpersonal conflict with pupils that are fundamental in making or breaking a career in teaching. This kind of rite of passage experience, the baptism of fire in the classroom, is clearly embedded in the way in which teachers make sense, retrospectively, of their own development. It is part of the folklore of teaching and, as Measor describes in this volume, such *critical incidents* are crucial in the ways in which teachers account for the very process of becoming a teacher. Establishing oneself in the classroom, becoming a teacher, is clearly a two-way process. The teacher may be taming the pupils, as they see it, but in their proactive strategies the pupils are profoundly shaping and directing the teacher's self-concept and moral career. For those who fail in the baptism of fire, who are by definition unrepresented in the analyses presented here, the pupils may be decisive in forcing them out of teaching, or as in the case of Mr Smith, described by Measor, may force them to seek to pursue their struggle to survive and develop as teachers in other schools. The psychological stress and the critical significance of these experiences are clear in the symbolic power and delivery of the stories which the teachers tell.

Several writers (Werthman, 1963; Rosser and Harre, 1976; Woods, 1979) have emphasized the ways in which pupils seek to establish some control over the activities of their teachers and subvert and colonize teachers' intentions and practices. Werthman's American high school gang members had a particular concern with the ways in which their teachers assigned grades, what grades and on what criteria. If the gang felt that the criteria being used were illegitimate, taking into account student demeanour and behaviour rather than effort and ability, then sanctions were applied, like coming late, ignoring the teachers' attempts to teach and a carefully judged insubordinate demeanour referred to as 'looking cool'. The British pupils investigated by Rosser and Harre also judged their teachers by a set of rules of conduct, if their teachers broke these rules then principles of retribution were brought into play either in the form of reciprocity, paying back in kind, or equilibration, which involved tactics to offset any loss of self-esteem or personal indignity which may have resulted from the teachers' offence, an insult or slap or unfair punishment. In the process of action and reaction, offence and retribution pupils are involved in educating or re-educating their teachers, although like some pupils teachers do not seem to learn their lessons well. Riseborough's paper in this volume takes this analysis one step further by stressing the often underestimated symbiotic relationship between teacher and pupil. He argues that pupils can be seen as 'critical reality definers' in the classroom, acting in a competent and knowledgeable way to 'process' their teachers. In doing so, they critically affect the teacher's health and survival and the degree of stress that the teacher experiences. Those who do survive become 'hardened' on the chalk face, 'they become what they become'. They learn from pupils, they learn what is possible and what is not. They respond, retreat, and rethink. Teacher and pupils are each determined by and determine the others in the interaction. Pupils subvert the teachers' conceptions of their substantive self. Teachers type, channel and direct pupils' careers and may affect their life chances beyond school.

In less dramatic fashion pupils also shape and constrain the teachers' pedagogy and may engage in a resistance of or negotiation over matters of content. Measor (1984) found that pupil perceptions of subject status played a significant part in the degree of cooperation that they were willing to extend to teachers, Spradbery (1976) reported similar findings in the case of pupil resistance to teacher attempts to introduce maths for the majority work for the less able. This was regarded by pupils as 'not proper maths'. Clearly, however, for some teachers and perhaps in some subject areas in particular there are 'gaps' and possibilities within the educational system which allow for the development and maintenance of radical orientations to teaching. And on occasion there are circumstances or 'moments' which provide a focus for such radicalism either in a straightforward educational sense or in a wider political sense.

Smith, Kleine, Dwyer and Prunty (in this volume) indicate the ways in which radical moments and experiences fit into and have an impact upon the lives of those involved. They isolate several factors which recur in perspectives and subsequent career of teachers involved in innovative schooling in the 1960s. This experience made a long term impact on working lives and personal lives of these teachers in profound ways.

In a somewhat different way the shadow of the 1960s looms large in the career histories and perspectives of some of the teachers attracted to work in Croxteth Community School (Carspecken and Miller, 1983). People with experience of political movements at college or university, who had experimented with alternative lifestyles and new religions, who had journeyed, literally and figuratively, in search of personal fulfilment were attracted by the combination of direct action, community politics and cooperative involvement that Croxteth offered. They brought their commitment and their experience and found the satisfactions and frustrations of putting political and personal theories into practice. For others, some of those people from the Croxteth Community who became involved in teaching or others working at the school, this experience provided a new beginning, a significant change of life course, a new sense of meaning and purpose against a background of alienation and aimlessness. The long term implications for these people will remain to be seen but Smith *et al's* Kensington study provides some pointers as to likely directions.

Identity, Commitment and Allegiance

The ways in which teachers achieve, maintain, and develop their identity, their sense of self, in and through a career, are of vital significance in understanding the actions and commitments of teachers in their work. Identity is also a key to apprehending the divisions between teachers. Ball (1972) suggests a useful separation of the *situated* from the *substantive* identity, a separation that is between a malleable presentation of self that differs and alters according to the specific definition of the situation and a more stable, core self perception that is fundamental to the ways that individuals think about themselves. Analyses of teaching and the folk wisdom of practitioners often stress the peculiar necessities of impression management in the dynamics of classroom interaction. Teachers often talk of the usefulness of feigning anger 'going in hard and easing off later', 'not letting them see that you are nervous', all of which highlight the need to achieve particular presentations of self in particular contexts. The staffroom may provide another context in which such presentations are required, as Cole argues in his paper in this volume. The separation is between teacher and person. Student teachers frequently complain about being unable to be 'themselves' in the classroom. As initiates into teaching they are acutely aware of this dichotomy of the self. For some a career in teaching becomes an odyssey in search of forms of teaching work where this dichotomy can be abandoned or reduced. Bennett's art teachers are one group which come closer than many others. to achieving this. Many of Nias' primary teachers are clearly in search of such a closing. Kensington and Croxteth provided institutional occasions within which resolutions were, for a time, possible. Furthermore, over time, identity becomes invested in particular aspects or facets of the teaching role. For many secondary teachers their subject specialism plays a crucial role. They see themselves as scientists, geographers, historians, mathematicians, etc. This is not surprising in that teacher training in the broadest sense tends to prepare and socialize aspirants for separate and ideologically distinct social and institutional roles. As Lacey (1977) puts it, professional induction to teaching is not single stranded 'but a multi-stranded process in which student teachers are moving towards a profession which is itself still striving towards common understandings in vital areas of its professional practice' (p. 76). In the secondary sector this separation and distinctiveness of subjects is maintained by the strong classification of the school curriculum. Not only does the teacher in preparation acquire identity but also, in many cases, a subject specific set of norms and values. They are invested in subject sub-cultures. We can see the evidence of this in Bennett's account of the perspectives and training of art teachers. The importance of subject sub-cultures has led a number of researchers towards the study of the historical development of school subjects (Goodson, 1983). Historical analysis can uncover the range of conflicts and influences which have played their part in defining subjects in particular ways. These definitions channel and constrain the sorts of identity available to the subject teacher.

In relation to identity vested interests develop in maintaining and reinforcing particular aspects of role and particular self confirming ways of existing in teaching. For some therefore innovations or reforms in teaching or school organization can represent a threat to identity or the possibility of humiliations associated with a spoilt identity. Riseborough (1981) has highlighted this in the case of secondary modern teachers caught up in the reorganization of Phoenix Comprehensive. The experiences of seventeen teachers from the secondary modern school, upon which a new comprehensive was based, all long serving, many two-year trained, all but one non-graduates, are documented in detail by Riseborough. With the appointment of a new Headteacher and the influx of new, younger, university-trained staff these 'old' staff found their careers brought to a complete halt. Indeed as posts of responsibility were shared out in the new school they found themselves demoted in the status hierarchy and dispossessed of previous positions and duties (their salaries were protected). Further, the new Headteacher quickly made it clear that he saw no future for them in what was now 'his' school.

> The Head's idea of a good teacher is everything I'm not. Just look at the ones he's appointed. That's what he thinks a good teacher is. Their rating is really on academic qualifications and examination record. This man has a tremendous fear that he has to show results. From the beginning I realised the writing was on the wall. (Ex-secondary modern teacher aged 56, p. 359)

The old staff found themselves effectively barred from top set teaching and allocated instead to 'dirty work' among the bottom stream groups. The system of streaming pupils in the school came to be paralleled by a system of streaming the teachers. Like the bottom stream groups they taught these teachers began to develop an anti-school culture.

> The 'old' staff's orientation to work is thus centred around an utter personal antipathy to the head; to teaching and to the school as defined by him; and to any kind of conception of comprehensive education. They define their role in opposition to the head's expectation. (p. 363)

Among the many strengths of Riseborough's study is that it puts the concept of career into the context of a particular institution which has its own ideological structure and micro-politics. It demonstrates the role of the headteacher as 'critical reality definer' and gatekeeper of teachers' careers whose 'strategic choices constructs and sustains through interaction the professional identities of teaching staff' (p. 367).

In a similar case study approach to the examination of careers Ball (1985) found grammar school teachers experiencing a loss of prized aspects of teaching work and a devalued sense of self when faced with comprehensive reorganization and the subsequent possibility of the loss of the school sixth form. However, in contrast to the secondary modern teachers at Phoenix, these grammar school teachers continued to offer skills and capabilities (especially with examination classes) which were valued by the new Headmaster. They were able to use their influence in the school to defend many traditional practices and to oppose some at least of the innovations they saw as undesirable. And significantly those grammar school teachers who at the point of reorganization suffered status demotion were able over a period of time to recover and resume their vertical and horizontal career progress.

Fundamental to the establishment of identity in teaching is, as Nias argues in her paper in this volume, *the reference group*. For those sixth form college teachers described by Burke in this volume their reference groups clearly lay in the university disciplines for which they prepared pupils and to which some at least aspired personally. Their commitments to and the satisfactions received from preparing students for university led to willing acceptance of heavy teaching loads, long hours of preparation and marking, as well as attempts to keep up with the recent developments in research in their subject area. Not all teachers display this kind of intense personal involvement with their work, indeed Lortie (1975) suggests that the occupation of teaching is geared to 'recruitment rather than retention and low rather than high involvement' (p. 99). And Woods (1981) argues that the degree of strength and commitment among teachers can be considered in terms of three primary types of commitment, which he refers to as *vocational, professional,* and *career continuance.* The vocational type we have met already among Nias primary teachers. This is usually based on a broad personal commitment to a set of ideals and beliefs related to 'service' and helping and or changing society for the better. Lacey (1977) found this sort of commitment well represented among his sample of Postgraduate Certificate in Education (PGCE) students, and at this stage it bears many similarities to the ideal doctor commitment evidenced among the beginning medical students studied by

Becker *et al.* (1961). As we have seen already in the case of radical teachers, this idealism may be fragile when tested against the exigencies of classroom life and can be compromised away by the adoption of short term survival strategies. This kind of commitment may also come under pressure from the expectations of colleagues about what constitutes good practice. Nias' idealists were notably tenacious, stubborn and successful in their own classes but they were also acutely aware of the difference between themselves and many of their colleagues. In the broadest sense the vocationally committed are educators rather than scholars. They see their interests as primarily with caring for the pupils and encouraging their intellectual development. In contrast professionally committed teachers are much more likely to see themselves as subject specialists and to see their subjects as providing an avenue for advancement as well as a source of personal satisfaction. They are in general terms academics who wish to teach their subject and, perhaps as a result, see their role relationship with pupils more narrowly. Lacey (1977) found that students of this type in his PGCE sample tended to rate their teaching ability very highly as well as having a long term career perspective. It is presumably within this group that Lyons (1981) found his 'map makers', those cue seeking teachers who established for themselves a career map or a career timetable by which to guide and measure their progress over time, who sought out 'sponsors' and cultivated an awareness of appropriate 'benchmarks' and 'gatekeepers'. These two groups may be said to have, in different ways, a positive commitment to teaching (we must be aware that these are ideal types; not all teachers can be neatly fitted in to these categories and individual teachers' motives may be mixed, or one person may change the nature of their commitment over time). They have normally made a firm and decisive choice to enter teaching, although the vocationally committed teacher may also see the possibility of pursuing their mission outside of school. For many entrants into teaching however, the decision to become a teacher is best described as a negative decision or a series of non decisions. For some, a teacher training institution is a second best alternative to university or a way of marking time while searching for a positive interest elsewhere. Once in college the inertia of continuance commitment carries the unsure, and even the alienated, along and leaves them with a non–negotiable qualification. Even entry into teaching may be made on similar grounds — the outcome of a combination of inertia and a lack of viable alternatives. To this group may be added a number of university graduates uncertain of how to make positive use of their degree or who postpone their career decision by embarking on a PGCE course. Cole's study of college of education students in this volume, contains both negatively and non-committed teachers of this kind and they represent an important counterpoint to the radicals described above and to Nias' idealist teachers. Clearly, while some of these waverers drift out of teaching, perhaps failing to survive when their commitment is tested by critical incidents in the classroom, others become trapped by the side bets made over time into a teaching identity. Some undoubtedly acquire a more positive orientation to their role as they find satisfactions in new challenges or new aspects of their work or in relationships with colleagues. But our knowledge of this group is particularly limited and teachers themselves have a vested interest in not betraying these kind of reluctant commitments. The ideology of professional work stresses the altruistic and missionary aspects of commitment over and against the utilitarian or pecuniary or alienated.

Sikes, Bennett and Nias all point to examples of teachers who find more substantial commitments and identity reinforcement outside of the normal work of teaching and outside of the school. Some develop concurrent careers which provide forms of status or economic recovery or provide a channel for psychological withdrawal from the travails of teaching. For some of Bennett's art teachers it was possible to cash in their training in commercial art work or to attain personal satisfaction and reinforcement of substantive identities as artists by exhibiting and selling their personal work. Beynon describes a teacher whose local reputation and personal satisfactions derived from his historical writing and research. Nias also points out that for some women teachers a career as mother may provide an alternative to a career as teacher and pregnancy may be a deliberate means of escape from teaching work.

Certainly the concept of career as used in common parlance to describe a commitment to promotion and professional development through work over a long timescale is not relevant to all teachers, or all groups of teachers. Lyons (1981) found that not all the teachers he interviewed held a clearly conceived 'career map' and that many work towards short-term objectives, be it getting through to the end of term or capturing a scale post of responsibility. Others judge their careers in terms of long-term stages and did not expect rapid movement from one benchmark to another. They felt that they might in the long term hope to become a head of department or a year tutor, but they did not necessarily measure their progress towards these goals against timetable norms set by contemporaries and did not see themselves in any sort of direct competition with their colleagues for scarce promotion possibilities. It will be interesting to see to what extent these perspectives are altered in the current context of 'cuts' and falling rolls.

Bennett's art teachers certainly do not identify themselves with the norms of promotional striving which they see in other subject groups. Indeed the norms of their own subject subculture discourage such striving. Although we must also recognize that the status of art in the hierarchy of school subjects tends to preclude art teachers (as well as other teachers in areas like craft design and technology, physical education, domestic science and needlework) from the normal routes of promotion to senior management positions in schools. Neither did Nias' primary school teachers normally talk about or see themselves embarked on a career in teaching *per se*. They may have been discouraged from this both by factors related to gender biases in promotion and the absence of a highly developed system of scales and posts of responsibility. And it would be unusual to find radical teachers committing themselves to teaching in terms of a career. Indeed, such a notion may be antithetical to their sense of personal development and social equality.

The concept of a career in teaching, as commonly understood, is problematic for many individuals and groups. This may be particularly true in the case of women teachers. For many women teachers careers are constructed, in both objective and subjective senses, in radically different ways from those of male careers. And these 'deviant' constructions often severely disadvantage the women in the competition for promotion in schools. Marland (1983) has recently collated the striking pattern of under-representation of women teachers in senior positions across all the sectors of education. The extent of awareness among women of these inequalities and the extent to which individuals feel themselves to be disadvantaged is of course itself problematic. Clearly, some women do see teaching simply as a means of providing a second income and, like many men, are committed only in calculative terms to their work. However, recent financial cuts in spending in education have had a disproportionate impact on women in one area in particular. In many schools faced with financial restrictions and/or falling rolls part-time posts have often been the first to be cut. The vast majority of part-time teachers in schools are women. Apart from such obvious inequities women 'career' teachers may find themselves further disadvantaged when compared with men who are part of what Acker (1980) refers to as joint-career families. As a result of their different patterns of career both in relation to things like maternity leave and child-bearing and reduced promotional prospects many women are likely to experience the phases of the teaching career, as Sikes represents them, in rather a different way from men. And it is important to recognize that even those women who follow a 'normal' career pattern will experience their careers differently from men. One aspect of difference relates especially to those women who are successful in gaining promotion to senior posts in schools and this is discussed by Kanter (1977) in a study of the working lives of women in an American industrial corporation, namely the numerical distribution of men and women in such positions:

> The numerical distribution of men and women at the upper reaches created a strikingly different interaction context for women and for men. At local and regional meetings, training programmes, task forces, casual out-of-the-office lunches with colleagues, and career review or planning sessions with managers, men were overwhelmingly likely to find themselves with a predominance of people of their own type — other men . . . the culture of corporate administration and the experiences of men in it were influenced by this fact of numerical domination, by the fact that men were the *many*. (p. 206)

This question of numbers had its impact in a whole variety of ways on the personal experiences and likely success of *the few*, the women. They were often highly visible as a result of their minority, which could have its advantages in terms of being noticed for promotion but disadvantages in terms of the additional pressures it brought for those who had 'only women' status and who 'become tokens: symbols of how-women-can-do, stand-ins for all women' (p. 207). Some found themselves cast as outsiders, unable to enter the culture of an alien social world, constantly left out or ignored. This can lead to a *fear of visibility* and attempts to play down differences. Women in these positions may hide or minimize traits or behaviours that they see as distinctly feminine. Or specific women's roles may be carved out for the token few which embody various stereotypes of female behaviour and male-female relationships; Kanter (1977) suggests mother, seductress, pet and iron maiden. Clearly, we have as yet little research evidence on these sorts of issues as they affect women in teaching but there are certainly hints in the available literature that these processes and problems do exist for women in teaching. We need only think of the contradictions inherent in the common role in comprehensive schools of third deputy head responsible for girls discipline and matters of staff welfare.

In the first section of this chapter we have argued that research into teachers lives and careers has substantially reflected the political and ideological climates in which those lives are embedded. We have also argued that the career must be studied in the context of the whole life (and that life histories can help in exploring this relationship). Account must be taken of the increasing numbers of teachers who say things like 'recently, I've been thinking more about life and less about career' or 'you don't understand my centre of gravity is no longer here' (ie. in the classroom). When the climate of schooling is changing as rapidly as at the moment we need methodologies and concepts which sensitize us to these changes of gravity in teachers' lives. For much of the impact of those who currently seek to 'cut' education can only be assessed by methods which map the teachers' changing perception of their work; the delicate balance of commitment between teaching and life.

Notes

1   Some recent examples of plans for such cuts and their effects on jobs are: Newcastle-upon-Tyne, cuts of £1.7 million including 180 teaching jobs and 100 non-teaching jobs; Devon, cuts of £1.4 million including 134 teaching jobs; Doncaster, cuts of £1.8 million including 138 teaching jobs; Leicestershire threaten to cut 357 teaching jobs including making 75 teachers on fixed-term contracts redundant; Warwickshire propose to axe 200 teaching jobs; Hertfordshire have cut 482 secondary teaching posts since 1979 and 52 per cent of ancillary and clerical posts have disappeared in this period; Ealing plans to cut 40 middle school posts; Harrow plans to cut 15 teaching posts.
2   At the time of going to press attempts are being made to restructure salary scales, with a two year entry grade and a main professional grade with higher levels of pay for those with particular, substantial responsibilities.
3   However, this may be less true in the sixth form colleges; see Burke in this volume.

References

ACKER, S. (1980) 'Women, and other academics, *British Journal of Sociology of Education*, 1, 1, pp. 81–82.
BALL, D. (1972) 'Self and identity in the context of deviance: The case of criminal abortion', in SCOTT, R. and DOUGLAS, J. (Eds) *Theoretical Perspectives on Deviance*, New York, Basic Books.
BALL, S.J. (1981a) *Beachside Comprehensive*, Cambridge, Cambridge University Press.
BALL, S.J. (1981b) 'The teaching nexus', in BARTON, L. and WALKER, S. (Eds) *Schools Teachers and Teaching*, Lewes, Falmer Press.
BALL, S.J. (1984) 'Becoming a comprehensive? Facing up to falling rolls', in BALL, S.J. (Ed.) *Comprehensive Schooling: A Reader*, Lewes, Falmer Press.
BALL, S.J. (1985) 'School politics, teachers' careers and educational change: A case study of becoming a comprehensive school', in BARTON, L. and WALKER, S. (Eds) (forthcoming).
BALL, S.J. and LACEY, C. (1980) 'Subject disciplines as the opportunity for group action', in

WOODS, P.E. (Ed.) *Teacher Strategies,* London, Croom Helm.

BECKER, H. *et al.* (1961) *Boys in White,* Chicago, University of Chicago Press.

BECKER, H. (1966) *Sociological Work, Method and Substance,* Aldine, Chicago. Especially the article 'The life history and the scientific mosaic', pp. 63–74.

BENNETT, N. (1976) *Teaching Styles and Pupil Progress,* London, Open Books.

BERLAK, A. and BERLAK, H. (1981) *Dilemmas of Schooling: Teaching and Social Change,* London, Methuen.

BERNSTEIN, B. (1981) 'On the classification and framing of educational knowledge,' in YOUNG, M.F.D. (Ed.) *Knowledge and Control,* London, Collier-Macmillan.

BERTAUX, D. (1981) *Biography and society,* London, Sage.

BOGDAN, R. and TAYLOR, S. (1970) *Introduction to Qualitative Research Method,* New York and London, Wiley.

CALLAHAN, R. (1962) *Education and the Cult of Efficiency,* Chicago, University of Chicago Press.

CARSPECKEN, P. and MILLER, H. (1983) 'Teachers in an occupied school', paper presented at the *Teachers' Careers and Lives Conference,* St. Hilda's College, Oxford.

CLEGG, S. and DUNKERLEY, D. (1980) *Organization, Class and Control,* London, Routledge and Kegan Paul.

CORTIS, G.A. (1975) 'Seven years on — a longitudinal study of teacher behaviour' Educational Review, **28**, 1, pp. 60–70.

DELAMONT, S. (1980) *Sex Roles and the School,* London, Methuen.

DENSCOMBE, M. (1980) 'The work content of teaching', *British Journal of Sociology of Education,* **1**, 3, pp. 279–292.

DENSCOMBE, M. (1984) 'Control, controversy and the comprehensive school,' in BALL, S.J. (Ed.) *Comprehensive Schooling: A Reader,* Lewes, Falmer Press.

DES (1977) *Education in Schools: A consultative Document,* London, HMSO.

DES (1981) Her Majest's Inspectorate 'Report by HMI on the effects in the education service in England of local authority expenditure policies financial year 1980–81', London, HMSO.

EVANS, J. (1982) *Teacher strategies and pupil identities in mixed-ability curriculum: A case study,* unpublished PhD thesis, Chelsea College, University of London.

GOODSON, I.F. (1981) 'Life Histories and the Study of Schooling', *Interchange,* Ontario, **11**, 4.

GOODSON, I.F. (Ed.) (1983) *School Subjects and Curriculum Change,* London, Croom Helm.

GOODSON, I.F. (Ed.) (1985) *Social Histories of the Secondary School Curriculum: Subjects for Study,* Lewes, Falmer Press.

HARGREAVES, A. (1977) 'Progressivism and pupil autonomy', *Sociological Review,* **25**, 3, pp. 585–621.

HARGREAVES, D.H. (1967) *Social Relations in a Secondary School,* London, Routledge and Kegan Paul.

KANTER, R.M. (1977) *Men and Women of the Corporation,* New York, Basic Books.

LACEY, C. (1970) *Hightown Grammar,* Manchester, Manchester University Press.

LACEY, C. (1977) *The Socialization of Teachers,* London, Methuen.

LORTIE, D. (1975) *Schoolteacher,* Chicago, University of Chicago Press.

LUNDGREN, U.P. (1972) *Frame Factors and the Teaching Process,* Stockholm, Almquist and Wiksell.

LYONS, G. (1981) *Teacher Careers and Career Perceptions,* Windsor, NFER-Nelson.

MARLAND, M. (1983) 'Staffing for sexism: Educational leadership and role models', *Westminster Studies in Education,* **5**, pp. 11–26.

MEASOR, L. (1984) 'Pupil perceptions of subject status', in GOODSON, I.F. and BALL, S.J. (Eds) *Defining the Curriculum: Histories and Ethnographies,* Lewes, Falmer Press.

MORGAN, C., HALL, V. and MACKAY, H. (1983) *The Selection of Secondary Headteachers,* Milton Keynes, Open University Press.

POLLARD, A. (1982) 'A model of classroom coping strategies', *British Journal of Sociology of Education,* **3**, 1, pp. 19–38.

RISEBOROUGH, G. (1981) 'Teachers careers and comprehensive schooling: An empirical study', *Sociology*, **15**, 3, pp. 352–80.

ROSSER, E. and HARRE, R. (1976) 'The meaning of trouble', in HAMMERSLEY, M. and WOODS, P.E. (Eds) *The Process of Schooling*, London, Routledge and Kegan Paul.

RUTTER, M. *et al.* (1979) *Fifteen Thousand Hours: Secondary Schools and Their Effects on Children*, London, Open Books.

SALAMAN, G. (1978) 'Towards a sociology of organizational structure', *Sociological Review*, **26**, 3, pp. 519–54.

SCRIMSHAW, P. (1975) 'Should schools be participant democracies?' in BRIDGE, D. and SCRIMSHAW, P. (Eds) *Values and Authority in Schools*, London, Hodder and Stoughton.

SHARP, R. and GREEN, A. (1975) *Education and Social Control,* London, Routledge and Kegan Paul.

SHAW, C. (1930) *The Jackroller*, Chicago, University of Chicago Press.

SPRADBERY, J. (1976) 'Conservative pupils? Pupil resistance to a curriculum innovation in mathematics', in WHITTY, G. and YOUNG, M. (Eds) *Explorations in the Politics of School Knowledge*, Driffield, Nafferton.

SUTHERLAND, E. (1937) *The Professional Thief*, Chicago, University of Chicago Press.

THOMAS, W.I. and ZNANIECKI, F. (1927) *The Polish Peasant in Europe and America*, New York (2nd Edition).

TROPP, A. (1957) *The Schoolteachers*, London, Heinemann.

WALLACE, G., MILLER, H. and GINSBURG, M. (1983) 'Teachers' responses to the cuts', in AHIER, J. and FLUDE, M. (Eds) *Contemporary Education Policy*, London, Croom Helm.

WATTS, J. (1977) *The Countesthorpe Experience*, London, George Allen and Unwin.

WEBER, M. (1968) *Economy and Society*, London, Bedminster.

WERTHMAN, C. (1963) 'Delinquents in schools', *Berkeley Journal of Sociology*. **8**, 1, pp. 39–60.

WHITESIDE, T. and BERNBAUM, G. (1979) 'Growth and decline: Dilemmas of a profession', in BERNBAUM, G. (Ed.) *Schooling in Decline*. London, Macmillan.

WILSON, B. (1962) 'The teacher's role — A sociological analysis', *British Journal of Sociology*, **3**, 1, pp. 15–32.

WIRTH, A. (1983) *Productive Work — In Industry and Schools*, New York and London, University Press of America.

WOODS, P.E. (1979) *The Divided School*, London, Routledge and Kegan Paul.

WOODS, P.E. (1981) 'Strategies, commitment and identity: Making and breaking the teacher', in BARTON, L. and WALKER, S. (Eds) *Schools, Teachers and Teaching*, Lewes, Falmer Press.

The Life Cycle of the Teacher

Patricia J. Sikes

Editors' Note: This paper draws in part on data from an ESRC funded project on teachers' careers, directed by Peter Woods. Measor's paper, in this volume, also arises from the work of that project. Sikes follows the life cycle of the teacher from probationary year through to retirement.

> They stay young, they stay young and they stay young, and you get older and older and older, it's the same old pattern. That's what I dislike about teaching. (Emlyn, 33, Scale 3).

Pupils, like policemen, continually get younger — or so many teachers say. By virtue of the nature of their job it is difficult for teachers, as it is for obstetricians and lollipop people, to avoid recognizing their own mortality. As social systems, schools are affected and influenced by the processes occurring within them. The aging of members is but one of these processes and, as a consequence of falling rolls and contraction the teaching profession becomes, on average, older, is one which is likely to assume increasing significance for the cultures, ethos and outcomes of schools.

This chapter presents an overview, *not* an exhaustive description, of the ways in which secondary school teachers perceive, experience and adapt to growing old. It draws on evidence collected in the course of research into teacher careers using life history method. Male and female, art and science, retired, mid-career and new secondary school teachers, with ages ranging from 25 to 70, approximately 48 teachers in total, were involved in this project. Although every possible age group was not represented in the sample, information about perceptions and experiences at all stages of a teaching career was available as a consequence of the methodology. Insofar as, within its parameters, the sample is biased, it is probably so with respect to female career patterns. It has been thought that it is usual for women teachers to have 'split careers', taking at least five years off to have and bring up children. This was not the experience of the women in the sample who either had no children or if they had had only stopped teaching for a relatively brief period.

Owing to the relatively small number of informants usually involved, life history research is open to criticisms on grounds of validity and typicality. The major safeguard for the life historian is triangulation. In this particular research, space and investigator triangulation were used (see Denzin, 1970). I was also able to refer to evidence collected for an inquiry I had previously conducted into secondary school teachers' perceptions, adaptations and motivations in a contracting secondary school system, which had involved teachers of all ages.

Age and Occupation

Aging is both a unique and a universal experience and as such is an important source of personal and social identity. In western culture, and particularly for men, paid work tends to take up a large proportion of the life cycle and occupation can, and often does, confer identity (see Mulford and Salisbury, 1964; Havinghurst, 1964; Super, 1981). Aging, occupational development and identity are inextricably linked. Sofer (1970) suggests that 'the variations in meaning attached to work at different phases of the personal life cycle can be expected to be associated with variations in what the person expects at different phases and what is expected of him. We associate particular ages with particular statuses and with each status go characteristic and legitimate hopes, expectations, rights and duties. Age-status expectations constitute an important link between the personality system of the individual and the social system in which he participates' (pp. 118 and 119). These meanings and expectations are likely to be further differentiated when, as in teaching, there is an hierarchical career structure and 'position mobility follows patterned sequences (and) different motivations . . . become appropriate and inappropriate at each stage' (Strauss, 1959).

Research (eg. Peterson, 1974; Newman, 1979; and Rempel and Bentley, 1970) has variously shown that different experiences, attitudes, perceptions, expectations, satisfactions, frustrations, concerns, etc. appear to be related to different phases of the teacher's life and career cycle. This is the case for other workers (see Glaser, 1968, for examples). However, teachers are in the almost unique position of working with a fixed generation, which they progressively move further and further away from.

There is no standard definition of the age span of a generation. In this chapter, age parameters are of only relative importance because 'generation' is conceptualized as being essentially subjective and experiential. Thus, a generation share a culture and similar experiences during a specific period of time, ie. within the same historical context. We move out of one generation and into another when, because of various extra-and intra-personal influences it no longer feels appropriate or comfortable, physically as well as psychologically perhaps, to share and participate in particular cultural activities. For example, reflecting on his, relatively brief, teaching career, one man said:

> It's interesting, the sort of changing relationship with children. When I first started, when one was, sort of, young, 22 or 23, children treat you as an

older brother, whereas now they start to look on one more as a parent, sort of thing. You know I find, particularly in this school, where the parents are often not much older than myself, there's a change in the sort of relationship and I suppose that will come about more. (Arnold, 31, Scale 2).

At the same time, and more usual within the work situation, age relationships *vis à vis* younger colleagues shift from child to parent. Cain's (1964) concept of age status asynchronization usefully describes the imbalances or discrepancies which can occur and can be a source of personal and social strain if a teacher is in a low scale, low status post that is generally regarded as being appropriate for a younger person.

Framework for Comprehension

Teachers do not all follow the same occupational career path, nor are their lives necessarily similar in other respects — each has their own idiosyncratic biography. Yet their accounts do suggest a common developmental sequence of stages or phases each of which seems to be associated with an evaluation and perhaps a redefinition and/or re-ordering of interests, commitments and attitudes, frequently in response to events and experiences not directly connected with the work situation.

In considering these different stages in context — ie. in terms of the teacher's total life experience it did seem that Levinson *et al*'s (1979) conceptualization of life development could serve as a useful framework for comprehension and also provide a structure for the coherent presentation of evidence. Drawing upon sociology, anthropology, history, political science, psychology and psychiatry these authors take a broad based social-psychological view of male adult development, characterizing phases in the life cycle as 'seasons'.

On the basis of empirical research, using a biographical interviewing technique Levinson argues that 'the life structure evolves through a relatively orderly sequence (of eras) during the adult years' (p. 49), (brackets and contents are my addition), and that each era is characterized and identified by 'its own distinctive and unifying qualities which have to do with the character of living' (p. 18). Levinson's study was limited to males and the sample was really too small to justify the prescriptive calendar described. Yet, because the 'character of living' encompasses all aspects of life — biological, psychological, social — the model can accommodate differences of gender, race, occupation, culture, historical and geographical contexts etc., which can be expected to influence the individual's life experience. Indeed, research[1] has indicated that women go through the same developmental periods as men, although some of the particular incidents are different.

The rest of this chapter will be concerned with outlining what appear to be definite, identifiable phases of the teacher's career. These phases have not been rigidly defined in terms of age and therefore fit loosely into Levinson's model which will be used as a supporting, rather than a confining framework.

Phase 1: 21–28 age group

According to Levinson *et al.*, the major tasks facing those in the 21–28 age group are '(a) to explore the possibilities for adult living: to keep options open, avoid strong commitments and maximize the alternatives ... and (b) ... to create a stable life structure: become more responsible and "make something of my life"' — (p. 58). This phase, which he calls *Entering the Adult World*, is in many respects something of a trial period and it seems that teaching is a career which allows scope to attempt and to accomplish both of its tasks.

Even among those for whom actually becoming a teacher is the realization of a long term ambition[2], many young teachers do not see themselves as committed to a life-long career in teaching (see Nias and Cole in this volume). Intention to leave, and numbers actually leaving teaching, is considerably higher among the under 30s than for any other age group (Kyriacou and Sutcliffe, 1979; Lortie, 1975; Lacey, 1977). School teaching is something they are trying out before going on to other things, which they may or may not have ideas about:

> I am now wanting to get, still with an element of teaching but being able to carry on with things, personal, individual work of my own at the same time. My ideal is to get a job part-time teaching in an art college — like it is for most other art teachers. (Chris, 28, Scale 1, art teacher)

Jan was less specific.

> I don't know whether I see myself being in school in ten years time. It depends a lot on circumstances, personal circumstances. I just don't know yet. I don't plan that far ahead. (Jan, 25, Scale 1, art teacher)

Pete (25, Scale 1, biology teacher) hoped to go into business and Margery (45, Scale 3, chemistry teacher) had chosen teaching rather than take up an offer of a job as a research chemist because she was getting married and saw her career becoming relatively unimportant. Very few actually have any specific career plans (Lyons, 1981); this is probably because they are unaware of the possibilities, for, those who do, often have a family background of teachers — they know the culture (see Super, 1981).

It is also true that at the present time when there is teacher unemployment and when many teachers can only get temporary posts, actually having a Scale 1 job is something to feel fortunate about and can seem to be sufficient career. Promotion, especially when opportunities are so limited and the future so uncertain, may appear as an extremely remote prospect. For the majority, if not all new teachers, the immediate concern is coping, and being seen to be able to cope with the job itself.

> It worries me, it still worries me ... when you go into English classes or whatever, they're all sitting down, quietly working, but they don't in art, they're all over the place, and I don't like people coming in and thinking they're not working. I mean they all are. (Sarah, 25, Scale 1, art teacher)

In order to survive they have to learn the skills, the craft technology of teaching. But first, if they are to succeed they have to come to terms with the reality of the situation.

The majority of the teachers we have talked to had had grammar school educations. Their first contact with comprehensives or secondary moderns, and their pupils, whether it was on teaching practice (TP), in their first job, or later on ('old' teachers can still be young in experience) came as a bit of a surprise. It seems that, as Peterson (1964) found among Chicago teachers, 'there occurs in early teaching experience, a "reality shock" in coming to terms with problems of disciplining and motivating students' (p. 268). (See also Cole, this volume; Grace, 1978.)

> I did a TP in a secondary modern and it was like a new world. Here were people who didn't care about doing well or doing better than others like I'd done throughout school and college ... (but) I enjoyed the experience. I used to go home and tell my mum and dad about what the children got up to and they wouldn't believe some of the stories. (John, 45, Scale 4, art teacher)

> For my first five years I worked in a grammar school. It was a new experience teaching non-grammar school kids. I was aware of the difference, because my wife worked in a secondary modern but I'd never actually taught kids who were secondary modern kids and meeting these turned me upside down ... but I survived, I learnt an awful lot. (Dave, 45, Scale 4, chemistry teacher)

It was perhaps an even greater shock for Keith who went into teaching straight from industry without any training:

> I thought, I'll be a grammar school teacher. It'll be just like it was when I was a kid, and I was all sort of nostalgic, it'll be just like going back to school again ... the kids were not like I'd expected. Even though it was a grammar school it was in no way the sort of grammar school I'd been to ... I was shattered by the kind of boys that I met who couldn't care tuppence about learning, and all they seemed to want to do was mess about all the time; and by the girls who were not at all like I'd thought. They weren't at all ladylike. In fact many of them were cruder than the boys. (Keith, 38, Scale 1, chemistry teacher)

Discipline maintenance seems to be the area which causes young teachers the most anxiety. It is a curious phenomenon that particularly, although not exclusively, for women, first impressions of pupils are of how physically big and of how mature they seem.

> My first 6th form group all seemed enormous. (With regard to their maturity) I think I just got them wrong just as I think all young teachers do; they looked mature and you thought they were but they weren't any different really ... I think it was just me really, or anyone whose inexperienced. (Margery, 45, Scale 3, chemistry teacher)

Lacking the natural authority of age, keeping order is often perceived as a frightening and difficult task. In the past when more authority was, seemingly, attached to the teachers' role some were, perhaps, a little more confident.

> In the first school, the grammar school, that I was in, even the 6th form, and our ages weren't all that much different, I was 23 and they were 18, 19, even then they had to be told what to do and disciplined. And they accepted it, it was what they expected. (Dave, 45, Scale 4, chemistry teacher)

But even teachers who experienced a similar situation to that Dave describes, along with those working in schools where discipline is comparatively strict, still tended to be apprehensive and usually experienced and were aware of pupils 'trying it on' and 'seeing how far they can go' with a new teacher. Jan's experience is typical:

> I found the pupils higher up the school, my first week in this place, were all out to get me, the likes of the 4th years and the 5th years. I was new. And they do it with every new teacher I've since found out because I say to people, 'well did that happen to you?' 'Oh yeh! They do it to everyone just to test you out' . . . They answer back, try and put one over on you if you . . . explain something they'll say 'Oh, why is that?' as if to say 'Well do you really know what you're talking about?' They test you out on that. They usually heave one at the beginning where they try and paint each other . . . It's all annoying little things, ripping up a sheet of paper, just to see what reaction you'll get . . . I did it with young teachers when I was a kid. (Jan, 25, Scale 1, art teacher)

During their training and when they first start teaching quite a number have been advised that it is a good plan to be very strict, firm and even distant for the first half term in order to establish an identity as a teacher who will brook no nonsense (cf. Waller, 1932 — where it is upheld that the effective teacher maintains a marked social distance). After this, it is said, it should be possible to 'let up' a little and approach and respond to pupils, who hopefully have learnt that it is not worth taking 'liberties' and 'advantages', in a more relaxed and friendly manner. Jan followed this advice:

> Once I've got the discipline I can relax and go round and talk to them individually. But I won't get involved with them until they are at a stage when I can go round and know if I talk to one person somebody else isn't going to start yelling . . . so that's about the first half term before I really start to get to know a class. That's what they advised me to do at college . . . We have a system in this school where if they're too bad we send them to a year tutor. Well I was warned straightaway, don't do that too much because the children know, as soon as you send them out of the classroom, you've lost . . . If you're prepared to set one detention a year, you're prepared to set one essay and make sure you get it all in, nine times out of ten they won't do it again. (Jan, 25, Scale 1, art teacher)

There are those who try, unsuccessfully, to follow this advice, or who reject it, because it goes against their personal nature. For example:

> I'd rather be too friendly than the other extreme, so I'll go to that way. It seems to be more pleasant . . . and it's the easiest for me to do, so I won't go against what I'm personally like. (Chris, 28, Scale 1, art teacher)

> I'm sure I have more discipline problems than I should because I like to relax too easily, and relaxing, you can relax too much and the kids soon take advantage of it. (Pete, 25, Scale 1, biology teacher)

> I try to follow the plan of starting off strict and then soften up later . . . but I'm not very good at being authoritarian so I soon soften up, 'cos I can't remember to keep doing it . . . (Ann, 43, Scale 1, art teacher)

At some time during their first year teachers often experience 'critical incidents' which are to do with discipline (see Measor and Cole, this volume). Frequently these incidents take the form of a direct challenge to their authority, and thereby their professional identity. If the teacher keeps control and resolves the situation, or if they lose their temper and verbally or even physically assault pupils, and by so doing show themselves to be human, it seems that their identity as a competent teacher is strengthened — both in the eyes of pupils with whom they are likely to have 'easier' relationships, and of other staff who begin to respect them as fellow professionals. However, this will only be the case if their anger is controlled. Teachers who can be easily riled are fair game for pupils who feel like a diversion and a spot of entertainment in a lesson. Nor are they highly regarded by colleagues who are likely to see them as inept, lacking in self-control and, therefore, unprofessional. In the following account Sarah outlines the scene she staged after pupils had misbehaved on an out of school visit. She suggests a potential gender difference, when she reflects that the scenario and the teacher's role in it might have been different had she been a man.

> I told them off, and I organized a sort of demonstration of disgust . . . so I just, basic acting, threw a tantrum and walked out . . . I thought I wonder what'll they do now? So I came in a few minutes later . . . and they were completely silent and so they realized by that demonstration of something that is not normal for me, that I was really annoyed . . . That was drastic action, something I've never done before . . . A man might have done something different but that's how I thought I could shock them, a shock tactic. . . . The situation developed and as (it) developed this was my end plan. It worked though! (Sarah, 25, Scale 1, art teacher)

The chances of her having to use such a strategy again are probably slight. Teachers often report that following a 'critical incident' they experience fewer difficulties. This is partly because pupils respond differently learning via their grapevine that they will not necessarily 'get away' with disruptive behaviour, and partly because their confidence in their ability to cope is strengthened. Such incidents appear to be a crucial part of learning to cope with being a teacher, and it seems that those who continually 'fail' get reputations of inadequacy and, if they do not leave, are not regarded within that particular school as being competent teachers.

For the majority, on the whole, as time passes, while it continues to be an important area of concern, discipline tends to become a slightly less intimidating aspect of the job. There are various explanations for this. For instance, teachers gain experience and fairly soon establish an identity and a reputation within their school.

> After three years you'd have learnt the technique or learnt some techniques that work for you. And you begin to know the kids, which makes a difference, and they you. When you're new, you're the sort of pebble that sticks out and they react to you more. When you're sort of part of the wallpaper, you're part of the scene, part of the background, it's different . . . You're a member of the school, you've always been there. Or, at least they can't remember a time when you weren't. And it just goes on then. You've got no real, major problems. (Jim, retired biologist)

In addition, pupils are diminished in all respects, they resume normal proportions — as Dave remembers.

> I taught for five years in one school, and when I think about that the 1st years that I'd started teaching were then in the 5th form. But, I taught them as 1st years so, they grow with you and you see them growing up so they're not so much of a threat, physically in size or in personality . . . when you can remember them as tiny 1st years. (Dave, 45, Scale 4, chemistry teacher)

Furthermore, and perhaps even more reassuring they may be surprised to learn, from a variety of sources including pupils who talk freely to them, and when they cover other people's classes, that older teachers do not necessarily have the degree of control that the young teacher had attributed to them. Here Chris explains how he was enlightened:

> I have, you know, been through other lessons and I've seen lessons happening. A lot more recently some of the older teachers here have not been sort of ashamed to admit that they had (discipline) problems. (People started discussing their problems at the time when the authority abolished corporal punishment) . . . I found it reassuring, I don't know whether it surprised me or not, yeh, I think it did because some of them I thought were so confident in their appearance that they couldn't possibly have any problems. In outward appearance in the staffroom. Most of the lessons that I've taken (covered) have been their lessons and pupils have a certain, you know, thing about certain teachers and say 'oh so and so's tricked we never do anything what we're told, you know, it's so boring.' I think, ah yes! it must be, they must have a few problems. (Chris, 28, Scale 1, art teacher)

In some ways coming into possession of such knowledge represents and can be regarded as a status passage, and an initiation into the 'teacherhood', because at least part of the mystique of the 'experienced teacher' is lifted and they are revealed as pretty ordinary mortals not dissimilar to oneself!

After discipline the next major aspect of becoming a teacher would appear to be concerned with the subject. At this stage the subject is usually personally very important. Most teachers have, to a greater or lesser degree of intensity, a special fondness for, and get a great deal of enjoyment from, their subject. It is because of the subject, in order to stay in contact with it and perhaps because of a desire to pass it on that some are motivated to become teachers (see Lyons, 1981, p. 94). 'I really enjoy my subject, and when I was thinking about other jobs I immediately thought of what else I can do in my subject'. (Pete, 25, Scale 1, biology teacher).

> I wanted to do something with art . . . and it was while I was in the 6th form that I decided on teaching. I hadn't wanted to be a teacher ever since I was young. (Jan, 25, Scale 1, art teacher)

The subject can provide a sense of security. It is an area the young teacher is, as Pete says, comfortable with:

> I think it's very much a question of wanting to do the things that you feel comfortable at doing. And I think I know my subject well enough to be able to teach it pretty well. (Pete, 25, Scale 1, biology teacher)

With regard to the subject they are specialists, experts in the field, and it gives them an identity (cf. Lacey, 1977; Bernstein, 1971). In school, however, they are inexperienced novices and one way of coping with this is to put the emphasis on the familiar. Thus the subject is likely to be perceived as the most important part of being a teacher. Teachers of all ages and lengths of experience may use the subject as a personal defence. For instance, a teacher who finds it difficult to cope with mixed ability classes may say that his subject is too difficult for the less able (see Elbaz, 1983, p. 122). It seems that those with a subject degree and a PGCE put greater emphasis on the importance of the subject than do these who trained at a college of education. A possible explanation is that the latter have made higher investments in their self as teachers and, therefore, have a greater incentive, and/or find adapting to the role easier (see Grace, 1978, p. 200).

Learning how best to communicate the subject to the various groups of pupils tends to engage a large proportion of the young teachers' attention: 'It's such a struggle, especially with the older ones, to get them to sit down and to sweat over it, which you need to do. I haven't got the expertise *yet* to get it out of them' (Sarah, 25, Scale 1, art teacher); although Chris' concern to communicate effectively is perhaps more to do with his interest in the general problem of communicating ideas and his view of the teachers' role, than with his relative lack of experience:

> It is difficult to start with, a challenge if you like, but I can see things . . . you know, goals, that I'd quite like to reach, being able to communicate successfully and so on. . . . getting across certain complicated things, you know, sort of ideas, being able to share those ideas, that are of a very complicated, sometimes, personal nature . . . You just have to some way

improve and cut down the time it takes you to get to some more important things that I am interested in and want to understand . . . Everything's got to be so obvious and laid in front of them without any doubts about it . . . well most of the time, you can't leave too much that can be interpreted wrongly . . . You have to plan and go through all the possibilities before, or at least work out what could happen . . . in terms of interpretation, the way they might interpret ideas that you're telling them . . . how they might misinterpret or the directions they might go off in from the ideas that you give them. (Chris, 28, Scale 1, art teacher)

Usually they evolve their own pedagogy through a mixture of trial and error, from observing others (on the rare occasions when this is possible) by remembering their own teachers (who, incidentally often serve as models of bad practice) and from their own idea of what it should be like. The majority say that their professional training, apart from teaching practice, was of very limited practical value. Sometimes, in the face of cynicism from older members of staff, and an initially unpromising pupil response (often due to pupils' expectations based on experience in that particular school) they need great persistence in order to carry on with their strategies. This was Pete's experience:

It's a strategy that I've always tried to do and I've always worried about whether it's working. And recently I seem to be getting evidence that it is working . . . Basically it's be positive . . . you don't slang kids, you're never sarcastic to kids, and the way to motivate people . . . is to try and find occasions when they're doing something right, and tell them it's right and say how pleased you are, and really encourage good things and don't gripe on about bad things.

I went on a course which advocated this type of approach and it gave me a conviction that it's the *right* thing to do in teaching . . . and recently it really seems to be working . . . I look around at other members of the staff and I see that they're doing the opposite and that makes me feel that I'm right. And they tell me that I'm stupid and that my way will never work! And I was beginning to believe them. Not now though. (Pete, 25, Scale 1, biology teacher)

Socialization into the occupational culture, learning to be a professional and a proper teacher also takes place on the job. By observation and experience the young teacher learns the appropriate codes of conduct which relate to such things as: how to address another member of staff in front of pupils: how to talk to, relate to, and associate with pupils: What constitutes acceptable dress for a teacher: in-school expectations about marking, involvement in extra-curricular activities, and so on. If one is to have a smooth running career it is as well to fit in (see Hanson and Harrington, 1976, pp. 5–6) to internalize or at least strategically comply (see Lacey, 1977, pp. 72–3) with these informal although very important rules. As Lacey (1970) notes, beginning teachers who fail in their attempts to strategically redefine and change the rules regarding professional behaviour, can experience 'serious problems in qualifying' (p. 96). These rules are rarely verbalized or defined, for instance:

> There are certain things, I don't think about them any more, I just, if I think it's wrong I don't do it. (Chris, 28, Scale 1, art teacher)

> I think that teachers should adopt certain standards, but what those standards are I don't know, but I must admit, when I see other teachers I think, Ugh ... I spose it's the middle class thing ... just the way they conduct themselves, just that, that special thing. (Sarah, 25, Scale 1, art teacher)

This lack of definition allows schools to develop their own idiosyncratic rules and codes of conduct, which means that teachers can easily miscue. Once again, Keith's experience as a late entrant provides a particularly clear example:

> When I first started teaching, I came straight from industry. My first reaction when kids messed about in class was to give them a smack round the head. And I was soon told that that was unprofessional conduct ... but, this is it, ... what *is* professional conduct then? ... I don't think I've ever seen a job specification ... But what I'm getting at is that to my recollection no one had ever said a professional teacher does this, this and this and doesn't do that, that, and that ... What does the profession entail? What are the criteria? What are the norms of behaviour? ... because when I was a pupil, to inflict corporal punishment was considered to be quite a professional thing to do ... now, twenty five years later it's an unprofessional thing ... I now appreciate that it was unprofessional conduct to belt a kid ... but until they tell me the rules of the trade as it were I don't know what's considered professional or unprofessional. (Keith, 38, Scale 1, chemistry teacher)

At some schools young teachers quickly learn that it is perhaps not wise to talk too much in the staffroom about problems, particularly disciplinary ones.

> In the staffroom teachers vocalize problems that they don't really need any help for, but, just need to say it ... They're not prepared to talk about proper problems ... I'm not, not in the staffroom as a whole. To some people, yes, the people who I know perhaps could help me, like a head of year ... I mean, if it is known that a member of staff is having problems then ... the opinion goes down ... I've seen that happen to someone. (Sarah, 25, Scale 1, art teacher)

What Sarah (and most other teachers) says throws an interesting light on Hammersley's (1980) findings that the staffroom offers a 'ritual of self-exposure and repair and thus an expression of solidarity' (p. 48). Teachers say that the majority of staffroom conversations are at the anecdotal level and it may be that accounts of terrible classes and awful pupils are the tip of the iceberg. Telling such stories, which can often have a humorous aspect and hence entertainment value, and sharing the problem is reassuring both for the teller and the listeners who have had similar experiences. But, the real problems, the ones that cause most anxiety, are kept either to oneself, or are told to the people one trusts, and who it is felt safe to be open with. In Sarah's case, her head of year. However, even if only at a superficial level, it does seem that there has been a definite change in attitudes, and that it is easier for young teachers to seek help. Jim and Arthur, starting teaching just after and just before the war, felt that they simply had to get on with it.

> I can't ever recall sort of going to another member of staff and saying 'I just can't control this lot'. You wouldn't have dreamt of admitting your inability. (Jim, retired, biology teacher)

> There was an unwritten law that you didn't talk shop in the staffroom. You kept your worries to yourself. (Arthur, retired, art teacher)

Margery, who began her career in a grammar school in the late 1950s compares her experiences with the present day:

> I think actually a big difference is that ... one hid one's incompetence, very much, from everybody I think, from oneself. I think nowadays the young teachers we have are much more happy to talk about it, and I'm not sure it's always to their advantage ... When I started, any problems were your own affair. (Margery, 45, Scale 3, chemistry teacher)

Nowadays, in many schools, or within specific departments, new, inexperienced teachers are encouraged to talk about their problems and are given constructive, positive help. Yet, even in such atmospheres where young teachers are told they can talk freely, it seems that there are fears (perhaps not unreasonable if there are many teachers at your school with similar views to Margery's) of appearing incapable, of a reluctance to 'emphasize their powerlessness *vis à vis* their colleagues' (Nias this volume), and feelings and suspicions that problems and difficulties are worse than anyone else's.

> You imagine it's happening, you know, everybody's in the same place, but unless they actually tell you, you know, you think oh, they're not having half the problems I am ... they're (actually) having worse ones (laughs). (Chris, 28, Scale 1, art teacher)

These feelings are partly a consequence of the secrecy that surrounds the classroom and they are likely to be more commonly experienced as fewer probationers are appointed because of falling rolls. Both Pete and Chris had been the only probationers and the youngest members of staff at their school and both said that for a while they had felt rather isolated and depressed because of this. Chris was lucky to stay in touch with his friends from college:

> When I came here I was the only probationer ... I had friends outside the school who were teaching, who were in their first year, and I could share a lot of the things with them ... It's a great talking point, the first year of teaching ... It's very reassuring that everybody faces the same problem ... (Chris, 28, Scale 1, art teacher)

If a group of young teachers start at a school together they may form a mutual support group, wherein they can share experiences, tips, ideas and information about pupils. This was Christine's experience:

> When I came here there were three probationers in the department. We'd all started together, all got the same problems and we all used to sit after school sorting ourselves out. It was very much a self help type of group .... (We were all scientists) so we very much could identify with each other's problems ... It was quite important to me. At the end of the day we'd just collapse into a chair and thrash out the problems ... We used to discuss lesson content, pupil ability, discipline ... It was moral support to a great extent ... but there was practical help as well. (Christine, 34, Scale 3, physics teacher)

They may also joke about, and criticize as 'old fashioned' more senior teachers (cf. Peterson, 1964, p. 285), and this can serve a therapeutically cathartic function. As Peterson suggests, it seems that young teachers form 'generational cliques' partly in order to protect themselves from 'uncomfortable situations with mature teachers' (p. 296). In some schools there may be a group of teachers who are extremely vocal in expressing their dissatisfaction, cynicism and/or career frustration — others can be affected and even influenced by their scepticism. Pete was lucky to find a safety valve:

> There's all these people in the staffroom, absolutely moaning and moaning about what they've been asked to do and what they've got to do etc ... On the last week of last term, I just had to walk out of there ... I just couldn't cope with all those people moaning and moaning about what they had to do, it just cheesed me off so much I just had to say something to someone. And it developed into ... spilling out (to my head of department) about how hard I'm having to work and how I just can't cope etc. (and he agreed with me, said I was doing fine and is changing things so that I'm less pressurized). (Pete, 25, Scale 1, biology teacher)

Edelwich with Brodsky (1980) noted that 'attitudes like germs, spread rapidly in a stuffy atmosphere' (p. 76), and it might be that some experienced teachers try to ensure that the young teacher catches their 'disease'. New, enthusiastic workers in any occupation pose a threat to the *status quo*. In order to avoid being shown up and made to work harder, re-examine methods, etc. the older workers socialize the tyros into their ways and put pressure on them to conform. This happens in schools just as it does in factories (see Woods, 1981, p. 30; and Edelwich with Brodsky, 1980) and an increasingly static teacher population may well exacerbate the situation.

Even those who have universal-type ideas about education being able to have far reaching social effects are not exempt. Indeed the idealistic face potentially greater and more painful disillusionment, especially if they lack like-minded colleagues who can help them sustain their ideals.

Within a school, teacher age distribution is not only significant in purely educational terms. Young teachers, perhaps especially if they are new to an area and if they do not have personal commitments locally, may look to the school for their social life. They may be disappointed if most of the staff are older and concerned with their homes and families. Both Chris and Pete found this:

> I'd moved to this area to get the job so I didn't know anybody in the area. I think I expected everybody to be in the same position as me, people of about my age, that they'd go to similar sorts of places and do similar things. But I found there was nobody like that ... everybody was married ... they didn't want to do the same sort of things. (Chris, 28, Scale 1, art teacher)

> When I first came there seemed to be a big gap in age between me and everybody else ... It's a very old staffroom so there's very little social activity anyway ... it used to worry me for a time ... that there was no social life in our school. They were all talking about their mortgages and their kids and I was growing up far too fast. (Pete, 25, Scale 1, biology teacher)

If the teacher does join a school-based social group their whole life can revolve round the school, with boy/girl-friends, husbands/wives and children being progressively incorporated. Young teachers are often of the same generation as many of their pupils and are, therefore, likely to share similar interests and concerns eg. fashion and music. However, because it does seem that pupils tend not to regard teachers as people (see Blackie, 1977) it may be necessary to make sure that they realize this. As Jan commented:

> I think you've got to let them see you're human on occasions because they tend to think you're not human in some ways. They tend to think you're just a teacher, that you don't have a life outside. (Jan, 25, Scale, art teacher).

Such comments contradict Waller's (1932) assertion that, to his pupils the effective teacher must be 'relatively meaningless as a person'. On the whole, teachers said that they felt if pupils did recognize them as people it was usually easier to establish good relationships, which generally meant that discipline was less of a problem. Friendship, as Denscombe (1980) notes, can be a successful control strategy which, for the young teacher, goes some way to compensate for the lack of age and experience based authority. Ann's point of contact, which her subject allowed her to exploit, was, and still is, clothes:

> My first job was in a girls' secondary modern ... being young I got on well with teenage girls ... they identified with me, and they generally like art anyway ... Most of them didn't do 'O' level so there was no syllabus that had to be followed, no training that had to be done and so I often did things about fashion and things that they were interested in; so I managed to get them interested and then I could slip in a few things that I felt were worthwhile and they might not have seen. Plus the fact that I always made my own clothes, and they'd come and say 'I like your dress, Miss', and I'd say, 'Well, you make it like this', and they'd go home and make it; and I had a good relationship with them. (Ann, 43, Scale 1, art teacher)

The extent to which teachers want to share their interests and identify with pupils, obviously, differs. In some schools there are few, if any, similarities between pupil and young teacher (ie. 'educated', 'middle class') cultures (cf. Peterson, 1964, p. 271). While within such schools there may well have been 'constructed an identifiable middle ground between teacher and pupil cultures upon which the official business of the school (is) conducted' (Measor and Woods, 1982, p. 3), it is likely that there is little desire on either side to associate on a social basis. Pete's feelings were that: 'We're ever so friendly but there's always that distance and I've no wish for it to be any different'. (Pete, 25, Scale 1, biology teacher)

As has already been seen, during teacher training the importance of keeping 'that distance' in order to maintain discipline is often emphasized and, in any case, some personally prefer to be seen primarily in the teacher role. There are exceptions. Although none of the teachers I talked to said they had ever mixed socially with pupils they said that they had heard or knew of those who did. The ones who said that they definitely would not choose to do so suggested that those who did 'were perhaps lacking something in their personal lives'. (Chris, 28, Scale 1, art teacher)

American female high school teachers, who had started teaching in small rural schools were found to be more likely to report high job satisfaction from close social relationships with pupils than those who initially worked in urban areas (Peterson, 1964, pp. 71–2). Relative geographical isolation and community strength seem similarly to have been a factor in this country. Older teachers like Mrs Castle who taught in the Welsh valleys, and Arthur, working in a fen-land village, did not, in their early days before the war, have easy access to transport and were, therefore, thrown back on the same social life that was available to pupils and their families. Margery however, lived some distance from the school and she thought that this might have made a difference.

> I didn't mix socially with pupils. I didn't live in the town so I suppose that hindered . . . I lived about ten, twelve miles away, so (social life) tended to be separate . . . if I'd lived closer it might have been different. (Margery, 45, Scale 3, chemistry teacher)

It appears that it is part of the culture, the tradition, at some schools for pupils and teachers to meet out of school. For instance, Mr Count had worked at a relatively formal grammar school where teachers and pupils were expected to take equal turns at hosting the bridge club, and Ann's daughter, like I myself did, went to a school where it was usual for young teachers and 6th formers to be on Christian name terms and to meet socially.

One area where there is likely to be contact and a common interest is sport, where relationships which are not pupil-teacher but fellow-team-mate may develop.

> We played basket-ball three or four lunchtimes a week and I got to know that group of lads exceptionally well, and one or two of the girl hangers-on who'd come, and score for us: I was almost on an equal footing with 6th formers then . . . Just as my wife had a netball team. She was 21 and they

were 15 and they'd chat to her about their boyfriends and what have you, just as if she was one of them. (Dave, 45, Scale 4, chemistry teacher)

Marriage and long term relationships between male teachers and their pupils are, and always have been, far from rare: 'Once in a blue moon some member of staff would marry a 6th form pupil, and that happens even now'. (Margery, 45, Scale 3, chemistry). But teachers have to be careful. Men are usually warned, at college, to avoid situations which could possibly be misconstrued. Dave admitted to getting quite paranoid when he was a young teacher and it seemed that he was likely to get into a situation where he was alone with girl pupils. Sally, on the other hand, who, perhaps relevantly, had no teacher training, found the role compartmentalization expected of her as a young teacher, problematic.

> I think the social thing at first I did find a bit difficult . . . some of them (6th formers) wanted to come round in the evening and see me and discuss things they were doing and so on (as they had done with the previous older teacher) and an older member of staff advised me against this. Said he didn't think it was a good idea, I ought to be careful . . . it was difficult to be very friendly and familiar on one side and then go back to the school teachers' role on the other side. (Sally, 41, Scale 3, art teacher)

Young women, especially if they are attractive, may find themselves particularly popular. Not surprisingly this is especially likely to be the case when they work in boys' schools. This was Sally's experience:

> (When I first started, at a boys' secondary modern) there was a bit of a problem with being a novelty . . . with being one of two women and the other was coming up to retirement anyway, . . . and when I ran a club after school about seventy people turned up for it the first session. And we got the odd graffiti and that sort of thing. But it seemed to sort itself out fairly soon . . . when the novelty wore off it was better. (Sally, 41, Scale 3, art teacher)

Mrs Castle, quoted in Measor's paper (in this volume), gave a similar account. Yet, as Measor points out, the character of such incidents is not always as gentle. Less pleasant are sexual innuendoes which are, perhaps, particular occupational hazards for those teaching art, 'You always tend to get it a bit in art of course, with nudity being rather connected with art', (Sally, 41, Scale 3, art teacher); and biology. Women tend to adapt by using a strategy of ignoration: 'The more upset you are the more likely they are to do it', (Sally, 41, Scale 3, art teacher). For the most part, however, young teachers just enjoy being with pupils. They tend to have fewer personal and domestic commitments which along with their 'youthful energy' enable them to spend more time with kids doing things that they both enjoy. In John's (48, Scale 4, art teacher) case this had meant going out into the country to sketch; for Sarah (25, Scale 1, art teacher) it had been hiking trips, and in Pete's own words: 'I go birdwatching anyway. I might as well go birdwatching with other people and help them to learn things and share the pleasure' (Pete, 25, Scale 1, biology teacher) Those who do spend a lot of time taking part in and organizing extra curricular activities might have half an eye to being seen to be committed and involved and thereby hopefully improving their chances of promotion, but this is unlikely to be their sole motivation. Pete, for instance, has been able to accommodate, and hopefully further both his birdwatching and his career interests:

> From the promotion point of view it definitely helps ... when I ran the football team I thought 'Oh no, I don't fancy doing this', but, on the other hand, I felt quite definitely that I ought to get involved in something, and I'd been asked by the head of PE if I'd run a football team and I'd said 'yes' and when I went back to him I said, 'Well, look, rather than run a football team I'd rather run a birdwatching club'. (Pete, 25, Scale 1, biology teacher)

Sarah actually received confirmation that her involvement in extra-curricular activities was helping her career. When, on one occasion, as she frequently did, she found herself leading a walking party supposedly organized by another, more senior teacher, a deputy head was present:

> He said 'Well, it'll be mentioned in despatches that you did this, that and the other.' But the times you do it and there's nobody there to see you do it, you know I often wonder whether it is noted. (Sarah, 25, Scale 1, art teacher).

Promotional ambitions are typically to become head of a subject department. Indeed this was the aim of all of the young teachers I talked with. Pastoral posts of responsibility do not initially seem to be as popular. Reasons for this include (i) young teachers are less aware of career possibilities within the pastoral structure; (ii) as has already been noted, they tend to identify with their subject and are less willing to consider spending less time working with it (see Lacey, 1977, pp. 61–64); and (iii) they are too close in age to pupils to consider taking on a parental-type guidance role.

During the expansionist phase of the 1960s and early 1970s regular and frequent promotion came to be expected and it was not unusual for people of 27 or 28 years old to be Scale 3 or 4 heads of departments. In the early 1980s they are less likely to achieve such posts. Even so young teachers may be anxious to meet socially appropriate age associated career stages. The implication is that there is something 'wrong' with the teacher who is still on a Scale 1 after six or seven years' experience (see Cain, 1964).

> It doesn't look particularly good on a record for somebody to be teaching seven years on a Scale 1. It's a bit of a death knell. The natural question is 'Why has that person been on a Scale 1 for seven years?' Possibly because of certain incompetencies in certain respects the interviewers might feel. (Tom, 28, Scale 1, maths teacher)[3]

For a man, unless he is a late entrant, or there is another apparent acceptable reason, Scale 1 at twenty eight is not regarded as really appropriate. For a woman, however, particularly if she has children, there is little social shame attached to an entire working life spent in Scale 1 posts.

Phase 2: 28–33 Age Group

During this phase, which Levinson *et al.* (1979) call the *Age Thirty Transition*, 'the provisional exploratory quality of the twenties is ending (and there is a) sense of greater urgency' (p. 85). For many people life begins to get more serious now, commitments and responsibilities are increasing and it becomes more important to establish a stable basis and work out and plan a life structure for the future. It can be a stressful period, particularly because after the age of thirty it usually becomes increasingly difficult to start out in a new career. In various respects the years of the *Age. Thirty Transition* are a last chance to assess and subsequently confirm or change one's provisional life structure.

At this point gender differences can become particularly apparent. Women, who throughout their twenties had pursued an occupational career and had not had children frequently report that they experienced their thirtieth birthday as something of a watershed. They felt that they had very little time left to decide whether to have children and, depending on such variables as personal orientation, cultural norms and economic circumstances the choice may have appeared to be an either/or one (see Sheehy, 1976, chapter 1b).

Another very important factor to be considered is the state of the jobs market. All the mid-career women teachers I talked with who had children had been happy to interrupt their careers because they were confident that they could get a job when they wanted to start again. In the event, none of them were out of teaching for more than a year at a time. Nowadays the situation is different and women are more reluctant to resign. It seems that more of those who decide to have chidlren are taking only the statutory period of maternity leave before returning to their protected jobs.

During the *Age Thirty Transition* it may be that some teachers will leave or begin to consider or explore alternatives to teaching. For others promotion becomes a more important issue than it perhaps has previously been. By this time, teachers are likely to feel sufficiently experienced and capable of taking on greater responsibility. They no longer find their present job as satisfying or challenging as it initially was and they begin to look for a new one. Some will already have received promotion and may, therefore, be relatively satisfied for the moment. Others may believe that they have been 'overlooked' and may feel bitter and dissatisfied when they see older people on high scales apparently, and actually, not doing anything to earn their salaries. Their discontent is likely to partly be due to their increasing anxiety to achieve age appropriate positions. Teachers in this age group frequently say that they are afraid of becoming like older colleagues who 'failed' to do so, who have responded by withdrawing their effort and commitment and who are among the leading grumblers and cynics of the staffroom. For example:

> I know lots of teachers who've become rather embittered because they've served many years and rightly or wrongly feel they should have gained a promotion. Maybe they didn't deserve promotion ... but it does tend to make people embittered I think, when they could see other people who had

taught the same time as them, or even fewer years than them gaining promotion . . . I think people like them tend to do the minimum . . . they become sour, bitter and cynical, and I hope I don't find myself in that situation. (Phil, 32, Scale 3, physical education teacher)[3]

Riseborough (1981) describes how at Phoenix School the majority of male teachers gravitated either towards the clique or the cabal (cf. Burns, 1955, pp. 474 and 480). Clique members were 'bad' deviant, low-status teachers, who were anti-the-institution and who had a negative orientation to work; cabal members were the opposite. As Riseborough suggests, cliques appear to be part of the reality and culture of schools and represent and offer teachers a main line of adjustment to career disappointments. By the time they reach thirty many teachers suspect that they will qualify for clique membership.

Another reason why promotion may become particularly significant around this time is that domestic and familial commitments are increasing and money becomes more important. Chris was just finding this out at first hand.

As soon as I heard my wife was pregnant I thought 'Oh! Money.' Mainly 'cus my wife's working now . . . but she won't be able to do that after a couple more months so it's going to be pressure, moneywise so I've got to think about that . . . so I am looking for a Scale 2. (Chris, 28, Scale 1, art teacher)

Research shows that money also becomes more important if the job is proving unsatisfactory in other respects — eg. if promotions felt to be deserved are not forthcoming — (see Edelwich with Brodsky, 1980, p. 17). The wish for and assumption of greater responsibility is representative of 'growing up' and moving away from pupils' interests. Some teachers may deliberately make an effort to stay in touch with youth culture, but on the whole, their concerns are no longer similar to those of their pupils. Although like Elbaz's Sarah (1983, especially p. 153) they may retain, and even consciously hang on to, an ideal image of themselves as the 'young teacher' on the same side as the kids, the kids are less likely to see them in this light. As Peterson (1964) notes pupils 'seem to age-grade teachers by age distancing teachers, away from them', and this is experienced as 'a matter of loss . . . of some kind of intimate, friendly contact with pupils' (p. 273). Jim put it like this:

When you get a bit older, being familiar with them doesn't work. They know very well they can't be familiar with you . . . because the age gap doesn't allow it really, and so they don't appreciate you trying to bridge it'. (Jim, retired, biologist).

In effect pupils can be seen to be forcing teachers to grow up and acknowledge their age. In these circumstances perhaps it becomes easier to be the 'teacher', the mentor who is concerned from above, from a position of greater experience, rather than on the level. From this time on pastoral jobs begin to seem more appropriate than they previously did. Some who don't want to totally lose the satisfactions they get from informal contact may incorporate pupils, as friends, into their new family life, involving them in gardening, decorating, baby-sitting, and so on. For instance:

When we moved into our first house I used to invite kids round at the weekends. We'd do some digging or some painting, sketching as well as house painting. They'd have their teas with us. We'd just have them around. (John, 48, Scale 4, art teacher)

It is interesting that if teachers mention having been motivated to enter teaching by a teacher of their own who served as a career model, it was usually someone who gave them an insight into their out-of-school life. This had been so for John (quoted above) who was perhaps reproducing the situation for his pupil-friends and it had also been Pete's experience:

I think the biggest influence on me when I was coming to (career) decisions was my own biology teacher ... I used to go round to his house, spend time with him and his wife ... He seemed to have a life style that I would have enjoyed. He didn't seem to be working particularly hard; he had lots and lots of outside interests and he had lots of time in his holidays. And it seemed to be alright moneywise. (Pete, 25, Scale 1, biology teacher)

Unfortunately there is evidence which indicates that those with such career models are likely to be disillusioned and to become dissatisfied when they find that few pupils are as responsive and cooperative as they were as pupils (Edelwich with Brodsky, 1980, p. 50). My evidence tends to support this hypothesis, for to some extent John and Pete had both been disappointed in this respect, nor had they found career prospects, working conditions or wages to be as good as they had initially appeared.

While they may be especially prone to experience frustrations and stress concerning their objective career prospects and developments, in terms of actually teaching and coping in the classroom, teachers in this age group tend to have become more relaxed. Many like Ann, no longer feel as much need to rely on tight structures:

I think I was more formal when I first started because I didn't feel secure ... I think if a teacher's not secure if they can stand at the front of a class and dictate and have everybody do as they say it improves their feeling of security ... their feeling that they're in charge. (Ann, 43, Scale 1, art teacher)

They have begun to 'develop', to experiment and use their own ideas based on experience rather than relying exclusively upon what they have been taught and advised. Chris describes this process of working out his own ideas as one of unlearning.

I'm trying to forget everything (ideas about art in school) I started with because a lot of it was me repeating what I'd read; I mean Herbert Read and things. I never knew really if that was what I thought or if that was what I'd just read. I know that you do both, gain things from what you're reading but it sounded, to start with, not like me really. I was just picking them up, and I think it sounded like that when I said them to anybody. So as

I said, I've tried to forget what I've learnt in a way, and try and formulate something from actual teaching and try and work out something from that. Things like Reade are always pleasant to come back to because they're safe things that somebody else has said and you think, if you agree with them, there's two people who think the same and you're OK, you know, somebody else thinks like that. It's harder to come up with your own (ideas) but, I don't know, they feel a bit better. (Chris, 28, Scale 1, art teacher)

Some become more interested in curriculum development and innovation. In the early 1970s involvement in these areas was one way of enhancing promotion prospects (cf. Whiteside, 1978) but in the 1980s when fewer promotions are available personal satisfaction and maintaining interest when a change of job seems a remote possibility is more likely to be the central motivation.

Teachers of this age often begin to become more interested in pedagogy, rather than their subject. Helen remembers that she did.

I think I started teaching as a subject-based teacher, where the subject always came first, that was when I started, I think, perhaps until I came here really (when aged 28). I'm not quite sure of the reasons for it. But I think even more so as time has gone on I've got more of an, yes, OK, I teach art but I think of myself more as a teacher than artist, so I think it's changed to thinking of art as the motive for it as the fact you're thinking of being a teacher. (Helen, 41, Scale 3, art teacher)

Young teachers anticipate this happening. This may partly be because their subject, or rather its culture, as experienced at college or university (cf. Lacey, 1977) is becoming increasingly distant. Furthermore, subject knowledge, perhaps especially in the sciences, grows outdated, and there is little time or opportunity to keep up (cf. Burke's sixth form college teachers, in this volume). All the science teachers, except for twenty five year old Pete made a comment similar to the following quote from Margery:

Of course you very quickly get out of date, within nine or ten years at the most. And though you do try to keep up you don't have the time, or the money, to read the specialist journals. One starts off with good intentions, but it's something that I think you have to accept. (Margery, 45, Scale 3, chemistry teacher)

It therefore gets more difficult to maintain an identity as a specialist, particularly in the world outside school, and 'teacher' offers an alternative. Perhaps not as prestigious or exclusive an identity but in many respects, a more secure one.

Phase 3: 30–40 Age Group

Throughout the thirties the conjunction of experience and a relatively high level of physical and intellectual ability mean that in terms of energy, involvement, ambition and self-confidence many teachers are at their peak. Levinson *et al.* (1979) characterize this period as the *Settling Down* phase in which a man faces two major tasks:[1] (i) He tries to establish a niche in society: to anchor his life more firmly, develop competence in a chosen craft, become a valued member of a valued world; (ii) He works at making it: striving to advance, to progress on a timetable' (p. 59). It is usually during this period that the male teacher's career is established and, what is likely to be the terminal point is reached, or at least comes into view. People at this stage of life often have to do a lot of adapting to and coping with 'reality'.

Women's experience can be quite different. Many will have chosen to make their occupational career secondary to their career as a wife and mother. This is what is expected of them and those who do not conform may well face social censure. Women who have a family and who continue to work are often under great pressure insofar as they have two jobs. In many schools the attitude towards women teachers is often that they are working for 'pin-money',[4] and in few secondary schools are they equally represented in senior posts.

Those, men in particular, who are following the career path will be working towards major goals, deputy headship, headship. They will probably set themselves deadlines after the expiration of which they expect their chances of success will decrease. These deadlines are frequently extended! The amount of time and energy they devote to their pursuit may be detrimental to other aspects of their life. For instance:

> Dave and Ray, they work bloody hard, they drive themselves into the ground, and they're brilliant teachers. But just talking to their wives, ask them what they think about how much work their husbands do and they're not impressed at all. (Pete, 25, Scale 1, biology teacher)

Furthermore, rising aspirations can result in *Burn Out* (see Edelwich with Brodsky, 1980).

Once again career concerns and sources of job satisfaction change. Interest in management and organization is common among teachers at this stage. Ray's account gives some indication of the network of reasons which contribute to this change in orientation and commitment.

> I'm now prepared to leave teaching, or rather get out of the classroom full time as it were. Because my interests now are in learning theory and pedagogy and in organizing schools and, managing teachers you might say, in order to get the best out of them — their job satisfaction is crucial of course ... I would really like a deputy head curriculum type role ... to have the time to get into teachers' classrooms and to help them, to influence them perhaps ... It's partly your own career image, I'm not saying that doesn't come into the equation ... in order to get more status, get more influence in schools you've got to go into this area ... and on another level, if we lived in a situation where one's salary as a head of biology just kept on increasing as it were, then the situation might be very different. (Ray, 39, Scale 3, biology teacher)

On the other hand, some teachers say that they are not interested in promotion because it usually means less time in the classroom actually teaching. Professing a strong desire to stay in the classroom and an equally strong dislike of managerial and administrative work may be a contingency coping strategy used to protect both public and personal self image in the event of failure to achieve promotion. That some teachers do use such a strategy is suggested by the following quote:

> What I wouldn't like to do is to become an administrator as such, within the usual career structures. I don't think it's because I couldn't be one, so I'm not saying this defensively if you know what I mean, it's sort of conscious. (Roland, 38, Scale 3, metalwork teacher)[3]

Those who haven't reached the positions they hoped for have to come to terms with where they are. By this time they will probably have made significant personal investments and accumulated considerable personal valuables; for instance, marriage, children, a home, friends, and these factors may make it very difficult to make a geographical move should promotion seem possible elsewhere. Thus they find they have to make, what are in effect, 'final' decisions and adaptations which take into consideration their long term future. Some adapt by altering their perception of and thereby the nature of their commitment to their job, eg. from seeing it as a career in which they can work up to a senior position to viewing it as a worthwhile, interesting job (cf. Nias, 1980; Woods, 1979; Silverman, 1970, on commitment). Within school a change in commitment can be publicly and personally indicated and confirmed by joining, and being seen to join, a clique. Some decide that the returns are not worth the effort and so cut down on what they do, while others build up an alternative career. John (48, Scale 4, art teacher) for example, set up a small publishing company when, in his late thirties, he felt that his teaching career had reached a dead end. He no longer found his job satisfactory for a number of reasons but neither did he feel that he could move. Once he became involved in his company he found that he was able to 'juggle' his interests (see Pollard, 1980; Woods, 1981), enjoying those parts of the teaching job he found satisfying and, to a large extent, disregarding the aspects he found frustrating because the satisfaction he obtained from his alternative career more than compensated. Other teachers I have met had started shops, restaurants, a market garden, a travel agency, and an antique china repairers.[5]

Not all teachers possess the capital, the marketable skills, or the inclination to start a business, and they may juggle their interests by investing more in their families, homes or hobbies. There is a gender difference here for it tends to be expected that women will make by far their largest investments in their families. It is perhaps significant that Helen (41, Scale 3, art teacher) was the only mid-career woman who was both unmarried and who felt that she had sufficient time to follow her hobbies and interests.

Obviously generational status does not only alter *vis à vis* pupils, and once they are in their thirties it is no longer appropriate to regard themselves, or to behave as young, inexperienced teachers. Depending on how successful they have been they may see younger teachers who are in relatively senior posts as 'Whizz Kids', a term generally used in a derogatory sense. Heads of department, faculty, year, house, etc., common positions for those in this age group, have some responsibility for guiding and helping young staff. They often complain that they have no training for this — hence one reason for the interest in management. On the whole, those who are concerned about this aspect of their job say that they draw on their own experiences, whether good or bad, as junior teachers.

With respect to pupils, the relationship has definitely changed. Teachers in their thirties no longer belong to the same generation as pupils and, even if they should wish to, they can no longer participate as equals in youth culture. Dave remarked on how thirty seems to be a critical age.

> Kids do adopt a different standpoint as you get older. You can't equate with their ideas, I mean I'm long gone and past it, I'm over thirty, I should be buried up to my neck and left there as far as a lot of these kids ·are concerned, because I don't understand their problems. I'm not in their world, they're quite sure that I don't listen to pop music and to imagine me dancing would be a laugh, the fact I do this every week doesn't matter. (Dave, 45, Senior Teacher, Chemistry)

Around this age teachers seem to start to make more frequent adverse comments about pupil standards, attitudes, behaviour etc. They also compare kids 'today' unfavourably with kids in the past. Peterson (1964, p. 276) reports similar findings which seems to suggest that this change in perception of younger people is, to a large extent, a function of aging and changing generational status. But it is not all negative, for at the same time, teachers all say that discipline becomes easier as they grow into the natural authority of age. By becoming older and maybe more prone to be judgemental and authoritarian they perhaps become more like the 'proper teacher' (and less like an ordinary person) as perceived by pupils and some young teachers.

Women who have returned after having children often come back into school as 'mums'. 'You must come back as more of a mother figure, I suppose, than a "mate" and that has some advantages' (Margery, 45, Scale 3, chemistry teacher). The 'advantage' mentioned by all mid-career women with children was that of greater understanding and sympathy.

> Having your own children must change the way you see children ... you get an understanding of children but you don't really know where you get it from or how you get it ... I think having a child of my own helped. And I'm sure I must be more understanding than when I first started to teach. (Ann, 43, Scale 1, art teacher)

Teachers who have children of their own often develop a different perception of and attitude towards pupils. The relationship becomes more parental and perhaps, in some ways, more relaxed and natural. Mother/father teachers see their own kids in the pupils and become more sympathetic.

> I think I gradually have come to see pupils differently ... at the beginning really there's a tendency to assert some superiority over them, when you

first start teaching, when you're young I suppose but I tend to feel rather sorry for them now, I don't know that that affects my teaching of them very much in some ways, but you know the world is a very hard place for them now. I feel, by and large, rather sorry for them, apart from the rotters ... I suppose inevitably, whether I do it consciously or not I see my own children in them really, and realize that they're having a struggle in some areas, jobs and qualifications and the world generally. It's harder I think than it used to be. (Margery, 45, Scale 3, biology teacher)

The sheer disregard that many (pupils) have for themselves in terms of self respect, respect for others, their general unwillingness to want not just to *learn*, but to want to experience things. They have a very narrow view of life, most of them, far narrower than I had, and my kids have ... And sometimes the sheer disregard that their parents seem to have for them. It makes me more protective and more concerned for my own ... and it makes me want to do right by the kids in school. It's the comparison, I think, between their lives and my kids that's had this effect. (Brian, 45, Scale 3, art teacher)

For their part pupils see older teachers differently. The relationship has changed and, as Margery found, this is reflected in the confidences they entrust and the things they talk about to teachers.

Now they undoubtedly regard me more as as mum and sort of chum up along me. And they tell me incredible things like that they're moving house, or that their granny's ill. You know, things that it's very strange that old pupils would tell you. I'm talking about post-16 pupils. When I was younger I used to hear all about their boyfriends and girlfriends, their romances, but that seemed to stop when I came back ... I was only thirty three, it made me feel quite old. (Margery, 45, Scale 3, chemistry teacher)

Male teachers may find that they are no longer so attractive to young girls, which may be a blow to the ego but means that it is not quite so necessary to be on guard against potentially compromising situations. As Dave explained:

I'm onto the safe area. I think I am the father/uncle figure now (and I have been for five or six years). A lot of the worries I had as a younger teacher are no longer there; I'll keep anybody in by themselves, it doesn't worry me. I'll sit and talk to a 6th form girl, by herself, for an hour and a half, it doesn't worry me any more. I've passed the danger area in that sense ... (Dave, 45, Senior Teacher, chemistry)

Phase 4: 40–50/55 Age Group

In terms of the hierarchical career structure the 'successful' teachers of forty plus are in senior management positions and generally have relatively little classroom contact with pupils. This study was not concerned with these people and the teachers in this age group who we talked to were generally in 'middle management' ie. Heads of department, Heads of House, posts.

For male teachers, promotion after forty grows increasingly unlikely, although contraction may have had some effect in slowing down promotion rates and altering perceptions of what constitutes an age appropriate position. By contrast, women whose families are no longer quite so dependent on them may start considering, applying, and, being appointed to senior pastoral posts. Kath (retired, chemist) for example became a Senior Teacher in her early forties, and Margery (45, Scale 3, chemist) and Sally (41, Scale 3, art) were seriously considering applying for deputy headships with responsibility for girls' welfare. Both felt that they stood a reasonable chance of success. Even so, it seems that the major task for the age group (male and female) is of coming to terms with and adapting to what can be seen as a plateau in the life career. It is the time which follows the hurriedly incremental phases culminating in the peak years and comes prior to the pre-retirement phase.

There is considerable evidence which suggests that between the approximate ages of thirty seven to forty five individuals experience a phase which can be at least as traumatic as adolescence (see Jung, 1971; Vaillant and McArthur, 1972; Sheehy, 1976; Erikson, 1959; Levinson *et al.*, 1979; Bromley, 1974; Dicks). Crucially it is during this phase that it becomes apparent whether or not the work of establishing occupational career, family and identity begun in the twenties and thirties has been successful; and it tends to involve self reappraisal, questioning what one has made of one's life and searching for ways of expressing, fulfilling and satisfying oneself in the future. It is the transitional phase from youth to maturity and, according to Jaques (1965) the central issue is accepting and coming to terms with one's own mortality. This task is not made any easier for teachers who are constantly surrounded by young people.

Their relationship with kids is now definitely parental, indeed they may be closer in age to their pupils' grandparents.

> I do seem ancient to some of these kids. I mean round here they get married early and I'm actually older than some of their grandparents, I mean I go to Toyah concerts with my youngest daughter, I'm a real head banger, more with it than most of them. But they see an older man, like grandpa, and it affects their attitudes. It's bound to. (Brian, 45, Scale 4, art teacher)

It may come as a bit of a shock to realize that young teachers are the same age as their own children, as the following quote from a forty eight year old teacher suggests:

> As the years go on I realize that I have in my department teachers who in fact are only as young as my own children. This brings me up with a start sometimes but then I think it's all simply a matter of staff relationships. (48, Senior Teacher, English)[3]

Some are conscious of adopting a parental-type interest in and guidance role *vis à vis* their younger colleagues. For example:

> I had this young girl from Cambridge as a probationer in my department. I took quite a fatherly interest, I suppose you might say, in her. I helped her out with any problems she might have and so on. And she and her husband came to tea here once or twice and we went to them. She's moved now but we keep contact and meet occasionally. (Mr Count, retired, chemist)

Peterson (1964) found that unmarried older women teachers sometimes sought to extend their services as mothers or aunts to young teachers (p. 295). It may be that a role of this type enables them to feel pleased for and proud of 'their' young teachers who are more successful, in promotional terms, than they themselves have been. Perhaps anticipating and defending themselves against how they expect young teachers perceive them, those in this age group often mention that they've come to recognize how good the mid-career teachers they criticized when they were young actually were!

Adapting to 'maturity' can mean a new life structure, and new roles. By virtue of their seniority and age, within a school, teachers of forty plus are often authority figures, having taken on a role as maintainer of standards and guardian of school tradition (see Lacey, 1970). In some ways they can be regarded as the dependable backbone of the school. They are not 'paid' for this work but it is nevertheless a recognized position within the school's internal, informal status hierarchy. Dave sees himself as one of these teachers:

> If I go into the hall with 144 kids to sit an exam, they know what to expect. They know they're not going to be moving around, they're not going to be talking ... now that might not be so with every member of staff. Not every member of staff might want to live that way. But in a community, to get order you need somebody, or a number of people who will do that, otherwise you'd have chaos ... The staff recognize what I'm about ... they recognize the strata, or they recognize the control that is needed. (Dave, 45, Senior Teacher, chemistry)

Those who adopt such roles, whether they say they have done so consciously or unconsciously, often stress that they are not doing anything special and are only behaving as professionals should. At the same time some of them may also hope that they are making a point: ie. if they have not had the promotions they think they deserve they aim to show that they can do the job better, and more 'professionally', even without the scale and the salary.

By and large the teachers who take on authority roles have made relatively successful adaptations and are content to identify with and be identified in terms of their job and their school. Despite the turmoils of the mid life transition, research indicates that many teachers view the period between thirty five and fifty as a time during which their morale was high, second only to the first three to five years in teaching in terms of job satisfaction and contentment (Rempel and Bentley, 1970; Peterson, 1964; McLeish, 1969; Lortie, 1975). This is likely to be due to a combination of factors which include relative confidence in their ability to do the job, and declining ambition — when they have accepted that further promotion is unlikely they can stop striving for it and concentrate upon actually doing and enjoying the job.

However, not all adapt so successfully. There are those who find it difficult to accept and come to terms with their position and their age. In some respects these people may be coasting, they are not working towards any goal in their occupational or other aspects of their life. They are, in terms of Erikson's (1959) model, stagnating rather than generating. Even so those who are cynical and bitter about how things have worked out for them can become central figures in the grumbling cliques which were mentioned earlier.

Phase 5: 50–55 plus Age Range

Bearing in mind that as a consequence of contraction many LEAs are offering early retirement, teachers in this age group can be considered to be experiencing a phase in which the major task is that of preparing for retirement. From around the age of fifty, even if their morale is high, energy and enthusiasm for the job often are felt to be declining. Jim's feelings seem to be typical:

> The kids are always the same age and you gradually get older and older and older, that's very true . . . they do. And unfortunately too their capacity for life, their energy remains the same and yours diminishes . . .
>
> I think I had some of the best teaching experiences and pleasure when I was round about thirty five . . . you've got lots and lots of energy and you're prepared to spend all the time in the world on it, but as you get on you haven't got quite the same amount of energy or time. And it's no good blinking the fact that you're not so eager to take up the challenge of the next trip abroad and so on. Or at least I wasn't and I'm sure it applies to the rest. (Jim, retired, biologist)

Retirement becomes as increasingly attractive prospect (see Morse and Weiss, 1955). Those have ceased to enjoy teaching and who have been 'time serving' now have a goal to look forward to and this, paradoxically, may give them an enthusiasm that they have lacked for some time. Towards the end of their career, teachers often say that they become freer in their attitude and discipline (see Newman, 1979; Rempel and Bentley, 1970; Peterson, 1964; Lortie, 1975). This is partly because they have authority; because their experience has led them to the opinion that 'trivialities' are unimportant, that the kids learn is the main point.

> I became less bothered about things like copying. I thought well, it doesn't really matter where they get the information from, whether from me or their friend, as long as they get it. (Jim, retired, chemistry)

Arthur (retired, art) and Kath (retired, chemistry) both said that they came to a similar opinion. Another reason for a more relaxed approach can be because the value of the rewards to be gained by inhibiting their individuality and conforming are now negligible (see Miner, 1962). As Arthur pointed out:

> Well, they weren't going to promote me during my last three years or so,
> well, long before that really, so I had nothing to lose; I did more or less
> what I wanted to with the kids. (Arthur, retired, artist)

Teachers of fifty plus will probably have been at their present school for some
time, and may have taught pupils' parents. Thus their reputation precedes them.
They may welcome this sense of continuity but can also experience it as a constraint.
Jim felt this:

> If you've been at a school for a while you become known. There's a sort or
> mythology about you that's passed down by pupils you've taught, to their
> kids. And they come into school with all sorts of ideas about you. In some
> ways it's nice but people change and things change, courses change and
> methods, and so on, and it's sometimes very difficult if people have these
> expectations about you. (Jim, retired, biologist)

Arthur just felt old!

> I had kids coming and saying 'Eh, you used to teach my grandma didn't
> you?' and I thought 'By Heck! I must be getting on'. They married young
> mind you, but the first time a kid said that to me ... I nearly dropped
> bow-legged! (Arthur, retired, art)

As is the case at any age pupil: teacher relationships are dependent (to a large
extent) on personalities. However, unless they come to see them in a grand-parental
role, it seems that many kids have a tendency to reject and to distance themselves
from the old, and teachers in this age group may find it harder to get close to pupils.
For instance:

> The way in which they treat you changes ... when you get older they
> treat you with what they believe is respect, but they never really take you
> into their confidence in a sense. They don't really appreciate it when you've
> got a few years on your back, over the last five years that I had, if you use
> their common nickname they used among their friends. Now, twenty or
> thirty years ago that would have been easy ... with a younger teacher
> there isn't quite the same gap and they would accept (use of nicknames)
> ... you could, or I could, pull their legs, in other sorts of ways but that one
> didn't seem to go. (Jim, retired, biology)[6]

Young teachers likewise, may regard them as 'past it', outmoded in terms of
pedagogy and values. Older teachers tend to be in senior posts as head of department
or faculty and, particularly if they exercise a high degree of control, younger teachers
can become frustrated and dissatisfied because they are unable to put their own ideas
into practice.[7] These feelings are exacerbated if, as they frequently do, they perceive
older teachers as having eased up. It seems that the knowledge and experience of
older teachers is rarely sought and made use of. The fault and lack of communication
is not only on the side of the young, for, on the whole, older teachers are critical of
what they perceive to be the low professional standards of the new generation of

teachers, which they also usually add, reflect general social attitudes. The following comment is typical:

> I was having this session with probationers or young ones just into the school, on . . . I don't know if you'd call it 'successful teaching' or what you'd call it, but, I was trying to give some advice or, the sort of things that I did in certain situations and so on and so on. And I was absolutely floored at a young teacher who turned round and told me that lesson preparation was a waste of time. Well, we were talking about good and bad teachers, how is anyone going to develop if they think lesson preparation is a waste of time? Now, I'm not saying all young teachers are like that, of course not, but that sort of attitude isn't all that uncommon these days. (Kath, retired, chemistry)

Some teacher in their fifties and sixties (and perhaps a few in the preceding age group) started off their careers as class teachers in elementary schools. Without exception, those who did say that they are grateful for this experience and that it made them more-capable and more able to adapt to comprehensivization when it came. These teachers often say that they feel that grammar school and younger teachers are very limited in skills and that increasing specialization has not been a good thing for schools, pupils and education in general. As Arthur explained:

> When I started I taught everything except music . . . specialist teaching in those days (1935ish) was unknown (in an elementary school) . . . I'd taught all types of ability, others who've never had that experience find they've got problems . . . some of them had a terrible time when we went comprehensive . . . It happens very often now that somebody's off sick and you're asked to step in if you've got a free period. 'Will you take so and so?' And you walk in this classroom, there's a gang of kids there, 'What should it be now?' 'Oh, we're doing English', or 'we're doing geography' or 'we're doing this', and through all this earlier training you found out that you were able to sort of pick it up from there and carry on. You didn't altogether waste the time of this period you'd got with somebody else's kids in a subject that wasn't yours, cus you can fall back on the experience you'd got, which is something the modern chaps going into the profession can't do. They're highly specialized. They know their own subject p'raps inside out, but stick 'em in front of a class on some other subject or topic and they haven't a clue what to do. So it's 'Silent reading for you lot'. (Arthur, retired, art)

Teachers of all ages often remark that it is difficult to get any indication of how well they are doing their job, and this is perhaps one reason why many teachers are in favour of examinations — results provide some feedback. Much of the satisfaction that can be obtained from teaching is in a sense vicarious. It arises from seeing what ex-pupils have made of their lives, and, because few people achieve eminence, fame, notoriety and so on, teachers look to being part of the process whereby a child becomes, in Jim's words, 'a responsible, decent citizen'. Even, and perhaps especially, when they retire teachers can continue to meet and hear about how ex-pupils are getting on and thereby get a great deal of satisfaction. All of the retired teachers I talked to had a fund of such stories, and they were an important source of pleasure. The message the stories apparently hold for the older teachers was that, after all, being a teacher had been worthwhile. On this account Jim and Arthur shall have the last words.

> Occasionally you pick up little bits from people who've passed through your hands. You hear about what they're doing. And you say, well it wasn't completely lost. Yes we *did* do something worthwhile ... that sort of thing keeps your flame burning a little bit. (Jim, retired, biology)

> I can't go into a bank or building society or anywhere in (town) with any privacy, because the old grammar school kids are the ones who went to went to work in banks and building societies. 'Hello, Sir. How are you?' and I think 'Oh my God, here we go again!'. I like it, I think it's a compliment if a kid'll come and talk to you ... The other day I met a lass, she's started up a nursing home for old folk, and she said to me 'You needn't worry Sir, I'll look after you, you can come to my place'. And I thought that was great. (Arthur, retired, artist)

Conclusion

Pupils are not the only ones who sometimes forget that teachers are human. (In this country at least, the body of information on teacher careers grows very slowly). Teachers are first and foremost people who just happen to be in the job of teaching. Like everyone else they are subject to biological and psychological changes which are associated with aging and how the process is viewed in this society.

An investigation of the ways in which certain aspects of the occupational culture appear to influence teachers' experiences of growing old contributes to our understanding of schools as social systems, and enables teachers to compare and share and learn from each others' experience and feelings about a personal although absolutely central and universal aspect of their lives. In addition, it gives some indication of the effect that age and experience can have upon motivation and commitment and, therefore, of ways in which teachers' job satisfaction and effectiveness are (and might be) influenced.

This study only involved teachers of art and science. Although subject culture differences have not been emphasized in this chapter, it does seem that they have a significant influence upon teachers' career experiences and perceptions and, thereby on their experiences of aging. Physical education teachers provide an obvious example for the nature of their subject tends to make them acutely aware that they are getting old. Scientists too, know that their specialist knowledge and expertise dates them. While this is perhaps less apparent in terms of the science they teach in school, than it would be at, for instance, a conference on what was their specialist area, it is harder to avoid recognizing it when young teachers join the department and talk about what they did at university. Art is subjective and intimately associated with time, and perhaps art teachers are more likely to be conscious of their age when they begin to feel that they haven't the energy to fight for resources or to improve the status of what in many schools is a marginal subject. It seems likely that teachers in other subjects also face specific subject/age related situations, as well as the more common, if not universal, personal developments associated with the aging process. This, therefore, is an area requiring further research.

Acknowledgement

I am indebted to the teachers involved and to Lynda Measor and Peter Woods for their observations on this paper and their help in writing.

Notes

1 Levinson refers to doctoral research by Wendy Stewart with a small sample of women in their mid-thirties. No titular or publication details are given.
2 Hanson and Herrington (1976) note that it is difficult to determine the real degree of commitment among student and probationary teachers for research findings vary considerably. For instance, about 50 per cent of the students studied by Lomax (1970) 'drifted' into teaching, while a further 25 per cent had really hoped to go to university. Smithers and Carlisle (1970) found that over 50 per cent of their students would ideally like to enter another occupation. Yet Carr (1972) and Taylor and Dale (1971) found that teaching was the first choice career for around 75 per cent of their respective samples of students and probationers.
3 These are teachers I interviewed in 1981 in the course of an investigation into how teachers perceive and adapt to the reduction in promotional opportunities which is a consequence of falling rolls.
4 This is definitely the impression to be gained from staffroom and other informal conversations with women teachers.
5 In the course of a study I conducted into secondary school teachers perceptions of and adaptations to reduced promotional opportunities consequent upon falling rolls, I found that approximately eleven of 105 male teachers had business/commercial interests. I say approximately, because I later learnt informally, that some craft teachers occasionally did paid work for colleagues and other acquaintances. They did not declare these earnings which perhaps explains why they did not mention them.
6 This account supports Woods and Measor's (1982) observation that 'peer group nicknames (are) for use only by "approved" teachers.' By and large the (relatively) old are not approved by the young.
7 In the investigation referred to in note 3 the most frequent reason teachers under thirty five gave for wanting promotion was to have more freedom and responsibility.

Bibliography

BERNSTEIN, B. (1971) 'On the classification and framing of educational knowledge', in YOUNG, M.F.D. (Ed.) *Knowledge and Control*, Collier-Macmillan, London.
BLACKIE, P. (1977) 'Not quite proper', *Times Educational Supplement*, 25 November, pp. 21–2.

BROMLEY, D.B. (1974) *The Psychology of Human Ageing*, Harmondsworth, Penguin.

BURNS, T. (1955) 'The reference of conduct in small groups: Cliques and cabals in occupational milieux', *Human Relations*, 8, pp. 467–86.

CAIN, L.D. Jr. (1964) 'Life course and social structure', in FARIS, R.E.L. (Ed.) *Handbook of Modern Sociology*, Chicago, Rand McNally.

CARR, R.F. (1972) 'Recruitment for teaching: Problems and possibilities', *London Educational Review*, I.1.

COLE, M. (1985) 'The tender trap?' Commitment and consciousness in entrants to teaching'. (this volume).

DENSCOMBE, M. (1980) 'Pupil strategies and the open classroom,' in WOODS, P. (Ed.) *Pupil Strategies: Explorations in the Sociology of the School*, London, Croom Helm.

DENZIN, N.K. (1970) *The Research Act in Sociology: A Theoretical Introduction to Sociological Methods*, London, butterworth Group.

DICKS, H.V. (n.d.) 'Personality' *The Seven Ages of Man*, New Society Publication.

EDELWICH, J. with BRODSKY, A. (1980) *burn-Out: Stages of Disillusionment in the Helping Professions*, New York, Human Sciences Press.

ELBAZ, F. (1983) *Teacher Thinking: A Study of Practical Knowledge*, London, Croom Helm.

ERIKSON, E. (1950) *Childhood and Society*, New York, Norton.

ERIKSON, E. (1959) 'Identity and the life cycle', *Psychological Issues*, 1, pp. 1–171.

GLASER, B.G. and STRAUSS, A.L. (1968) *The Discovery of Grounded Theory*, London, Weidenfeld and Nicholson.

GLASER, B.G. (Ed.) (1968) *Organizational Careers: A Sourcebook for Theory*, Chicago, Aldine Publishing Co.

GOULD, R. (1972) 'The phases of adult life: A study in developmental psychology', *American Journal of Psychiatry*, **129**, 5, pp. 521–31.

GRACE, G. (1978) *Teachers, Ideology and Control: A Study in Urban Education*, London, Routledge and Kegan Paul.

HAMMERSLEY, M. (1980) *A peculiar world? Teaching and learning in an inner city school*, Manchester, University of Manchester, Ph.D. Thesis.

HANSON, D. and HERRINGTON, M. (1976) *From College to Classroom: The Probationary Year*, London, Routledge and Kegan Paul.

HAVINGHURST, R.J. (1964) 'Youth in exploration and man emergent', in BOROW, H. (ed.) *Man in a World at Work*, Boston, Houghton Mifflin.

JAQUES, E. (1965) 'Death and the mid-life crisis', *International Journal of Psychoanalysis*, **46**, pp. 502–14.

JUNG, C.G. (1971) *The Portable Jung*, (Ed. Joseph Campbell) New York, Viking Press.

KYRIACOU, C. and SUTCLIFFE, J. (1979) 'A note on teacher stress and locus of control', *Journal of Occupational Psychology*, **52**, pp. 227–8.

LACEY, C. (1970) *Hightown Grammar*, Manchester, Manchester University Press.

LACEY, C. (1977) *The Socialization of Teachers*, London Methuen.

LEVINSON, D.J. with DARROW, C.N., KLEIN, G.B., LEVINSON, M.H., and McKEE, B. (1979) *The Seasons of a Man's Life*, New York, Alfred A. Knopf.

LOMAX, D. (1970) 'Focus on student teachers', *Higher Education Review*, Autumn.

LORTIE, D.C. (1975) *Schoolteacher: A Sociological Study*, Chicago, University of Chicago Press.

LYONS, G. (1981) *Teacher Careers and Career Perceptions*, Slough, NFER.

McLEISH, J. (1969) *Teachers Attitudes: A Study of National and Other Differences*, Cambridge, Cambridge Institute of Education.

MEASOR, L. and WOODS, P. (1982) *Cultivating the Middle Ground: Teachers and School Ethos*, unpublished paper, School of Education, Open University.

MEASOR, L. (1985) 'Critical incidents in the classroom: Identities, choices and careers' (this volume).

MINER, J.B. (1962) 'Conformity among university professors and business executives, *Administrative Science Quarterly*, June.

MORSE, N.C. and WEISS, R.S. (1955) 'The function and meaning of work and the job',

American Sociological Review, **20**.

MULFORD, H.A. and SALISBURY, W.W. (1964) 'Self-conceptions in a general population', *Sociological Quarterly* **5**, pp. 35–46.

NEWMAN, K.K. (1979) *Middle-Aged Experienced Teachers' Perceptions of their Career Development*, paper presented at Annual Meeting of the American Educational Research Association, San Francisco, California, April.

NIAS, J. (1980) *Further Notes on the Concept of Commitment*, unpublished paper, University of Cambridge, Institute of Education.

NIAS, J. (1985) 'reference groups in primary teaching: Talking, listening and identity (this volume).

PETERSON, W.A. (1964) 'Age, teachers' role, and the institutional setting', in BIDDLE, B.J. and ELENA, W.S. *Contemporary Research in Teacher Effectiveness*, London, Holt, Rinehart and Winston.

POLLARD, A. (1980) *Towards a Revised Model of Coping Strategies*, paper presented to Middle Schools Research Group, Woburn, April 1980.

REMPEL, A. and BENTLEY, R. (1970) 'Teacher morale: Relationship with selected factors', *Journal of Teacher Education*, **21**, Winter, pp. 534–9.

RISEBOROUGH, G.F. (1981) 'Teacher careers and comprehensive schooling: An empirical study' *Sociology*, **15**, 3, pp. 352–381.

SHEEHY, G. (1976) *Passages: Predictable Crises of Adult Life*, New York, E.P. Dutton.

SILVERMAN, D. (1970) *The Theory of Organizations*, London, Heinemann.

SMITHERS, A. and CARLISLE, S. (1970) 'Reluctant teachers', *New Society*, 5 March.

SOFER, C. (1970) *Men in Mid-Career: A Study of British Managers and Technical Specialists*, Cambridge, Cambridge University Press.

STRAUSS, A.L. (1959) *Mirrors and Masks: The Search for Identity*, Glencoe, Free Press.

SUPER, D.E. (1981) 'Approaches to occupational choice and career development' in WATTS, A. G., SUPER, D.E., KIDD, J. (Eds) *Career Development in Britain*, Cambridge, published for CRAC by Hobsons Press.

TAYLOR, J.K. and DALE, R. (1971) *A Survey of Teachers in their First Year of Service*, University of Bristol School of Education Research Unit.

VAILLANT, G.E. and McARTHUR, C.C. (1972) 'Natural history of male psychologic health. I. The adult life cycle from 18–50', *Seminars in Psychiatry*, 4, 64.

WALLER, W. (1932) *The Sociology of Teaching*, New York, John Wiley.

WHITESIDE, T. (1978) *The Sociology of Educational Innovation*, London, Methuen.

WOODS, P. (1979) *The Divided School*, London, Routledge and Kegan Paul.

WOODS, P. (1981a) *Careers and Work Cultures*, Milton Keynes, Open University Press.

WOODS, P. (1981b) 'Strategies, commitment and identity: Making and breaking the teacher role' in BARTON, L. and WALKER, S. (Eds) *Schools, Teachers and Teaching*, Lewes Falmer Press.

Critical Incidents in the Classroom: Identities, Choices and Careers

Lynda Measor

Editors' Note: This paper draws on data from an ESRC funded project on teachers' careers and lives, directed by Peter Woods. The data arise from life history interviews with experienced teachers who are looking back on their early days in the classroom and the problems they faced.

Critical Phases and Critical Incidents

In the research on life history and sociologically read biography, the issue of 'critical phases' has already emerged as an area of importance. Strauss and Rainwater (1962, p. 105) for example, discussed 'periods of strain' in the lives of the chemists they were researching. During these critical phases, particular events occur, which are important. Rob Walker (1976) in his work on teachers' careers used the term 'critical incidents' to describe such events.

I want to argue that there are 'critical incidents' which are key events in the individual's life, and around which pivotal decisions revolve. These events provoke the individual into selecting particular kinds of actions, they in turn lead them in particular directions, and they end up having implications for identity. Becker (1966) wrote of 'these crucial interactive episodes, in which new lines of individual and collective activity are forged ... and new aspects of the self brought into being' (p. xiv). They are a useful area to study, because they reveal, like a flashbulb, the major choice and change times in people's lives. In this chapter, I want to pinpoint the 'critical incidents' in some teachers' biographies and to give detailed descriptions of them. From that data we can begin to move toward theory, to find whether there are any common patterns in different biographies, so to work toward 'the developmental, generalized formulation of careers' that Glaser (1964) called for (p. xv).

In the data presented here, it becomes apparent that 'critical incidents' are most likely to occur at particular times in the individual's life. These are the 'periods of strain' that Strauss identified. I have termed them 'critical phases', they can be provoked by a number of different factors, and fall into extrinsic and intrinsic, as well as personal types. 'Extrinsic' critical phases can be produced by historical events. In the biographies of the older teachers we interviewed, the Second World War showed up as an example, where conditions forced decisions and actions upon people. More localized changes, like policy turnabouts in education, for example comprehensivization, also forced actions and decisions on teachers.

The second type of 'critical phase' is 'intrinsic'; within the natural progression of a career, there seem to be several critical periods. They are important, because the individual is confronted by choices and decisions. A number of intrinsic critical phases can be identified within the careers of teachers.

1 Choosing to enter the teaching profession
2 The first teaching practice
3 The first eighteen months of teaching
4 Three years after taking the first job
5 Mid career moves and promotion
6 Pre-retirement

The third type is 'personal', family events, marriage, divorce, the birth or illness of a child, can also provoke critical phases and project an individual in a different direction. For older, female, unmarried teachers, parental demands and pressures had determined and frequently constrained their actions and choices.

It is during these periods, which are times of changing and choosing, that critical incidents are most likely to occur. The incident itself probably represents the culmination of the decision making, it crystallizes the individual's thinking, rather than of itself being responsible for that decision. This chapter takes as its focus the kind of 'critical incidents' that occur in one 'critical phase', the first eighteen months of teaching.

The data which follows is taken from a research project which began in 1982. We were interested in teachers' careers, and used a life history methodology, together with what ethnographic techniques we could, to study them. The research selected secondary school teachers, who taught art and science subjects. Three separate age groups were involved, retired, mid-career, and young teachers (those with about five years experience).[1] During their first eighteen months of teaching, the majority of teachers we interviewed had serious trouble controlling the pupils they taught. Discipline difficulties are one of the defining characteristics of this critical phase. The problems are moreover experienced in the context of an extreme form of exhaustion. Mr Shoe's comments were typical, 'I must admit that the first six months of my real teaching was very, very hard'. Mr Quilley agreed, he had begun his career in an elementary school in the North of England in the late 1930s, both times and pupils were exceptionally hard. 'I think your worst feelings about discipline were in your first job. I went through Hell, for about five or six weeks'.

There were individual teachers who did not experience such difficulties, but they form an important exception and need separate attention. We also need to take gender into the account, for it is teachers who taught male pupils who had most difficulty. Women teachers in girls schools faced no such problems. Miss Coal recalled, 'Oh yes, I mean the children were a bit naughty, but it was alright'.

The background against which critical incidents occurred was also interesting; it revealed the pressures and the constraints upon the young teacher entering the profession. It became clear that the young teacher was usually under the tutelage of an older, more experienced member of staff. The older teacher exerted pressure to show a 'heavy hand' to pupils. Mr Shoe described the experience of teaching in a small rural school, staffed by himself, and a much older Headmaster. A glass partition was all that separated their classrooms; and Mr Shoe remembered the eagle-eyed observation with horror:

Mr Shoe: He kept popping in to tell me how to do it ... he was one of the old school, strong disciplinarian, no nonsense, he was the boss in his school. His advice to me was, if you have any trouble with any of the kiddies, impose your authority. Smack them down. He'd got a very hard, horny hand there.

It is in this context, that the critical incident occurs. It involves a confrontation between teacher and pupils. Quite frequently that confrontation is violent, and leads to the involvement of senior members of staff at the school. One account, gathered by Pat Sikes from a Glasgow woman teacher, gives a particularly clear view of the outline and character of such episodes. The woman began her career in a tough elementary school in Glasgow in 1939. During her first year there she experienced considerable discipline difficulties, which culminated in one day's events. The teacher entered the classroom to find that each of her male pupils had displayed their genitals on the desk in front of them. She told the pupils to put them away, and then frog-marched one of the boys out of the classroom. Her classroom was on a first-floor balcony and somehow the woman teacher pushed the boy in such a way that he fell over the balcony and on to the floor some distance below. A now carefully buttoned-up group of boys watched his fall in a hushed and respectful silence. The woman had no further discipline problems. This incident, while perhaps particularly colourful (blue?) is a good example of many of the issues involved. The general properties are that a class is disruptive over quite a long period of time. At some point, a threat is made by pupils, a response is made by the teacher, and there is a violent outcome.

The other point about these incidents is their long term effects. The Glasgow teacher reported that as a result of the events, she was able to establish a reputation and an identity, which enabled her to gain reasonable discipline in the school from then on. It is significant that all the accounts we collected of these kinds of encounters had successful outcomes for the teachers. Presumably those who fail such tests give up teaching. Riseborough (1981) began questioning the effects that pupils have on teachers' careers, accounts of critical incidents given insights into the processes at work.

A comparison of the accounts of 'critical incidents' revealed a number of common features, in terms of the ways they were staged by pupils; but this is not the end of the story. All of the teachers in the accounts we collected, survived the pupils' tests, but, their response to the incidents varied considerably. As a result the teachers established quite different kinds of reputations and identities. The episodes worked to set many of the teachers' attitudes for the remainder of their careers, in ways that must be documented.

I would like to compare two teachers' accounts of their 'critical incidents' to show the common patterns, but also to contrast their different responses. First, Mr Quilley:

Mr Quilley:	And I've been bashed by kids about a quarter my size, and one of them got bashed back (laughter) and I ended up on the mat about it.
R:	Tell me.
Mr Quilley:	Well yes, it was near the end of the lesson, and I walked past a child who was working, and he'd take a swing at you. In the tummy, or even further down.
R:	This was the colliers' sons?
Mr Quilley:	Oh, yes, yes — well what do you do — wop them one then and there, at least I did that, and so I was sent for. Eventually the Head said I mustn't bash them up. I wasn't a bully, but I said, personal violence, foul-mouthed cheek is not on, because most of the staff were wopping them one occasionally, or taking them to be wopped. Mmm! Eventually the Head said, 'No more, that's it. The next time and you're going in front of the Director'. (Laughs) And I thought, My God, my old man, teaching in town, me in front of the Director, this will be terrible.
R:	[Laughs]
Mr Quilley:	This will be ghastly, because my father was running two departments in the local Tech. (Said in a highly animated way).
R:	[Laughs again]
Mr Quilley:	Well I went to see my NUT bloke. Anyway there came a time when a bloke was absolutely terribly disobedient, so I said 'Come out here, I'm gonna cane you in front of all, everybody'. And I rushed into my store room, and I had lots of little sticks in there, and I unfortunately grabbed the first, and it happened to be the black one, and it was about twelve inches long, and I came out, and I said . . .

I was transcribing Mr Quilley's account from the tape, myself, and realized at this point, that I was having serious difficulty in getting down what he had said. On reflection I realized that this was because Mr Quilley had increased the pace of delivery of his sentences, so that I was able to take down only one phrase at a time. His sentences were shortened and forceful. He piled up sentence upon sentence in a staccato fashion, it emphasized the drama of his narrative.

Mr Quilley:	. . . and I came out and I said 'Hold your hand out lad; now you know what you're getting this for?'

'Yes'.

'Do you deserve it?'

'I don't know'.

'Yes you do; hold your hand out'.

So he held his hand out and as I struck him, he turned it upward, so I bashed him across the thumb.

So I said 'Serve you right. And the other hand, and this one again, and that one'. And I sent him back to his seat.

[Draws a proper breath for the first time and relaxes the pace of the narrative]

And nothing happened. The next day the Head yanked me out and said 'You're as good as fired'. 'Got to go and see — the what's his name, Director — in the Town Hall, but I'm washing my hands of it. The only hurdle you've got to get past is the boy's father. He's coming to see you. You'd better watch it . . .'

R: [laughs]

Mr Quilley: '. . . but I've washed my hands of you, I'm speaking against you'. So the father came up, about the boy, and I thought ughm this is it, and the boy's father came in, and we had quite a nice conversation. We got on quite well, and to cut a long story short, I gave him ten bob — at his request [pause] — lot of money in those days.

R: Yes.

Mr Quilley: I only got paid £14 a month — but, er, he said er, next time Mr Quilley, get him out of school and knock his head off. I don't want him bashed in school. And that was the end of it.

Mr Tucks gave an account of a very similar incident. However his reaction to it was very different:

R: Did you have any real 'show downs' with kids, especially at the beginning.

Mr Tucks: I did yeah. I did at the beginning, yeah.

R: Do you want to talk about it or not?

Mr Tucks: Well . . . there was a very significant incident on the . . . last day of the first half term . . . when I actually came to blows with a student. Yeah, and . . .

R: This was in your first term?

Mr Tucks: And . . . he wasn't a student of mine, but he'd interrupted a lesson and gone out, and slammed the door, and various things [mutters] and, and didn't seem to [mutters, and his voice becomes quiet and indistinct] work at the time [mutters again].

R: Were you teaching him?

Mr Tucks: No, no, no! No — [takes a deep breath in].

R: He just came in and interrupted your lesson.

Mr Tucks:	Yeah, yeah, yeah [mutters, sighs] Er mmm! And in fact I was reprimanded by the Head, for that ...
R:	What did you do — chase him out of the room?
Mr Tucks:	I chased him and then I clocked him over the head ... yeah ... I completely lost control of myself.
R:	Yeah.
Mr Tucks:	I hesitate to repeat it, I can't, I don't know what ... you know ... it's difficult to repeat it, don't like it. Well that was crucial. I suddenly got the wrong sort of reputation amongst students who didn't know me, for some time the ones who knew me well, didn't learn anything from it. At least — well not — but it had the effect ... these students could perceive, from afar that I was slightly different style ... they weren't prepared to sort of it ... test it. I was prepared to be very informal with students I was teaching, but I was sufficiently unsure of myself to regard an assumption of students I wasn't teaching, of that informality as a threat.
R:	What effects has it had? Do you hit kids now?
Mr Tucks:	Noooh! Not at all.

For Mr Tucks the experience had been personally distressing, his facial gestures and tone of voice expressed his discomfort, he openly stated that he did not like even talking about the incident. The pace of his delivery slowed down discernibly and the researcher had to push for the full story. Mr Tucks' response to the critical incident was different from Mr Quilley's, the violence and tension were experienced differently by the two teachers. The discovery of such personal anger in himself discomforted Mr Tucks quite considerably and determined his future course of action. He sought to avoid any repetition of such incidents.

Mr Shoe gave an account of a 'critical incident', the details were the same, in a moment of exasperation he 'just banged their heads together you know'. He was able to draw out what was crucial in the experience for him:

| Mr Shoe: | I did it once — it was a salutary lesson, so I learned that if I ever wanted to hit out, I never did. I learned from that, and I think one of the things I learned was the fact that one of the worst things you can do is deal with a child in anger, when he's provoked you. I think I learned too that, if you begin to shout and you begin to rant and rave with the class, you lose your authority anyway. |

Mr Shoe gives an indication of one of the elements which make such incidents 'critical'. It is the discovery that a display of real anger in the classroom is genuinely counter-productive, and that teachers need to 'stage manage' a 'front' of anger if they are to cope as 'proper teachers'. Being provoked into a display of real anger by pupils represents not 'coping', it represents a breakdown in classroom interaction rules. It means a failure in classroom negotiation, it introduces a different ambience. Mr King recognized this:

> *Mr King:*   I think you have to pretend to be angry with children, but never to lose your temper, once you lost it, they sense it, something's transmitted, salt or something, is sent across the atmosphere. They know it, just like an animal. A horse will gallop through a wood if you're frightened of him and brush you off, if you really hold the reins he won't. So children are like that, they react intuitively or whatever, instinctively is better.

It may be that in these accounts we catch a glimpse of what pupils call 'trouble' (Furlong, 1976) feels like to teachers. These incidents cause 'trouble' for the teachers, they faced punishment or embarrassment of some kind as a result of their loss of control. The intervention of senior colleagues made the teachers' lack of coping a public matter, there is both a public and a private loss of face involved.

As a result of the 'critical incident', the teachers involved reached a number of decisions.

> *R:*   Did you go on hitting kids?
> *Mr Shoe:*   Not really, no . . . It wasn't my way really.

The teacher realized something about his own teaching style, and about the way he wanted to do things. When the teachers described this process, they usually employed a negative model, to help define their own choices. Mr Shoe compared himself with the horny-handed headmaster:

> *Mr Shoe:*   I learned by observing him in many ways.
> *R:*   Were you like him?
> *Mr Shoe:*   Well, I don't know. In his lessons there wouldn't be any messing. You hadn't got to think, now how can I make sure I've got their interest. What he did was purely imposing his will on them, that was that really.

Mr Redford used the same tactic, in reference to his first head of department:

> *Mr Redford:*   I quickly ditched any set rules he was passing on to me, and just taught in my own sort of way.

Hanson and Herrington (1976) in their research on teacher socialization, discuss the ways that senior members of the teaching profession, put pressure on younger teachers to conform and accept the *status quo* in schools. To borrow Riseborough's phrase (1981) Heads of Departments in particular may act as 'critical reality definers'. The 'critical incidents' show in detail the ways in which such pressures work, but also show the ways that teachers negotiate around them. The incidents are 'critical' because they force a move in the process by which the new recruit finds a way through to being the kind of teacher they want to be; they represent a jump in learning to 'do it my way'.

The researcher offered this analysis of 'critical incidents' to some of the teachers being interviewed. This was part of an attempt to get respondent validation, but also to involve teachers more fully in the work of analysis. The researcher suggested to

Mr Redford that a 'critical incident' had set the style of teaching and discipline he had held ever since:

> *Mr Redford*: Yes, I think it probably did, although I don't think it came as a great shock to me, do you know what I mean? I think I'd perhaps, I'd actually reached that stage earlier, but my lack of experience had encouraged me to, under the pressure of the situation, to accept the urgings of the Head of Department to take on *his* operations. Plus I was supply at that point. If I'd started in September, perhaps I wouldn't have done that you know, but er ... in fact ... er ...

The analysis can perhaps be taken one step further, with Mr Redford's account. It is not that the critical incident necessarily introduces anything totally new into the ideology or framework of practices of the teacher, rather it probably acts to crystallize, and set ideas, attitudes and actions that the teacher has more generally been considering.

Teachers did employ a negative role model to define their own choices more clearly, but this was not the only tactic they used. They also offered accounts of 'counter incidents' to explain themselves. In their biographies, most of the teachers gave an account of another incident, quite close to the first 'critical incident'. The 'counter incident' like the 'critical one', involved a challenge set up by the pupils. It is different from the 'critical one' because of the way the teacher handled it. The teachers made it clear that they much preferred their responses in the counter incident, their responses there reflected 'their way', the way they wanted to be in school. Mr Shoe, for example, offered an account of another confrontation situation he had encountered, but this time he had stayed in control, he had stage managed the interaction in a teacherly fashion.

> *Mr Shoe*: I realized that however I managed the class, I had to make sure that at all times I was in charge. Well, of course, kiddies will always tend to aggravate any new teachers to the limit. They'll try to see 'How far can we go?' It's either them or you, and there's some big lads and one had to decide how do you impose your authority on them? Sometimes it has to be even physical, some of them were big, and literally I did occasionally have to come to the decision that 'If you're going to behave in this way I'm going to get you out' and if he refuses to go out then 'I'm going to remove you out, if necessary physically'. And there were times when the tussles were, the kid's as big as you, if they don't go you've a problem; you're sort of, the authority's gone. So if you're going to take them out then you've got to get them out in no uncertain manner.
>
> *R*: So if you're going to take on a confrontation you've got to pick one you know you're going to win.
>
> *Mr Shoe*: That's right, yes.

R: Because I think teachers do try to avoid confrontation actually.

Mr Shoe: Well, I would have felt dreadful I think if I felt that I was losing the control and some kiddies wouldn't do what I wanted. I don't think I could live with that, and I think the worst occasion I had, or the best occasion maybe, and that was, she was a widowed mother, a very fine lady really, but John, her son, was not particularly able but tending to be a bit difficult at times and I know one day I had to remove him. I said 'Well if you're going to behave like this, I've had enough of this, it's going to be to the Headmaster'. And we were in a dining room then with a central corridor and this was used as a classroom, and he'd played and played and he'd been funny and difficult and I thought — well I'd better get rid of him. He wasn't going to go if I just said 'GO', so I think one of the best ways, really, you get them at a disadvantage very quickly to get them by the scruff of the pants and scruff of the neck, and you've got them then and they will go.

        I got hold of this lad and he was pretty big and heavy, and I said 'Well are you going out?' and he said 'No, I'm not', 'Oh, you are'. Well, of course, he went down the middle of the passageway and hitting desks and chairs as he went, there was an almighty crash, bang, wallop, doors open, out he went, and he was seen to go straight through, like that, across the playground and in front of the Headmaster's study. I said, 'Now you can tell the Headmaster what you've seen'. The kiddies had seen all this; heard all the noise and kerfuffle: 'what a tiger we have'! But I didn't do that very often, just that one occasion I think. You learn, well I'm not standing any nonsense, so, I'm not sure it works on every occasion.

R: Was this occasion you've just described, was that during that first six months of teaching?

Mr Shoe: Yes, actually end of the day, John Dewhurst and I were the best of pals. He didn't sort of resent me, no; I told him I wanted him out and, certainly I tried to tell the kids that 'Alright you misbehaved. I assure you that I'm not one to bear grudges and I would hope that all teachers would, once they've chastised or corrected, are not going to hold it against you — I'll remember you in future. As far as I'm concerned if you accept punishment, and it's accepted gracefully (and most of them did) as far as I'm concerned, then it's finished. I'm not going to treat you now any different from anybody else'.

Mr Shoe's 'critical' and 'counter' incident stories were told, closely following each other in the same interview. They were used to point up the teacher's choices of teaching and discipline style, and indicate the values and attitudes he sorted out for himself as a teacher. In Mr Shoe's case, his style did not entirely exclude a physical approach, the incident with John indicated that. Nevertheless, Mr Shoe learned from his 'critical incident' to pick both his pupil and the form of 'aggro', quite carefully. In the counter incident, the events are staged — to show 'what a tiger we have'. In the second episode, there is noise, kerfuffle, excitement, spectacle even, and all the pupils were aware of it. Yet there was no real physical violence, no pain. Mr Shoe was in control of the counter incident, unlike the critical one. His comment that John and he were later 'the best of pals' was also significant. No such truce would have been possible after the first incident.

Different teachers told different kinds of 'counter incident' stories, they showed the way different personalities make different choices about directions and behaviour, and how individuals read different meanings into a similar event in their life. Mr Redford provided a 'counter incident' story, in which his values were made particularly clear.

> *Mr Redford*: I had another quick incident. There was a cupboard, with the stock in, and some of the big 5th years, they were quite toughies were in the cupboard, and I said 'Come out' and the whole class went silent, and I said, 'Right, empty your pockets' and this lad said 'No'. [The first 'empty your pockets' was said quite gently]. So I said 'Empty your pockets'. [Mr Redford repeated the order, even more quietly and with real gentleness in his account]. He said 'No' and you know you've got this immediate confrontation. This lad was about six foot tall, and there's me — looking up at him. And he said 'You'll have to make me'. It was an *AWEFUL* situation. But I knew I couldn't back down. He walked towards me, and I put my hand out, and he slipped, his feet shot from under him, and he fell flat on his back. He said 'Right then' (his tone was very aggressive) and I said 'O.K. Come On' (Mr Redford's tone was very gentle). I realized he needed a way out. He said, 'Alright, I'll empty my pockets, but if you don't find anything I want an apology'. He got up and emptied his pockets, and there was nothing in there, and I apologized, and after that my relationship with the whole group was completely different.

This incident was important to Mr Redford because it showed his preferred way of dealing with discipline difficulties. He attempted to leave violent confrontation completely out of his teaching style. While he could not avoid confrontation in an all boys comprehensive always, he did attempt to meet such confrontations with the minimum of aggression, and in a way which refused to enter and cooperate with the macho style that is current in such schools in his view. He told a third incident, which is important for it reinforces the identity which he was trying for. In this incident, another individual reinforces this identity. A pupil approached him:

Mr Redford: 'Ere Sir', he said 'Ey you're alright'. So I said 'Oh thanks a
                 lot'. 'Yeh' he said, 'Yeh, what I like about you' he said 'you
                 don't try and be tough like the other guys, some of the other
                 teachers' and I said, 'Well I'm not'; an you could have heard a
                 pin drop. And he said, 'What did you say?' I said 'Well, I'm
                 not tough', and he said (loudly) 'Did you 'ear what he said?',
                 you know. And I was intrigued, and it seemed to me that a
                 lot of teachers, you can get drawn into a situation, where —
                 if you're not careful — where you have to act tough, and
                 you're pushing and pushing and pushing, and you never
                 allow them to see that there's no harm in not being tough
                 which probably contributes to the tendency for them all to
                 be little tough guys.

Mr Quilley also told a 'counter incident' which reveals some particular features
about his teaching style, which were in direct opposition to those of Mr Redford.
When Mr Quilley told his 'critical incident' he had shown none of the remorse about
his experience of violent confrontation, which the other teachers exhibited strongly.
He did not suggest that he avoided violent confrontations from then on in his career.
Other data gathered in the project supported this conclusion. We tried to choose
teachers for interviewing who knew each other, because they worked in the same
school, even at different times historically, or because they taught the same subject in
the same town. It was part of the attempt to validate data. Mr Tucks knew Mr
Quilley, he had done his student teaching practice at his school. He laughed when
Mr Quilley was mentioned, 'Oh he was renowned that guy, everyone knew him'.
The comment was confirmed by other teachers. Mr Redford knew him, 'Oh yes
everybody knew of him'. Mr King declared 'He was a bully'. Mr Redford told tales
of Mr Quilley's record of monstrous mass canings that had shocked parents, peers
and the educational community.

Nevertheless, this was not the full picture. Mr Quilley did not provide a specific
'counter incident' to reveal his teaching style, but he did make a series of comments
which showed there was another side to him. He was anxious to indicate that he did
achieve good relationships in some areas, with at least some of the pupils.

Mr Quilley: Colliers' sons, wonderful in the playground, great on the
                 football pitch, and in the swimming pool. I had no trouble
                 with them there, but in the classroom, you were a different
                 person, to be got at, if you were gottable at.

In addition Mr Quilley provided long accounts of the expeditions and trips he had
organized for pupils to go skiing or to visit art galleries abroad or sailing small boats.
Mr Tucks confirmed this view of a two-sided figure.

Mr Tucks: He was extraordinary, such a mixture. He'd organize all these
               super trips, skiing and painting, the kids loved it, and yet all
               this violence too. I don't know if the story is apocryphal, but
               there are tales of him playing games with knives, you know

boys had to splay their fingers out, and you dot between them with a big knife.

Woods (1981) has shown the balancing act that a teacher he named Tom did in school and community. He did certain things that weighed down the credit side of his account, and others that leaded the debit side. Tom carefully chose a display of strategies, and put them forward to enable him to keep afloat in the school. Mr Quilley engaged in a similar process. He secured excellent relationships with at least some pupils, through his proficiency in sport and by his energy and willingness to organize extra activities. Yet, he was renowned in the community as a bully with a record of severe classroom violence. The 'critical incident' revealed one set of strategies, he used real violence in an unrepentant spirit. The contrastive shadow episodes, where he described himself having a good time with kids at the swimming pool and taking pupils abroad on enjoyable trips to art galleries, show the second set. As a result of using both strategies Mr Quilley kept some sort of balance in his career, although perhaps not a very successful one. People were always aware of the dualism in what this teacher did.

I have given a description of three sets of 'critical' and 'counter' incidents in the careers of three separate teachers. I want to suggest that in the accounts issues of choice and identity are involved. The teachers are indicating which direction they took at a particular phase. They are trying to show what kind of teacher they became and therefore identity is involved. The mechanisms by which identity is communicated are interesting and something we have attempted to discuss before (Measor and Woods, 1983). We took Lewis's (1980) argument that values, attitudes, roles and identity are things which are very difficult for people to talk straightforwardly about. Indeed, in Lewis's view, they are precisely the things that people need symbols for. We suggested that adolescents employed myths to signal acceptable role models and identities for themselves (Measor and Woods, 1983). We also documented the ways that adolescent girls personified values into particular people around them and used them as positive or negative role models.

The same mechanisms were at work in teachers' accounts of their biographies. I have already indicated that negative role models were employed. 'No', they said, 'I wouldn't want to be like him'. The 'critical' and 'counter' incident accounts were another device where symbols are used to reveal choice and identity preferences. The 'critical' incident is described, the reaction to it is identified, and the confusion it engendered is emphasized. The choices that resulted from it are then made clear. The 'counter' incident is told, it acts like a contrastive shadow, it reinforces the choices that resulted from the 'critical' event, and it sets the identity.

Teachers gave more information about 'their way' in interviews. The critical incident sets the teacher off on a path, looking for another way to do things. Mr Shoe indicated the importance of discovering positive role models at this phase.

Mr Shoe: I think one of the teachers that perhaps interested me was a lady, deputy headmistress, and I used to admire her in some ways. She always used to seem to have — the kids in her class always seemed to be well occupied, always interested. I used to think, well — I used to see her sometimes coming to school in the morning, she'd get off her bike, and she'd be snatching a sample of this, a flower of that, and she'd come in armed with that, and suddenly you'd see that these were being used in a lesson. She always seemed to, never had discipline problems with the boys that I was having you see. It was just the fact that her lessons were ineresting.

As a result, Mr Shoe discarded his old role model, the Headmaster of his first school. He decided he had been wrong, that there was another way and that he was going to follow it.

Mr Shoe:	I think the first thing is that you've got to get the kiddies interested.
R:	Any other ways?
Mr Shoe:	I think bringing in a certain sense of humour, if you can break it up, have a laugh. Involve them.
R:	How else did you involve them?
Mr Shoe:	Talking, even though it wasn't necessarily relevant. Football, if they're a Chelsea supporter, or something. And 'Top of the Pops'. Knowing their interests, whether it be roller skating or skateboarding or any other interest.

Mr Shoe had by the time he had been in teaching three or four years found his own 'way' in school, and it was a way that was distinctively different from the first role models he had been provided with.

At the beginning of this chapter, I suggested that there were clear gender differences involved in critical incidents for teachers. All of the incidents described, except for the first, occurred when male teachers confronted male pupils. The women teachers we interviewed who had taught in all girls' schools did not report comparable experience, although women teachers involved in teaching boys or mixed classes did. The Glasgow woman teacher's story has already been told. Another woman, Mrs Castle, also had difficulties and the experience of violence in her first teaching job. She taught in a selective grammar school in a South Wales mining village. Mrs Castle described the school as 'nicely disciplined', nevertheless there were many challenges to her discipline, and once she cracked.

Mrs Castle:	I did hit a pupil once, in a temper, hit a boy of six foot.
R:	This was in the South Wales school.
Mrs Castle:	Yes, I felt ever so silly afterwards, very upset, I apologized.
R:	What had he done?
Mrs Castle:	I don't know. He was probably being a bit cheeky or something. I was horrified, I think I apologized almost straight away. He tried to cheer me up then.

Mrs Castle gave further accounts of the discipline challenges she received.

Mrs Castle:	As I say the boys did play me up at Christmas. I got chased

> round with the mistletoe and shut in the Art room with some
> of the 6th form, and they said things like 'Why don't you give
> in gracefully, or are you going to call for Sir'.
>
> *R:*   Which did you do?
>
> *Mrs Castle:* I gave in gracefully of course.

Recent classroom research has suggested that there are gender differences in pupil deviance (Ebutt, 1981; Measor, 1983). In addition, it may be that the gender of the teacher affects the nature of classroom deviance (Walkerdine, 1980). The kind of discipline challenges that Mrs Castle and the Glasgow woman teacher witnessed, varied also with the social class and the location of the school and the pupils. And the responses of the teacher were not the same. Nevertheless, in both cases there was a specifically sexual element to the challenge and it gained its point from being addressed to a woman teacher.

At the beginning of this chapter, I made reference to one negative case, to a teacher who felt he had never had any real discipline problems and who certainly had no 'critical' experience of violent confrontation. This was Mr King, and his account is interesting for the other kinds of historical 'critical incidents' involved. It may be that they were responsible for his lack of discipline problems. The account was set at the end of the Second World War.

> *Mr King:*   ... Well I was blown up, as I told you, and was asked if I
> would go into a garrison regiment, because that's for down-
> graded physique. In theory you strut about with a revolver at
> your hip, and look after a town as opposed to fighting. But no,
> this garrison unit piled into boats and sailed over to the Channel
> Islands, we were the liberating force. I remember being in the
> first landing boat, not a German in sight, but girls galore. I
> suppose I had been there about three or four weeks, the Civic
> Authorities had a big dinner, they invited some officers. I sat
> next to the Education Officer and he said 'Why don't you come
> to Jersey, you're just the sort of man we want'.
>
> *R:*   Was it just accident you were sitting next to the Education
> Officer?
>
> *Mr King:* Yes! I said 'I don't care to teach in the Channel Islands'. I saw
> myself with a good job in a public school. Or painting portraits
> in a posh studio of posh people.

Finally, Mr King agreed to take the job. His position as a man with a military background was to have a profound effect on his image, his experience of teaching and his eventual teaching style.

> *Mr King:* The Channel Islands public schools had suffered like hell
> because the Germans had imprisoned a lot of the teachers that
> hadn't escaped, so it was more or less run by the locals and
> senior boys. I remember being shown around by the HM and
> the first room he opened, he, not me, was hit in the face with a

book. He spread it around that I was an ex-commando, which I wasn't, and of course boys immediately moved to the other side of the corridor and said 'Morning Sir', and that was what I was really enrolled for, to impose discipline, there was none. I never hit a boy. I would grab him by the scruff of the neck and the trousers and pick him up, and say 'Now what are you going to do?' It didn't matter if he was eighteen years of age, because I was very strong then. I would put him down and say, 'Now behave yourself'. I never needed to hit the boys.

Mr King had finished up as the Senior Tutor at his school and he had been in charge of discipline. He had a reputation in the school and wider community for excellent, unquestioned discipline. He felt that these early incidents were crucial in enabling him to build a confident front, so his discipline was never questioned. They had set his image and given him his teacher style.

What is it then which makes these incidents critical for the teacher telling the story? The account involves a set of claims about the self. For the individual particular claims about their ability to maintain discipline and about their authoritative image are made. It represents a claim to the identity of being 'a proper teacher. The critical incident involves a challenge to this identity and image. As a result of the challenge, some of these claims are dropped, others are made real. Some parts of the identity are confirmed, others are renounced. In addition, the critical incident can involve a discovery about parts of the self, about one's capacity for anger, which can be difficult to cope with. The incident provokes a series of choices as the individual sorts out which kind of behaviour and which parts of the self are appropriate for display in the teacher role. There may be insights into role theory here, for all the data was drawn from the early period of the teachers' careers when they were being socialized into being a teacher. The individual begins with a general sense of what is expected from them in the new role, then they choose from amongst the alternative models they perceive and are presented with. Role in this data seems to be both constraining and flexible at the same time.

Strauss (1959) discussed the way a particular event changes the things an individual wants or sees as important, it can change their trajectory. The critical incident works in this way, it involves a reassessment of priorities; and we gain an insight into the processes by which identities are built for individuals at particular points in their life cycle. By focussing on critical incidents we place the actor's definition of what is important to the forefront. Hankiss (1981) wrote of the way 'people endow certain fundamental episodes with a symbolic meaning, by locating them at a focal point of the explanatory system of the self' (Bertaux, 1981, p. 205). This seems an accurate description of identity construction. On the basis of this data, the individual chooses 'a way' and by so doing makes a self.

It is open to question whether these changes and choices remain permanent. Hankiss felt that 'key events' were important because 'they constantly lead or force that person to select new models or a new strategy of life' (Bertaux, 1981, p. 206). I would want to question her use of the word 'constantly' here, coping with such 'critical incidents', 'constantly' or even quite often, would be far too exhausting. Critical incidents occur at intervals, probably during critical phases, and they have momentous consequences for the self: they don't happen constantly. Folks couldn't cope if they did.

Critical incidents then have a far reaching effect upon teacher's careers, but there are a number of critical phases in any biography. Teachers, if they survive this kind of test, find others later on in their careers. They have to negotiate their way through promotion hurdles once they are established in their role, and this represents an increasingly sophisticated set of strategies in the current economic situation. They always have to cope with senior colleagues, and have to set their own ambitions and career interests against those of their family. The last phase, as the teacher comes up to retiring age represents another critical period, a number of adjustments and problems have to be made and faced then as the teachers look back over what they have and have not achieved.

Note

1 Forty eight teachers in all were interviewed, two male, two female in each category. Half the teachers lived in the south east of England and the other half in Yorkshire. The methodology involved repeated interviews with each teacher; we aimed for about six interviews with key informants, but this was reduced where teachers had neither the time nor inclination to become so involved with the project.

References

BECKER, H. (1966) 'Introduction', in SHAW, C.R. *The Jack Roller*, Chicago, University of Chicago Press.

BERTAUX, D. (Ed.) (1981) *Biography and Society*, London, Sage.

EBUTT, D. (1981) 'Girls science, boys science revisited', in KELLY, A. *The Missing Half*, Manchester, Manchester University Press.

FURLONG, V. (1976) 'Anancy goes to school', in WOODS, P. and HAMMERSLEY, M. (Eds) *School Experience*, London, Croom Helm.

GLASER, B.G. (1964) *Organizational Scientists: Their Professional Careers*, Kansas, Bobbs-Merill.

HANSON, D. and HERRINGTON, M. (1976) *From College to Classroom*, London, Routledge and Kegan Paul.

LEWIS, G. (1980) *Day of Shining Red*, Cambridge, Cambridge University Press.

MEASOR, L. (1983) 'Gender and the sciences', in HAMMERSLEY, M. and HARGREAVES, A. (Eds) *Curriculum Practice: Some Sociological Case Studies*, Lewes, Falmer Press.

MEASOR, L. and WOODS, P. (1983) *Transfer to Comprehensive School: The Pupils Experience*, Milton Keynes, Open University Press.

RISEBOROUGH, G. (1981) 'Teachers careers and comprehensive schooling: An empirical study', *Sociology*, **15**, 3, pp. 352–80.

STRAUSS, A.L. (1959) *Mirrors and Masks: The Search for Identity*, Glencoe, Free Press.

STRAUSS, A.L. and RAINWATER, L. (1962) *The Professional Scientist*, Chicago, Aldine Press.

WALKER, R. *et al.*, (1976) *Innovation, the School and the Teacher (1)*, Open University Course E203 Unit 27, Milton Keynes, Open University Press.

WALKERDINE, V. (1980) 'Learning, Language and Resistance', History Workshop Conference, Brighton.

WOODS, P. (1981) 'Strategies, commitment and identity: Making and breaking the teacher role', in BARTON, L. and WALKER, S. (Eds) *School, Teachers and Teaching*, Lewes, Falmer Press.

Teacher Status Panic: Moving Up the Down Escalator

Rodman B. Webb

Editors' Note: The research upon which this chapter is based was conducted under Contract No. 400–79–0075 of the National Institute of Education, Washington, DC. It does not necessarily reflect the views of that agency. The chapter was published in slightly different form in the *Journal of Thought* (1983), 18, 4, pp. 39–48. It is reprinted here by permission of the *Journal of Thought*. While the paper is based on research conducted in the USA the parallels with the contemporary situation in Britain are inescapable.

It is an American shibboleth that teaching is a 'rewarding' (read personally satisfying) profession. However, a two-year study of middle and high school teachers gives reason to distrust the truth of this long-time truism (Ashton, Webb and Doda, 1983). Ethnographic analysis of observation data gathered in ten public school classrooms and interviews with more than forty teachers suggest that teaching is no longer the satisfying profession it once may have been. In fact, teaching has become a profession in crisis.

Status and Mobility

Dan Lortie (1975) has pointed out that in the United States 'teaching is clearly white-collar, middle-class work and as such offers upward mobility for people in blue-collar or lower-class families' (p. 35). Historically, teaching has provided an honourable route to the white-collar world of the middle class.[1] The education profession has offered its members an adequate and slowly increasing income, job security, and some degree of community respect. Rapidly expanding school systems have offered better-paying administrative jobs for teachers who wished to continue their ascent up the social status ladder. Today, however, the situation is changing.

Population growth has slowed dramatically and a sluggish economy has caused some school systems to lay off teachers and others to struggle along on shrinking resources. Inflation has cut deeply into the salary advances earned during the 1960s.

As shown in figure 1 starting salaries for teachers have fallen substantially while they have increased in most other professions (Sykes, 1984, p. 65).

Figure 1   Starting Salaries for College Graduates, in 1975 Dollars

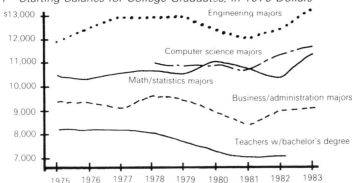

According to the National Center for Educational Statistics, teachers' buying power declined by nearly 15 per cent during the 1970s (Dearman and Plisko, 1982, p. 102). During roughly the same period, strongly unionized, blue-collar workers fared much better. For example, the after-inflation income of coal miners advanced 31 per cent, that of truck drivers 23 per cent and the income of plumbers over 11 per cent (Blumberg, 1980). Teachers who once prided themselves on their advancement into the middle class are alarmed that the income of many blue-collar workers has caught up with and even exceeded their own. Such a situation threatens teachers' sense of self worth and social location. Blumberg (1980) has shown however, that this problem is not unique to teachers; it effects many members of the middle class.

> Today, the middle-class struggle to maintain what have been for them appropriate income differentials is collapsing. Such salaried employees must inevitably develop the feeling that their income is no longer commensurate with their social worth (p. 83).

Blumberg asks:

> In a society where money is the measure of social worth, what happens when clerical workers and retail salespeople discover that factory workers are suddenly earning not merely slightly more, but 2–2.5 times more than they; when school teachers and librarians are being left behind in the factory dust; when unionized blue-collar workers are quickly closing in even on college professors who have invested up to ten years in graduate school ... to prepare for a career (p. 83).

He adds ominously: 'When rank — or *imagined* rank — no longer gets its due, social order is in danger' (p.83).

The teachers interviewed for this study discussed the problem of pay with great emotion. These comments are typical:

> I do get discouraged ... the pay is so low. I ask myself, Why am I doing this? Why did I ever go into teaching? I feel embittered.

I'm getting out of teaching. It isn't so much that I don't like teaching. It is because the pay is so low.

Occupational status is one of the most widely studied aspects of the social stratification system in America. Most studies derive from research conducted by the National Opinion Research Center in the 1950s. Since that time other studies have found a high degree of stability in the prestige assigned most occupations. Studies of occupational status show that teachers rank far below most other professions (physicians, pharmacists, lawyers, and so on) and in the lower third of white-collar occupations. In a ranking system that gave status scores as high as 583 and as low as thirty to various occupations in America, Coleman and Rainwater found that high school teachers had a rating of 131, or just barely above, 'the lowest level of managerial . . . and kindred workers' (p. 61).[2] Status-sensitive teachers are troubled by low salaries and by the relatively low status that their salaries reflect.

The social standing of teachers is further threatened by the growing public dissatisfaction with education in general and with the quality of teachers in particular. Over the past eight years, for example, growing numbers of Americans expressed worry over the quality of public schooling. In a 1974 survey, 32 per cent of the American public assigned grades of C or below to indicate how badly they thought schools were doing. By 1981, 54 per cent gave the schools such low grades (See Figure 2) (Weiler, 1982, p. 9).

Figure 2   Distribution of Aggregate Good (A–B) and Bad (C–F) Grades for Public Schools, 1974–1981

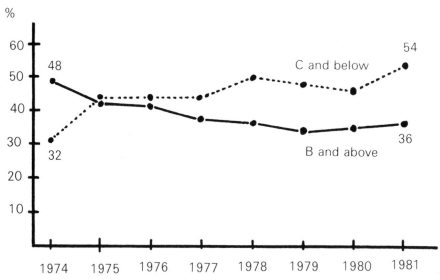

Sources: Stanley M. Elam, ed., *A Decade of Gallup Polls of Attitudes Toward Education, 1969–1978* (Bloomington, Ind.: Phi Delta Kappa, 1978); and reports on the 11th, 12th, and 13th annual Gallup Polls on the Public's Attitudes Toward the Public Schools found in the *Phi Delta Kappan* (September 1979, pp. 33–45; September 1980, pp. 33–46; and September 1981, pp. 33–47).

The reasons for the decline in public confidence have not been studied carefully so their exact causes are not known. However, scholars, critics, and the popular press frequently cite such reasons as the prolonged national decline in achievement test scores; the steady rise in educational expenditures; the escalation of school crime; the alleged failure of Great Society programs designed to improve education, and an increase in teacher militancy. For the first time, the 1980 Gallup Poll reported that a majority of Americans (52 per cent) would be displeased if a child of theirs decided to become a public school teacher. This figure is up from 25 per cent in 1969 (Gallup, 1980, p. 38).

Teachers we interviewed were aware of their flagging image in the community and were disturbed that the public didn't understand the problems teachers face or appreciate what they took to be the real accomplishments of the public education. As one teacher put it:

> In the [media] we have lost a lot of respect. They blame teachers because students don't do well on ... tests. We're getting the blame when [it] should be placed on the home. Pay us more. Pay us as professionals and let administrators treat us as professionals and then see what we can do.

A National Education Association survey in 1981 asked teachers to indicate the factors and forces that have had a negative effect on their job satisfaction. Well over 50 per cent of teachers surveyed indicated that the public's attitudes toward schools, the treatment of education by the media, student attitudes toward learning, low salaries, and the declining status of teachers have had a negative effect on their job satisfaction and professional morale (Dearman and Plisko, 1982, p. 105).

Teachers come to their work with aspirations of vertical mobility, but today they find little opportunity for advancement in their chosen profession. They come with the hope that they will earn an adequate income, but they find that their salaries are not keeping pace with inflation and that the pay of many blue-collar workers equals or exceeds their own. They come with expectations that white-collar work will afford them respectably high status in the community, but they find that their prestige is damaged by the decline of public confidence in education. It would appear that teachers are suffering what C. Wright Mills (1951) once called 'status panic' (p. 254–258). Such anxiety is damaging to their professional self-esteem and has diminished their commitment to education.

Given these conditions, it should not surprise us that there has been a catastrophic drop in the degree of satisfaction teachers report they find in their work. When a National Education Association (1982) survey of teachers asked, 'Suppose you could go back to your college days and start over again, and in view of your present knowledge, would you become a teacher?' only 25 per cent of female teachers and 16 per cent of male teachers indicated that education would certainly be their career choice (p. 74). These percentages are down from 57 per cent for females and 35 per cent for males in 1961. Today, less than half of the nation's teachers definitely plan to stay in the profession until retirement (*ibid.*, p. 76).

The teaching profession is not providing individuals with the financial and psychological support they need to sustain them in their work. As a result many teachers are leaving the field. According to Schlechty and Vance's (1981) research the most academically able teachers are the most likely to leave the classroom. Not surprisingly perhaps, the number of academically talented students entering teacher preparation programs has declined sharply. In 1972 there were 191,172 education degrees conferred in the United States. By 1980 that number had fallen to 118,102 (Dearman and Plisko, 1982, p. 96). Between 1973 and 1981 the Scholastic Aptitude Test (SAT) scores of high school seniors who aspired to teaching fell in the verbal area from 419 to 391 and in mathematics from 449 to 418 (*ibid.*, p. 88). True, SAT scores have been falling in the United States for some time, but the scores of prospective teachers have dropped faster than the national average (See Figure 3) (Sykes, 1984, p. 65).

Figure 3   SAT Scores by Intended Major

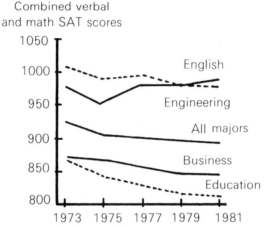

Teachers are showing more and more of the signs of anxiety that characterize other lower middle-class, white-collar occupations. Greater numbers of teachers appear to fit Beth Vanfossen's (1979) description of such workers:

> [They] perform necessary work activities and are essential to the running of bureaucracies. But they lack decision-making power and work autonomy. Their jobs are relatively secure, but dead-end. Their incomes are sufficient, but minimal. They have to be gregarious and sociable to please both boss and client, yet they receive little recognition for their placating functions. Their levels of self-esteem are higher than in the blue-collar stratum, yet they are more prone to a chronic dissatisfaction with their jobs, their incomes, and life in general. They neither prosper nor perish (p. 324).

Uncertainty and Teacher Satisfaction

Traditionally the major source of teacher satisfaction has been the act of teaching itself. Though many teachers still report that they find joy in teaching, many others express uncertainty that they are making a real difference in the classroom:

I thought I'd quit teaching. I just felt ... useless because I was going through long periods of time thinking that I wasn't doing anything for anybody.

I gave a test at the end of the year in which I reviewed material we'd gone over since the fall. Most of my students didn't do very well. It felt as if [I were running] a diploma factory.

As Dan Lortie (1975) has noted, 'teaching demands ... the capacity to work for protracted periods without sure knowledge that one is having any positive effect on students' (p. 144). Uncertainty is pervasive and cuts deeply into teachers' sense of satisfaction and accomplishment.

Status-Panic and Teacher Isolation

We might expect that the common problems teachers face would promote unity and cooperation within their ranks. We did not find that to be the case in most schools we studied. We found almost no evidence that teachers worked to bolster one another's flagging self-esteem. Instead, we found that teachers were generally isolated from one another and received little recognition from either colleagues or administrators. Some teachers complained that they were ignored, but no one we talked with felt that much could be done to diminish teacher isolation or promote a sense of community within the school. A teacher with ten years' experience complained about the lack of recognition at her school:

I think this year I have suffered from what they call teacher burnout. There is very, very little recognition here. Even a dog needs to be patted on the head, but we don't get that here. It makes you question whether it's worth it.

Another teacher told us that everyone needs to be 'told that he or she does something well.' She wished that administrators would pay attention to her accomplishments and let her know on occasion that she was 'doing a good job with these kids.' She thought if she could just 'hear that twice a year' she would feel her job was 'worth it.' She went on to say that administrators had:

never been [in my class] to really see what I've done and that hurts. You try, you really try and you take your profession seriously. You don't just sit on the job. But you never hear anything except complaints about your mistakes. You never hear anything that's worthwhile.

Teachers appear to be especially frustrated by the lack of recognition by administrators for their hard work and accomplishments. One teacher told us that her husband was encouraging her to leave teaching:

He sees how much teaching has devastated me over the years, and it has. A lot of these kids can break your heart. And he says I don't get much reward from teaching. I guess he's right, we certainly don't get much from the front office.

Nobody comes in and says, 'Thanks for stopping the riot at the basketball game.' That was something I did this year. And no one says, 'We think you're doing a terrific job.' I don't know of anybody in the school who has ever gotten that kind of recognition.

If it is true, as Rawls (1971) and others contend, that recognition from significant others is necessary for the establishment and maintenance of self-esteem, then teachers' self-esteem is put in jeopardy by the general lack of administrative and collegial support (p. 441). A teacher understated this point when she told us, 'It's awfully nice to get feedback from outside of yourself.' The literature from social psychology and sociology which bears on self-esteem would suggest that it is not simply nice that others evaluate one's work positively, it is essential to the maintenance of professional self-respect. Because teachers have difficulty assessing their classroom accomplishments and receive little recognition from the community, colleagues, or administrators, their professional self-esteem is kept in continual jeopardy (Webb, 1981, pp. 253–257; and 1982). Teachers' anxiety concerning their professional competence is heightened by a value system that links self-esteem with salary and social standing. Dedicated to the ethic of vertical mobility, teachers are discouraged to see their social standing beginning to slip and their relative economic advantages being eroded.

If teachers do not get support from the public or the administration, neither do they get help from their colleagues. One teacher complained that her fellow teachers were working 'in their own little world(s). Everybody is doing their own thing and nobody is helping anybody else.' As a consequence, she continued, the school becomes atomized and the educational enterprise hopelessly segmented. 'Nobody is working [with colleagues] to make this a whole school. I don't think a school can be effective that way. We're all in the boat together, and it's sinking.' Another teacher explained why colleagues do not cooperate:

We have the chance but we don't do it. I don't know why that is. I . . . think it would embarrass us if we hadn't thought of an idea ourselves and had to get it from another teacher.

Another teacher said:

Anybody's input would [have been] a help. If they would just share some of the things they have tried. But you know teachers get hold of a good idea and instead of sharing it, they hoard it. A lot of teachers are that way. They get some material and hoard it and won't let you see it. But I need some ideas and materials. I'm dying for information.

The psychological function of teacher insularity is to assuage the several uncertainties that teachers face; the social function of insularity is to decrease institutional disruption when teachers are absent, quit, or transfer to other schools. If teachers are self-contained and self-sufficient, no teacher or group of teachers will become indispensable to the smooth operation of the school. Every teacher is a unit unto him or herself and all units are functionally interchangeable. New teachers need little orientation and their work does not require long periods of initiation or the building of close professional relationships with fellow teachers.

We asked an experienced teacher how her colleagues would describe her if they were being candid. Although she has worked in the school for over a year, she was unable to answer the question:

> I think the majority of faculty don't know I'm here. The principal never introduced me. I don't even know the names of some teachers here.

When we asked another teacher the same question, she answered: 'I don't know ... I don't think they know whether I'm here or not'.

Teacher isolation functions to deprive teachers of the power to influence school-wide decisions that affect the conditions of their work. If teachers do not often speak of common problems, they are not likely to object to decisions that have a negative impact on their professional lives. Administrative decisions can be made at the top by principals, county administrators, or state officials without faculty consultation. Many teachers we talked to were disturbed by what they perceived to be their powerlessness within the school organization. One teacher said: '[We] aren't consulted as much as we should be by ... county officials or school administrators'. Many teachers express frustration over their inability to influence the decision-making process. One teacher told us, 'We are sometimes consulted, but it never seems to matter.' Another said:

> We talk [with administrators] to a certain extent, but I don't know that anybody listens. You tell your department head and he can pass it on to the principal, but it doesn't help. The administration starts planning and they don't think about our problems. They have problems of their own.

Self-estrangement Among Teachers

Our discussions with teachers have convinced us that for many the conditions of their employment promote an attitude of professional non-involvement with peers. Such conditions engender feelings of insecurity, status panic and self-protection through isolation and promote a form of alienation that social psychologists have called self-estrangement. Self-estrangement refers to a loss of meaningful connection between the worker and his work. According to Blauner (1964) 'When an individual lacks control over the work process and a sense of purposeful connection to the work enterprise, he may experience a kind of depersonalized detachment rather than an immediate involvement ... in the job tasks' (p. 26).

Many of the teachers we talked with and observed claimed that their profession was not fulfilling their needs or tapping their potentials:

> Teachers are not recognized the way they should be. I feel that with my

ability I could have been an engineer or . . . a scientist. I would have had
more recognition . . . and more financial reward.

Another teacher said that if she had it to do over she would not become a teacher
again because 'I have capacities that I haven't tapped, that can't be tapped in
teaching.'

To these individuals, and many of their colleagues, teaching provides only a
weak sense of accomplishment, satisfaction or success. Like most middle-class
Americans they desire success but have difficulty finding tangible signs of their own
accomplishment. They work long hours, sometimes facing more than 150 students a
day. They plan lessons, teach classes, counsel students, attend meetings, sponsor
clubs, correct papers, fill out forms, write report cards, coach sports, talk with
parents, and much more, and yet they have little way of knowing whether all this
work amounts to anything. They are keepers of the American dream, ·strivers,
carriers of middle-class values, but they have no tangible product to call their own.
They are unsure of their accomplishments on the classroom level and are
unsupported by colleagues, administrators or members of the community. In a sense
they are victims of their own values. They have difficulty reconciling their actual
achievements with their personal expectations.

Michael Lewis (1979) contends that most middle-class Americans are frustrated by
the mismatch between actual achievements and personal expectations. As he explains:

> If our quest of self-respect leads us to high aspirations, the chances are
> very great that in the overwhelming majority of cases there will be a con-
> siderable difference between what we think we are capable of and what it
> is we actually seem to be achieving. And if the maintenance of self-respect
> depends upon not only great expectations but great expectations realized,
> then such disparities are likely to pose a major threat to the self-esteem of
> many Americans (p. 15).

Lewis contends that aspirations by themselves are relatively unproblematic. However, 'convincing ourselves that we have indeed been successful — that our dreams
have been realized and that consequently we may respect ourselves — is extremely
problematic' (p. 15). The aspirations of teachers encourage them to lay claim to 'the
good life' and to personal achievement. But, as Lewis points out, those same values
make 'any perceived failure . . . a threat of significant psychological force to our
self-esteem' (p. 14). Failure or the hint of failure, in fact anything but the absolute
assurance that our accomplishments have exceeded our aspiration:

> threatens our self-esteem by causing us to doubt our character, our
> competence, or quite possibly both. To the extent . . . that our aspirations
> go unrealized (whatever the reason), we are threatened and troubled by
> personal guilt. Fearing that we have done less than we should, we are all too
> frequently haunted by the sense that we have done ill (p. 17).

Teachers are so haunted. They possess no personal or institutional means of
exorcising the ubiquitous worry that they have failed to fulfil their own middle-class

success aspirations. They are particularly vulnerable to the self-doubt and status panic that characterize many white-collar workers.

Like many white-collar employees, teachers are becoming increasingly estranged from their work. Many feel they have given up an essential part of themselves to pursue a task that provides little professional recognition, social status, remuneration, or personal satisfaction. They do not realize themselves through their work and are haunted by the knowledge that they have not become all that they once hoped to be. They form a negative occupational identity that threatens their already beleaguered self-esteem. Blauner (1964) discusses the connection between a lack of job satisfaction and self-identity:

> Self-estranging work compounds and intensifies [the] problem of a negative occupational identity. When work provides opportunities for control, creativity, and challenge — when, in a word, it is self-expressive and enhances an individual's unique potentialities — then it contributes to the worker's sense of self-respect and dignity and at least partially overcomes the stigma of low status. Alienated work — without control, freedom, or responsibility — on the other hand simply confirms and deepens the feeling that societal estimates of low status and little worth are valid (p. 31).

It is not suggested here that all or even most teachers are estranged from their work. It is suggested, however, that the pressure of isolation, status panic, uncertainty, and non-recognition make it difficult for teachers to avoid such estrangement. Until we find ways to increase the status of teaching and improve the working conditions of teachers, attempts to improve the quality of education at the classroom level are likely to fail.

Notes

1 According to the National Education Association, 51 per cent of today's male teachers and 41 per cent of today's female teachers have (or had) fathers employed as unskilled, semiskilled or skilled labourers or as clerical or sales workers. National Education Association (1982) *Status of the American School Teacher: 1980–81*, Washington, DC, National Education Association Research Division, p. 184.
2 Coleman and Rainwater included the term 'professional' in the above quote. The term was deleted because no 'professions,' as the term is generally understood, were include among
occupations that scored below 130.

References

ASHTON, P., WEBB, R., and DODA, N. (1983) *A Study of Teachers' Sense of Efficacy*, Washington, DC, National Institute of Education.
BLAUNER, R. (1964) *Alienation and Freedom*, Chicago, University of Chicago Press.
BLUMBERG, P. (1980) *Inequality in an Age of Decline*, Oxford, Oxford University Press.

COLEMAN, P. and RAINWATER, L. (1978) *Social Standing in America: New Dimensions of Class*, New York, Basic Books.

DEARMAN, N. and PLISKO, V. (1981) *The Condition of Education*, Washington, DC, National Center for Education Statistics.

DEARMAN, N. and PLISKO, V. (1982) *The Condition of Education*, Washington, DC, National Center for Education Statistics.

GALLUP, G. (1980) 'Gallup poll of the public's attitudes toward the public schools,' *Phi Delta Kappan*, **62**, 1, pp. 33–48.

LEWIS, M. (1979) *The Culture of Inequality*, New York, New American Library.

LORTIE, D. (1975) *Schoolteacher: A Sociological Study*, Chicago, University of Chicago Press.

MILLS, C.W. (1951) *White Collar: The American Middle Class*, New York, Oxford University Press.

NATIONAL EDUCATION ASSOCIATION (1982) *Status of the American Public School Teacher: 1980–81,* Washington, DC, NEA Research Division.

RAWLS, J. (1971) *A Theory of Justice*, Cambridge, Massachusetts, Harvard University Press.

SCHLECHTY, P. and VANCE, V. (1981) 'Do academically able teachers leave education?' *Phi Delta Kappan*, **63**, 2, pp. 106–112.

SYKES, G. (1984) 'The deal,' *The Wilson Quarterly*, VII, 1, pp. 59–77.

VANFOSSEN, B. (1979) *The Structure of Social Inequality*, Boston, Little, Brown and Company.

WEBB, R. (1981) *Schooling and Society*, New York, Macmillan.

WEBB, R., (1982) *'Teaching and the Domains of Efficacy'* a paper presented at the American Educational Research Association, New York.

WEILER, H. (1982) 'Education, public confidence, and the legitimacy of the modern state: Do we have a crisis?', *Phi Delta Kappan*, **64**, 1, pp. 9–14.

'The Tender Trap?' Commitment and Consciousness in Entrants to Teaching

Martin Cole

Editors' Note: This paper reports on a continuing longitudinal study of student teachers. In particular Cole examines the motivation of students who are weakly committed to a career in teaching and the pressures and problems they experience as they move through college and out into school.

The sociology of education has always given teachers a bad press. The pattern was established in Waller's (1932) seminal study which devotes considerable space to the elaboration of the theme that teaching is the refuge of 'unsaleable men and unmarriageable women' and explains the 'known failure of the profession to attract as large a number of capables as it should' by reference to the way:

> The nature of the work of teaching ... may both deter and attract to the ultimate damage of the profession ... may eliminate from teaching many of those virile and inspiring persons of whom the profession has such need (p. 379).

More recently discussion of the conservatism of teachers (as in Dale, 1977; Bartholomew, 1976; Hargreaves D., 1978; Hargreaves A., 1981; Mardle and Walker, 1980) seems tinged with a feeling of despair, a feeling aroused especially it seems by the belief that teacher training and the sociology of education in particular have little impact on the practice of teaching.

There is here less of the bitterness that marks some of Waller's remarks about the kind of people who choose to become teachers because an alternative explanation for teacher conservatism is favoured: that the structures of schooling, as experienced before, during and after training both create and sustain conservative attitudes in teachers.

There is thus a considerable degree of determinism in contemporary analyses of teaching. It can be detected, for example, in Hargreaves' (1981) discussion of a possible hegemony amongst teachers and in Mardle and Walker's (1980) emphasis on 'common structural parameters' and the 'apparent determination' whereby 'schools, colleges and university departments are highly functional in producing the right kinds of teachers' (p. 121). It could also be seen in Sharp and Green's (1975) assertion that teachers are 'unwilling victims of a structure' (p. 227).

This degree of determinism would have been unremarkable three or four decades ago when structural functionalism dominated sociology, but it is something of a surprise today when the sociology of education has recently shown intense interest in interactionist analysis and pursued phenomenological 'new directions'. It is also a disappointment, at a time when there is wide sympathy for attempts to integrate different sociologies, to see teachers portrayed so determinedly as passive victims of the structures of schooling (and training), having their consciousness constructed for them.

This deterministic structuralism has also tended to produce a crudely stereotypical assessment of the teacher. Thus conforming, moderately successful schoolchildren who have found their schooling congenial choose to become teachers. During training they are persuaded to discuss liberal conceptions of education which they reproduce (with a merely instrumental motivation) in some of their academic work. Meanwhile, the hidden curriculum of training reinforces the conservative assumptions with which students entered. in the probationary year survival in the classroom is achieved on the basis of familiar, pragmatic recipes (often learnt while still a pupil) and the emerging teacher soon joins maturer colleagues in the dismissal of liberal theory as irrelevant to the daily practice of teaching: the scene is set for a career of unreflective conservatism.

We may understand some reasons why sociologists might wish to sustain, at the level of their common sense, such an image of the teacher. Most of us engaged in sociology of education work as teacher-trainers and the critical nature of our discipline entails, implicitly at least, a prescription of innovation. Faced with a school system in which most sociologists find little evidence of teachers innovating there is a need to construct some account of the apparent futility of the sociological component in training. Concepts of 'structure', 'ideology', 'hegemony', and the stereotype I have sketched, assist in this accounting. There may be a counterpart here for the practice of teachers in favouring accounts of pupil failure that focus on alleged deficiencies in pupils, their pre-school and extra-school experiences.

This chapter starts, then, from a desire to redress the perspective balance a little by recognizing that teachers also assist in the construction and maintenance of those very structures that, it is so frequently argued, socialize and constrain them, and by stressing that teachers' participation is active not passive. In so doing the chapter aims to avoid the dualism most clearly defined by Giddens (1976 and 1979) in which determining structure and voluntary action are regarded as competing poles in social theory. Rather I shall attempt to follow the fundamental tenet of Giddens' theory of structuration that 'social structures are both constituted by human agency, and yet at the same time are the very medium of this constitution' (1976, p. 120).

Specifically, I shall suggest reasons for relinquishing the sociological stereotype of the teacher and adopting a less generalized and less deterministic picture. This picture will entail a typology of beginning teachers in terms of attitude and commitment to teaching. Finally, a challenge will be laid down to the widely accepted notion that what happens to teachers following training represents a change of attitude. In place of this again rather deterministic view that professional socialization changes attitudes I shall argue that the experience of teaching should be seen as supportive of a particular mode of consciousness. Such an analysis is able to embrace the active participation of teachers in the construction and maintenance of those structures which act back upon them, and thus avoids reducing them simply to passive, unreflective and 'over-socialized' dupes.

First, however, it is necessary to consider both the research methodologies which have contributed to the deterministic and stereotyped conception of the teacher, and those which have produced the data discussed in this paper.

I have referred elsewhere[1] to the irony whereby ethnographic studies of teachers in their staffrooms (such as conducted by Woods, 1979; and by Hargreaves, 1981) have served to support a rather deterministic or 'over-socialized conception'[2] of the teacher; an emphasis more readily associated with structural functionalism. The crucial mistake has been to believe that the exclusion of pupils makes the staffroom a 'back-region' (in Goffman's terms) when it should be seen as another 'front-region', with colleagues as audience, where teachers contrive a consensual common-sense which is continually reproduced by individuals' strategic present-ations of self. I side with Hammersley (1981) in his contention that staffroom talk:

> must be treated not as a straightforward reflection of the attitudes of individual teachers but as a perspective constructed and sustained in the particular circumstances of staff relations (p. 337).

The means of trying to uncover the attitudes of individual teachers in my own research has therefore emphasized the importance of getting teachers talking outside of the context of staffroom, and, indeed, of the school. Teachers have been interviewed privately and, wherever possible, both in their own homes and in circumstances that would reassure them of the confidentiality of the exercise (for example, the interviewer not knowing the identity of the respondent's school). Of course, interviews, like staffrooms, are interactional settings where participants may indulge in strategic presentations of self. The point is not that the data deriving from such interviews is necessarily or self-evidently *better* than that obtained by in-school ethnography, simply that it is a *different* kind of data. The differences may be instructive, both about teachers and about sociological methods.

The data which will be discussed here results from a number of distinct but inter-related projects:

1   A programme of interviews (averaging three hours' duration) with fourteen experienced teachers (ranging from twenty-six to late fifties in age). All were strangers to the interviewer, who did not know the identity of respondents' schools. Interviews took place in the teachers' homes.
2   Interviews with twelve BEd teacher-trainees in the final week as students in my own college (average duration one hour).
3   A substantial confidential questionnaire presented to all final year BEd

students of the college in their last week. There were forty responses, representing a rate of 61 per cent.

4 A programme of interviews with ten former students of the college between one and four years after entry to teaching.

All of the interviews were very loosely-structured and all were tape-recorded.

These projects represent the tentative beginnings of an attempt to construct a number of longitudinal case-studies. The data collected so far is, of course, of questionable status in terms of longitudinal analysis since the different stages of the entry to teaching are represented by different individuals (and the numbers are small). While the experienced teachers were asked to recall their attitudes towards teaching (motives, aspirations, etc.) from the initial decision to teach, through training and the early years in teaching, it is doubtful to what extent such recollections are reliable. To what extent are recollections of previous attitudes influenced by changing perceptions in the interim? It is in view of this doubt (and a lack of hypnotic powers) that I intend that the students interviewed in project 2 be re-interviewed at yearly intervals over the next few years. It is also planned to interview new recruits to a neighbouring college on entry, at intervals during training, and during at least the early years of their teaching careers.

The work to date should be regarded, therefore, not as an attempt to generate different generalizations, or a different stereotype, from those currently on offer, but rather to uncover some possibilities, subtleties and complexities, and perhaps to formulate some hypotheses, which future research might be designed to explore in greater depth and breadth. It is to these that I now turn, organizing them according to the longitudinal frame of reference.

Before Training

It has often been argued that one of the most potent, if not *the* most potent of influences on the teacher is his or her own experience as a pupil. Lortie (1975) has explored this influence in detail, asserting two key elements: first, the manner in which pupils imbibe taken-for-granted assumptions about schooling (using the term 'student' where a British reader would expect 'pupil'):

> Students rarely participate in selecting goals, making preparations, or postmortem analyses ... they are not pressed to place the teacher's action in a pedagogically oriented framework ... It is improbable that many students learn to see teaching in an end-means frame or that they normally take an analytic stance toward it. What students learn about teaching, then, is intuitive and imitative rather than explicit and analytical (p. 62).

Secondly, Lortie shows us the relation between school experience and the decision to enter teaching:

> the conservative force represented by teachers who entered with highly positive sentiments of identification is not offset to any appreciable degree

by people favouring discontinuity and change towards other conceptions of teaching (p. 46).

We ought not to be surprised if teaching attracts mainly those individuals who have found success and pleasure in their past involvement with schools organized as they are. Although teaching is unique in the degree of knowledge of the occupation entrants to training already possess, it would not be surprising if entrants to most occupations are mostly those attracted by the occupation as they believe it to be presently organized rather than those who believe the job ought to be organized differently. There is probably an inherent conservatism in the processes of self-selection for, and recruitment to, most occupations.

My own data does suggest, however, the need for some scepticism about Lortie's assertion (a now rather dated one):

If there are people who enter teaching because they wish to express negative sentiments through direct attack on conventional practice, they do not appear among the respondents in Five Towns; nor, in fact, are they evident in any studies I know of. If they do indeed exist they must be very scarce (p. 46).

The questionnaire completed by my students in their final week of training produced a considerable amount of negative reporting on experience as pupils. Asked to write a few sentences about how they had felt about their own primary and secondary schooling (at the time they left each stage of schooling) fifteen of forty students responding made some negative comments. Almost all of these related to secondary school only and, in quite a number of cases, it appeared that unsatisfactory secondary schooling had been a factor in opting to train for primary teaching. However, a number of remarks, in identifying for example 'boring teachers' or 'chaos following school reorganization', suggest that students now saw their dissatisfactions resulting from particular circumstances; such remarks do not necessarily represent a disaffection with the principles or practice of schooling in general. Nevertheless, four students making negative remarks about their own schooling did, in answering a different question about the reasons they had had for wanting to teach (at the time they entered college) state that a desire to reform particular aspects of schooling had been a reason for entry. Perhaps there are rather more negative identifiers among teacher-trainees than we have generally been lead, by Lortie at least, to believe.

The presence of negative identifiers in my own college was something I had originally become aware of largely by accident. Early in the programme of interviews with students in their final week of training, it had been decided to concentrate particularly on students who from the personal knowledge of myself and one or two colleagues appeared to be most likely of all the students we knew to enter teaching with a definite motivation to challenge conventional practice. Such students had rarely attracted the attention of researchers — indeed Lortie and others have virtually denied their existence; they were therefore of particular interest. Virtually all the students selected in this way volunteered information during their loosely structured interviews about bad experiences as pupils. In many cases there had been considerable open conflict with secondary school: one student had been a chronic truant; two others had, despite academic potential and pressure from school and parents, left school at age sixteen to start work. In almost every case there had also been a break between school and college of between one and three years. Some had done routine jobs they found unrewarding and one had done voluntary social work overseas; several had had to gain entry to college via evening classes to gain 'A' levels; two had entered by the University's process of 'mature matriculation'. The decision to enter teaching in all these cases had been a concerted one, and one that often involved some personal hardship; for these students teaching could be said with some justification to be a vocation.

These students' entry to teacher training was in marked contrast to that described by positive identifiers in other interviews and in questionnaire responses where there appeared to be a *drift* into teaching: respondents found it difficult to pin-point any particular time when a decision to teach had been made, or the reasons for it. Some used expressions like 'an assumption that I would be a teacher' to describe the gradual evolution of their choice of career during secondary schooling. A further distinction between positive and negative identifiers appeared to lie in the expect-ations of future commitment to teaching. Positive identifiers seemed to enter training with an optimistic assumption that they would enjoy teaching and expected it to occupy the rest of their working lives. Negative identifiers entered with some scepticism: they felt they had to 'give teaching a try' but, despite the investment of the hardships experienced in gaining entry, were prepared to give up teaching after a few years if they did not find it satisfying. The significance of this distinction will become apparent in later discussion of further stages in the progress into teaching.

There are, then, grounds for suspecting that entrants to teacher training are not quite the homogeneous body frequently portrayed. In terms of identification with their own schooling and related matters such as motivation and commitment on entry to teaching it seems appropriate to distinguish 'conservatives' from 'in-novators'. One further aspect of the background to the entry into teaching merits brief mention. Bearing in mind that the statistic derives from just forty respondents in one college, it may be of interest that exactly 50 per cent of students responding to the questionnaire had some 'family history' of teaching. (Of these twenty students, four reported both parents to be teachers, six mother only, five father only, five an elder brother or sister). Of most significance, however, may be the fact that of the eight 'innovators' interviewed, only one reported a family connection with teaching. Perhaps this finding is consistent with the picture drawn above of the 'innovators' making a concerted decision to become teachers, while the 'conserva-tives' were more likely to 'drift' into the occupation.

Training

The questionnaire completed by forty students immediately prior to leaving the college required them to place themselves on a ten-point scale of intention to teach at the time they entered college and at the end of each college year. (Thus a score of ten represented the response 'certain that I wanted to teach' and a score of nought meant 'certain that I did NOT want to teach'). Students were asked to explain the reasons for any change in score between stages of their college career. Unsurprisingly, virtually all respondents claimed to have entered college at least 'fairly certain' that they wanted to teach; the scope for upward movement of scores during training was therefore limited.

Two-thirds of respondents displayed either a small upward movement of score (no more than three points) or maintenance of the same score from beginning to end of training. There were no cases of a major reversal of trend during training. These students seemed generally to bear out the now common assertion that the effect of training is to confirm students in the attitudes with which they enter. Those who gave reasons for small increases in the certainty that they wished to teach frequently explained that they had entered with some doubts about their 'suitability' or 'ability to cope' and that training (especially teaching practice) had made them more confident of both suitability and competence. The remaining one-third of respondents displayed a downward movement of score during training. In several cases this was a small movement, but in six instances students who had entered college at least 'fairly certain' that they wanted to teach were, at the end of their final year, either 'in some doubt' or 'fairly certain that (they) did NOT want to teach'. The full impact of training on this small group is not, however, revealed by the questionnaire. Fortunately I was able to interview four of these six students since during their final year they had revealed their change of attitude to me (either in casual conversation or in the course of seminars in which teacher socialization had been discussed). On the basis of these interviews it seems appropriate to propose a further category to join those so far applied to students prior to training ('conservatives' and 'innovators'). This third category, which only becomes applicable *during* training, I shall call 'the disillusioned'. These are students who enter college as 'conservatives' and leave it with one of three orientations: (i) with no intention of teaching, despite having achieved the qualification to do so; (ii) intending to pass the probationary year and perhaps teach for a further year or two while looking for an alternative career; or (iii) feeling that their entry to teaching is under constraint.

The reasons given by 'the disillusioned' for their change of attitude to teaching as their chosen career focused particularly on teaching practice (TP). They were not alone, however, in citing teaching practice as the major influence. Almost all students and teachers involved in these research projects, when asked to recall their developing thoughts on teaching during training, referred first, and often exclusively, to teaching practice. For 'conservative' students especially the 'second year at college', for example, meant the 'second teaching practice'.

It might be thought that the 'disillusioned' students were reflecting unsuccessful teaching practice, with rejection of teaching as a desirable occupation serving as a rationalization of a failure to make the grade. I could find no evidence, however, that this was generally true of the 'disillusioned' students I came across. Rather the effect of teaching practice had been to show these individuals that the role of teacher, as conventionally defined, was not one they wished to identify with, as the following excerpts from the questionnaire responses of the six disillusioned students show:

Mary: Faced with a mould that I didn't fit.

Christine: I discovered especially after my final TP that I was irritated by spending long periods of time with children, and found teachers in general boring and hypocritical; I felt I definitely didn't want to end up like that.

Geoff: Not convinced that I could cope 'within system' without turning into an authoritarian.

Elaine: After my third TP I decided that adopting the role of the teacher was very difficult as I did not agree with what this entailed (discipline, irrelevant subjects, etc.).

Jayne: As a person and a potential teacher I have changed a lot in three years as a result of TP, studies and general college experience. My image of teaching as I would face it in September is very different to what I envisaged some years ago and I have to seriously question my personal role and task as a teacher.

Sarah: TP had shown me that I did not want to teach an unpopular subject (French) to recalcitrant adolescents.

Although teaching practice was central to the process of disillusionment several students in this category referred to academic studies, especially the sociology of education, as confirming the critique of teaching which teaching practice had evoked. It seems that the effect of college courses may be not just to confirm conservative attitudes but also to confirm (though not originate) emergent critical ones.

Students in the 'conservative' category made little mention of college courses as influencing attitudes to entering teaching. Perhaps the critique of schooling implicit in some courses was understood and successfully reproduced in essays and examinations (as Bartholomew, 1976, describes) but it was not personally relevant for these students. It was the lived experience of teaching practice that mattered in confirming the original identification with teaching and allaying any early doubts about aptitude or competence. It is easy to see here the seeds of the future support for the common sense rule of the staffroom that theory courses in college are irrelevant to the practice of teaching.

We might ask of the 'disillusioned' students why they do not join with the 'innovators' in entering teaching with a positive motivation to change aspects of schooling they find unsatisfactory. It is essential to remember here the crucial difference in the attitudes of the two categories of student on entry to training. The 'innovators' had entered sceptically, anticipating possible frustration and conflict, prepared to give teaching a try but not wholeheartedly committed to the idea of a lifetime in teaching. Few in this group were therefore surprised or disappointed by any experiences during training. The 'disillusioned', however, had entered with an unquestioning optimism; they now felt 'let down' and none, though they would like to be able to change aspects of schooling, seemed to have the stomach for the fight, that is, to have a motivation to teach which would need to be of a quite different kind from that with which they had entered training.

Of the six 'disillusioned' students only one was certain not to enter teaching: she, rather fortuitously, had found alternative and to her attractive employment. The question arises as to why the remaining five, despite their disillusionment and in some cases a definite desire *not* to teach, were nevertheless seeking teaching jobs. Part of the answer seems to lie in the process of investment. All six students had decided during training as they recognized their disillusionment that having got to college and spent some time there it would be foolish not to complete the course and obtain their degree: 'I thought it would be a waste of my three years — I just thought, well, at least get your degree' (Interview with Sarah). There were also references to a desire to show parents that the original choices of career had received a fair trial.

Now, at the end of training, the investment argument was taken a stage further: it would be foolish not to make sure that teaching was not for them by teaching for at least one or two years (at the same time perhaps as looking around for alternatives). It will be shown in some detail in the next section of this chapter that these early years in teaching could in turn become part of an investment which rationalizes continuance in teaching.

There was a general realization too that these students were qualified for no other work — certainly not for anything that would produce a teacher's salary. All spoke of the pressures of being surrounded by friends feverishly applying for teaching jobs and by staff encouraging these endeavours. The pressure had been resisted for some weeks but finally all but one of the 'disillusioned' had felt obliged to join the job-hunt. One seemed to have succumbed partly because of trepidation at revealing her disillusion to her paternalistic head of college department who was busily pointing out job-openings and encouraging application. It may be that the presence of the 'disillusioned' in our colleges has been largely unrecognized because of the way such students have been inhibited from revealing their true feelings by the belief that both staff and fellow students would feel they ought to have withdrawn earlier in their college career and not gone on to 'waste' their training.

A further factor in the progress of the 'disillusioned' into teaching may be personal commitments of a domestic/emotional nature. Students' estimates suggest that about a third of the (mostly female) students of my own college have, by the time they leave, made a permanent relationship with a partner they expect to marry. Such a situation creates an obligation for the 'disillusioned' student to find a teaching job for financial reasons; it may also distract them from anticipated job dissatisfaction. Hargreaves (1978) has suggested that married women with families may best be able to weather the stresses of teaching because of domestic distractions and the broad spread of personal commitments. Perhaps a similar point can be made about students anticipating marriage at the time of transition from training to the probationary year.

It has been suggested above that college academic courses can confirm both the conservatism of most students and the disillusionment of a minority. It appears also that they may confirm 'innovators' in their reforming zeal. Several students in this category singled out for mention courses in sociology of education which they saw as supporting their own critical doubts about schooling and in so doing helped to compensate for frustrations experienced in other aspects of training. These students were particularly aware of ambiguities and conflicts between college liberal theory and conservative practice. They were not, however, surprised or disillusioned: they had entered training critical and sceptical about educational institutions and with a conditional commitment to teaching. It appeared that each would go on into the probationary year with this orientation confirmed during training.

After Training

This section of the chapter will focus on the crucial early years of the teacher's career, although the data on which it is based has been derived from interviews with teachers ranging widely in age: from those in their first three years of teaching to those who have taught for more than thirty years. Before consideration of the three categories 'conservatives', 'innovators' and 'the disillusioned' it is appropriate to consider an aspect of commitment amongst teachers that may be applicable across the categories.

Woods (1979) has already applied to teachers the concept of 'investment' discussed by Kanter (1974). Investment refers here to the way present satisfaction represents the dividend earned from past actions or experiences particularly where these involved some form of sacrifice.

It has already been suggested above that training itself (particularly the rigours of teaching practice) may represent an investment. Interviews with experienced teachers suggest that the hardships of the first two or three years in teaching may also represent a kind of investment when the successful conquest of the challenge presented by classes, pupils or circumstances perceived as difficult pay a dividend in the form of what Lortie (1975) calls 'craft pride' felt in later years. There is reason to think this form of investment is a widespread phenomenon amongst teachers: a remarkable number of teachers seem to have spent their early years teaching in 'the toughest school in town' and staffroom banter, especially in secondary schools, often consists of anecdotes about rough children or classes taught in the past. It is almost as though there is a need for some teachers, whatever the circumstances earlier in their careers, to believe in a 'baptism of fire' myth as a means of sustaining their craft pride. Anecdotes sometimes show teachers' failures or humiliations during this baptism — these are like battle-scars to be shown to colleagues as evidence of how tough it was and how much professional honour is due to them for finally emerging victorious.[3] The almost ritual complaint of teachers that their training did not prepare them for the rigours of teaching might be partly attributable to the function of the 'baptism of fire', real or mythical, as a past investment in present craft pride: whatever the quality of their training, some teachers might need to believe they were inadequately prepared.

A teacher who has made this sort of investment and is receiving the dividend of craft pride may not be able to afford to turn his or her back on teaching: such a course might appear as an ultimate admission of defeat and would, in terms of self-esteem, mean the forfeiture of all the dividends received while at the same time removal from the professional environment would cut off the source of esteem from others. The attitudes and commitment of conservative teachers have been much discussed, in particular detail by Lortie (1975) in the United States and by Woods (1979) in Britain. The only contribution to this discussion suggested by my own data is that of the 'baptism of fire' investment I have explored above.

But what of that largely unacknowledged but interesting minority, the innovative teachers? How does the experience of the early years of teaching influence innovators' attitudes and commitment? Both the existing literature on teachers and the conventional wisdom of the staffroom encourage a belief that after a few years in teaching 'innovators' will have changed their attitudes in a conservative direction while, by implication, their commitment will have come to resemble more closely that of those with a conservative orientation from the outset. Such are the findings of, for example, Finlayson and Cohen (1967) and Morrison and McIntyre (1967), while Lacey's (1977) study of Postgraduate Certificate in Education (PGCE) students lends general support to this contention. Aware of this apparent unanimity that teaching encourages more conservative attitudes in teachers I entered the programme of interviewing with the expectation that the notion would be confirmed. Three of the fourteen teachers interviewed in project 1 chanced to fall into my subjective category of 'innovator', while five of the ten ex-students interviewed after 1–4 years' teaching (ie. project 4) had been selected because as students they had appeared to be 'innovators'. In practice, these interviews produced little evidence to support the established contention about attitudes and a good deal that seemed to challenge it. In particular, the five ex-students identified as 'innovators' appeared to be as exercised about what they saw as the shortcomings of the conventional practices of schools as ever they had been as students, in one case perhaps rather more so:

> I found it very hard when I went into teaching to accept things that go on in school, and I still find it very hard ... It really gets to me. I get upset, really angry ... It's nice being with the kids but the system really bugs me ... I feel myself getting dragged down by it all ... If anything I'm more dissatisfied with the system now than when I started teaching (Interview with Maureen).
>
> Although I've been helping to make the system work, in a way, for four years now, I don't feel any of my views about things needing changing have really altered at all. Maybe I'm clearer now that it's going to be a long, hard struggle but the desire to change things is just as strong I think (Interview with Philip).

There is clearly a need to consider the reasons for an apparent discrepancy between this data and the conventional view of attitude change in teachers. Of course it may simply be that my very small sample of teachers was unrepresentative. However, pending the availability of more extensive evidence it is worth considering another possible explanation — one that is consistent with an analysis of the consciousness of teachers which I have suggested elsewhere[4]. It is convenient here to employ the distinction made by Giddens (1979) as part of his theory of structuration, between 'practical' and 'discursive' modes of consciousness. 'Practical consciousness' refers to 'tacit stocks of knowledge which actors draw upon in the constitution of social activity', while discursive consciousness involves 'knowledge which actors are able to express on the level of discourse'. 'Practical consciousness' thus has a good deal in common with Schutz's concept of 'recipe knowledge' (quoted by Esland, 1977) in which 'clear and distinct experiences are intermingled with vague conjectures; suppositions and prejudices cross well-proven evidences; motives, means and ends, as well as causes and effects are strung together without clear understanding of their real connections' (p. 17). Giddens' route to this distinction is largely through the philosophy of language and it is convenient to refer to our use of language in order to illustrate the two modes of consciousness: thus it is possible to utter a complex sentence *without* being able to enumerate the linguistic rules instantiated in that sentence — in so doing it is the practical mode of consciousness which applies. The further step of making the rules explicit requires a discursive consciousness of the formation of the sentence.

It may be that what previous researchers have seen as a change of attitude in teachers after a few years' teaching experience is better described as a difference in the mode of consciousness employed by the two groups — students and teachers — responding to questionnaires (the method employed in all the studies mentioned).

To illustrate the point, one might consider questioning a student undergoing initial training as to his or her views on the relative worth of intrinsic and extrinsic kinds of motivation in learning. A student with what Barth (1972) would call 'child-centred' beliefs about children and learning, and answering in the mode of discursive consciousness, would logically emphasize the value of intrinsic motivation. That same person some years later and an experienced teacher, while still sharing child-centred beliefs, would, by answering in the mode of practical consciousness, be quite likely to stress the importance of extrinsic motivation. What has happened to this teacher in the intervening years is not necessarily a change of attitude, but rather a change in the mode of consciousness activated in answering questionnaires about teaching methods.

Students undergoing training are used to being called upon to discuss educational issues at the level of discourse; the expectation is part of the hidden curriculum of training. When during college courses students are sometimes asked to complete self-assessment questionnaires on pedagogical preferences it is not uncommon for them to ask: 'Are we to assume we're teaching in an ideal world?' The question is in effect a request for confirmation that the exercise is to be approached discursively. Serving teachers, in contrast, are rarely required to think or talk at the level of discourse about school practices. Rather, day-to-day survival in teaching is secured by the application of common-sense assumptions which answer the need to cope with the structural constraints of class-size, syllabuses, examinations, timetables, resources, etc. This is not to say that many teachers are not *able* to achieve a discursive penetration of educational issues (though clearly they will vary in their ability to do so); rather it is to argue that they are surrounded by structures that generally discourage them from exercising that ability.

It may at first seem that what is argued here is no more than a paraphrase of Bernstein's (1971) original theory of language codes — that teachers, in the solidarity of shared experiences and sentiments, have no need to communicate amongst themselves in anything more than a 'restricted code' which will 'emphasize verbally the communal rather than the abstract, substance rather than the elaboration of processes, the here and now rather than the explanation of motives and intentions' (p. 143). However, such a view would misrepresent teachers who, in most contemporary analyses, are seen to represent divergence rather than solidarity; thus Grace (1978):

> ... the occupational group is now more differentiated in terms of the social and cultural origins of its members; the contexts and contents of their socialization and the priciples which they are attempting to realize in their teaching activity (p. 215).

And Lacey (1977):

> ... individuals who hold divergent views as to how the institution should be run, indeed, as to what the purpose of the institution is! ... These tensions are reconciled but they remain as subterranean issues ... (p. 136)

Any apparent solidarity of shared sentiments amongst teachers should be seen then as a veneer interactionally contrived through the daily routines of school life which obscure differences in individuals' values and intentions and suppress discussion of them. In responding to researchers' questionnaires, then, serving teachers are likely to formulate their answers in the practical mode of consciousness: the frame of reference is not a notional ideal world but 'my classroom and what I did in it today and what I would do tomorrow'.

Those studies which claim to have uncovered changes in attitude by comparing students' responses to questionnaires with those of experienced teachers have not in effect, then, been comparing 'like with like' for the mode of consciousness exercized by the two kinds of respondent may well have been different. My own extended interviews with teachers, however, have, I believe, put them in a situation which has activated their discursive consciousness and therefore revealed the maintenance of attitudes which questionnaires have obscured.

If it is the case that the experience of teaching does not necessarily change attitudes in the way or to the extent that has been commonly accepted there arises a problem of explaining how individuals with an innovatory orientation cope with structures which are generally regarded as particularly resistant to change. The interview data indicates some aspects of the commitment of the innovators in teaching.

There were examples of fairly high and low job satisfaction among the 'innovatory' teachers interviewed. The particular school in which each teacher was employed was clearly a crucial factor, with the dominant ethos amongst the staff the single most important consideration.[5] Several of the 'innovators' employed two categories to describe their staffroom colleagues: there were those who were open to critical discussion about teaching and tolerant of innovation, and there were those who appeared to find critical discussion threatening and who disliked innovation. Not surprisingly the most contented innovatory teachers interviewed were those working in schools where they saw the first category of teachers as dominant (generally because the most powerful members of staff were in this category). Conversely, the least satisfied innovators worked in schools in which the second category of teacher predominated and the innovators were reduced to furtive *tête-à-têtes* in the corner of the staffroom.

There was evidence, too, that the most satisfied 'innovators' were those who, whether consciously or by chance, had found ways of spreading their personal commitment to teaching to include areas beyond the mainstream of curriculum and pedagogy wherein there was more opportunity to express an innovatory orientation: pastoral duties, school plays, sport, school youth club, etc.

> I'm really hooked on producing school plays now; it's what I teach·for really . . . It gives me the opportunity to do my own thing in my own way . . . you can make the sort of relations with kids you want to (Interview with Karen).

> that's why I do so much *after* school with the kids: you're not tied down by syllabuses and exams (Interview with Philip).

Of the three categories of entrants to teaching discussed in this chapter, one, the 'disillusioned', cannot be considered in this final section on the experience of teaching. None of the teachers interviewed appeared ever to have occupied this category as students.[6] This does *not* necessarily mean, however, that disillusioned new teachers soon remove themselves from the occupation (as my 'disillusioned' students anticipated they would so do) and are not therefore available for interview. It is possible that, for some at least, disillusionment is a transitory phase experienced particularly towards the end of training when teaching is viewed most discursively and at the same time the individual is asked to make the momentous and irrevocable commitment to the first teaching post. Once this critical juncture is passed we might expect the processes of commitment through investment and through side-bets[8], the distractions of domestic relations and financial obligations to obscure if not resolve the disillusion. Subsequently the earlier disillusion may be forgotten or perceived so differently as to be redefined. This possibility, and others, can only really be assessed by a genuinely longitudinal study which follows entrants to teaching over a number of years. By maintaining contact with the disillusioned students (in project 2) over the next few years and interviewing them at intervals I hope to make a tentative start to just such a longitudinal study.

Conclusion

The small-scale exploratory projects described here seem to demonstrate the desirability of confidential interviewing and of longitudinal studies as part of our repertoire of methods for analyzing the occupational group teachers. They also suggest that such methods will lead us toward an altogether more subtle and complex picture of teachers than that previously portrayed in the sociology of education. Essential elements of this picture will be the processes of career and commitment and the way in which these both facilitate and are facilitated by particular modes of consciousness.

Notes

1 Cole M.H. (1984).
2 The echo of Wrong's (1961) classic paper 'The oversocialized view of man in modern sociology' is a conscious one.
3 The analysis here appears to be generally in line with Measor's discussion of 'critical incidents' elsewhere in this volume.
4 Cole M.H. (1984).
5 Cf. discussion of primary teachers by Nias, in this volume.
6 There was, of course, a number of cases of teachers who had become disillusioned *after* some years' experience, but these had entered teaching as 'conservatives'.
7 There may be some similarity between this analysis of modes of consciousness and Keddie's (1971) discussion of 'educationist' and 'teacher contexts'. The two analyses cut across each other, however, in that the former focuses on the actor and the latter on structure (ie. 'context'). Although the analysis of consciousness recognizes that different structures may facilitate or discourage the exercise of particular modes of consciousness, it remains possible, if unusual, for actors to be discursively conscious in the 'teacher context', and for them to exercise only practical consciousness in the 'educationist context'; school staff meetings I have witnessed which seemed simply to celebrate taken-for-granted assumptions and recipe knowledge exemplify the latter.
8 The concept of 'side-bets' derives from Becker (1960). Examples of side-bets for teachers would be (i) rewarding informal relations with colleagues, and (ii) leisure pursuits made possible by relations with colleagues, by school facilities, or by the hours and holidays peculiar to teaching. It is debatable whether domestic commitments (to wife, children, building society, etc.) constitute side-bets in Becker's terms. Becker's (1960) definition describes a situation where 'the committed person has acted in such a way as to involve other interests of his, originally extraneous to the action he is engaged in, directly in that action' (p. 34). It is doubtful whether domestic commitments can be said to be 'directly' involved in teaching since taking up a different occupation need not necessarily affect domestic affairs. However, since a teacher's qualifications and experience are barely transferable to another similarly remunerated occupation teachers may well *feel* that there is a direct link between domestic commitments and continuance in teaching.

References

Barth, R.S. (1972) 'So you want to change to an open classroom?' in Sobel, H.W. and Salz, A.E. (Eds) *The Radical Papers*, New York, Harper and Row.
Bartholomew, J. (1976) 'Schooling teachers: The myth of the liberal college' in Whitty, G. and Young, M.F.D. (Eds) *Explorations in the Politics of School Knowledge*, Driffield, Nafferton.
Becker, H. (1960) 'Notes on the concept of commitment', *American Journal of Sociology*, 66, pp. 32–40.
Bernstein, B. (1971) *Class, Codes and Control*, (Vol. 1), London, Routledge and Kegan Paul.

COLE, M.H. (1984) 'Teaching till two thousand: Teachers' consciousness in times of crisis', in BARTON, L. and WALKER, S. (Eds) *Social Crisis and Educational Research*, London, Croom Helm.

DALE, R. (1977) 'Implications of the rediscovery of the hidden curriculum for the sociology of teaching', in GLEESON, D. (Ed.) *Identity and Structure*, Driffield, Nafferton.

ESLAND, G. (1977) Open University Educational Studies, Second Level Course: *Schooling and Society*, (Unit 6: Schooling and Pedagogy), Milton Keynes, Open University Press.

FINLAYSON, D. and COHEN, L. (1967) 'The teacher's role', *British Journal of Educational Psychology*, 37, pp. 22–31.

GIDDENS, A. (1976) *New Rules of Sociological Method*, London, Hutchinson.

GIDDENS, A. (1979) *Central Problems in Social Theory*, London, Macmillan.

GOFFMAN, E. (1959) *The Presentation of Self in Everyday Life*, Harmondsworth, Penguin.

GRACE, G. (1978) *Teachers, Ideology and Control: A Study in Urban Education*, London, Routledge and Kegan Paul.

HAMMERSLEY, M. (1981) 'Ideology in the staffroom? A critique of false consciousness' in BARTON, L. and WALKER, S. (Eds), *Schools, Teachers and Teaching*, Lewes, Falmer Press.

HARGREAVES, A. (1981) 'Contrastive rhetoric and extremist talk', in BARTON, L. and WALKER, S. (Eds), *Schools, Teachers and Teaching*, Lewes, Falmer Press.

HARGREAVES, D.H. (1978) 'What teaching does to teachers', *New Society*, 9 March, pp. 540–542.

KANTER, R.M. (1974) 'Commitment and social organization' in FIELD, D., *Social Psychology for Sociologists*, London, Nelson.

KEDDIE, N. (1971) 'Classroom knowledge' in YOUNG, M.F.D. (Ed.) *Knowledge and Control*, London, Collier-Macmillan.

LACEY, C. (1977) *The Socialization of Teachers*, London, Methuen.

LORTIE, D. (1975) *Schoolteacher: A Sociological Study*, Chicago, University of Chicago Press.

MARDLE, G. and WALKER, M. (1980) 'Strategies and structure: Some critical notes on teacher socialization', in WOODS, P. (Ed.), *Teacher Strategies*, London, Croom Helm.

MORRISON, A. and McINTYRE, D. (1967) 'Changes in opinions about education during the first year of teaching', *British Journal of Social and Clinical Psychology*, 6, pp. 161–3.

SHARP, R. and GREEN, A. (1975) *Education and Social Control*, London, Routledge and Kegan Paul.

WALLER, W. (1932) *The Sociology of Teaching*, New York, Wiley.

WOODS, P. (1979) *The Divided School*, London, Routledge and Kegan Paul.

WRONG, D. (1961) 'The oversocialized view of man in modern Sociology', *American Journal of Sociology*, 26 pp. 183–93.

Reference Groups in Primary Teaching: Talking, Listening and Identity

Jennifer Nias

Editors' Note: This paper is the latest in a series based upon Nias' study of a group of 100 primary school teachers. Here Nias explores the teachers' search for social and cognitive support for their educational views and commitments. This also provides a useful counter-point to the secondary experiences reported in the majority of the other papers in the collection.

> It's the teacher's disease. You have to talk about it all the time, get someone
> to listen, tell you you were right . . . It's a wonder we still have any friends,
> isn't it? But I couldn't manage without them . . .

In the tradition of symbolic interactionism, the individual knows of herself both as 'I' and as 'me'. The self is a social yet reflexive product, shaped by the responses of others but capable of initiating behaviour and reflecting upon it. Mature actors are self-conscious even though, paradoxically, they know themselves through their social identities. In the formation and maintenance of this reflexive relationship a crucial part is played by 'significant others', that is by those who have the most intimate socializing capability for the individual. It is through the responses of, for example, parents, siblings, and teachers to the actions of the developing 'I' that we come to see ourselves as others appear to see us and begin to incorporate this 'me' into our growing concept of 'I'. Cooley's 'looking glass self' is both the 'ego' formed through perceiving how others view the 'alter' and the 'alter' shaped by the initiated actions of the 'ego'. A distinction is also sometimes made between the self as 'ideal' and as 'real', although in this chapter I have not explored the potential of this difference.

As we grow older and our range of interaction increases the 'significant other' is supplemented by the 'generalized other', a term which Mead coined to describe an individual's understanding of the organized roles of participants within any defined situation. It does not refer to an actual group of people but to the supposed attitudes and opinions of others which are then invoked by the self for the regulation of behaviour. These views are often mediated through the beliefs and behaviours of 'reference groups', that is, groups which individuals use for self-evaluation and as a source of personal goals and values. Significant others are distinguished from the generalized other and from reference groups by their crucial role in early socialization and by the fact that normally they are or have been in direct contact with the person to whom they are 'significant'. By contrast, reference groups need not be friendship or membership groups and may indeed exist only in the individual's imagination. Their importance lies not in their physical but in their symbolic presence and their influence is transmitted by communication rather than by face-to-face contact. Membership of such a group is thus a question of identification, not of affiliation or allegiance. Indeed, it is possible for an individual's actions, taken in response to the norms of her reference group, to run counter to the interests of her membership group.

In addition, we all encounter many different social settings or are called upon to play varied roles. Symbolic interactionists therefore posit the existence of 'multiple selves' which reflect the individual's perception of herself (as both 'ego' and 'alter') in relation to the different groups in which she participates or with which she identifies. As these multiple selves are formed and negotiated, reference groups change, over time and with alterations in circumstances. They may even conflict, inducing the need for the resolution within the individual of dissonance between the warring 'selves'.

In an attempt to explain the relative consistency of much human behaviour despite such varying referential pressures, social psychologists (notably Katz, 1960) have suggested that as they mature, people develop, through contact with significant others, an inner self or core. This 'substantial self' (Ball, 1972) which is highly resistant to situational changes comprises a person's most salient and most valued views of and attitudes to both her 'ideal' and her 'real' self. It is more persistently defended than any other aspect of the self-image.

It follows that this substantial self too will be supported and defended by reference groups since identification with such groups is of crucial importance to the process of 'ego-anchoring' (Sherif and Wilson, 1953). However, the concept of the reference group has come to be used by sociologists in an all-embracing fashion whose very scope reduces its analytic value. One can distinguish three main meanings given to the term since its first appearance in 1942, in the work of the American social psychologist, Hyman. The first is comparative, to indicate a group serving as a standard for comparison in the self-appraisal of, for example, status or material rewards. The second is normative: within a decade it was also established, notably by the work of Merton and Kitt (1950) and of Newcomb (1950) as a phrase describing any group by whom a person wishes to be accepted and treated as a member and thus by whose norms and values she evaluates herself. Used in this sense, it was quickly accepted by some sociologists as a very potent force (eg. Stogdill, 1959, claims that reference group identifications may determine an individual's satisfaction with a membership group, her support of its activities, acceptance of its norms, perception of the legitimacy of its role system, her aspirations for status and chances for upward social mobility within it). Others have however tempered these claims with an appeal to utility (eg. Jackson, 1960, argues that reference group orientations are significantly affected by the extent to which dominant motives are matched to available gratifications within the membership group).

Thirdly, there has been considerable discussion of the influence of reference groups on perception. In particular, Sherif and Wilson (1953) speak of reference groups as groups whose norms are used as anchoring points in structuring the perceptual field, and claims that they are used as organizing devices with which to order experiences, perceptions and ideas of self. Shibutani (1955, p. 63) takes this argument further, claiming that one's perspective ('an ordered view of one's world') is 'an outline scheme which, running ahead of experience, defines and guides it'. Thus once one has internalized the particular outlook of a reference group, it becomes a 'frame of reference' which is brought to bear on all new situations. Most powerfully, it determines what is accepted as information about reality. However, since we all participate simultaneously in a variety of social worlds, we are all likely to be confronted from time to time with the need to choose between two or more conflicting frames of reference. It is in such situations, where alternative definitions of reality are possible, that problems of loyalty arise. According to Shibutani, the concept of the reference group is therefore an indispensable tool for understanding the behaviour of men in large, pluralistic and technologically sophisticated societies. Such understanding requires that we can ascertain 'how a person defines the situation, which perspective he uses in arriving at such a definition, and who constitutes the audience whose responses provide the necessary confirmation and support for his position ... (The use of this notion allows us to focus) attention upon the expectations the actor imputes to others, the communication channels in which he participates, and his relations with those with whom he identifies himself' (p. 171).

In this chapter, I explore the normative and perceptual reference groups of ninety nine primary teachers as these relate to the defence of self. Elsewhere (Nias 1981a and 1984b) I described the varying self-perceptions and types of commitment which characterized these teachers' substantial selves. I argued that many of them chose teaching because they believed that as primary teachers they would be able to propagate or at the least live consistently with the values which formed the core of their professional activities. Here I show that values and personal identities were anchored in and sustained by in- and extra-school reference groups. For each individual, discussion with members of these groups served the interrelated functions of defending the substantial self and defining the reality to which that self had to react. As a result teachers who failed to find referential support within their schools — that is, who had no-one to whom they felt they could talk — came progressively to deny the social reality of adult life within them and, in many cases, left the profession. Those who found confirming responses within school from at least one other person gained the confidence to continue behaving consistently with their sense of self-image, even when this was divisive for the school as a whole. A few felt able to take the membership group of the school as a reference group, a development which strengthened their commitment and increased their job-satisfaction. For all except the last group, extra-school groups were of critical importance in defining and sustaining the individual's sense not just of personal but also of professional identity. Although primary schools are relatively simple in organizational terms, members of them evidently experience the conflict between frames of reference which for Shibutani characterizes complex societies. That they do so is a reflection both of their social isolation within school and of their access to others outside school who share their values and beliefs.

Data Collection

Full details of the methodology are available in Nias (1981a and b). My enquiry relied heavily upon the personal accounts of ninety nine graduates who trained in one year Post graduate Certificate in Education courses for work in infant and junior schools and who had, at the time of interview, taught for between two and nine years. Two-thirds of them had attended, over five years, a course of which I was tutor. The remainder were a random sample who had between them attended similar courses at seven universities, polytechnics or colleges of education. Altogether there were thirty men, and sixth nine women the balance of sexes in each group being roughly the same.

I knew all the members of the first group very well, and three-quarters of them had been in touch with me between the time that their course ended and my enquiry began. Few of the second group knew me previously. To my surprise I found that members of both groups were not only equally keen to talk to a neutral but interested outsider about their professional experience, but that all of them were free (sometimes to the point of indiscretion) in their comments. Twenty two members drawn from both groups also kept a diary for one day a week for one term and the perspectives revealed in these accounts were very similar across the groups.

I contacted all the members of each group by telephone or letter. Six of the first group did not wish to be included in the project. With their prior consent, I visited in their schools (in many different parts of England) fifty three of the remainder and all the second group. I spent roughly half a day with each of them in their classes, making unstructured observations which I subsequently noted down before each interview. I also visited in their own homes twenty of the first group who had left teaching and were bringing up families. I had long telephone conversations with a further eight from the first group (six were at home, two teaching outside England).

The purpose of the school visit was to provide a background against which I could interpret subsequent interview data and not to undertake any formal observation. Afterwards I conducted semi-structured interviews taking rapid notes in a personal shorthand. Respondents were encouraged to give long and if necessary discursive replies and I often used supplementary questions. Thus the shortest of the interviews took one and a half hours, the longest five hours. Most took about three hours. Many interviews of those in the second group were completed in the pub or members' homes. All of those in the second group took place at school. Respondents talked equally freely both in and outside their places of work.

The data used in this chapter are drawn from responses to questions used throughout the interview. The questions which yielded the most evidence relevant to this analysis were: Who do you talk to about what happens in school/about educational ideas and issues? Have you had as much support within (each) school as you wanted? Who gave it to you? Do you see anything socially of people from (each) school? How do you know if you're getting it right/doing the job well? What would have to happen in school to make you give up? What do you like/dislike about your job? Who/what has been the greatest influence on the way you see teaching?

The diaries were chiefly used to triangulate individual accounts of perspective and practice. It is of course a matter for speculation whether these teachers' responses reflect the different nature of the occupational socialization experienced by graduates as distinct from three or four-year trained teachers (usually in colleges of education (Shipman 1969; Nias 1972)), or whether the divisions which their comments suggest may be found within the profession as a whole. I also contacted by letter, telephone or visits about 70 per cent of the headteachers of any school in which any of the sample had taught during the previous ten years. The purpose of these enquiries was to cross-check factual information and sometimes statements of opinion, and to provide an institutional context for teacher replies. They have not been a primary source of data for this paper.

Pupils as Reference Groups

The most frequently invoked reference group of these teachers was pupils. Teaching is (notionally at least) a client-centred occupation, so children naturally become a potent influence in shaping and reinforcing teachers' values and the actions which stem from them. In addition, teachers spend more time with their pupils than with their colleagues. It was common therefore to hear them say, 'I didn't much mind about anyone else, I had to make it work for them'; 'It doesn't matter that I don't agree with the rest of the staff, I can cut myself off from them by working with kids'; 'Blow the other (teachers) — I keep going because the kids enjoy what I'm doing and that tells me I'm right'. Since however many teachers work in physical isolation from each other and are protected even in open-plan schools by the 'norm of disregard' (Hitchcock, 1982), it was difficult for anyone to challenge their claims about client-satisfaction. In short, as long as classroom processes remain largely hidden from all except participants, pupils may be invoked as a reference group to justify many different decisions and types of behaviour.

Referential Support for 'Commitment'

Pupils then were the joker in the hand of every teacher, capable of being used to confirm any number of beliefs and practices. However, other reference groups specifically supported teachers in particular views of themselves. Earlier (Nias, 1981a) I distinguished five senses in which these teachers were 'committed' to their occupation. Many were motivated by the desire to 'care and give' and about half of the total number expressed their debt to referential support for their political or religious views. This they received either through their own involvement in extra-school activities (eg. 'I am a Christian first and everything else is shaped by that'; 'I couldn't keep going in teaching if I wasn't politically involved') or through their families. Many spoke of a Christian or Hebrew upbringing or of parents who were socially or politically active. Sustained by these forces they believed, for example, 'Most of what I do is because I think it's *right* to do that. It doesn't matter what the others do'; 'My own upbringing, my family especially — that's stronger than any influence in school'.

The lasting influence of such groups is encapsulated in the career of one particular talented and hard-working young woman, a convent-educated Catholic who had been actively involved in student protests at her university. She entered teaching believing strongly in the importance of cultivating creativity and individuality in her pupils, and her first teaching post, by her own choice, was in a self-styled 'progressive' school in a large city. There she was inescapably confronted by the dissonance between her frames of reference. All of the rest of the staff were committed to encouraging autonomy and creativity in their multi-ethnic, inner-city pupils. When she decided, at the end of her first year to give up teaching, she explained: 'The real problem for me was not being able to decide how much was up to the teacher. I'd spend the weekend making reading materials for (a seven-year-old) because he needed to learn his phonics, and give them to him on Monday morning. When he turned round and said, "Piss off, Miss, I want to make a monster", I honestly didn't know whether he'd learn more about reading if I insisted he do the cards, or if I let him make a monster and then write about it. The rest of the staff were quite happy — they believed in the monster — but I could never completely see it that way. I felt I had a responsibility to teach him what he needed to know ... It happened to me'.

Most were also committed to the pursuit of 'occupational competence'. In interviews they expressed their need for one or more reference groups which would help them to work out and maintain their own professional goals and standards. Ashton *et al.* (1975) have suggested that the factor most likely to distinguish among primary teachers in terms of orientations to teaching is their views on teachers' control over children's behaviour and learning. There is an alternative view, that teachers themselves see 'commitment' (and, in particular, acceptance of teaching as a professionally demanding occupation), as the most distinguishing characteristic. Certainly, it was the latter and not the former for which these teachers looked to the headteacher to 'set a standard' or 'to help shape my ideas' and were disappointed if he/she did not live up to this expectation (Nias, 1980). In default of the head they turned to senior teachers. As one said, of an older colleague in her first school, 'He wasn't a model for the way I behaved, but it was tremendously supportive to find someone else on the staff who thought the way I did and was prepared to say so. That helped a lot'.

In addition, they frequently confirmed their own professional views and attitudes by using others as negative reference groups (Newcomb, 1943), that is, as groups of which they would not want to become members. Sometimes this took a general form (eg. 'It's easier to find teachers you wouldn't want to be like than ones you would . . . You don't meet many teachers who make you feel "That's the sort of person I'd like to be", do you? Usually it's the other way round'.) More often they located 'the opposition' or 'the enemy' (two phrases in frequent use) within their own school. However, as with negative role-models (Nias, 1984a), such polarization was normally made without intimate knowledge of the values of the teachers of whom they spoke. Moreover, teachers employing negative reference groups spread out along a wide political and ideological continuum. To assume, as sometimes happens, that graduate teachers see themselves as more 'progressive' than their fellows is to oversimplify their individual complexities and the rich variety of motivation which they bring to the job.

A minority were also committed to teaching because they saw 'being a teacher' as part of their self-image. The contact which they maintained with their own ex-teachers and tutors and sometimes with teachers in their families served to support them in this view. One said, 'All my family teach, and I didn't want to be the only failure — I *had* to keep on trying'. Another claimed, 'My family used to say, "You'll be a marvellous teacher one day", so I can't go back to them and say I've failed, can I?' This type of reinforcement was summed up by the man who said, 'Whenever I have doubts about whether it's for me, I go and see my old primary school head, he's retired now and he says "I've always seen you as a teacher — how's it going?", and I sit down and tell him'.

By contrast, three teachers bound by financial commitments and similar 'side bets' (Becker, 1960) but disillusioned by teaching, had rejected the teacher self-image. Instead, they had become privatized workers (Goldthorpe *et al.*, 1968). In the process they had adopted reference groups within their own and other schools which supported their psychological separation from their work. One man put it his way: 'It's a job — nothing more. I need the money, but I don't put more into it than I have to. My real life is with the band. That means I often come in exhausted in the morning — my main aim is to keep the kids quiet — off my back . . . I'm not the only one who sees it this way, you know . . . we talk about it . . . If society doesn't put itself out for us, why should we bother for them?'

In addition, a few teachers were, as Woods (1979) argues, 'committed' in the sense of being entrenched in an occupational structure. These alluded to reference groups which supported their aspirations in this or other concerns. Four teachers had begun seriously to aspire to senior posts and were invoking the real or imagined standards of their local Deputy Heads Association or of headteachers generally. By contrast, others were using alternative groups to plan futures in educational psychology, community and social work or in parenthood. Such normative groups helped individuals move from one career stage to another, but they do not seem to have been especially influential in determining subsequent educational policy or practice. Teachers who shaped their behaviour by reference to a specific occupational group (eg. deputy heads) still needed, once they had attained their new status, to seek or maintain a 'frame of reference' which would help them translate their beliefs into action.

My interviewees did not see themselves simply as teachers. They also regarded themselves as people with intellectual interests and capacities. Unfortunately, although they looked for appropriate referential support within their schools, they tended to find it outside them. The cumulative effect of this was to alienate many of them from teaching. One of my interviewees put it this way, 'I didn't identify with (my colleagues) as people like me. I'm more aware of other things outside school than someone who has been trained as a teacher and to do the things teachers do'. Similar comments were: 'They're not like me, and I'm not like them'; 'My educational reference group is certainly not in school — it's a few intimate friends from university and scientists generally'; 'I'm intellectually lonely at school. I'm the only one who reads *The Guardian*, the only one interested in politics or literature and there is only one other who's ready to talk about art and music'; (from a man teaching in an infant school) 'I love the children and the work, but I have no contact with any adults with whom I have any ideas in common. I feel intellectually starved'; 'For me, it was the three years at university that counted'; 'All our friends are doing postgraduate work, I've begun to feel left out.'

It was this felt-need to maintain contact with the world of ideas and of passionate debate that led several teachers towards advanced courses, kept them actively involved in politics or para-political organizations (such as the Child Poverty Action Group), reinforced their ties with non-teacher, graduate friends, caused them to remember their university teachers or PGCE courses with enthusiasm (eg. 'It was there that education became ideals, not just ideas in the file'; 'My course made me interested in ideas — even more than in practicalities'). Two had begun to write for educational journals, three were actively seeking posts as college lecturers or advisers. Three left junior school work for posts in further education and two took jobs as specialists in secondary schools 'because I miss the stimulation of my subject'. Ebbutt (1982) has suggested that teachers can be sustained in an intellectual view of themselves by an academic reference group which they initially find through advanced courses and research projects. Many of this sample were seeking such a group and, failing to find it, were looking for ways of leaving teaching, despite the fact that they found the work affectively and occupationally satisfying.

In-School Reference Groups

Reference groups within the school varied considerably in size. Many teachers appeared to need the referential support, 'to confirm my values', of only one other, be it colleague, headteacher or sometimes adviser. The mutual support afforded by such a person was out of all proportion to either the size of the group or the time spent in communication. The existence of 'just one other' confirmed their goals and aspirations, kept them from leaving the school, supported them in innovation or retrenchment, deepened their satisfaction and fuelled their discontents. As one teacher said of such a reference person, 'We fed each other'. Such pairing may be a launching pad for new ideas or a powerful obstacle to change within the pair and amongst their colleagues. It can also have a destructive effect upon social relationships within the school as a whole.

Indeed, the influence of school-based reference groups upon their members was not always seen as working in the direction of greater professional commitment. A few teachers candidly said, for example, 'We make each other lazy'; 'It's difficult to work hard if no-one else does. The norm here is about putting teachers' interests first'; 'It was better when she left . . . I'd begun to share her lack of commitment to the job', and 'I know I'm a worse teacher than I was three years ago. It's difficult to do what you think you should do when you know you're an island. If only there was just one other person in the school who shared my ideas'. They described themselves as 'feeling less worried by my own conscience', 'learning to grow a skin when things aren't perfect,' 'learning to compromise'. Siegel and Siegel (1957) argue that individuals are particularly strongly influenced by membership groups which become reference groups. These comments may reflect, for some teachers, attitude changes resulting from a realignment of this kind.

In a few instances, individuals were able to point to a group of like-minded colleagues. When such a group existed, it tended also to be seen as a membership group. As such, it had a social dimension which strengthened its referential impact (see also Sherif and Sherif, 1964). Members could identify one another and indicate where they usually interacted (eg. 'We have a pub lunch once a week'; 'We stay behind after school'; 'We don't talk in the staffroom but we often meet in (the year leader's) classroom'; 'We're the mob in the corner — you'll see us there at lunchtime most days').

Moreover, when a reference pair or group developed an affective (as distinct from social) dimension it could become a potent force within a school. Three examples make this point very clearly. In one case, a value difference brought to the surface by a new headteacher led to the formation of a forceful staffroom group ('There's four of us — all women. We share the same political views, we do a lot socially together and two of us live together. He'll find it hard to break us up . . .'). In another, a married couple who taught together in a double unit, each independently said to me, 'I don't listen to what anyone else on the staff says. They all think differently to me, and now I'm working with (my spouse) I can just talk to him/her and we support each other'. Thirdly, two teachers working as a team — each married to teachers in other schools — began to live together. They explained: 'To make the team work we had to talk a lot, and that meant we spent a lot of time together and we began to realize how many ideas we had in common and how much we liked each other . . . well, team-teaching, especially in a shared unit, has to be a bit like a marriage if it's going to work, you have to want the same things, have the same values, and if one of you is male and the other's female and you obviously get on well together, the kids begin to treat you like mum and dad . . .'.

On the rare occasions that a whole staff was perceived as being concurrently a membership and reference group, it had a powerful effect upon its members. Five teachers spoke of being at schools where 'we accept that we all have common beliefs and that gives us a common basis for discussion,' or 'there's a basic level of understanding and therefore we can disagree and there's lots of lively talk in the staffroom'. By contrast, I was given three examples of staffs which were so tightly knit, philosophically and socially, that other teachers felt 'driven out — they had to leave if they wanted to survive'. In all of these cases, shared goals and standards were reinforced by joint social activities (eg. staff parties, theatre visits) and by a good deal of open discussion.

Extra-School Reference Groups

Unfortunately, at some point in their careers, the majority of my interviewees found themselves in a school in which there was no group other than pupils by reference to whom they could affirm their values. So great was their felt-need for referential support that, lacking it in one school, they actively sought for it outside. They went on courses (see also Schools Council, 1981). Some claimed: 'I don't care whether or not the rest of the staff approves of what I'm doing, but I do wish I had someone to discuss my ideas with. I'm so desperate I've signed up for a course at the Polytechnic' and 'I go to courses for reassurance/to listen to people agreeing with me/to find someone like-minded to talk to'. Others became involved in politics or union activities (eg. 'Branch meetings give you a chance to meet people who think like you do'), returned to their training institution or the friends they made there (eg. 'I don't see all that much of them, but I'd hate to lose touch with them because they're there to talk to if I need them'; 'I draw a lot on the PGCE course. It's there in my mind and bits come back . . . I suppose that's why I keep in touch with (my tutor). It keeps me from losing all my ideals which I would if I just listened to the teachers (in my school)'. This piece of research really started when an ex-student from my PGCE course came back three years later from 300 miles away to talk about her work and said, 'I do wish you could come and see what I'm doing now. No-one at my school seems to care and I'm losing heart'. Many others telephoned, wrote, dropped in at half-terms or in the holidays. 'No,' said one, 'I didn't really want your advice. I just wanted someone to tell me I was right'. It appears to have been for that reason too that several turned to educational books and, especially later in their careers, sought confirmation for their ideals in the writing of educationalists as widely disparate as A.S. Neill, Chris Searle and Rhodes Boyson. As one said, 'You need to know that someone else shares your views — someone with a wider view than teachers can have'.

Individuals also looked to teachers in other places — different schools, family and university friends, their own families. Ten teachers had kept in touch with a particular teacher or headteacher from a previous school at which they had taught, either before or after training, and regarded him/her as a 'very influential person in my development'. Most had teacher friends whom they perceived as very important (eg. 'If you're isolated you begin to question whether you're right'; 'I've got one friend from another school and we meet in a pub once a week . . . it helps reinforce your belief that you are right'). Four referred to people who had taught them at school (eg. 'I still keep in touch with her, I'm always interested in what she has to say about education'). Eleven of the men were married to primary school teachers and eleven of the women to secondary school teachers (none to primary school teachers). Despite the relatively small number of spouses in like employment most (but not all) of the sample cited their spouse as someone with whom they discussed their educational problems and ideas 'all the time'. One said, 'He's never been inside the school and I don't think he'd want to, but he really helps me sort my ideas out. He's a sort of touchstone, I suppose. If he thinks it's OK then it usually works'.

Parents were important too (eg. 'My father (a retired HMI) — I ring him a lot'; 'My mother still teaches and I talk to her a good deal') and even more frequently cited were parents-in-law (eg. 'Richard's mother kept me going. We used to go to see her in the holidays and she used to support me in what I was trying to do'; 'Frank's father is a headmaster of a junior school (in another part of the country) and I rely a lot on his reassurance.') Siblings (especially sisters) were occasionally mentioned. Five referred to their own children (eg. 'I think — would I want that to happen to them?').

Importance of Talk

Throughout this study talk emerges as the critical element enabling the formation of individual values and related reference groups. First, it was through discussion during their early experiences of teaching that individuals hammered out their aims and priorities. As one woman said, 'The staff (in my first school) included several exceptional people, people who were prepared to talk about what they were doing and listen to me'. Another said of a colleague, 'He was particularly influential in shaping the way I work now. We used to chat after school and compare notes'. By contrast, others complained, 'It's been hard to get teachers in this school to talk about their philosophy; I always wanted to talk and they wouldn't,' and, 'I left soon after she did — I couldn't cope without somebody to talk to — I lost sight of what I was trying to achieve'. Indeed, the absence of opportunity or appetite for discussion emerged as a major source of dissatisfaction among these teachers, especially in their early years (Nias, 1981b). Secondly, staffrooms in which probationers 'found it difficult to get to talk to people' tacitly encouraged them to seek extra-school reference groups. It is no coincidence that many of the experienced teachers who were cited as 'important influences' had classrooms near, travelled with or lived close by those who adopted them as reference persons (Nias, 1984a). (See Sikes, in this volume, for further discussion). Physical proximity made them accessible not so much for observation as for discussion. I also became aware of the importance which my interviewees attached to their telephones and of the amount of communication which went on, across the country, through this medium. It enabled the maintenance of many far-flung referential networks.

The phenomenological view, that it is through talk that participants create and make sense of a shared social order, offers a means of understanding this need for talk. Working in isolation from other adults, many of these primary school teachers failed to find in their schools the means of forging a negotiated understanding or the incentive to do so. A vicious circle existed. Needing referential support for their values, they turned to those who would readily provide it. Often such groups already existed outside their schools, so they talked to them. The more they interacted with the latter, the fewer understandings did they share with their colleagues and the less desire they had to talk to them, particularly when they spent the bulk of their working day with their pupils. Thus the reality which sustained their substantial selves came to exist anywhere rather than in the adult life of the school. Lortie (1975) and Hargreaves (1982) have drawn attention to the lack of a common technical culture among teachers. I would suggest that the individualistic nature of the profession, particularly in the primary sector, goes deeper than this, that teachers' reference groups result in and reinforce multiple realities which give individuals a false sense of having achieved within their schools agreement over ends and means. In short, teachers neither wish nor are able to talk to one another. They are not able to because outside their reference groups, they lack a shared language by which to attach meanings to their common experience. They do not want to because the process of creating such a language would threaten the social context which sustains and defends their substantial selves.

However, teachers need the affective and affiliative support of their colleagues, especially in circumstances where they feel themselves to be under threat from pupils. They may therefore be under strong material or emotional pressures to conform to the norms of the staff membership group, even though they lack the desire or the opportunity to make them their own. In Nias (1984a) I have described in greater detail the strategies that are commonly adopted in situations like this to preserve a sense of identity without disrupting staffroom life. Sometimes the resulting behavioural conformity does result in a change of attitude, with the individual internalizing the values of the membership group. More commonly, open conflict is avoided, a false consensus is achieved but the individual is able to go on behaving within the classroom in ways that are consistent with her self-image.

Conclusion

Members of this group of primary teachers were characterized by a strong sense of personal identity which, was by definition unique to each individual, but which contained many common elements. In particular, they saw themselves as 'committed' to teaching, especially as an occupation which would enable them to pursue humanitarian ideals and as a job which they wanted to do well. Some also saw themselves as 'being teachers' and a few as entrenched in a career structure. Most also perceived themselves as people with intellectual interests and concerns. These attitudes to themselves appear to have been deeply embedded; certainly individuals used a number of strategies to defend them from influence or assault by their colleagues and headteachers. Chief among these was the use of reference groups, especially as a perspective-confirming device. In Shibutani's (1955) terms, they defined reality through, communicated with and directed their actions towards selected audiences, many of whom had existed long before they made the decision to teach. The traditional isolation of the classroom teacher and the reluctance of many primary school teachers to engage in a potentially conflictual debate about ends served to confirm them in membership of these groups. Lack of appetite and/or opportunities within school for the discussion of values impeded the negotiation of new attitudes so, needing the confirming responses of others, they sought contact (often by telephone, if meeting was difficult) with those who they knew would provide such support. The more ego-gratifying this reinforcement, the less incentive there was to talk to their colleagues, and the more isolated they became within school, fortified in their personal convictions by contact with those outside it.

To be sure, these teachers were not impervious to the pressures of the membership group. In particular, they found it hard to sustain social isolation. As a consequence, they sometimes aligned their frames of reference more closely with those of their colleagues; more often they changed schools or left the profession. In addition, pupils became very important to them as a reference group. However, the presence on the staff, or among those very closely associated with the school, of only one other person with similar aims and values, frequently enabled individuals to sustain their sense of personal identity, to preserve their substantial selves. A reference group need not, it appears, be numerous, as long as the reality it stands for can be symbolically confirmed within the adult world of the school by a single representative.

Reference groups, it seems, may simultaneously promote and impede the development of the profession and of the individual within it. On the one hand, they are crucial in establishing and maintaining shared values among groups of teachers, a state which, if achieved, facilitates mutual understanding and provides encouragement and support in a lonely occupation. On the other, they may frustrate the negotiation of shared collegial norms. Reference groups used for the defence of one set of values can obstruct the open discussion of and agreement on others.

Viewed this way the notion of reference group membership is an important key to our understanding of schools' often-reported imperviousness to change. When these teachers reported having modified their practice they usually claimed it was out of a felt-need to survive socially within the staff group, or because they found identification with a particular sub-group in school to be in other respects reinforcing of their sense of identity. In most cases they did not change but continued to act in ways which were consistent with their view of their substantial selves. In this they were supported by referential contact, within the school or outside it. In other words, opposing views of reality, confirmed by communication with distinctive groups, led to actions which were directed to different audiences (whether real, imaginary or potential).

In short, teachers may hear what is said to them but not respond to it because they are listening to other voices. There are times, of course, when such deafness may be beneficial to the development of the profession as a whole. Equally however the formation within one school, or across many, of well-defined sub-groups with divergent aims may impede collective progress or distract attention from the need to tackle common problems. The problem then becomes one of helping teachers to overcome this kind of selective inattention to their colleagues' voices. One answer may be to provide opportunities and encouragement within primary schools for teachers to talk to one another about those aspects of their jobs which really matter to them. If the person makes the agenda, the practitioner may join in the debate.

References

ASHTON, P. *et al.* (1975) *The Aims of Education*, London, Macmillan.

BALL, D. (1972) 'Self and identity in the context of deviance: the case of criminal abortion', in SCOTT, R. and DOUGLAS, J. (Eds) *Theoretical Perspectives on Deviance*, New York, Basic Books.

BECKER, H. (1960) 'Notes on the concept of commitment', *American Journal of Sociology*, **66**, pp. 32–40.

EBBUTT, D. (1982) *Teacher as researcher: How four teachers coordinate action research in their respective schools*, TIQL Project, Working Paper 10, Cambridge Institute of Education.

GOLDTHORPE, J. *et al.* (1968) *The Affluent Worker: Industrial Attitudes and Behaviour*, Vol 1., Cambridge, Cambridge University Press.

HARGREAVES, D. (1982) *The Challenge for the Comprehensive School: Culture, Curriculum and Community*, London, Routledge and Kegan Paul.

HITCHCOCK, G. (1982) 'The social organization of space and place in an urban open-plan primary school', in PAYNE, G. and CUFF, E. (Eds) *Doing Teaching*, London, Batsford.

JACKSON, J. (1960) 'Reference group processes in a formal organization', in CARTWRIGHT, D. and ZANDER, A. (Eds), *Group Dynamics: Research & Theory*, 2nd edition, London, Tavistock.

KATZ, D. (1960) 'The functional approach to the study of attitude change', *Public Opinion Quarterly*, **24**, 163–204.

LORTIE, D. (1975) *Schoolteacher: A Sociological Study*, Chicago, University of Chicago Press.

MERTON, R. & KITT, A. (1957) 'Contributions to the theory of reference group behaviour', in MERTON, R. (Ed.) *Social Theory and Social Structure*, Glencoe, Free Press.

NEWCOMB, T. (1943) 'Attitude development as a function of reference groups: the Bennington Study', in MACCOBY, E., NEWCOMB, T. and HARTLEY, E. (Eds) *Readings in Social Psychology*, London, Methuen.

NEWCOMB, T. (1950) *Social Psychology*, New York, Dryden.

NIAS, J. (1972) 'Value-persistence and utility in colleges of education', *Education for Teaching*, **89**, pp. 29–34.

NIAS, J. (1980) 'Leadership styles and job-satisfaction in primary schools', in BUSH, T. *et al.* (Eds) *Approaches to School Management*, London, Harper and Row.

NIAS, J. (1981a) 'Commitment and motivation in primary school teachers', *Educational Review*, **33**, pp. 181–90.

NIAS, J. (1981b) 'Teacher satisfaction and dissatisfaction: Herzberg's 'two-factor' hypothesis revisited', *British Journal of Sociology of Education*, **2**, pp. 235–246.

NIAS, J. (1984a) 'Learning and acting the role: in-school support for primary teachers', *Educational Review*, **36**, 1–15.

NIAS, J. (1984b) 'Definition and maintenance of self in primary teaching', *British Journal of Sociology of Education*, **5**, 267–280.

SCHOOLS COUNCIL (1981) *Making the Most of the Short In-Service Course*, Working Paper 71, London, Methuen.

SHERIF, C. and SHERIF, M. (1964) *Reference Groups: Exploration into Conformity and Deviation of Adolescents*, New York, Harper & Row.

SHERIF, M. and WILSON, M. (1953) *Group Relations at the Crossroads*, New York, Harper & Row.

SHIBUTANI, T. (1972) 'Reference groups as perspectives', in MANIS, J. & MELTZER, B. (Eds) *Symbolic Interaction: A Reader in Social Psychology*, 2nd edition, Boston, Allyn and Bacon.

SHIPMAN, M. (1969) *Participation and Staff-Student Relationships: a Seven-Year Study of Social Changes in an Expanding College of Education*, London: Society for Research into Higher Education.

SIEGEL, A. and SIEGEL, S. (1973) 'Reference groups, membership groups and attitude change', in WARREN, M. and JAHODA, M. (Eds) *Attitudes*, Harmondsworth, Penguin.

STOGDILL, R. (1959) *Individual Behaviour and Group Achievement*, Oxford, Oxford University Press.

WOODS, P. (1979) *The Divided School*, London, Routledge and Kegan Paul.

Paints, Pots or Promotion? Art Teachers' Attitudes Towards their Careers

Carey Bennet

Editors' Note: This paper is drawn from an on-going research study of art teachers in school. It employs both questionnaire data and interview materials to explore the 'life world' of teachers within one subject area.

It is common amongst those employed in the professions to invest a great deal, in personal terms, in their jobs; work is often the central area of their lives in which they strive for satisfaction and success. It is also a common cultural expectation that professional people will seek upward mobility in terms of prestige and remuneration. However, in the education system the present political and economic situation is such that shortage of resources increasingly constrains and obstructs teachers in their jobs, and falling rolls, amongst other factors, result in insecurity of tenure and decline in promotion opportunities.

The career structure in teaching basically presents two options for the pursuit of the usual career goals of promotion and the like:

1 The subject/academic option, where progress presupposes increasing professional excellence in a subject area and also a willingness to take on organizational responsibilities in a subject department.
2 The pastoral/administrative option, where progress involves reduction or loss of subject teaching, increase in administrative or organizational work and/or assumption of formal pastoral responsibilities. Responsibilities for curricular processes and staff development would be included in this option.

As Lyons (1981) points out, teachers may pursue various career strategies to enhance their careers in these respects, such as making themselves visible to influential others; recognizing the necessity of career planning; taking on extra-curricular duties; involving themselves in inservice training for professional development in pedagogic, pastoral or administrative areas. The interesting thing about the strategies Lyons describes is that they are largely *intra*-professional; they involve teachers

120

manoeuvring *within* the system in pursuit of conventional promotion-related career goals associated with the subject and pastoral options outlined above.

But do all teachers respond in the same way? Even more to the point perhaps, is it right to assume with Lyons that they should? To begin with, as an empirical question, it is worth asking whether the career strategies described by Lyons are typical of all groups of teachers, and whether all groups employ them to the same extent. The strategies described by Lyons assume common goals and common values among teachers which relate primarily to prestige and income, and also to increasing responsibility, and improvement in working conditions. But teachers are not a homogenous group. They are differentiated, at the secondary level for instance, by subject specialisms and by the relative status of those specialisms. The existence of a status hierarchy of school subjects which disadvantages the so-called 'practical subjects' is particularly important in this respect. As Goodson (1983, p. 37) remarks, 'Academic subjects provide the teacher with a career structure characterized by better promotion prospects and pay than less academic subjects'. Goodson summarizes Byrne's (1974) findings on resource allocation in schools: 'The implications of the preferential treatment of academic subjects for the material self-interest of teachers are clear: better staffing ratios, higher salaries, higher capitation allowances, more graded posts, better career prospects' (p. 83).

Clearly, differences in subject status may influence teachers' careers generally and their responses to adverse career conditions in particular. In times of contraction, low status subjects tend to receive the 'hardest knocks', not least because they lack representatives in positions of influence who can direct resources and decisions to their advantage (Goodson, 1983). There is therefore good reason to study different groups of teachers separately if we are to gain a clearer understanding of teachers' career needs and responses.

In this chapter, I shall focus on art as one such low status subject and assess the career implications for those who teach it, and to some extent, for career-blocked teachers in other parts of the school system also.

Art teachers, like teachers of certain other subjects such as drama, physical education and home economics, are rarely to be found holding senior posts in schools.[1] Certainly the status of art is an important factor in accounting for this, but my research suggests additional factors which the teachers themselves feel are more important. These factors concern their orientations towards their 'careers' in the broadest sense, their satisfactions, dislikes and priorities concerning the central involvements of their lives, that is their 'subjective careers'. The idea of 'careers' having two dimensions, the 'objective', concerning movement within a system of statuses and clearly defined offices, and the 'subjective', concerning a person's own moving perspective, was proposed by Hughes (1971, p. 137). The research reported here focuses predominantly on the subjective aspects of art teachers' careers, that is to say, their feelings about, rather than their formal positions within, the teaching profession and its career structure.[2] Nevertheless, as the analysis will show, these personal perceptions do have important links with the objective opportunities, thus relating the two dimensions.[3]

Teachers who are subject to adverse conditions regarding promotion and career development, such as secondary modern school teachers working in reorganized comprehensives (Riseborough, 1981), or most teachers currently working in circumstances of contraction, constraint and falling rolls (Hunter and Heighway, 1980), could be expected to suffer from low morale and/or to engage actively in strategies to counteract adversity. One might expect teachers of low status subjects who permanently experience restriction of career opportunities to respond in just this way. Yet, contrary to this, the group of art teachers interviewed by me were not, generally, frustrated and depressed; neither did they appear to employ deliberate strategies for the advancement of their careers, such as those described by Lyons.

It is clearly worth asking why this should be the case. More importantly, it is worth asking what implications the unexpected response of the art teachers to their apparently depressing situation might have for that increasing number of career blocked teachers outside art who are trapped within a contracting system. Analysis of art teachers' careers might thus have important things to say about teachers' careers generally.

Three Facets of Art Teachers' Careers

The following extract is one art teacher's analysis of the career structure for art teachers:

> You see, there can be two kinds of situation for art teachers. There's the 'Art' person who has to make some kind of personal, emotional break between himself as an artist and self as a *career* teacher, in order to go for top posts — ie. he has to lead a double life, admin. and creative. And the 'Art' person must decide if he or she can reconcile the *power* position of, for instance, Headteacher, with the role as art teacher. Then there's the 'Teacher' type person, it's mainly a matter of training the BEd-type, who usually *wants* to advance vertically but is blocked because specialist trained art teachers hold the Head of Art posts. (T26).

Whilst referring to the formal structure of objective career options of the sort outlined earlier this teacher also highlights a number of other important career related issues in the wider, more subjective sense of the term. He talks of 'the Art person' and 'the Teacher person', and implies that these types have particular sets of interests, priorities and values which have implications for their careers. The idea of 'dual identities' is raised — 'himself as an artist and self as a career teacher', and the potential conflict between these two identities and their associated roles is suggested. Whilst a teacher may desire success in the conventional career terms of remuneration and status, s/he may not feel able to make this 'emotional break', nor wish to sacrifice other rewards such as the social relationships enjoyed in classroom teaching. This point addresses the long standing problem that the formal career structure as it is currently constituted does not serve those teachers who have a firm commitment to classroom teaching and to their subject, and who have no inclination towards organizational and pastoral duties. The validity of T26's suggestion that his 'Teacher type' art teachers wish to climb the career ladder but find themselves blocked by art college trained teachers in head of department posts will be tested later. But the suggestion also points to another important factor influencing teachers' careers — type of training.

Like most subject departments, art departments are composed of teachers with specialist subject qualifications in Art and Design and those with first degrees and Postgraduate Certificates in Education. One might expect those who have received a four or five year training at an art college (followed in most cases by a one year art teachers' training) to arrive in teaching with different career orientations to those trained as teachers for three or four years at a college of education.[4] Furthermore, research has pointed to the fact that teachers' objective careers in terms of rates of promotion etc. are related to such factors as graduate versus non-graduate status and specialist versus non-specialist training of the people concerned, (Hilsum and Start, 1974; Lyons, 1981). Teachers' awareness of this fact might well affect their career considerations.

To sum up: when we begin to examine why there are so few art teachers in top posts in schools, three factors seem to be important: the low status of art in school; art teachers' own subjective career orientations and attitudes; and the nature of their training. In all these things the complicated links between the subjective and the objective aspects of teachers' careers should be constantly borne in mind. For instance, training may influence subjective orientations as well as objective career outcomes, so too may the status of art as a subject both restrict opportunities and dampen career aspirations. The data reported here derives from interviews with seventy-two secondary school art teachers in one English county, (65.5 per cent of the estimated population of all secondary art teachers in that county).[5,7]

Art Teachers' Perceptions Regarding Promotion within Teaching

Do art teachers feel that their chances for promotion to senior posts and for promotion generally are affected by their particular subject specialism? When the art teachers were asked, 'How available do you think top posts — Headships and Deputy Headships — are to art teachers in schools?', over half of them felt that their chances were 'non-existent' and only 12 per cent thought their chances equal to those of other subject teachers (see *Table 1*). CE teachers (college of education trained) rated their chances more highly than did AC teachers (art college trained) a surprising tendency in view of the fact that more subject graduate teachers occupy the higher scale positions in teaching than do BEd and certificated teachers. This tendency may indicate a stronger orientation towards promotion amongst CE teachers.

Several factors inhibiting art teachers' promotion were mentioned frequently. These included the low status of art in the hierarchy of school subjects, and the low regard for art teachers' capabilities; the non-academic nature of their subject and their lack of academic qualifications; and the abundance of art teachers 'on the market' which reduces the need for schools to offer art teachers incentives to stay. The following comments illustrate some ways in which teachers felt disadvantaged:

Art teachers don't get promoted as readily as academic disciplines. You may get shortlisted, but somebody with an academic training will always get given the job. They seem to think that someone with a degree in Maths is going to be more intelligent than someone with a degree in Art — which is ridiculous! It *is* more difficult to get promoted if you're an art teacher. (T42)

We're not looked upon as people who could cope with administration. Running a department like this, obviously we can. (T13)

Art teachers are too discomforting in schools — subversive — and the subject, by its very nature, is about the development of individuals, and that's not what schools are about ... Top men are 'Yes' men. (T16)

Art teachers have this license and therefore, because of this, they may not have access to higher positions. You lose one because of the other. (T44)

However, a most frequent type of comment was 'art teachers don't *want* those sorts of jobs'. These implied that the problem is as much to do with motivation as it is to do with availability of posts.

Responses to the question, 'Do you think that your opportunities for advancing your career in teaching generally are as favourable as they are for other subject teachers?' indicated that nearly three-quarters of these teachers felt that their opportunities were *not* as good (see *Table 2*). CE teachers, again, were more optimistic than AC teachers. Despite perceiving themselves at a disadvantage regarding promotion, this did not come across as great cause for concern. An early research hypothesis was that senior posts would not appeal to art teachers as career goals. The underlying assumption was that art teachers would, firstly, be reluctant to reduce time spent involved in art activity in school and, secondly, would be averse to taking on a position which necessitated conformity to a 'conventional' teacher role. (The extent to which art teachers nurture and value an image of themselves as 'unconventional' and 'different' to other teachers is pursued elsewhere in the research).

When I asked the question, 'Do such posts (senior posts) appeal to you?' the majority (82 per cent) answered with an emphatic 'No'. A small number said 'Yes', or gave a qualified yes answer, for example:

Yes, I'd like to be head in a *special* school, but not in an ordinary comprehensive.

The power which such positions offer appeals — power to change things — but not really.

All but two of those saying 'Yes' or 'Qualified Yes' were CE teachers. 92 per cent of the AC teachers said 'No'.

My expectation of art teachers' disinclination towards top posts was confirmed, but were the original assumptions valid? Is involvement in art activity in school such an important reward for art teachers that it makes them reluctant to seek promotion to senior posts? I asked the art teachers why senior posts did not appeal to them. Their answers fell into four categories: 'social' — loss of contact with children; 'Art' — loss of involvement in art activity; 'administration' — dislike of administrative work and bureaucracy; 'authority' — dislike of the discipline and authoritarianism associated with senior post holders.

The most frequently given reason for the lack of appeal of senior posts was their administrative nature (see *Table 3*). Next was the loss of involvement in art, although while over half of the AC teachers feared this, only 27 per cent of the CE teachers did so. On the other hand, more CE teachers cited loss of contact with children as an important deterrent. A subject/pastoral split associated with type of training emerges here. There was also some aversion to the type of teacher-pupil relationship art teachers associated with such posts. There is a sense here, in which the art teachers are saying 'I'm not like that'; they are emphasizing a distinction between themselves and top post holders:

> You'd be losing your teacher pupil contact, losing your subject and you'd be becoming a pen-pusher. The money is there, and the time, but, no. (T26)

> It would restrict one's personality, one's social life, and would be an *alien* sort of life. Art teachers have a certain licence in schools. They're not necessarily expected to conform — which is lucky for art teachers otherwise a lot of them wouldn't be in schools. (T44)

> The higher up you go, the greater the threat to your creativity. (T32)

The last two quotations illustrate an important link between status and identity. These teachers regard senior posts as a threat to, and incompatible with, their selves.

Loss of involvement in art activity is therefore an important inhibitor of teachers' ambitions within school, but the characteristics of top posts, particularly the administrative nature, and the demands they make upon the self, are perceived even more negatively.

Clearly, though, these findings are by no means self evident. The rejection of conventional career goals and the advancement of noble reasons for doing so may just be an attempt to rationalize potential failure in the promotion stakes — 'sour grapes' no less. For this reason, I asked the teachers, 'If you were offered a higher scale post which involved more administrative work and less classroom teaching, would this be attractive to you?' While the differences between AC and CE teachers suggested in the previous data emerge even more clearly here (see *Table 4*), the great majority still answered 'No'.

I also asked the teachers what they valued most, found most satisfying, about their jobs. I expected one of the most important satisfactions would be the opportunity to be involved in practical art during their working day. The responses will be summarized here, since there is not space to discuss them in full.

The most frequently cited satisfaction was the 'social' kind, the majority of these answers referring to contact with children and the actual teaching process, a few referring to relationships with staff. Next most popular was the 'freedom and flexibility' in the job and 'conditions of the job' (money, holidays, security, location). 'Art involvement' was mentioned by only 25 per cent of the teachers, fewer than expected. More surprising still, perhaps, was that *more CE* than AC mentioned this. Yet it may be that for AC teachers, art in school is not an ideal substitute for the practice of their own work; AC teachers frequently mentioned 'the long holidays' which allowed them to pursue their art. What these teachers appear to *value* most about their jobs is the social aspect. However it is not loss of this satisfaction which is uppermost in their aversion to top posts, but rather, the administrative nature of such roles, and the loss of art activity in their working day.

In summary: the teachers do not rate their chances of obtaining senior posts highly; they do not wish to give up involvement in art activity or contact with children and, perhaps most important, they are simply not attracted to the kind of work or type of role associated with such positions. The possibility that professed aversion is partly rationalization for not pursuing paths perceived denied to them did not come across strongly in the interviews. A number of teachers' comments suggest that there may also be a more subtle process operating to discourage art teachers from aspiring to top posts:

> If the art teacher is worth his salt, he won't be interested in being a head or a deputy head. In my last school the head of art became Deputy Head but that was only because he was a real smoothie and a good talker.

> I've never fallen for that trap. It could have been easy to do that, for money reasons. Sadly, most teachers do. I saw that trap.

Could it be that within the art teacher culture, subtle pressure is put upon teachers *not* to hanker after promotion? These comments certainly imply that such an orientation is discreditable, and suggest the belief that if one had such base desires, one would not be a 'real' art teacher/artist-teacher. The constraint exerted by the subject subculture may take a no more substantial form than a taken-for-granted distinction between 'teachers like them' (top post holders, career teachers) and 'teachers like us'.

From the data presented so far we might presume that since art teachers are not interested in climbing the promotion ladder, they will not be unduly dissatisfied with poor opportunities in teaching. However, in response to the question, 'Are you satisfied with your career opportunities within teaching?' the majority of AC teachers said 'No', whilst the majority of CE said 'Yes' (see *Table 5*). This result is surprising given the professed lack of interest in promotion and, if anything, one would expect the *CE* group to be less satisfied than the AC, given their apparently greater orientation towards promotion. How might we explain this?

To some extent the 'No' response may result from the feeling that they *are* 'badly done by' and ought *not* to feel satisfied with a system which discriminates against them. The following comment suggests this: 'I'd have to say "No", but it really doesn't bother me that much'. However, the 'No' answers provide insights into the career perspectives of these teachers. It seems that 'career opportunities' is not necessarily understood as 'promotion opportunities'. In a similar way to that identified by Becker (1952), in his study of Chicago School Teachers, 'career opportunities' for these art teachers are opportunities to fashion a satisfactory life-style and to secure conditions which meet their in-school and out-of-school needs; these might or might not involve promotion. Some teachers felt that teaching lacked sufficient *diversity* to hold them in it for a long period of time. Others spoke of restricted opportunities for *professional development* in their subject through in-service training:

> No, I'm not satisfied, because I'm human! I'm entitled to secondment, but what could I do? I'd have to go off and write bits of paper, and I don't want to. I wish I could have a year off and maybe work in an art college and freshen up on my ideas. As an art teacher, I cannot, under this system, have a year to develop my own work — which is so personal — not like a maths teacher where you could go off and develop a maths curriculum, or whatever. We can't do that. People would think it was a holiday to go off and do my own work. (T6)

Another problem particularly pertinent to *art* teachers, many of whom have taken time out of teaching to practise their art or craft, or who would like to, was raised by this teacher:

> I've a feeling that my leaving teaching to do three and a half years working for myself has put me at a disadvantage. I got a *lot* out of that, not only skills-wise, but also running a business and meeting different sorts of people. Whether that stands as a qualification or not — it doesn't seem to — whereas if you've got an MA or something to stick after your name, that is valued *more* than practical experience. (T16)

The response provides a further example of how 'career opportunities' involve out of school opportunities for personal development (Lortie, 1975).

Two Heads of Department described the frustration of blocked careers. The following extract suggests, as a response to this situation, the development of a concurrent career, ie. investment of time and energy, and possibly emotional investment, in an enterprise outside teaching, from which material and/or psychic rewards are derived:

> I know one or two people in art who've tried it (going for senior posts in schools) and not succeeded. But it's the next logical step for me, and one I won't be taking, because what pleasure I get out of the job is from talking to kids in a quiet, friendly, social context, and also it strikes me that you get not much more money for a hell of a lot more commitment and work. And I still do work on my own art, so I don't want the extra hassle. I was fortunate, through circumstances, that I achieved promotion early and quickly. But I can really only move sideways now. So I am stuck. The only way for me to diversify is to do things outside school, which I'm starting to do. Perhaps I can see my career expanding that way. I also do a bit of freelance work. I haven't got a plan. If the right opportunity came along and if I had enough capital, I might consider starting on something else. I

don't like the thought of sitting here for the next thirty years, but at the same time, I can't see anything else which is going to give me the time, the lifestyle etc. that I enjoy at the moment. (T58)

This discussion has been primarily concerned with attitudes towards and perceptions of promotion *within* the *school* system. If this is a limited area for career development, do art teachers look to higher education as an alternative potential career arena?

Perceptions Regarding Opportunities in Higher Education

I asked the art teachers how available they thought teaching posts in colleges of art are to school art teachers. They were very pessimistic. The most common response was 'not good' (40 per cent), followed by 'non-existent' (29 per cent) (see *Table 6*). Their various comments are perhaps more illuminating than the raw figures. Four separate (but some interrelated) issues were raised as factors which contribute to their perceived lack of opportunity in higher education.

1   Most often discussed was the perceived requirement to be a practising artist in order to obtain art college posts. These teachers realized that they would need to have a substantial body of artwork to show for themselves and yet their mostly full-time commitments in secondary school teaching made this very difficult to achieve:

> ... they'd expect you to be a practising artist with lots of work to show, and links with the outside world, which I haven't got at the moment as a teacher. (T9)

> I think they're looking for commitment to one's own work, rather than to art teaching in schools. (T8)

2   The last comment also expresses another feeling amongst the art teachers — that school art teaching is not considered by those appointing art college personnel, as a particularly important experience or qualification:

> They're more likely to be looking for exceptional students or artists of reputation. I think that if you're an unexceptional, straightforward, successful art teacher, you wouldn't be in line for an art college job. (T71)

3   A strongly held belief is that appointments in art colleges are largely a matter of having the right connections. The teachers spoke of being outside the 'in scene', of 'backscratching' and of a 'closed world' where 'one has to know the right people and cultivate contacts':

> Those posts are not available. It's fairly difficult to go from one sector of education to another. 'Coincidentally', there seems to be a preponderance of people who know one another in certain art

schools . . . a mini public school system, shall we say, is operating. (T44)

4   Several teachers spoke of the need, if one wished to get into higher art education, to do so early on in one's career:

> You'd have to have your sights set on going into art school teaching as soon as you left college. It's a bit like academia; once you've gone into teaching you've scratched your chances. (T24)

> My impression is that whatever you get into directly on leaving art school, you tend to stay in it . . . if you go into school teaching you don't go into HE. I don't see twenty years of school teaching as being seen as a tremendous qualification for FE and art school posts, especially art school.

And from a Scale 1 teacher in her fourth year of teaching:

> I think you have to be either a head of department or have just left college; at *my* stage I'd find it very difficult. (T5)

However, if art college was not felt to be a viable sector of higher education to which these teachers could aspire, what about colleges and polytechnics with interests in art *education*? Comments in response to the question, 'What about posts in colleges of education — how available do you think these are to you — ie., jobs teaching teachers?', suggest that although teacher education is perceived as a potentially more accessible avenue, there is some antipathy towards this sector of higher education.

> You have this terrible feeling on the ATC course (now PGCE) that they don't really know what's going on inside schools. (T32)

> That's what I like about art schools, because you're taught by craftsmen — not like these silly courses where you learn everything about Piaget and nothing about art. (T6)

There seemed little motivation towards teacher training as a career avenue. When teachers mentioned higher or further education in discussing future plans (not reported here) it was always with reference to art college teaching, whether on degree, foundation or other Art and Design courses; it was never with reference to BEd or PGCE teaching. Only one teacher expressed an interest in advisory work, but this, he felt, was an even 'longer shot' than art college teaching.

Attitudes Regarding Career Development

We have established that art teachers' perceptions of career opportunities within the educational system are poor, but that this is not necessarily cause for great dissatisfaction, and that teachers may understand 'career opportunities' in broader terms than advancement in the formal hierarchy. The following comment reminds us that notions of 'advance' in a career are subjective:

> I think the only step forward, *if you can call it that*, for an art teacher is to go into HE or an art college. I've never met any art teacher who'd go for headships. (T38) (my emphasis).

That careers are not always experienced or planned as long term ventures is expressed by this teacher:

> I've never thought about pursuing a 'career'. I don't like the idea of *thinking* in terms of 'careers' — it's alien to me. It's fixed and long term, and not how I've always wanted to see life. (T44)

Search for challenge, openness regarding future possibilities and eventualities, and tolerance of uncertainty characterized such career perspectives. Several teachers indicated willingness to move from one type of job to another without particular concern for increasing status or income. Teaching was variously presented as an interim solution to earning a living; as an interlude to other types of work; as experiment, ('I may stay, I may not; it depends how I like it'), and as a last resort; as well as a first choice and long term career.

Some teachers seemed to assume that they were typical in their low level of planning.

> I think you just enter it. I don't think a lot of people really think about what they're going to do in the future. I just entered it (teaching) to see what it was like. (T32)

Others suggested awareness of differences between themselves and those they called 'career teachers'. The following comment illustrates this as well as describing a fairly typical orientation amongst this group of art teachers:

> It suits me for what I want, but were I to be a career teacher I think I'd have trouble advancing from here . . . I'm doing this because I like it. I'm not seeking a career. Previously I had more career ambition, when I worked in commerce; I knew where I was going then. Now, in teaching, I've less ambition. (T45)

Income and prestige do not appear to be primary career considerations. A few teachers had actually taken a drop in salary and/or status in order to achieve a satisfactory work situation. One teacher had been a year head, on the pastoral side, for eight years, but took a drop in salary to take responsibility for the art department. Another was moving down in scale and becoming part-time in order to develop her art work. Another had decided not to take up a post offered to her in higher education. Some teachers had moved into teaching from more lucrative and prestigous employment in design, commerce and industry.

> I have a delightful sense of freedom in *not* being career oriented, and *not* having to resort to strategies. (T24)

Art and Art Teaching: Two Concurrent Careers

I can't imagine life without making pots. It keeps me sane. (T16)

What is it that enables art teachers to be so 'delightfully free' in this way? Whilst, obviously, teachers who do not have high aspirations in teaching and who seek other rewards than those associated with promotion are to be found in other subjects, and whilst it is not intended to imply that *all* art teachers are completely lacking in ambition, it appears that *as a group* they do differ in these respects from 'other subject teachers'.[7] One teacher offered this suggestion:

Art teachers don't seem to be 'into' promotion. Perhaps it's because teaching isn't 'it' for them. (T30)

There are more important things in life than one's job. My job is only *part* of my life. (T8)

The data have suggested that amongst art teachers 'career' is understood in broader terms than simply the teaching job, and that career needs and satisfactions are met through involvement in activities outside teaching, not simply as an extension of the teaching career, but, in some cases, as a concurrent career. Art teachers, along with teachers in certain other subjects (such as Music and English), are in the special position of being able to pursue their subject interest whilst in teaching. In addition, it is possible to take up a career in art late in one's career, and there are role models available in individuals who have left teaching to become successful writers, musicians, artists, (Colin Welland, Barry Hines, Sting, for example). An alternative career in art or design is always *potential* for the art teacher in a way that it is less so for, for instance, a chemistry teacher in mid-career who would like to be a research chemist, or a biology teacher who dreams of a career in medicine.

The nature of their subject is such that art teachers may continue to extend their subject knowledge and experitise. As already noted, extension of knowledge for most teachers in schools tends to be in pastoral and organizational/administrative areas, rather than in the areas of their academic disciplines. For art teachers, continued development in their subject area may hold open or create opportunities for career development outside teaching whilst other subject teachers respond with intra-professional strategies for career development, which may tie them to teaching ever more securely.[8]

The implications of this are various; there are opportunities for concurrent careers *with* teaching and for alternative careers *to* teaching. A teacher with a successful concurrent career is in a greater position of choice regarding staying in or leaving teaching. Not all of this teacher's 'career eggs' are in the 'teaching basket'. In some cases, it seems quite deliberately thus; two teachers used the term 'escape route' in reference to their outside involvements in art and design. Maintaining satisfying involvement in their work improves the quality of their total careers, and if the conditions in teaching are not too frustrating, and the pull of art not too strong, teachers may have good reason to stay in teaching, where they derive satisfaction from their relationships with children.

Satisfactory involvement in a concurrent career in art and potential opportunities for art work as an alternative to teaching have implications for the art teachers' 'emotional investment' in teaching, as suggested in this comment:

> A lot of people here have a disproportionate interest in what goes on in the school. They don't have any other interests ... working with people outside has given me a new perspective — schools are very artificial, strange environments really — and if you never leave school then you begin to see it *as* the real world ... I do bits and pieces of artwork and painting. I also do some car restoration. Anything that pays really! I'm doing some paintings for Daler who're introducing some new paints, and I'm doing a large sign for someone who's setting up a stall in the market. I've recently done some coach lining on a Rolls Royce and a Bentley; I'm marking 2000 'O' level scripts, plus I've got a commision to do three large paintings for someone's swimming pool — stuff like that ....
>
> Its just as important as teaching. It's all part of the same thing. Teaching is a job. That's the difference between me and some other staff. I teach in order to pay the mortgage and support my family. While I'm here I'll do it to the best of my ability, but when I leave I won't think any more about it ... I'm lucky, it's a job I enjoy — but it's not a mission for me. (T58)

Summary

Art teachers present an orientation towards their careers which is not specific to teaching. They recognize the disadvantages, in terms of promotion opportunities within teaching, which accrue from the low status of their subject, but this is more often a cause for cynicism than dissatisfaction. 'Career opportunities', for them, implies opportunities to meet their personal requirements. Teaching is not necessarily the most important aspect of their lives, nor a substitute for it, but just one aspect through which they fulfil certain needs and satisfactions; important amongst these are the satisfaction of social relationships with pupils (a satisfaction often discovered once in teaching), and that of continued involvement in art (frequently a motive for entering teaching). They have, in many cases and to varying degrees, concurrent (and potentially alternative) careers in art, craft, design and other activities outside school. Higher status, greater responsibility and increasing remuneration are not necessarily their primary career goals.

Conclusion

Whether or not this orientation of art teachers towards careers is a reaction to poor opportunities within the education system, there are implications here for the way we interpret all teachers' needs in a period of contraction, and for the strategies employed to improve teacher motivation and morale.

It may be that intra-professional strategies, such as encouragement of staff to take active roles in school decision-making; involvement of staff in curriculum development; creation of new posts of responsibility in school; secondment for higher degrees in Educational Studies, have been myopic. If art teachers derive enjoyment, refreshment, fulfilment, challenge and a sense of choice and control in their careers through involvement in their own work, which is not directly related to school or teaching, could not other subject teachers benefit from opportunities for personal development in extension of their subject knowledge and involvement, or other non-school interests? Up until now, 'staff development' has consisted almost solely in development of 'the teacher', with little consideration for 'the whole person'.[9]

An interesting development in schools in the past decade has been the *Artists in Schools* schemes, which have placed dance artists, musicians, poets, writers, actors and visual artists in schools, for varying periods of time, to practise their art on site and thereby to extend their specialist interests and knowledge to pupils (and staff). These schemes appear to have been successful in most cases, but perhaps their very conception has bypassed the fact that schools already contain subject specialists who could benefit from the opportunity to devote time to personal development and research in their field of interest, and to present aspects of this work to pupils in a different way to that normally employed in teaching their 'subject'. There are wider-ranging implications here for change in pedagogy and pupil-teacher relationships. Other implications of concurrent careers have already been noted. The latter could have favourable effects upon teaching quality, not only through extension of subject knowledge but also by keeping teacher morale high. Alternatively, success in concurrent careers could lead teachers *out* of teaching, in pursuit of an alternative career.

Discussions of concepts such as 'commitment', particularly in the context of teacher turnover, frequently present or imply the *institutional* viewpoint — that low commitment to staying in teaching is dysfunctional to continuity and stability in the system. But why always this institutional view? Art teachers use schools and teaching as a resource, just as schools use teachers.[10] Art teachers utilize the conditions which teaching offers (holidays, facilities, security, regular income and relative freedom and flexibility in their working conditions), which enable pursuit of their own interests. Could other teachers take a lesson from this?[11]

Tables

Question: 'How available do you think top posts — Headships and Deputy Headships — are to art teachers in schools?'
Answers were categorized:

1 Non-existent — eg. 'They're not available'
                         'Basically Zero'.
2 Not good   — eg. 'Well, your chances are low, but I suppose it's possible'.
3 Average   — eg. 'As open to art teachers as to anyone else.'
4 Don't know.

Table 1

		Percentage			
	Non–existent	Not good	Average	Don't know	N
AC	62	30	8	0	37
CE	41	41	16	3	32
ALL	52	35	12	1	69

(AC: art college trained   CE: college of education trained)

Question: 'Do you think that your opportunities for advancing your career in teaching generally are as favourable as they are for other subject teachers? Responses were categorized 'Yes' and 'No'.

Table 2

	Percentage		
	Yes	No	N
AC	17	83	36
CE	37	63	30
ALL	26	74	66

Question: 'Why do they (senior posts) not appeal to you?'
Responses were categorized:

1 Social — loss of contact with children.
2 Art — loss of involvement in move to senior post.
3 Characteristics of senior posts —
   (a) Dislike of administration and bureaucracy.
   (b) Dislike of discipline, power and authority associated with such roles.

Table 3

			Percentage Administration (a)	Authority (b)	
	Social	Subject	Characteristics	Characteristics	N
AC	26	54	54	14	35
CE	45	27	59	18	22
ALL	33	44	56	16	57

(Per cent refer to percentage of teachers mentioning this reason. Some teachers gave more than one reason therefore some total percentages equal more than 100%)

Question: 'If you were offered a higher scale post which involved more administrative work and less classroom teaching, would this be attractive to you?'[6]
Responses were categorized:

1 Yes
2 Qualified yes — eg. 'Yes with reservations',
 'It would have to be in the right proportions'.
3 No

Table 4

| | Percentage | | | |
	Yes	Qual Yes	No	N
AC	9	18	74	34
CE	31	7	62	29
ALL	19	13	68	63

*6

Question: 'Are you satisfied with your career opportunities in teaching?'[6]

Table 5

| | Percentage | | |
	Yes	No	N
AC	43	57	35
CE	65	36*	31
ALL	53	47	66

*6

Question: 'What about posts in higher education, for instance, how would you rate your changes of getting a job teaching in a college of art?'[6]
Responses were categorized as for *Table 1*.

Table 6

| | Percentage | | | | |
	Non-existent	Not good	Average	Donot know	N
AC	32	40	26	3*	38
CE	25	41	19	16*	32
ALL	29	40	23	9*	70

*6

Notes

1 DES statistics (March 1982) indicate that 3 per cent of all full time secondary art teachers in England and Wales held senior posts in schools (Headteacher, Deputy Headteacher or Senior Teacher); this was the lowest percentage of all the subjects listed.

2 The broader issues of this research which provide the context for this discussion include: motivations towards entering the profession; satisfactions, adjustment and commitment; identity and normative reference groups; the significance of art activity out of school; the nature and extent of career plans and planning.

3 The two dimensional conception of career has not gone unchallenged. CORRIE (1981) criticizes Hughes for failing to question the subjective nature of the objective career structure, arguing that the latter is constructed from the subjective preferences and values of individuals. BERGER and LUCKMANN (1966, p. 33) described this process as 'objectivation', wherein taken for granted reality 'originates in (peoples') thoughts and actions, and is maintained as real by these'.

4 For instance, to have different reasons for entering teaching, and different intentions and aspirations regarding staying or leaving. Teaching may be viewed as a first choice career or a 'last ditch', a long term commitment or an interim solution to an employment problem.

5 The target 'sample' was the total population of art teachers in that county. This decision was based on information regarding the composition, in terms of training, sex, specialism, route into teaching, and number of years in teaching of art teachers in the county's secondary schools. There was an 81 per cent response to the short questionnaire seeking this information. Not all of the ninety-five respondents were able or willing to take part in the interviews. In this respect the seventy-two interviewed were self-selected.

6 Where percentages do not total 100 per cent this is because they have been rounded to the nearest whole number.

7 It remains for research into some of these other subjects to refine our knowledge of subject variations in teachers' subjective careers.

8 WOODS (1977) describes how commitment to teaching increases as alternatives recede. BECKER (1964), in discussing 'commitment' as a set of side-bets placed on a particular line of activity, emphasized not only the *stability* derived in this situation but the *constraint*. A person may stake so much that is important to her or him on a particular enterprise that the consequences of inconsistency are too expensive, and alternative courses of action become unfeasable.

9 TAYLOR (1980, p. 338) has argued for recognition of the value of 'all those other self-improving activities in which teachers participate as individuals or in groups', besides those activities 'formally' designed for staff development.

10 LYONS and McCLEARY (1980) describe how top post holders 'use' the organization and make it work for them.

11 In this analysis, AC and CE teachers' responses to questions concerning promotion have been presented separately. Implicit in this presentation is the expectation that the two groups would differ in their attitudes towards promotion and careers. To some extent a tendency to differ did emerge; however, there was a large degree of consensus in their attitudes. On other issues (not reported here), differences were far more marked. There is no doubt that *other* divisions — other facets of the subject subculture exist — and have important implications for issues pertinent to art teachers regarding eg. pedagogy, subject definition and content. SMITH (1980) has identified seven art teachers types (with subgroups) on the basis of the values and concerns they espouse. HANSON (1971) discusses a subgroup of art teachers whose concern is to upgrade the status of the subject and its teachers through collective action and the academicizing of the subject. One could identify other groups associated with various lobbies in art education, such as those for 'Design Education', 'Critical Studies', 'Media Studies', and, rather dated now, 'Free Expression' and 'Basic Design'. Finally, one could differentiate between art teacher groups at different

stages of their careers, or by other objective factors such as sex, age, or specialism in art and design. The art teacher subculture is obviously a multifaceted one. The data reported here, however, do not support analysis in terms of all of these types.

References

BECKER, H.S. (1952) 'The career of the public school teacher,' in HAMMERSLEY, M. and WOODS, P. (Eds) *The Process of Schooling*, London, Open University/Routledge and Kegan Paul.

BECKER, H.S. (1964) 'Personal change in adult life', in COSIN, B.R. *et al.* (Eds) *School and Society*, London, Open University/Routledge and Kegan Paul.

BERGER, P.L. and LUCKMANN, T. (1966) *The Social Construction of Reality*, Harmondsworth, Penguin.

BYRNE, E.M. (1974) *Planning and Educational Inequality*, Slough, NFER.

CORRIE, M. (1981) Unpublished working papers for SSRC project: 'The Social Construction of Teachers' Careers' (End of Grant Report number HR/5423/2).

DES (1982) *Statistical Bulletin* (Issue 5/82), London, HMSO.

GOODSON, I.F. (1983) *School Subject and Curriculum Change*, London, Croom Helm.

HANSON, D. (1971) The development of a professional association of art teachers, *Studies in Design Education*, **3**, 2.

HILSUM, S. and START, K.P. (1974) *Promotion and Careers in Teaching*, Windsor, NFER.

HUGHES, E.C. (1971) *The Sociological Eye: Selected Papers*, Chicago, Aldine Atherton.

HUNTER, C. and HEIGHWAY, P. (1980) in BUSH T., GLATTER, R., GOODEY, J. and RICHES, C. (Eds) *Approaches to School Management*, London, Harper and Row.

LYONS, G. (1981) *Teachers' Careers and Career Perceptions*, Windsor, NFER.

LYONS, G. and McCLEARY, L. (1980) 'Careers in teaching', in HOYLE, E. and MERGARRY, J. *World Yearbook of Education 1980: The Professional Development of Teachers*, London, Kogan Page.

RISEBOROUGH, G.F. (1981) 'Teachers' careers and comprehensive schooling', *Sociology*, **15**, 3, pp. 352–381.

SMITH, F. (1980) in STRAUGHN, R. and WRIGLEY, J. (Eds) *Values and Evaluation in Education*, London, Harper and Row.

TAYLOR, W. (1980) 'Professional or Personal Development', in HOYLE, E. and MEGARRY, J. *op. cit.*

WOODS, P. (1977) 'Teaching for survival', in WOODS, P. and HAMMERSLEY, M. (Eds) *School Experience*, London, Croom Helm.

Concord Sixth Form College: The Possibility of School Without Conflict

John Burke

Editors' Note: Burke presents an account of teachers' work in a sixth form college, a series of significant contrasts are established between college work and teaching in the comprehensive school. This paper like that of Beynon highlights the importance of understanding careers in institutional context.

Different institutional settings help shape and modify the processes through which teachers play out their career. The sixth form college is one particular context which exhibits several unusual features. The absence of younger pupils makes for a markedly different ethos (Macfarlane, 1978; Watkins, 1982). The increased maturity of students and their subject-mindeness (Crowther, 1959); the fact that attendance is voluntary (cf. Corrigan, 1979); and, above all, the absence of discipline problems (Watkins, 1982) — combine to produce an atmosphere where the traditional skills associated with professional expertise in classroom management and control are not called into question (Hirst, (1971); Musgrove, 1971; Shipman, 1968; Hargreaves, 1975; Woods, 1977).

In this context, however, other somewhat different demands are experienced by the teacher. On the one hand there are the special demands of the teacher's subject discipline and the level of expertise required together with the heavy load associated with marking 'A' level scripts in some volume. On the other hand there are certain tensions produced by the nature of the institution. The three roles which traditionally differentiate the three major routes through which a teacher may develop a career, subject specialisms, pastoral concern and administration, are subsumed under the one identity of sixth form teachers. Whilst it is true that virtually all teaching roles involve elements of all three, emphasis on one normally characterizes the role identity ascribed to or claimed by individual teachers. Thus, 'History Specialist', 'Head of Third Year', 'Curriculum Coordinator' typically describe one set of concerns which has particular salience in the perception of the individual teacher. Within the case study college described here this is not so. Virtually all full time staff are tutors with a direct responsibility for the pastoral welfare of their students. On a day to day basis they deal directly with students, fellow teachers and parents, participating in this role in a manner normally associated with a Head or Deputy within the pastoral system of a school. They are also, quite clearly, administrators. This is a particularly heavy burden as all are directly involved with UCCA[1] forms etc., career counselling and admissions procedures. As the vast majority of their tutees are either in their first or last year following two-year courses, there is little respite from this preoccupation. Finally, all staff are obviously subject specialists as all are involved with 'A' level teaching.

Over the past fourteen months I have been carrying out field work at Concord Sixth Form College in a fairly large town in south east England. As each sixth form college appears to be very much a product of its recent reorganization or foundation process, much of the data recorded in this chapter may have very limited application to other institutions but this is an acknowledged limitation of all case studies. Nonetheless, Concord does appear to be typical of one of the broad 'types' of sixth form college. These may be distinguished along four axes:

1 In terms of foundations: ex-grammar school — new foundation.
2 In terms of access: selective — open
3 In terms of academic orientation: examinations — new sixth.
4 In terms of size.

Concord is an ex-grammar school (therefore, in part, a tradition-carrier) heavily oriented towards traditional examination success in terms of 'O' levels and 'A' levels and exercises a selective access policy in terms of basic entry requirements.[2] One of the most striking features of the sixth form college which quickly becomes evident to the participant observer is the enormous pressure of work experienced by both students and teachers, a case of Lacey's (1970) 'highly pressurised academic environment' writ large. The special circumstances which gave rise to this pressure for teachers may be delineated by comparing and contrasting the experience on offer at a sixth form college with the traditional sixth form in a grammar or comprehensive school.

The formative influences of Butler and Arnold in the nineteenth century were largely instrumental in establishing sixth form teaching as a separate category (Taylor *et al.* 1974, p. 74). In this tradition teaching the sixth was normally entrusted to senior members of staff, often including the Head. Such teachers would normally teach one subject at 'A' level, their degree specialism. Thus in a traditional grammar school, a sixth form teacher might spend up to ten or twelve hours per week teaching the sixth, lower and upper. Indeed, at the time of the Clarendon Report (1864) Westminster had eighteen sixth-form pupils, Eton twenty, Rugby forty one and Harrow, the largest, sixty two. Peterson (1973) recalls the average size of the pre-war grammar sixth form as being about twenty (pp. 61–62). After the 1944 Education Act the state grammar schools 'grew tops' and by the time of the Crowther Report (1959) it was recorded that a boy in a grammar school was likely to find himself one of about eighty in the sixth form as a whole. King's (1968) submission to the Croydon Education Committee revealed that in four out of the five grammar schools in Croydon the average lower sixth form class consisted of 8.9 pupils across all subjects. In the preliminary discussions leading to the establishment of Concord and its sister college, a working party committee pointed out that of one hundred and forty-six sixth form teachers in the authority, only fourteen taught more than ten hours of sixth form work. The current sixth forms in the three all-through comprehensive schools in the area number 104, 148 and 167 respectively. These figures compare with 611 and 400 in the two sixth form colleges.

When we compare these features of the traditional sixth form (TSF) with the sixth form college (SFC) three facts are immediately apparent:

1   The number of 'A' level periods taught in the TSF per teacher are many fewer than the SFC.
2   The number of pupils or students per set tends to be far fewer in the TSF than the SFC.
3   As a consequence, the marking load generated by contact time is far higher in the SFC.

A *typical* teacher at Concord SFC teaches between fifteen and eighteen fifty minute 'A' level periods. The *average* tutor in fact teaches 15.5 periods per week, the actual variation being between eight (an exceptionally low figure for special reasons) and twenty two. Typical sets varied between eighteen and twenty-two students per tutor. The added concentration on 'A' level teaching has wide ranging implications in the SFC in terms of preparation, teaching and, in particular, marking. In purely quantitative terms, this places considerable stress on teachers but there are other qualitative aspects which need to be taken into account.

Preparation

The preparation time required by sixth form teachers varies little between different types of institution. The fact that an individual teacher may teach two or three sets within the upper sixth does not normally significantly alter or increase the amount of preparation time required in preparing one set within most subjects. The main problems centre on somehow fitting in the necessary preparation to a personal schedule which is already stretched by commitments in teaching and marking. In particular, the time required for updating knowledge and keeping abreast of the subject brings about problems which are common to all types of sixth form teaching but which are further exacerbated by other demands for time arising out of the 'rounder role' of the sixth form college teacher mentioned earlier. This type of preparation is probably the most demanding and yet most satisfying aspect of subject-based work undertaken in the sixth form. It is, of course, common to all teachers in sixth forms but again it is the necessity of fitting this into an overburdened personal timetable that makes for special problems in the sixth form college. It obviously affects different subject cultures in different ways but it appears to affect the science subjects more particularly. A biology teacher explained:

> You see, the subject is constantly moving on. Take the human brain, for instance. There is a new approach now. Instead of endlessly cutting it up and finding out what the various bits do as when I was at university [fifteen years ago] the new approach is to make an artificial model and see what that

reveals. That all involves first, keeping abreast of developments and, second, updating my materials. I find it takes about seven years for the latest research to percolate down to the 'A' level examination. Yes, that's about right — the life cycle of a good textbook.

A physics teacher tended to concur but claimed the percolation period was shorter in physics:

In a recent 'A' level Physics paper more than half the questions were the subject of Nobel Prize awards. Not only that but you have got to be light years ahead of them [the upper sixth] just to keep on top. It's no good being a few pages on. They want to know what are the applications of lasers to defence systems or micro-surgery. If you don't know — you haven't worked it out — you can't expect to sustain their interest.

How, then, is it possible to keep on top of a developing subject and update teaching notes? Different teachers had devised different strategies. Two general observations may be made:

1 Most tended to think in terms of cycles over several years.
2 Everybody reported the intellectual excitement and satisfaction in keeping up, given time.

Biologist: I simply haven't the nervous energy to do anything worthwhile [as preparation] during term time. I read the journals, of course, but I don't actually do any real preparation during the year. I simply haven't got the nervous energy left. What I do do, is to pack away several books — especially Open University materials, which are excellent — and take them on holiday with me to Denmark. I always have a folder with me in my briefcase. What I do is revise two subjects a year thoroughly. I have about fifteen topics. It might be homeostasis in animals, the ultra structure of a cell, or the biochemical and physiological aspects of photosynthesis or whatever. Last year I did 'plant hormones' and 'immune systems'. That way I hope to revise everything every seven years.

The Head of Economics, with probably the hardest pressed department in the college, having two thirds of the students enrolled on 'O' and 'A' level courses, had hit on another strategy:

When I'm interviewing a new teacher I'm not looking for someone with a 'first'. He has obviously got to know his stuff but what is more important, if anything, is that he should be a good teacher with a genuine concern for the kids. I've got to feel he will work well within the department and really care for the students. But with Henry [a recent appointment who has just completed an MSc in Economics] I was actually looking for someone who was really 'spot on' in the subject. I wanted someone who could enliven things up, who would say: 'There's an interesting paper on that in such and such a journal', or 'Have you read the latest report on so and so'. In fact I wanted someone who would keep us all on our toes and make sure we were aware of what was going on in the latest research. That's why I wanted him.

Acquaintance with the latest research results was seen as an essential part of their teaching obligation, rather than a scholarly or dilettante past-time.

The sixth form teacher is very obviously a subject specialist. Stenhouse (1975) has shown how subject specialists tend to legitimate their knowledge in terms of their subject discipline allegiance in the university. It is not surprising, then, that standing on the threshold between school and university many staff should have a Janus-like attitude to both, using both as reference groups in seeking to assess their own status and condition of work. Though SFC teachers may compare their present lot with their TSF colleagues (and recall their previous experience as TSF teachers) they also covet the conditions under which their near-colleagues work in the university or polytechnic. We are reminded that Crowther (1959) describes the ideal sixth form teacher as having 'another but kindred career' to the career of the university teacher:

> Intellectually, he can hold his own with a university teacher except in the latter's speciality. It may not be lack of opportunity but a difference in ambition that has placed him in another kindred career (p. 233).

This feeling of mild envy and slight resentment was well expressed to me by one teacher who had researched an MPhil some five years earlier:

> I know of no other practitioner in education who has to sustain such unremitting pressure . . . A university lecturer has time between lectures to reflect on his work. What does he teach a week? A maximum of two or three lectures? A person who wants to teach in a sixth form college has to have a higher degree of stamina — more than you'll find in a university or polytechnic teacher. Someone who can pump the stuff out and still keep student interest and enthusiasm. No, it is not an easy option. I'm not sure it is such a good trade off for the lack of discipline problems — though there [in schools] you require a different sort of stamina, not so much intellectual stamina as physical stamina.

Teaching

The notion of relentless or unremitting pressure was one that surfaced frequently in staffroom talk. Purely quantitative differences experienced in the SFC place considerable burdens on the teacher. But qualitative aspects need to be taken into account as well. Because most staff in TSF are *senior members* of staff, they frequently have other administrative tasks which are timetabled throughout the week. These may be burdensome or uncongenial but they do represent 'recovery time', a concept often mentioned in staffroom talk at Concord. The remainder of their time-tabled teaching might typically be taken up with younger pupils, again representing 'recovery time'. One teacher remarked:

In the days of the old grammar school it was a sheer delight to teach the odd first year class. I couldn't stand teaching them day in day out but, as Bill Shakespeare remarked: 'when occasions seldom come they wished for come and nothing pleaseth but rare accidents'.

A cursory glance at the time-table reveals that many staff frequently teach five 'A' level sets of fifty minutes each in succession during the extended morning period. Not only is sixth form work intellectually stimulating, it is also very demanding (Macfarlane Report, 1980, p. 30; Macfarlane, 1978, p. 118). When this is regulated into a succession of fifty minute periods broken only by registration and an all too short coffee break it is easy to see why so many of the staff find the pace so unrelenting.

Marking

This is probably the most burdensome aspect of SFC teaching (Macfarlane, 1978, p. 118). Marking is rarely a congenial activity for anyone but when it comes in avalanches throughout the term dealing with it becomes a survival problem. In these circumstances it is not surprising that various strategies have been devised to help meet this contingency. They range from the development of highly skilled skimming techniques, the provision of model answers and self marking, to the division of sets among teachers and occasionally the loss of a batch of scripts which are simply never returned, although it has to be said this appeared to be a last ditch strategy seldom employed in my experience. When teachers reported an average of two or three hours marking per evening I was at first very sceptical. But these claims went unchallenged in staffroom conversation. They were born out by careful examination of students' marked exercises chosen on a random basis. The sheer volume of work marked and returned provided irrefutable evidence that in the cases I examined the claims were not exaggerated. This heavy load of marking was accepted as inevitable by virtually all the staff in view of the numbers they taught; what they resented was not the marking but that somehow they had to cram in this activity to an already overburdened personal schedule.

Pastoral and Administrative Aspects

The pastoral and administrative aspects of the SFC tutor's role are seen by many as being of at least equal importance as teaching (Cf. HMA 1976, p. 5.).

> *T.* I wouldn't want to teach if I was simply a subject specialist. I'd very much resist any attempt to remove these other responsibilities because they *make* the job what it is.

Similar responses were frequently made by tutors across all subjects. Virtually everyone claimed to be overworked and many articulated well rehearsed complaints about their treadmill existence but when questioned as to how they would like to trim their role nobody was prepared to drop any part of their main duties. 'Less of the same' seemed to sum up the attitude of most staff, again expressed by the teacher quoted above who went on to add in the next breath:

> I wouldn't mind if they reduced the number of people I have to do it for. It would be better with fifteen or sixteen but I'd be doing the same job as I am now.

There is not sufficient space in this chapter to fully illustrate the nature of pastoral and administrative functions but something of the quality of the experience and a cross-validation of this account can be gauged from one sixth form college teacher's response to an earlier draft of this paper.

> Very representative — sums up the satisfaction and the difficulties faced by SFC teachers — they are being 'punished' by over-loading for having well motivated students and job satisfaction in the academic sense and in that they can see the 'end product'. The over-loading can be desperate at certain times of the year. The first half term (September–October) involves:
> 1 Induction for all first year and second year students, after having, as a tutor, most of the responsibility for seeing that they are undertaking courses suitable to their ability and their ambitions and therefore requiring a depth of knowledge of what course and career requirements are;
> 2 Settling in these students and initiating any necessary changes of course, while chivving upper sixth re UCCA and other career matters — they simply wouldn't get round to applying for anything otherwise;
> 3 Starting career discussions with first year people and nagging them to consider, and find a place for, work experience in early September and all the enormous shower of admin. that accompanies these . . . All this is a background to the establishment of 'A' Level and 'O' Level and other courses for a large number of students, initiating records for each, getting to know them, etc. and coping with the (belated) anxieties of returning upper sixth who realize for the first time that they have to start working hard. In the first half of the term there is a meet-the-tutor evening, an upper sixth parents' evening, and open evening for contributory schools and a first year evening — all compulsory for most staff.

In view of these pressures and the pressure related to preparation, teaching and marking described earlier, we may well ask: 'What are the attractions of working in such an institution?'

Focus on any particular aspect or theme tends to distort the broader reality. In the first part of this chapter I have focussed on the 'unremitting pressure' which is undoubtedly a feature of sixth form college life for both staff and students. In the second part, I want to examine why teaching in a sixth form college is deemed by its teachers to be such a satisfying experience.

In essence I want to argue four points:

1 Teaching in a sixth form college is professionally rewarding. The organization among staff promotes professional well being which runs counter to the increasingly common experience of teachers where professionalism is threatened and proletarianized (Lawn and Ozga, 1981, pp. 52–54; Bowles and Gintis, 1976) by bureaucratization and managerialism.

2 The college is a pleasant place for work. The ethos of cooperation and consensus reduces much of the strain and stress associated with secondary school teaching. I want to examine how this arises and how it affects both teacher and student.

3 Arising out of the second consideration, the students are eager to learn and it *is* possible to teach. Most of the energies of the teachers are therefore directed to doing their job. This has important implications for the teacher's sense of identity and general well-being.

4 Because of the cooperation and maturity of the students, the teachers are able to negotiate a role *vis-à-vis* the students which enables them to 'be themselves.'

Organization

Lacey (1983) explored the rhetoric which attended the creation of scale posts for teachers as the result of an arbitration award in 1971. Differentiation was equated with a move to professionalism and scales were represented as an increase in opportunity with enhanced career prospects. At a time of expansion and rapid change that was perceived as an attractive possibility; in an age of cutbacks and recession Lacey identifies the sour reality as stultifying bureaucratization and a sense of increasing frustration as teachers generally have come to realize that for many stasis has replaced career movement and advancement.

The situation at Concord is noticeably different. The short term gains in salary have been eagerly accepted. It is easy to appreciate that they have fed into the sixth form teacher's sense of self esteem and may be read as an institutionalized acknowledgement of their relative status. All full time staff are above the minimum scale (See Table 1). (Cf. Macfarlane, 1978, pp. 116–7).

Table 1 Comparison of teachers' salary scales as in 1982.

	% of teachers nationwide	% of teachers at Concord
Scale 1	31.5	0.0
Scale 2	32.3	28.6
Scale 3	14.9	45.7
Scale 4	6.3	25.7

Although comparative figures are not generally known among teachers at Concord, each individual is aware that their contribution has been recognized in a tangible way.

In spite of this process of status differentiation in terms of scale, there has not been a concomitant or consequential development of bureaucratization. As reported earlier, the teacher role at concord is very multifaceted and cuts across the traditional paths to career specialism. Thus each tutor is a subject specialist, an administrator and has a clearly defined and developed pastoral role. There is a managerial super-structure with Heads of Department, Senior Tutors and Assistant and Vice-Principals, but each is also a subject teacher with a class timetable. They are clearly seen as practising teachers with administrative responsibilities rather than remote managers who make infrequent sallies into the classroom as a more or less symbolic gesture. They are seen as facilitators of the role of tutor who is recognized as an executive member of staff, with a very wide range of executive responsibilities.[3] Decisions, taken at the level of tutor, have profound implications for the careers of in-dividual students. One teacher expressed the satisfaction which derives from this role:

> Teaching at Concord is much more than being a subject specialist, although that is important too, of course. What really matters is the all round involvement the job demands. Compare that with FE or university — or even an ordinary school. The pressure can be intense at times but I don't think I would enjoy teaching anywhere else [ie. in any other type of institution]. In fact, I'm sure I wouldn't. In fact, I actually look forward to coming here in the morning!

The individual tutor's perceptions of the scope and importance of these decisions was summed up succinctly:

> A tutor can make or break a student's application [UCCA]. He has great power. This sort of responsibility is only given to a Headmaster or a Deputy in an ordinary school.

What we see operating at Concord, then, is an organic style of interaction among equals, similar to the process of collegial cooperation described by Blau (1955).

The arena in which this action takes place is the staffroom, especially during the mid-morning break. The image which immediately springs to mind is that of a 'polite commodities exchange'. The whole staff assembles for the two morning breaks. In my experience at Concord these were the only occasions when I felt slightly uncomfortable. I felt ill at ease because I was largely outside this frenetic exchange. Unlike a conventional staffroom (cf. Woods, 1979, pp. 211–12) which tends to present a static image of teachers relaxing and momentarily 'turning off' from the pressures of teaching, the crowded staffroom at Concord during the mid-morning break presented a picture of most teachers milling round, balancing a cup of coffee in hand and, almost invariably a fist full of papers, report slips, messages from their trays, and other documents. Of course the picture here presented is exaggerated. Not all staff all the time are engaged in these activities, but the enduring image is one of quick snatches of conversation, requests, acknowledgements, agreements 'to action' some requirement. These exchanges are frequently interspersed with banter and good humour or moans, but most staff are 'on the move'. Most have some business in mind, few are totally relaxed or, indeed, sitting down.

The upshot as far as the tutors are concerned is that although they may be under pressure they experience a level of satisfaction which is increasingly denied in other educational settings. They enjoy collegial support in an egalitarian give and take atmosphere with much banter going on where accommodation and cooperation are the currency and where reputations built on these exchanges, become capital for later use.

Even within departmental meetings, where hierarachies are formally recognized, the shared experience of the same pressures tends to make for a collegial atmosphere. There also appears to be a 'carry over effect' from the habitual mode of decision making which characterizes the rounded role of tutor. The fact that all the members of staff teach both 'O' and 'A' level courses ensures that factional interests do not feature overtly or covertly as important issues although, within a large department, there may be self interested bids for certain specialized resources.

What I am reporting, then is a situation where all members share a common core experience of teaching, administration and pastoral care; the mechanism of exchange is the common staffroom where relatively inexperienced members may freely consult and are consulted on a range of issues which are vital to the smooth running of the college. In this situation supervisors — Heads of Department, Senior Tutors — are inside the dynamic process but on an equal footing as colleagues. They step outside the process only in infrequent formal exchanges which may take place in the Principal's study or some other back region. In this sense, then, nobody is in isolation. Although the staff are formally differentiated in terms of career hierarchy and the extent of specialized administrative responsibility, responsibilities in general are diffused throughout the staff and the differentiated tasks are much less obvious and even, sometimes, invisible. In this way, the dysfunctions of hierarchical differentiation noted by Blau and Scott (1963, pp. 121–122) are largely avoided. As Lacey (1983) notes:

> If examples of schools are found where change is successfully integrated, or where isolation and strain is successfully dealt with, or where there is a lack of conflict and polarization; and these features are associated with a managerial policy that specifically attacks the hierarchical elements of the career structure and promotes collegial, egalitarian demarcation methods of administration [then the damaging effects of bureaucratization and managerialism would not obtain].

One such example is Concord College and this, of itself, makes it a pleasant place to work.

Cooperation and Consensus

Blumer (1969) insists the cardinal principle of empirical science is to respect the obdurate character of *that* empirical world. He goes on:

A second important methodological implication that comes from seeing that human interaction is a process of designation and interpretation is the lack of warrant for compressing the process of social interactions within any special form. Such compression is an outstanding vice of social science, both past and present. We see it exemplified in the quaint notion that social interaction is a process of developing complementary expectations ... serving as the basis of [Talcott Parson's] scheme of human society as a harmoniously disposed social system. *We see it illustrated, also, in the contrary premise that society is organized basically in terms of a conflict process* ... To see all human interaction ... as organized in the form of some special type of interaction does violence to the variety of forms that one can see if he wants to look ... It is my experience that the interaction usually shifts back and forth from one form to another form depending on the situations that are being met by the interacting parties. (p. 16. My emphasis)

I want to argue that whilst all human groups, exhibiting different perspectives, will necessarily exhibit *some degree of conflict*, it is possible to envisage a situation where the weight of consensus and the degree of cooperation outweighs the conflict. Such a situation would be characterized as harmonious. Such a situation tends to exist in Concord Sixth Form College. The key to understanding this situation, which is markedly different from the situation generally reported,[4] lies in (i) The voluntary nature of sixth form attendance; (ii) the attainable reality of student expectations; (iii) as a consequence, the removal of the identity crisis identified by Hirst (1971) and elaborated by Woods (1977) as an increasing feature of secondary school experience.

Voluntary Attendance

Although some students are undoubtedly constrained to attend for a variety of reasons (eg. parental expectation and pressure or lack of alternative occupations), the vast majority of students elect to attend because they *want* to attend. This fact was born out in my own research by innumerable conversations, in informal settings where students were unconstrained and were willing to 'speak their minds' Virtually all other forms of school experience are marked by coercion. Shipman (1968, p. 79) makes the point boldly:

The imposition of schooling is a form of coercing applied by teachers, however humanely ... Inevitably many children resent the accompanying pressure ... Their reluctance to conform and resistance to the teachers means that schools are centres of active or passive conflict. Coercion not consensus is likely to be the basis of order.

Corrigan (1979, p. 46) goes as far as to reject Lacey's (1970) and Hargreaves (1967) notion of pro-school pupils internalizing school values; coercion and power differential are, he argues, the crucial factors:

Almost immediately after coming into contact with the boys I could see the errors in this explanation. There seemed to be no real acceptance of school values by a lot of the boys *at any time*. In fact the whole emphasis on 'values' as a guide for action seemed to be wrong. The boy's actions were not created by such consistent things as 'values': the crucial factor to explain classroom interaction seemed to be much more to do with the power differential between teachers and pupils.

He goes on:

> Most importantly, this power relationship was played out between groups of people who were in the institution for different reasons ... boys were only really at school because they had to be. (p. 41)

In contrast, not all pupils who wish to go to Concord can be accommodated. In 1982, for instance 369 applied for 330 places. In 1983, the college swelled its numbers to 611, well over its agreed quota in response to student demand. Prospective students have to attain certain basic qualifications to enter. They have to demonstrate a desire to succeed at interview. And those who obtain entry for 'O' level courses have to perform at a satisfactory level at the end of their first year to be allowed to enter the upper sixth. 'There is no automatic right of re-entry', as they are frequently reminded. Those on 'A' level courses have to make satisfactory progress throughout their course or they are obliged to leave. At the very lowest level of compliance, then, there is a strong instrumental conformity to the requirements of the college. They are not constrained to stay by the college authorities; rather, the onus is on them to demonstrate a willingness to work hard in an academically pressurized environment in order to ensure their continued presence.

Expectations

Lacey (1970) comments on the effect that impending examinations had upon the Express Stream (highest ability form) at Hightown Grammar.

> In the 1959 intake I had witnessed the levelling and concentrating effects of the impending GCE examinations ... the mock exams after Christmas, and the subsequent official ones, had produced an atmosphere of purpose and dedication that inhibited anti-group development. (p. 119)

The fact that no student at Concord is ever more than a few months away from examinations certainly has its effect. But this, on its own, is not sufficient to explain the atmosphere of cooperation and interest — and even, at times — enthusiasm that characterized many of the classes I observed at Concord. It is true that I also observed yawns, and low levels of attention at times, but these were remarkable for their comparative rarity. I never observed or heard of any 'incident' in class which was even mildly threatening.

Commenting on the quality of interaction in Band 1 and Band 2 classes at Beachside, Ball (1981) notes:

> From the very beginning of observation these forms appeared different from each other in their work performance and their behaviour in lessons. The general conduct of the lesson by the teachers was also very different. Teachers found 2CU [Band 1] generally easy to control, easy 'to teach', cooperative, lively (in the positive sense in which teachers used the word) enthusiastic, and interested. On the other hand, 2TA were described as difficult to control, difficult to teach and to get to work, uncooperative, lively (in the negative sense . . .) dull and uninterested. In each case these descriptions were typical of the Band as a whole. My observations in other Band 1 and Band 2 lessons demonstrated a similarity between all the Band 1 forms and all the Band 2 forms in terms of attitude, behaviour and pupil-teacher relationships. (p. 26)

It would appear, then, that the type of pupil Ball is describing as a Band 1 pupil approximates to the type of student one typically encounters in the sixth form college: 'easy to control', 'easy to teach' and 'co-operative, lively . . . enthusiastic and interested.' In these circumstances, it is not difficult to understand why teachers enjoy teaching at Concord. Who, in a comprehensive school, would not enjoy exclusive association with Band 1?

Where ethnographers explicitly deal with the pro-school pupil, he or she is usually found in the top stream or band, an examination candidate who apparently internalizes the values promoted in the school or else has a very strong instrumental adaptation.[5]

When I come to examine the typical sixth form college student, this is precisely what I found. In the main these are students who have negotiated a relatively very successful school career to date. Their experience of the pupil role has been reinforced and reaffirmed as a 'successful pupil identity'. Certainly the 'A' level candidates have enjoyed a large measure of success, the average 'A' level student having obtained at least five 'O' levels. Typical 'O' level students have been less successful but their examination orientation is equally — or in many cases — more marked. Their continuing presence in college is contingent not only upon their external examinations success at the end of one year but also upon a satisfactory performance as monitored throughout the year. There is a strong peer group pressure to do well and stay in college with their friends, many of whom are typically 'A' level candidates. Those who do not measure up to the requirements are either invited to leave early or are refused registration for the following year. In contrast to the situation obtaining in most secondary schools the majority of students do succeed. In Willis's (1978) terms, there is no question of 'penetrating'. The time in college is of short duration, the reality of a future contingent upon certified success is apparent to all. What the college holds out in terms of goals is perceived to be attainable and worthwhile — all the more so in an age of high unemployment.

Within the recognizable student subculture, which develops within the 'greedy' institution[6] most students accept the necessity to work hard. Undoubtedly some do seek to negotiate the load, to avoid 'unnecessary' work, to get by with the minimum but the choice is bleak: either succeed or leave.[7] Some measure of the internalized work ethic may be gauged from a questionnaire I administered to ninety students across a variety of tutor groups in the Easter term. In an open-ended question I asked: 'Now that you know the ropes, what advice would you give a friend who comes to college next year?' I fully expected a somewhat cynical response. Indeed one student replied: 'I would tell him what he *had* to do and what he could get away with.' Against this, 20 per cent used the construct 'work hard'. The full response is given in Table 2.

Table 2   Advice to a friend attending college next year

Work hard	21
Get involved in college activities	9
Mix/make friends	7
Choose your subjects carefully	7
Come (simply)	4
Come it is enjoyable	7
Respond to what the teachers say	1
Be yourself, grow up	1
Avoid certain named staff	4
Don't expect too much — the college is under school regulations	1
Beware lack of incentives	1
Tell him what he can get away with	1
Rely on yourself	2

In response to the open-ended question: Why did *you* come to Concord? the answers were equally revealing.

Table 3   Why did you come to Concord?

Get qualifications	22
Study for 'A' level	16
Study for better grades on 'O' level	2
Because of the wide range of subjects	5
Reputation of Concord	14
To widen outlook/because of better social life	4
Hope to get a better job	1
Didn't like old school	20
Friends or brothers at Concord	6
Liked timetable	2
Nearer/easier to get to	3
Nice atmosphere on visit	2
Couldn't find anything else to do	1

The majority of students reveal a strong academic orientation. Significant, too, is the large number who didn't like their old school. Although this questionnaire was carried out anonymously I was able to clarify this response to some extent in connection with different groups. With one exception every student interviewed claimed he or she was happier at Concord and enjoyed it better than his or her old school. (The one exception, a girl, recalled her old single sex school as very friendly.) Nine of the respondents who had previously given the advice 'work hard' had claimed they had disliked their old school, confirmation of Wood's (1980) assertion that a new start offered a kind of redemption (p. 18).

If any doubt about the orientation of the students at Concord still lingers, this may be dispelled by one further answer to the open ended question 'What is your main criticism of Concord?'

Table 4   Main criticisms of Concord

No criticism (explicit statement)	20	
No comment made — a dash	10	
Satisfied	2	The students
Very satisfied	1	had misread the
Fairly satisfied	1	instructions and
Not allowed out in free periods	17	ticked the answer
Smoking rule	7	as instructed
Lack of heating in one block	3	in the space above
General studies a waste of time	2	
Too much freedom	1	
Place is disorganized	1	
Treated like children	4	
Lack of college feeling	3	
Lack of personal attention	1	
'Cold' staff	3	
Staff don't really know you	1	
Staff too strict	1	
Run like a secondary school	1	
Too many 16 yr old (?)	1	
Lack of incentives	2	
Not enough teaching periods	1	
Too much pressure to succeed instantly	1	
Not allowed to do I only A level	1	
The whole notion of examinations	1	
G.S. not interesting, choice too narrow	2	
Lessons too long	1	
Lack of follow up on easy	1	

Given then the questionnaire's guaranteed anonymity and that students are normally characterized as being fairly vociferous in complaint, it is a remarkable fact that they had so few criticisms.

Woods (1979) and Hargreaves (1978) and many other commentaries have analyzed the stress associated with teaching. Although the Concord teachers may have to work very hard, they are free of most of the stress associated with survival and conflicts of identity. One teacher already quoted remarked that the stress was essentially different. In a secondary school, he observed, you needed physical stamina.

Hirst (1971) has demonstrated that the concept of teaching is totally dependent on learning since the intention of all teaching activities is to bring about some learning. He goes on:

> If therefore, a teacher spends the whole afternoon in activities the concern of which is not that his pupils should learn ... he cannot have been teaching at all ... In these terms, it could be the case that quite a large number of professional teachers are, in fact, frauds most of their lives.

At Concord, teachers can and do spend most of their time in the classroom teaching. Their control is neither contested nor challenged. This clearly has important implications for their self esteem and their own feeling of identity. They clearly do not feel themselves to be frauds. In this situation, therefore, the sixth form college is obviously a pleasant place to teach, inspite of its pressures, precisely because they *can* teach.

To postulate an ethos where cooperation and consensus obtains is to point up *one* of the most salient features of the institution. It arises out of a shared understanding of the major purpose and aims of the institution where the major interests of both teachers and students are mutually perceived to be promoted by such cooperation. It reflects a strong instrumental orientation on the part of both teachers and taught. This is not to postulate a Parsonian 'complementarity of expectations' or to offer a neo-structural functionalist account. There are centres of conflict, there are divergent perspectives, both students and teachers do continuously seek to redefine individual situations to their own advantage.[8] But both students and teachers are constrained by an appreciation of the reality of external examinations which dominate short courses in an academically pressurized environment where success in these examinations is perceived to affect intimately the life chances of the student.

On a purely theoretical level, unless one is locked into an extreme conflict perspective which denies the possibility of consensus, it must be allowed that consensus and cooperation may result if the major sources of conflict are removed, negotiated away, successfully circumvented or rendered inoperative. This is exactly what has occurred at Concord.[9] By conscious decision the petty constrictions which regulate school life in innumerable detail have been abolished in almost every case. The seeds of antagonism do not flourish on such strony ground.

The Teacher as a Person

Durkheim (1961) sums up the moral commitment of the teacher.

> ... The teacher must therefore be committed to presenting [the rule] not as his own personal but as a moral power superior to him, and of which he is an

instrument, not the author. He must make the student understand that it imposes itself on him as it does on them; that he cannot remove or modify it; that he is constrained to apply it; that it dominates him and obliges him as it obliges them.

Meighan (1981, p. 209) commenting on Durkheim, focuses strongly on this view of the teacher as model of moral order.

Teachers must not lose sight of the fact that, although they are agents of transmission, they themselves are under obligation to the same societal requirements. *Teachers then are simultaneously moral models and moral beings, constraining and constrained.* (My emphasis)

Shipman (1968) goes further. He describes the teacher as a 'super moral agent'.

The school is organized to surround children with moral influences to regulate behaviour. This is not just the maintenance of normal civilized behaviour, for the school tries to be a super moral agent in which actions accepted or ignored outside are actively discouraged ... A teacher, therefore, is always stressing what is right and wrong. He is a moral agent and under the strain of having to sustain this through the day. (p. 68)

The tensions associated with this front are not experienced at Concord. Teachers do not have to act as moral guardians or arbiters of dress or hairstyle.[10] They are not disturbed if a student runs in the corridor. Teachers can be themselves. In fact any such 'posturing' would threaten the ethos of adult or semi adult interaction which is demanded by the students and forms the basis of many control strategies implemented by teachers. Students are very conscious of and sensitive about their emergent adult status. As revealed in the questionnaire, they resent infringement of this status even when it is not intended. Teachers, on the other hand, appreciate the possibilities that this open approach provides for getting to know their students and developing that special relationship which Crowther (1959) character-ized as one of the essential marks of the sixth form.[11]

The sixth form college enjoys many advantages which arise from the age and maturity of its students and their general orientation. It remains a final intriguing question whether any of the special circumstances which make for such an atmosphere of trust and cooperation — and enjoyment — can be extrapolated and applied to other institutions.

Notes

1 UCCA: Universities Central Council on Admissions — the central clearing-house for university applicants.
2 Virtually all Sixth Form Colleges advertize themselves as 'open access' (cf. Compendium of Sixth Form Colleges 1982) but in fact Concord has operated a form of selection process in that up to and including 1983 applications have always exceeded places. Places have

therefore been offered on a basis of: 'best applications first' all other things being equal. In 1982 there were about forty unsuccessful applicants. In 1984 a much reduced roll will necessitate a different policy.

3 This was described to me in interview with the Principal as '. . . a deliberate policy to maintain morale. I believe in encouraging all my staff to share responsibility.'

4 I argue elsewhere (Burke, 1984) that the concentration on conflictual situations especially in secondary education, has brought about a 'paradigmatic tilt', which is based on ungrounded metatheoretical assumptions and may lead to theoretical distortion within the interpretative paradigm. Whilst secondary schools *are* characterized as sites of conflict, it is inappropriate to characterize all schooling as conflictual, especially post compulsory schooling which has been almost totally neglected in the sociology of education and lacks any account of ethnography.

5 Cf. Woods' (1979) adaption of Werthman's topology and Ball's (1981) adaptation of Lambert *et al's* topology.

6 The concept of 'greedy institution' is derived from Coser (1974) am indebted to Geoffrey Walford who expanded this concept in a paper at the St Hilda's College conference on the sociology of education 1983.

7 'The Principal reserves the right to terminate the course of any student whose progress is inadequate or whose behaviour is unsatisfactory (Introductory Programme notes issued to every student before he or she is finally registered).

8 In a short paper such as this it is not possible to do justice to the variety of views and orientations of either students or teachers. Lacey (1977) forewarned us against treating student sub-cultures as homogeneous groupings and Downes (1974) issues a similar caveat in relation to teachers.

9 This situation is not unique to Concord. In January 1983, HMI began an inspection of Esher College. They report:

> The *overwhelming impression* gained by HM Inspectors from their visit to the College is of a group of young people *who in the large majority are content to be there and who believe that the College is serving their needs.* The atmosphere is happy, relaxed and generally purposeful.
>   . . . Although in some lessons students seemed unduly reticent, *the good relationships operate within and outside the classrooms and are founded on mutual respect.* HMI consider that they have been *a significant factor* without which College life could not have developed as successfully as it has done so far and promises to do in the future. (p. 7) (My emphasis)

Widnes Sixth Form College was inspected in November 1982:

> . . . a happy and hardworking community based on excellent relationships and mutual respect . . . (p. 52, 15:1)

Greenhead Sixth Form College, November 1982:

> . . . a friendly community in which relationships appear to be based on mutual respect and tolerance. (p. 10, 8:1)

10 Students are free to dress as they please. Most, in fact, conform to a 'student uniform' of jeans and sweater etc. although even within these groups students are aware of stylistic differences which were largely invisible to me until they were pointed out. The Assistant Principal related that she had sent two students home for unacceptable dress in nine years. One, a girl, had been wearing a provocative 'see through' blouse. The other, a boy, had a tee-shirt decorated with a picture of an intoxicated cat. Below this was the legend: 'Happiness is a tight pussy.'

11 Cf. the HMI reports quoted above.

References

APPLE, M. (1981) 'Social structure, ideology and curriculum' in LAWN, M. and BARTON, L. (Eds) *Rethinking Curriculum Studies*, London, Croom Helm.

BAILEY, A.J. (1982) *The pattern and process of change in secondary schools: A case study*, unpublished D. Phil thesis, University of Sussex.

BALL, S.J. (1980) 'Initial encounters in the classroom and the process of establishment', in WOODS, P. (Ed.), *Pupil Strategies*. London, Croom Helm.

BALL, S.J. (1981) *Beachside Comprehensive*, Cambridge, Cambridge University Press.

BARTON, L. & MEIGHAN, R. (Eds) (1979) *Schools, pupils and deviance*, Driffield: Nafferton.

BECKER, H. (1964) 'Personal change in adult life,' *Sociometry*, **27**, 1.

BLAU, P. (1955) *The Dynamics of Bureaucracy*, Chicago, University of Chicago Press.

BLAU, P. and SCOTT, W.R. (1963) *Formal Organizations*, London, Routledge and Kegan Paul.

BLUMER, H. (1969) 'The methodological position of symbolic interactionism', in HAMMERSLEY M. and WOODS, P. (Eds) *The Process of Schooling*, London, Routledge and Kegan Paul.

BOWLES, S. and GINTIS, H. (1976) *Schooling in Capitalist America*, New York, Basic Books.

BURKE, J. (1984) 'Paradigmatic tilt: Ungrounded metatheoretical assumption and theoretical distortion within the interpretive paradigm', unpublished paper, University of Sussex.

CORRIGAN, P. (1979) *Schooling the Smash Street Kids*, London, Macmillan.

COSER L.A. (1974) *Greedy Institutions, Patterns of Undivided Commitment*. New York, Free Press.

CROWTHER, Sir G. (1959) *15 to 18* vol. 1. Report of the Central Advisory Council for Education in England, Ministry of Education, London, HMSO.

DOWNES, A. (1974) 'Relationships among teachers' in HOLLY, D. (Ed.) *Education or Domination?*, London, Arrow.

DURKHEIM, E. (1961) 'Moral education' quoted in HARGREAVES, D. 'Durkheim, deviance and education' in BARTON, L. and MEIGHAN, R. (Eds) (1979), *op. cit.*

HARGREAVES, D.H. (1967) *Social Relationships in a Secondary School*, London, Routledge and Kegan Paul.

HARGREAVES, D.H. (1975) *Interpersonal Relationships in Education*, London, Routledge and Kegan Paul.

HARGREAVES, D.H. (1978) 'What teaching does to teachers', *New Society*, 9 March.

HIRST, P.H. (1971) 'What is teaching?' *Journal of Curriculum Studies*, 3.

HMA (1976) *Sixth Form Colleges*, Headmasters Association.

HMI (1982, 1983) Inspection reports. DES, London, HMSO.

KING, R. (1968) *The English Sixth-Form College*, London, Pergamon.

KING, R. (1976) *School and College*, London, Routledge and Kegan Paul.

LACEY, C. (1970) *Hightown Grammar*, Manchester, Manchester University Press.

LACEY, C. (1977) *The Socialization of Teachers*, London, Methuen.

LACEY, C. (1983) 'Career: Opportunity or constraint?' A working paper given to St Hilda's Conference on Sociology of Education, Oxford.

LAWN, M. and OZGA, J. (1981) 'The educational worker? A reassessment of teachers' in BARTON, L. and WALKER, S. (Eds) *Schools, Teachers and Teaching*, Lewes, Falmer Press.

MACFARLANE, E. (1978) *Sixth Form Colleges*, London, Heinemann.

MACFARLANE, N. (1980) *Education for 16–19 year olds*, London, HMSO.

MEIGHAN, (1981) *A Sociology of Educating*, London, Holt, Rinehart & Winston.

MUSGROVE, F. (1971) *Patterns of Power and Authority in English Education*, London, Methuen.

PETERSON, A.D.C. (1973) *The Future of the Sixth Form*, London, Routledge and Kegan Paul.

SHIPMAN, M.D. (1968) *The Sociology of the School*, 2nd ed. London, Longman.

STENHOUSE, L. (1975) *An Introduction to Curriculum Research and Development*, London, Heinemann.

SWIFT, D. (1969) *The Sociology of Education*, Milton Keynes, Open University.

TAYLOR, P.H., REID, W.A. and HOLLEY, B.S. (1974) *The English Sixth Form*, London Routledge and Kegan Paul.

WALFORD, G. (1983) 'The mediaeval baron in his castle — the public school housemaster'. A draft paper given at St. Hilda's Conference on the Sociology of Education, Oxford.

WATKINS, P. (1982) *The Sixth Form College in Practice*: London, Arnold.

WILLIS, P. (1978) *Learning to Labour,* Farnborough, Saxon House.

WOODS, P. (1977) 'Teaching for survival' in WOODS, P. and HAMMERSLEY, M. (Eds) *School Experience*, London, Croom Helm.

WOODS, P. (1979) *The Divided School*, London, Routledge and Kegan Paul.

WOODS, P. (1980) *Pupil Strategies*, London, Croom Helm.

Institutional Change and Career Histories in a Comprehensive School

John Beynon

Editors' Note: This paper examines teachers' careers in a single institutional setting, using life history techniques, and Beynon is able to demonstrate the importance of institutional history in the making and breaking of teachers' lives and careers.

Teachers' careers and professional identities have, in the past, been too readily taken-for-granted, with teachers depicted as carrying out role demands but with scant attention being accorded to how they actually experience schools, colleagues and staffrooms. Conflicts between teachers, whether on a personal and/or ideational level, have rarely been deemed worthy of study in spite of the fact that such 'preference orders' (Arfwedson, 1979) can be crucial factors in policy formulation and pedagogy. Underneath the apparently settled face the secondary school shows to pupils, parents and outsiders, there are likely to be antagonistic teacher groups with very different historical traditions and training (Hargreaves, 1980; 1982.). However, hand-in-hand with the current resurgence in the life history method is a concern with teachers' changing experience and perceptions and, in particular, a growing awareness of the importance of the 'micro-politics' of everyday school life (for example, Ball, 1984; Hoyle, 1982; Hammersley, 1981; Riseborough, 1981; Beynon, 1981). To date remarkably little is known about, for example, the interplay between teachers' professional and personal lives; or about changes in their outlooks over time; or how individuals are currently reacting to severe curtailment of career prospects during the economic recession. Yet what Arfwedson (1979) terms teacher and school 'codes' cannot be divorced from personal and institutional life histories: in short, unless we first understand teachers we can hardly claim to understand teaching. In this chapter, therefore, my object is to show how the life history interview can sharpen the ethnographer's insight into an educational setting and its processes. Data is drawn from fieldwork at the start of the year in Lower School, which contained the first year (approximately three hundred and fifty boys) of a large urban comprehensive called Victoria Road. I first provide details of the secondary modern-grammar schism in Lower School and then make a number of claims for the life history method. I then bring these two concerns together to focus on the field data, which I explore in terms of 'personal domain' (namely Mr Pickwick's careers as a history teacher) and 'institutional domain' (Lower School's evolution as a bastion of schoolmastery and the implications of this for the drama teacher, Miss floral).

Lower School: The Grammar-Secondary Modern Divide

Lower School was a late nineteenth century red-brick building (originally an elementary school) some two miles from the purpose- built glass boxes of the main campus (which I have called Victoria Road). It was thus isolated from it both physically and, to a considerable degree, ideologically. My principle purpose there was to observe initial encounters between teachers and pupils (Beynon, 1985). I decided early on that a study which attempted to explicate initial encounters without reference to the biographical and historical features of the setting in which they were grounded (and of which they were an expression) would fail to provide a rounded picture. What Lower School teachers were attempting to do during the early weeks of term could not be divorced from the personal and institutional differences; divided loyalties; occupational divisions; ideological orientations and constraints which characterized Lower School and were rooted in its formation over a decade earlier. Interpersonal staff relationships are an important, but under-researched, area given that teachers' colleagues, along with daily classroom experiences, shape perspectives and classroom processes. In all schools there exists a web of formal and informal relations based on age; background; sex; experience; lifestyle and wider social and political issues. It is all the more surprising, therefore, that recent ethnographies of schooling have paid such scant attention to teacher biography; career progression; and institutional history (for example, Woods, 1979; Ball, 1981; Turner, 1983). As a result teachers appear as disembodied voices when quoted in the text, cardboard cutouts without flesh or substance. Burgess' (1983) study of Bishop McGregor goes some way towards rectifying the position in that he shows how the life history of a school can affect present operation. Furthermore, he focuses on selected (Newsom) staff autobiographies as these impinge on classroom actions and attitudes.

Of the Lower School staff of seventeen, ten were permanently based there whilst the others had the status of 'visitors' in that they travelled between sites. The majority were former secondary modern teachers (or their college-trained successors) doing what was seen by those in authority as necessary, highly laudible, but essentially low status, 'junior' work. During comprehensivization in the late 1960s the grammar school staff (and their university-trained graduate successors) had secured the positions of real influence in Victoria Road. The Lower School 'residents' felt, as a result, deprived of authority and remote from both the main site and the inner workings of even their own departments. This was even true of the Lower School head Mr Changeable) and his deputy (Mr Megaphone), both former secondary modern teachers (of art and PE respectively). For the former secondary modern teachers (and their BEd and non-graduate colleagues) their low status was a cause of both anger and frustration, especially since they regarded themselves as superior classroom practitioners:

> They (the authority figures) would never have survived in the sec. mods. There it was the quality of your teaching that mattered, not the paper qualifications you kept hidden in the sideboard drawer (Mr Stern).

They resented the fact that teaching skills and pupil control appeared to carry little weight in gaining promotion and, as I shall show, Mr Changeable was especially concerned that there was now scant respect for the master teacher and for 'schoolmastery'. Indeed, there was considerable support amongst them for Mr Megaphone's oft-repeated and disgruntled assertion that 'most teachers graft away and at the end of the day all they've got is a bloody big mortgage and a sore throat.'

A decade after the formation of Victoria Road, the former secondary modern teachers still saw themselves (and were recognized as) a distinct group. Stripped of their former positions how had they responded? How had they maintained a cultural and physical unity and presence (Becker and Geer, 1960); coped with career truncation; and asserted new personal and professional identities? A number of strategies were evident:

(i) *Parallel careers* Many of the original secondary modern staff had diversified and developed interests outside teaching. These fell into two main categories. Those like Mr Stern (who repaired radio and telvision sets in his spare time) who had developed other skills to compensate for career demotion and boredom; and those like Mr Pleasant (who worked in a garage after school) who had to increase their income but were debarred from vertical promotion through lack of qualifications, age, or through having become too closely identified with the low-level 'childminding' reputation of Lower School. A third category like Mr Dancer (who was a leading member of a well-known local folk group) had an involvement which predated their entry into teaching but which they had expanded in the light of career decline. I shall return later to the notion of 'parallel career' in connection with Mr Pickwick and Miss Floral.

(ii) *Advocacy of mixed ability* The secondary modern staff as a whole were held responsible for the pattern of mixed ability (with some banding) that had emerged in the first three years of Victoria Road. They had energetically advocated it, seeing it as a means of horizontal promotion in that it enabled them to teach a cross-section of pupils and not be confined, as formerly, to the less able.

(iii) *Covert curriculum innovation* They were fiercely critical of the domination of departmental machinery and syllabuses by 'absentee' heads of department who rarely set foot in Lower School. They felt excluded from decisions made over the allocation of budgets, resources, content and pedagogy. Many had entered into protracted and acrimonious arguments, got nowhere, and had been fored into more devious manoeuvrings to get their way. Whilst they paid lipservice to official demands and syllabuses, they covertly introduced their own topics, materials and approaches. This covert curriculum innovation was repeatedly celebrated in Lower

School staffroom lore as a 'putting one over' on the superior status figures of Middle and Upper School and was a source of considerable humour, fellow feeling and solidarity.

(iv) *Claiming superior expertise* Victoria Road's secondary modern contingent could not boast of examination pass rates as a badge of their identity since very few taught examination classes. Instead, they openly flaunted their expertise in teaching pupils rather than subjects and their ability to impose order and win the respect of even the most intractable. They were proud of being hard task-masters and disciplinarians and, furthermore, were highly critical of 'weak', incursionist teachers (from Middle and Upper School) who could not mobilize the same degree of coercion. They also claimed superior expertise in remedial education and site supervision, being especially proud, for example, that the Lower School truancy rate was a third that of Victoria Road as a whole.

(v) *Lower School as home base* As I shall show, Mr Changeable had obtained his position as Lower School's principal reality definer through comprehensivization and was daily engaged in the 'quality control' of teaching. Like the headteachers in both Ball (1984) and Riseborough (1981) he assumed the key role of amplifier of teacher normality and deviancy as he sought to safe-guard the holy grail of schoolmastery. As a result Lower School became a secondary modern stronghold whilst Victoria Road as a whole was dominated by a grammar school-type staff who took the important decisions. Even the former secondary modern teachers who worked extensively in Middle and Upper regarded Lower School as their spiritual home, a bastion of certain (schoolmasterly) values. One of them, Mr Piano, explicitly referred to this when he said:

> Sometimes I jump in the car and tear down here for morning break or come down for a lunch hour chat. In the Middle School staffroom unless you're a head of department, or on the way to becoming one, you're nothing. It's all very serious, people watching what they say and buttering up the head, whereas down here there's a far friendlier climate because we see things in the same way and respect Bill (Changeable) for running things as he does. We're teachers, not theorists or academics — that's the difference. Up there a lot of them sound good outside the classroom, but inside they're a dead loss. The kids treat them as doormats, yet they could write a book when it came to theory.

(vi) *Recruitment of staff* Finally, as many of the old secondary modern staff retired they kept up their numbers by recruiting from the ranks of college-trained teachers (cf. Hargreaves, 1982) who, on joining Victoria Road, were posted to Lower School or drafted to cover the low status teaching in Middle School. Many of these young entrants soon began to sympathize with the grouses of their seniors concerning blocked advancement and the unduly heavy emphasis placed on university qualifications by the Victoria Road leadership. They resented the increased horizontal and vertical career openings available to their university-trained contemporaries and were more able to identify with strict discipline and schoolmastery than with the academic, subject culture of the grammar school-type appointments.

John Beynon

The grammar-secondary modern divide is not, of course, unique to Lower School as recent literature demonstrates. For example, Reynolds and Sullivan (1979) report its existence in the South Wales comprehensives they studied. It is strongly evident in the Ball (1984) and Riseborough (1981) studies of the creation through amalgamation of new comprehensives, both of which show some staff being demoted and, thereby, alienated. The former contradicts the view that grammar school staff inevitably land the academic posts and the secondary modern the lower status pastoral ones. He shows how the staff of one of the 'parent' secondary moderns (Shottsford) were highly successful in capturing posts of responsibility. Meanwhile the ex-grammar teachers formed themselves into an influential cabal and, whilst being dismissed as reactionary diehards by the ex-Shottsford contingent, employed an effective, albeit passive, strategic maintenance of identity. They opposed mixed ability and defended their own interests and commitments to teaching, implying that their former secondary modern colleagues were neither competent to teach the able nor the sixth form. The staff of the third amalgamated school, Egdon Heath, suffered from the poor relation image of their secondary modern; lost out in the re-organization; and ended up as 'skidders' (Wilensky and Edwards, 1959) with no further career prospects and diminished status. In the earlier study Riseborough (1981) links teacher groupings in Phoenix Comprehensive with the streaming of pupils and the differential distribution of knowledge. It has been repeatedly noted (for example, by Hilsum and Start, 1974) that promotion is most rapid for graduate teachers in key subject areas, and both Hargreaves (1967) and Lacey (1970) talk of the 'better' teachers being given the abler forms and the 'weaker' or more inexperienced inheriting the less able. In Phoenix the secondary modern teachers at first saw the prospect of both vertical and horizontal promotion (Becker, 1952) through comprehensivization, but found that in the new environment they were classed as 'bad' teachers and given the lower status jobs. The 'new staff', with better formal qualifications and teaching records in public examinations, monopolized the higher status work. In response, the former secondary modern staff formed an assertive, uncooperative and subversive clique and pitted themselves against the new head, his appointees, and their perceived 'treadiness'. Deprived of a worthwhile place in the Phoenix hierarchy they discovered their 'career aspirations outstripped career realities' as they experienced a severe 'truncation of their careers' (p. 365). In both studies the headmasters emerged as key, but embattled, figures at the nexus of the conflicting ideologies of the teacher factions. The aims they set themselves rendered them unpopular, even hated, amongst some sections of the staffs they inherited. In Ball's Casterbridge, the head felt the grammar and Egdon Heath teachers were holding up the development of his new school along shottsford lines, and in the Riseborough's Phoenix the head regarded the secondary modern staff as obstructive and ill-equipped to teach in the 'pressured' academic environment he was intent on fostering.

It is clear that comprehensivization through amalgamation can result in what Woods (1981) terms 'spoiled careers', with promotion being handed to the more highly qualified newcomers (or, in Lower School terms, the 'grammar school types'). Woods (1983) talks of the older teachers attacking their younger colleagues for being idealistic; ambitious; unable to control pupils; or to teach. In the meantime they had often lost their attachment to teaching and were involved merely in 'career continuance' until they could retire. Moreover, Hargreaves (1982) advances an analysis of comprehensives in which old divisions have been retained and where a hierarchy has emerged based on age; training; professional socialization; ex- periences and roles. Contemporary comprehensives are seen to combine two distinct occupational cultures, namely the grammar school and elementary school traditions, the former emphasizing subject knowledge, the latter pedagogic expertise. He argues that the secondary moderns fell into two ideal types: those which aped the grammars through traditional teaching and subject expertise; and those which focussed on pupil-centredness and relevance. The former are observed to have triumphed in comprehensive re-organization, with grammar school teachers securing senior academic and administrative positions. Former secondary modern teachers, meanwhile, have taken responsibility for CSE; non- examination work; junior work; and pastoral care. He concludes that comprehen- sives have bundled together teachers who have very different cultural antecedents and an all-graduate profession is being achieved by preserving that same split between those who place subject expertise foremost (conventionally trained university graduates) and those who base their identity on social-psychological theories of learning (the college BEd products). Divided by these traditions teachers have been unable to discover common ideological ground and have grown increasingly dissatisfied with their professional standing.

Before examining how life history data can aid the ethnographer to explore the inter-relation of critical events in the institutional and biographical domains (and how these translate into classroom actions and, thereby, add to our understanding of process and situation) I want briefly to survey the claims made for the life history method.

The Life History Method

After its Chicago heyday during the 1920s and 1930s, the life history method had, until recently, fallen on relatively hard times as a research procedure. The reasons for this demise are many, amongst them being the drive by the social sciences for respectability and status through the adoption of 'scientific' methods; the respect paid to positivist theory — testing and abstract theorizing; the time-consuming nature of life history data collection; and the individual life's lack of representative- ness and generalizability. With the strengthening of educational ethnography in this country in the 1970s, however, a new generation of researchers has started to explore the possibilities of the life history in helping to further understanding of school processes; generate theory; and forge links between individually and collectively lived experience and wider society. They hold that the interactionists' emphasis upon situations and strategies, whilst admirable, can obfuscate the importance of previous experience (the individual's autobiography) in influencing those actions and responses. Moreover, sociology is seen as being in danger of divorcing lived experience from structural issues and ignoring what Thomas and Znaniecki (1927) term the 'laws of social becoming' discernible from life history documentation. Furthermore, it frequently glosses over the complexities of lives by prematurely super-imposing researcher order and rationality upon the often chaotic personal worlds of its subjects.

It is in this spirit that Goodson (1983), for example, accuses interactionists of persistently neglecting the biographical. He argues that teachers and their actions cannot be divorced from their socio-historical context. He illustrates how changes in an individual career can echo changes in the life histories of collectivities (for example, occupational groups within teaching) and institutions (the organization, administration and ethos of a particular school). The fact is that in much educational ethnography previous career and experiences (including lives both within and outside school) are not researched and are not held to be significant in shaping teacher views or actions. It is, however, salutary for classroom researchers to bear in mind that all teachers and pupils have lives that are largely spent outside classrooms and which strongly influence (even determine) activities and reputations. Certainly the connections between these lifestyles and how they actually impinge on classroom processes have been underplayed. It is clear that the life history method can fill in the huge gaps in our understanding of the shifting sands of careers and professional lives. Only then will researchers arrest the tendency to treat teachers as a static, depersonalized mass and, moreover, tentative links can then start to be drawn between levels, between the evolution of the education system; the curriculum; the school; and the impact of external influences on the individual teacher's working life. Two notable contributions which further the resurgence in interest in the life history for this purpose are the restudy of the Smith and Keith (1971) classic on innovation in Kensington School in which they chart changes in teachers' life histories and attitudes (see Smith *et al.* in this volume), and Goodson's (1983) portrait of the development of environmental studies based on the life histories of key personnel.

The claims made for the life history data can be expressed in terms of three functions, namely the subjective; the contextual and the evaluative.

The Subjective Function Faraday and Plummer (1979) argue that the life history method is uniquely placed to grapple with the individual's subjective reality, assumptions and beliefs. It emphasizes the interpretations people place on their every day experiences as an explanation of behaviour. Bogdan and Taylor (1970) advocate life history documentation as essential to appreciate stages in a life and Becker (1966) sees it able to throw light on key interactive episodes when new aspects of self are brought into being and new lines of individual and collective activity forged. Each of these writers asks sociologists to acknowledge that lives are full of turning points, confusions, ironies and contradictions and that the life history method is the most suitable for exploring the ambiguities, nuances, changes and richness of lived experience.

The Contextual Function The life history grounds the individual life in both the context of lived experience as well as within the broader social and economic system in which s/he lives. Person-centred data, it is claimed, throws light upon both the historical changes which have occurred during a life time, as well as the constraints bearing down upon any one life (Faraday and Plummer, 1979). Dollard (1949) makes a similar point: the life history allows us to contextualize the individual within the wider framework of historical continuity and holds out the prospect of exploring the relationship between the cultural, social structural and individually lived experience. The life history, then, whilst adding to our knowledge of processual detail by focussing on personal reality and changing interpretations, can nevertheless link the individual life and the contemporary history of society by tracing the choices, contingencies and options open to that person (Bogdan, 1974). Advocates see in the life history the prospect of formulating models which help bridge the biographical and psychological; the situational and structural; and the economic and socio-political functioning of capitalism. The individual is seen coming to terms with changes in conditions and attitudes which encompass both personal and public issues. The life history gives added meaning to the immediate by contextualizing it in the totality of a life or lives. In this view the adoption of a particular set of strategies by a teacher is wedded to autobiographical, historical and situational circumstances and can only be fully understood by reference to them.

Evaluative Function Faraday and Plummer (1979) castigated sociologists for predominately focussing on mass phenomena at the expense of the individual life histories which comprise them. They claim the life history method reasserts the complexities of lived experience and alerts researchers to issues of which there is, as yet, a poor conceptualization (for example, 'going comprehensive'). It can explore and build up sensitizing hypotheses and concepts and such data can correct, test and extend existing theory by throwing up valuable leads for future research: voices out of a particular culture or work situation can, for instance, correct the deep biases, unverified assumptions and superficiality which often clouds our thinking (Dollard, 1949). It is worth remembering that Robert E. Park held individual life history documents to be part of a wider research scheme and single contributions were evaluated in the light of the grand overall enterprise: a theory of city life. Only by building up the detailed mosaic could the interconnections of seemingly unrelated phenomena be spotted.

It is clear then, that life histories are far more than 'good stories', but can generate sensitizing concepts and contribute to conceptual frameworks and theory-building. Indeed, Becker (1966) presents life history data as a theoretical touchstone to test current theories and indicate the direction research might take. A useful concept for my purposes is that of 'critical incidents', which is elaborated by Measor (in this volume). They can set the individual off in a new direction and occasion a change of style, even identity, thus setting the tone and pace of a future career. In retrospect subjects reinterpret and bestow these with meaning so that they come to hold deep subjective truths. In talking about them people may tell us less about the event than the meaning that has been, or is being, attributed to it (Bertaux, 1981). Through them the individual reassesses priorities, gains insights, and decides on a path ahead: they help establish ideas and attitudes and, as special events, can be seen as putting meaning, organization and shape into a career and/or life.

For many Lower School teachers, comprehensivization, with its attendant changes in organization, administration, policies, location, values and norms, had been a crucial watershed in their careers and their present positions were continuously reevaluated in the light of this event of twelve years before. I intend now to examine some critical incidents in Lower School teachers' lives by drawing a distinction between the personal and institutional domains (which, in practice, interpenetrate). I hope to show how:

- life history data can deepen the ethnographer's understanding of visible, observable forms;
- critical personal and institutional shifts can have a direct impact on pedagogy and classroom processes;
- past events and those outside the ethnographer's vision can survive and be crucial touchstones for actors and their present actions;
- actors interpret and re-interpret these events and invest them with subjective truths and significance.

Below I draw on two sources of life history data: that detailing critical incidents in the career of one teacher, Mr Pickwick; and the survival in Victoria Road of the grammar and secondary modern traditions of schooling as a direct outcome of the manner in which comprehensivization had taken place over a decade earlier.

The Personal Domain: The Embittered Mr Pickwick

In talking to Lower School staff it was evident that personally memorable events, some pre-dating their teaching careers, had exerted a strong influence on those careers, guiding future actions and shaping attitudes. Sometimes a whole philosophy could be attached to a particular, clearly-recalled incident. Here is Mr Changeable, the head of Lower School, talking about his conception of himself as a schoolmaster as opposed to 'just any teacher' and recalling something which held, in retrospect, great significance for his future career:

> I remember walking through the town with my father. It was 'Good morning, sir' every few steps. He was very highly regarded and everyone knew him. He never raised his voice. When he walked into that school he had *instant* respect. He was an inspired teacher and I remember thinking that he was the kind of teacher I'd like to be. He was a schoolmaster down to his bootstraps and, as such, had high status in the community. All that's gone. Today teachers are sloppy in comparison and as a result they've lost the public's respect. The old schoolmaster ideals and skills have all but disappeared and that, to my mind, is why schools are in such a pickle.

Others located teaching in the wider context of their lives, re-evaluating their present position in the light of chance events which had impacted on their school careers. Mr Union, for instance, spoke regretfully of possible missed opportunities earlier in life:

> Teaching has always been second best for me. After the war ... I fully intended studying accountancy and insurance. I started, but it was a long

haul and I needed a secure job there and then, so I jumped into teaching. I've always been fascinated by insurance and I've always pottered around with it for NUT members, but I often think, 'If only I'd made it a career'. Then in 1948 I had the chance to go and work in insurance in South Africa, but my wife fell ill at the time. Then, over the years, she's become more and more disabled and so I've stayed in teaching, first in the sec. mod. and now in the comp. It's all been a bit of a botch-up, but I've no real regrets — or just a few perhaps!

In similar vein Mr Stern regarded teaching as an anticlimax after an earlier career as a professional footballer in the years immediately before and after the war.

A lot in life ended for me when I stopped playing league football. I've tried to replace it — I enjoy photography and I'm interested in electronics ... but teaching doesn't mean much to me, not really, although it has its moments. If I had my time over again I'd not teach. It has all been a big let down.

In Mr Pickwick's case childhood memories of attending a secondary modern and then being transferred to the grammar were still vivid and the basis for advocacy of the comprehensive (egalitarian) ideal:

I'd never been out of Stonebridge until I was 15. I went to the sec. mod. because I failed the 11 + . I'd never seen a gown until I was transferred to the grammar school. It was another world. I went home and told my mother that the kids actually worked in class, behaved themselves and that there was discipline. I said 'I've got a lot of work to catch up', and so that first term I worked and worked and I came top and they lowered my mark in history because it embarrassed them! That taught me a hell of a lot: it's one of the reasons I'm so pro-comprehensive. In the summer I came top again, but they couldn't do anything about it then! I'm still very bitter about the years I wasted in the secondary modern. Many of the teachers treated us like idiots. That is why I treat all the kids exactly the same and try to give them all something they'll succeed at. I remember just what it was like to be told you were dull. In fact I'll never forget it: I'm one of the very, very few teachers in this school to have experienced a sec. mod. as a pupil. Most of them were learning Latin in their grammars when I was working every minute of the day hoping I might catch someone's eye and get a transfer.

Mr Pickwick, on whose career I now focus, was a controversial member of the Lower School staff. Popular in the staffroom as a vociferous critic of the policy-makers in Victoria road, he was also critized for his unco-operative attitude and the fact that he put minimum effort into his teaching. His cynical, acerbic humour was a feature of staffroom life. The principle charge levied against him was that he was unprofessional, that he created an 'easy time' for himself in classes so that he could get on with his own research as a much-published local historian:

It can be easy teaching here. The same lesson can last a week. He isn't here to do a job, just to get on with his own stuff. If you ask me that's all wrong.

In fact, it's a scandal that he is allowed to use school time to do his own work. I don't know how he gets away with it! (Mr Megaphone)

The trouble with school teaching is that it depends on goodwill and co-operation. If that is withdrawn then things quickly become a mess. Mr Pickwick has withdrawn all sense of co-operation: he does the minimum and so cannot be sacked. He appears in the classroom and he keeps the kids quiet and occupied, but he doesn't actually teach much and he does absolutely nothing outside the classroom. We finish at 4.00 and he's in his car one minute later. He's last in and first out and is openly critical of staff who put their backs into the job and give their all. (Mr Changeable)

These charges were, in fact, amply borne out by my observation of his classroom and staffroom incidents I witnessed. For example:

Worksheets litter the desks: they remain a fixed feature as classes are ushered in and out. It is streamlined, production line teaching, geared to the maximum efficiency for the least teacher effort. When I mention this to Pickwick he comments: 'How else could I get on without interruption? I'm a human micro-chip! I just sweep them in and out while I try to do my own thing.' (Fieldnotes, week 3)

There was great discussion in the staffroom at break as to how long the PTA meeting would last. Pickwick made his position clear: 'I'll be here from 7.30 to 8.30, no longer! I'm not prepared to give up my own time for this place. There's nothing in my contract that says I've got to attend at all. Anyone who stays longer is a sucker!' (Fieldnotes, week 6)

Mr Pickwick readily admitted to being an embittered and frustrated teacher. After sixteen years in Victoria Road he had failed to be promoted and had, in recompense, developed a successful career as a local historian and author. He claimed that he needed to remain in the locality to carry out his research and, moreover, he was a great believer in 'roots' and had no inclination to move from his home town. As a result he no longer saw any point or purpose in teaching other than to earn a salary:

Being here is like a life-sentence. It's like being in a Russian labour camp. I've got no prospects. Megaphone was appointed over me (as deputy head of Lower School) and I've got no hope of ever being head of the history Department now, not with the present headmaster around anyway. I've got no promotion hopes here, but I don't want to leave the town. I'm stuck grinding away until I'm sixty! It's a nightmare really, a terrible predicament all round. I feel as if I've become a monk. I've resigned myself to twenty years of boredom. All that I can say for teaching is that it gives me a base so that I can do my own work. I've given up now. I don't bother anymore. I no longer regard teaching as my work. I just go through the motions.

His failure in the promotion stakes was attributed to the fact that he had consistently challenged Mr Headmaster's (himself a historian and, before his appointment, the head of History in the grammar school) definition of history teaching. History in the grammar school had been highly academic and, from the standpoint of Oxbridge entrance, highly successful. Mr Pickwick, on the other hand, had wanted to change the focus to local and industrial history and develop a range of courses which took the junior forms out of school to 'do history'. He resented the way in which the present head of Department and Mr Headmaster had combined to force him to conform to their wishes and definition of history teaching:

> 'You must have a syllabus' — that's their attitude. The Academic Registrar spends most evening propping up the bar down the Rising Sun while I'm working on my books and yet he has the sheer audacity to tell me what to teacher! You think what I could do with them if only I could do my own stuff. I could get them really interested. Instead I'm forced to teach all his crap. The trouble is that I got on with my first Head of History. He was an ideas man and he valued local history and my ideas. He encouraged me to do my own thing and innovate. He taught me a lot about teaching history, but I just can't get on with this bloke: he's just the Headmaster's stooge, his lackey. They're not interested in history, but in pumping kids full of facts for 'O' and 'A' Levels.

He presented himself as an enthusiast who had been ignored:

> I used to be keen and interested. I wrote piles of worksheets . . . it took hours, weeks, months. Now I just go through the motions, I couldn't care less. You could get a machine to do what I do now.

This claim was upheld by his colleagues. For example:

> In the early days, when he first started, he was far too easy-going and he had some discipline problems. On top of that he wanted to change things overnight. He wouldn't listen, just wanted to reform history in the grammar school. He alienated a lot of people including Mr Headmaster. They overlooked him for promotion and now he's suffering the penalty of staying here. He should have satisfied his ambitions in other schools. (Mr Jovial)

Pickwick's case was that he had been unjustly overlooked for a succession of posts:

> After years of being overlooked I turned elsewhere for my *raison d'etre*. When I first came here I was determined to make a massive success of teaching. I couldn't wait to get here. I had all sorts of ideas. I went on courses and spent evenings and weekends developing resources. What happened? Mr Headmaster never took me seriously. I've been overlooked for the head of department post on two occasions, but I thought I was sure to get the deputy headship down here (Lower School). But when Megaphone landed it that was the final straw. That's when I finally gave up. I do the bare minimum now, no more.

Furthermore, he felt he had been unjustly treated when Victoria Road had gone comprehensive:

When we became comprehensive they gave me all the low-ability history forms even though I was a graduate and teaching in the grammar school. They stuck me down here (Lower School) with all the sec. mod. rejects. They punished me because I tried to shake the History department out of its complacency. I told them (senior staff) that I couldn't do it, that I had no experience of teaching thick kids. And do you know what they said? 'You've got to learn to live with it, son!' Well, I blew my top! I told them that they were hypocrites sitting on their fat backsides pontificating and telling me I'd have to 'learn to live with it' when they themselves had no idea how to deal with low-ability kids. I got nowhere and I learned that you either take the crumbs they throw at you in this place and make the best of it, or you lump it and get hurt. That's why I'm so cynical both about teaching and the people who mismanage this school. That's why I knock it all the time.

The outcome was that he was locked in an acrimonious conflict with Mr Megaphone, a non-academic, college-trained PE teacher whom Pickwick looked down upon as unworthy of the deputy headship of Lower School:

The highpoint of this term, besides all the lovely time we had off because of the snow and the NUPE action, was when Bill Changeable was off with a bad back and that idiot Megaphone tried to assert himself. He started to strut around here as if he owned the place! He ticked me off one day for not going into assembly to hear him make a fool of himself. I told him to get stuffed! I said I didn't want to embarrass him by bursting out laughing! No one took any notice of him. No one liked the obvious way he put himself forward as the big chief. The place started to go to pieces, it was great! He was ignored, cold-shouldered and the kids got the message too and started to run wild. In the end the headmaster had to write down from Upper School saying that Megaphone was in control and would staff please obey him! When Bill Changeable came back it took him a week to clear up the mess.

By the time I observed his classes he had developed his outside interests to such a degree that they had replaced teaching as his principal interest in terms of enthusiasm, commitment and time, so much so that teaching was no more than an irksome necessity to earn a salary. His real career now lay elsewhere:

I just haven't got a moment to spare. I've got more than a lifetime's work ahead of me . . . But, God, I get depressed! I'm losing out to people who've got more time and resources. I'm stuck wasting my time here trying to fit my own work in around lessons, reports, parents' evenings, staff meetings and all that crap!

The Institutional Domain: Echoes of the Amalgamation

The formation of Victoria Road had been achieved through the amalgamation of a number of secondary moderns with the grammar school to form a comprehensive of over 2,000 boys. A true understanding of the undercurrents and staff relations in Lower School was only possible in relation to that event, which still impinged on the lives of teachers, many of whom had not been there at the time. It was still talked about, both directly and obliquely: for example, on the second day of my fieldwork I was introduced to Mr Union and the following, at the time mystifying, exchange took place:

Mr Union:	Are you an art teacher?
JB:	No.
Mr Union:	Craft — woodwork, metalwork all that?
JB:	No, I'm afraid not. Why?
Mr Union:	Well, if you were, you'd be head here (in Lower School) by now! [Laughter] Tell me, what is your subject by the way?
JB:	English.
Mr Union:	I see! Well, you'd be like me — helping the caretaker! [Laughter]

Mr Jovial was later to explain what had been meant:

Peter Montgomery was the first headmaster of the new comprehensive in 1966. He had the difficult job of integrating the grammar staff and the sec. mod. teachers. He had a great belief in the value of the practical arts and so he appointed craft and art teachers and such like to be head of year, and of Lower and Middle School. He saw them as blending the imaginative and the practical — something naive like that! That's how Bill (Mr Change-able) got his job — he used to teach art. It was little to do with talent, but being in the right place at the right time. The next thing was that people who'd been wielding a paint brush or a chisel one term were sitting behind a desk issuing orders the next! The whole business caused a lot of bitterness and a number of good people were overlooked.

Comprehensivization left a teacher like Mr Jovial with split loyalties: a former secondary modern teacher, he was a also an old boy of the grammar school and held its reputation in nostalgic awe:

This used to be a famous school. The headmaster was a national figure and Dr Fleming wrote science textbooks that were used throughout the country. It was one of the first schools to introduce economics onto the curriculum. Its Oxbridge record matched many of the smaller public schools.

The passing of the tripartite system, of which he had been a supporter, had deprived him of what had been his main inspiration and purpose in teaching:

I was known in this town as Mr Transfer. Nothing gave me more pleasure than to push on bright kids so that they got transferred to the grammar. I took enormous pride in that. The sec. mods. were chock full of bright kids and, in my view, instead of abandoning the tripartite system they should have made the transfer work more efficiently on a year by year basis. It was like the 11 +, it gave both teacher and kids something to aim for. Now there's nothing but this mixed ability mish-mash and there's no reward for excellence and that, my friend, is very wrong.

Mr Changeable, appointed as Lower School Head, commented on what had been a critical watershed both in his career and in the careers of all the secondary modern teachers swept up in the amalgamation:

Some of the senior staff look down on those, myself included, who were in the sec. mods. when we all amalgamated to form the comprehensive. They regarded us as a threat to what they held to be their province, their little academic empire! The jealousy when I took over as head down here was quite blatant! 'What, a sec. mod. man as Lower School head!' One chap, who is still here, said I was incapable of doing the job and was even talking of complaining to the Governors and involving the press and God knows what! And these attitudes still exist: twelve years later they still exist. They are perpetuated by the old grammar staff who landed most of the top jobs and came off by far the best in the amalgamation. Now they appoint new staff and the university people, the grammar school types, do all the exam work and the sixth form teaching; and the college teachers, the sec. mod. types, do all the general work with the lower forms. Yet Mr Headmaster will tell you that we are a fully developed, integrated comprehensive. If that's the case I'm Mohammed Ali!

Although the amalgamation had led to Mr Changeable's promotion, for other secondary modern teachers it resulted in demotion and spoiled careers:

If it had not been for the amalgamation I would have been a head. I was a deputy in Springfield (secondary modern) but when I came here it was back to the drawing board as a teacher of junior maths. Salary was safeguarded, of course, and there were promises, promises, but the money wasn't important. What was important was that I was still under fifty and I knew my career was finished. I was a sec. mod. man and when they did for them they did for me! It's been 'head down and roll on retirement' since then. (Mr Stern)

Some of the grammar school-oriented staff who taught in Lower School as 'visitors' kept alive the criticisms surrounding Mr Changeable's appointment:

What is he (Changeable) anyway? He's only a head of year, nothing more! The way he behaves you'd think he was important. He's got no degree, no formal qualifications for the job. It was only luck that got him the job in the first place. If it was today he wouldn't stand a chance. He hasn't got the temperament for the post — he's too tense and has to do everything singlehanded. (Mrs Fashion)

All of the former secondary modern teachers made it clear what a difficult period this had been for them as they had felt 'on trial', under scrutiny by their new and more prestigious colleagues:

They (the grammar school staff) were frightened of the less able and we were afraid of the very bright. They were tricky days I can tell you. There was very little fraternizing that September. (Mr Union)

The fact that they eventually won through and proved their worth was still a talking point amongst them:

At first we (secondary modern teachers) were seen as a liability. After six months the then headmaster came to me and said how impressed he was by the schoolmastery of many of the sec. mod. teachers. That was music to my ears, I can tell you. We'd proved ourselves. (Mr Changeable)

The consequences of the amalgamation still reverberated throughout Lower School, shaping its atmosphere and daily functioning. For example, Mr Changeable was in a position to impose upon his staff his particular definition of schoolmastery. He was fiercely dismissive of colleagues who:

- did not, or could not, keep order and decorum in class;
- did not engage in transmission teaching;
- threatened Lower School discipline and routine;
- were disorganized, unpunctual or untrustworthy;
- dressed or behaved in an unprofessional manner;
- were not committed to the job;
- did not support him and assist in the general smooth-running of Lower School.

He was highly distrustful of the female and younger members of staff on these grounds:

If you pushed me, yes, I'd have to say that women in my view do not on the whole, make as effective teachers as men. But before the *Women's Guardian* sends someone to stone me, let me add that there are very many exceptions, including one or two here, and that I am talking in particular about working in *this* school and not in schools generally. This school is a large boys' school, the majority of the staff are men, and the ethos is male. Women often prove to be a liability and that is why they are shunted off down here to me in Lower School. I have to find them jobs because they can't cope with bloody-minded third, fourth and fifth years! In my view a lot of the women and — let's be fair — some of the men, especially some of the younger, more irresponsible ones, let the side down. They're no longer schoolmasters or schoolmistresses, but teachers who couldn't give a damn as long as the cheque is waiting for them at the end of the month. The old skills, the old self-respect, are fast disappearing and the motivation for excellence on all the scores just isn't there.

Moreover, he remained an energetic defender of what he held to be the epitome of schoolmastery — the secondary modern 'tradition':

The head of Toryton School and his deputy came here sneering. 'We
don't want to make the same mistakes as you when we go comprehensive'
— that was their attitude. 'We want to retain the best of the grammar
school tradition', the Deputy said, 'and play down the secondary modern
side of things'. Well, I stood up for the sec. mod. tradition and I wouldn't
give an inch on that one! I wasn't prepared to see the real achievements of
the secondary moderns written off in that condescending, ignorant way. 'I
know, I was there', as Max Boyce would say.

Similarly, the other former secondary modern teachers in Lower School looked
back nostalgically on their pre-comprehensive days:

There's 120+ staff in this school, we seldom meet, we share three
staffrooms on three sites. What I miss is the community spirit of the old
secondary moderns. It's all impersonal now, it's all too big, and there's
barriers, barriers, barriers. In the sec. mod. we didn't have fancy buildings,
but we had a sense of purpose and cohesion that's lacking now. (Mr Union)

Nothing offended Mr Changeable's notion of schoolmastery as much as Miss
Floral's drama lessons. His open antipathy towards drama — its apparent dis-
organization, noise and ill-discipline — predated Miss Floral's arrival:

I'm afraid Bill (Mr Changeable) has pushed her from the start. There was a
huge clash of personalities between him and her predecessor. Marianne was
literally larger than life — she was huge and domineering. She'd stroll into
the school at all times and used to hold drama in the hall and make a
tremendous racket. She was a dance specialist and she'd jump around
banging a tambourine. Bill hated it all and he just couldn't see eye to eye
with her. When Karen Floral came he tried to control things from the start.
He moved drama out of the hall into a classroom and he makes no secret
that if he had his way it wouldn't be on the timetable. He just doesn't see
the point of it. In some ways I think he feels she's working against him and
being unprofessional. (Mrs Paint)

Both Mr Changeable and the Deputy Head, Mr Megaphone, regularly intervened in
drama to quieten classes. The latter related such an incident:

Karen Floral doesn't do that (establish teacher domination) and so she never
actually gets around to doing any worthwhile teacher. All the year she's
battling the challenges, she's never in control of her own classes . . . There
are quite a few like that — they can't cope and make the job more difficult
for Bill (Mr Changeable) and myself. All the women, with the possible
exception of Mrs Calm, ought to be sacked for their failure to control their
classes. They're bedlam! Many's the time this year that Bill or I have tapped
on a door with some trumped-up reason for entering in order to shut the
kids up. One day Bill had the chairman of the Governors in his room and
he was sitting about six feet from this guy and he couldn't make out what
he was saying because of the kids shouting and clapping in drama. He had

the embarrassment of having to go out, give Floral a rocket, belt a few kids' mouths shut, and then return to a bloke who all the time must have been thinking, 'What kind of place is this?' For as conscientious a schoolmaster as Bill Changeable it was a real smack in the chops and degrading. They let the side down.

Miss Floral, in turn, resented what she saw as a concerted anti-drama campaign orchestrated by Mr Changeable:

The other day I took my drama class out into the yard. The freedom was immense. I had a few funny looks from people passing, but the kids had a great time and really did some good work. I was pleased, but when I came back in they were all in the staffroom saying that they wished they could get out into the sun, but they had work to do, serious work to do, and a syllabus to follow, and it was okay if you were just entertaining kids rather than educating them. Okay, it wasn't said as openly as that, but it was implied. There's no way in which drama in this school is ever going to be seen as more than just a lark, a jolly knock around. It's sad, but that's the way it is: I'm forced to accept that as a sad fact of life . . . That I'm on a hiding to nothing . . . I'm just in the wrong school, doing the wrong thing, in the wrong way — at least that's the way I see it. In another school it might be the right thing, in the right way, but not here!

Against her wishes and better judgment she had been forced to tighten up on discipline and drop much improvization for writing and teacher-pupil discussion. After eighteen months in the school she concluded that:

What I'd like to do in drama and what I'm allowed to do I realize now are two very different things . . . A lot of them (pupils) misbehave because they are told by some teachers that drama is a laugh, a load of cobblers! So I'm forced to so-call 'discipline' them in a way totally opposed to the spirit and purpose of drama. What else can I do when every moment of the day Bill Changeable is snooping around checking up on me and wielding his noisemeter!

Mr Changeable interpreted this as promising evidence of successful socializ-ation into the ways of Lower School.

There's far less trouble in drama now that she's got over some of her delusions concerning drama. She's beginning to realize that some of the things they teach you in college just don't work in the classrom situation. As far as I'm concerned 1Y has made her grow up as a teacher. I see a glimmer of hope on the horizon now whereas a few months ago I must admit I was near encouraging her to 'move on', as they say. You see, I've seen all this happen before: it's a wonder what a bit of roughing-up, experience, maturity — call it what you will — can do to a young, idealistic member of staff. She was trying too much too soon with the wrong material. 1Y saw drama as a gold opportunity to run riot and make life hell for her. She's being far more realistic about things this term, I'm pleased to say.

Miss Floral, however, saw the situation in a very different light:

As far as I'm concerned I'm being forced to give up much drama because I've got no one to turn to for any support. All I get are sneers and cheap jokes from the staff and I'm being persecuted by Bill Changeable. He doesn't believe in drama and won't rest until I have them sitting in rows.

By the end of her second year in teaching Miss Floral was looking for another school. Moreover, annoyed by the constraints placed upon her she, like Mr Pickwick before her, was starting a parallel career;

I'm taking on a lot of production work in the Cityton Youth Centre — two nights a week. It keeps me going and reminds me that drama in this school is just a bad experience. Elsewhere it would be very different.

Mr Changeable could be seen to belong to the conservative wing of the secondary modern tradition, akin to Grace's (1978) authoritarian teachers with their emphasis on organizational ability, social control, domestication, and distrust of innovation. He sought to impose upon all Lower School staff his own code of pupil obedience and regimentation. Miss Floral offended all his 'good' teacher norms and so was pressured to tone down her 'experiments'. This is in line with Hammersley (1981), who shows the influence that could be exerted on individuals to adopt the predominant staff view concerning the treatment of pupils, the fear being that even minor deviations could undermine the whole moral order of the school. This clash was inevitable as long as Miss Floral accorded priority in drama to pupil collaboration, initiative and action in a context in which schoolmastery demanded silence, rote learning and the teacher-orchestrated response. In an institution pervaded by what Hargreaves (1982) has termed 'autonomous individualism', competence was attributed only to those who could be seen to manage alone: in these circumstances a high level of noise was interpreted as an indicator of gross incompetence (cf. Denscombe, 1980).

Conclusion

The micro-politics of teachers' daily lives and careers must, I have argued, be seriously examined not merely as background to classroom processes, but as an essential key to understanding them. Too often a wedge is driven between teachers and teaching and the latter reduced, unrealistically, to role performance divorced of subjectivity. Furthermore, such an approach ignores the phases and shifting perspectives within careers which reflect personal and institutional changes. Whereas Shipman (1973) warns researchers against becoming too embroiled in the 'trivia' of school life, educational ethnographers over the past decade have demonstrated the value of doing otherwise and committed themselves to 'grounded theory'. The life history, through its subjective, contextual and evaluative functions, can add a valuable dimension to this work, placing the people, personalities and events behind the situations, strategies and processes into the centre of the research enterprise. Better progress might then be made towards formulating theories that draw links between the circumstances with which teachers cope and the demands imposed upon them (what Woods (1983) sees as the 'second age' of educational ethnography). Although I started gathering the data quoted in this chapter as background to classroom observation, I came to regard it as necessary to explicate what I was observing in classes. Initial encounters revealed, for instance, Mr Pickwick intent on creating an 'easy life' for himself by establishing a rigid routine based on a bank of worksheets, whilst Miss Floral's attempts to implement an active, improvization-based drama pedagogy were tempered by the constraints imposed upon her in environment of schoolmastery.

Teachers, I have argued, should not be treated as if they are cardboard cut-outs: behind teaching lies a range of attitudes, motives and emotions, and life history material can tell us much about the socio-historical, institutional and personal influences on a career. It can help the ethnographer locate teaching in a wider temporal and inter-personal framework, incorporating external events that have diverted career trajectories (for example, chance domestic factors or changes in the national economy) and pinpoint crucial benchmarks and phases in a career (witness Mr Pickwick's move from teacher enthusiast to cynical time-server, and Miss Floral's from drama evangelist towards calculating realist). Little is yet known about such matters as:

- factors at work during comprehensivization and school amalgamation and their long term effects on teachers;
- the pressures (inter-personal, institutional and external) on teachers to modify their teaching;
- the processes by which young teachers (for example, Miss Floral) are socialized into the 'real world' of teaching;
- how teachers react to truncated careers and status deprivation;
- the development of the 'parallel' (compensatory) career and its effect on teaching;
- the means whereby a group (for example, former secondary modern teachers in Lower School) retains its identity in a hostile enironment;
- the influence of headteachers and other reality definers on individual careers;
- the historical bases for occupational splits, enmities and alliances in the staffroom;
- the impact of 'critical incidents' in an institution's history on its teachers;
- episodes in lives outside classrooms that occasion changes in attitudes and pedagogies.

We need to know far more about these and other matters before we are in a position to formulate adequately grounded theories about teaching and teachers.

Finally, this paper supports an accumulating body of evidence that suggests that comprehensivization has often involved teachers with very different ideologies and interpretative frameworks borne of long experience in the ways of the secondary moderns and grammar schools being summarily brought together under the roof of the 'common school'. Not only has this frequently proved a most damaging experience for individuals in personal and career terms (although for others, not documented in this paper, it was a very positive experience leading to career advancement) it can be claimed that it has skewed the whole development and operating of contemporary secondary schooling. Teachers brought different historical loyalties, values, educational goals and self-images with them: alienated, driven into a corner and suffering career stagnation, former secondary modern staff have often reacted by forming themselves into an obstructive pressure group. Furthermore, this ideological and occupational schism is often perpetuated by new recruits who enter divided staffrooms and are compelled to take sides, or find themselves placed in a particular camp through their training, qualifications and enhanced or depressed career prospects.

Acknowledgements

I would like to thank Stephen Ball both for his helpful comments on an earlier draft of this paper and for alerting me to Arfwedson's work; Helen Beynon and Aletha Powell for typing the manuscript; and the staff of Lower School. I can only hope that they would approve of what I have made of the data they so openly provided in my many conversations with them.

References

ARFWEDSON, G. *et al.* (1979) *Skolan och Lärana*, Stockholm, Institoner för pedagogik.
BALL, S. (1981) *Beachside Comprehensive*, Cambridge, Cambridge University Press.
BALL, S. (1984) School politics, teachers' careers and educational change. Paper delivered at Westhill College Conference, January.
BECKER, H. (1952) 'The career of the Chicago public schoolteacher', HAMMERSLEY, M. and WOODS, P. (Eds) *The Process of Schooling*, London, Routledge and Kegan Paul.
BECKER, H. and GEAR, B. (1960) 'Latent culture', in COSIN, B. *et al.* (Eds) *School and Society: A Sociological Reader*, London, Routledge and Kegan Paul.
BECKER, H. (1966) 'Introduction' to SHAW, C.R., *The Jack Roller*, Chicago, University of Chicago Press.
BERTAUX, D. (1981) *Biography and Society*, London, Sage.
BEYNON, J. (1981) *Poor Miss Floral: The micro-politics of drama teacher* (Paper delivered at St Hilda's College Conference, Oxford, September.).
BEYNON, J. (1985) *Initial Encounters in a Comprehensive School*, Lewes, Falmer Press.
BOGDAN, R. (1974) *Being Different: The Autobiography of Jane Fry*, London, Wiley.
BOGDAN, R. and TAYLOR, S. (1970) *Introduction To Qualitative Research Methods*, London, Wiley.
BURGESS, R.G. (1983) *Experiencing Comprehensive Education*, London, Methuen.
DENSCOMBE, M. (1980) 'The significance of noise for the practical activity of teaching', in WOODS, P. (Ed.) *Teacher Strategies*, London, Croom Helm.
DOLLARD, J. (1949) *Criteria For The Life History*, New Haven, Yale University Press.

FARADAY, A. and PLUMMER, K. (1979) 'Doing life histories', *Sociological Review*, **27**, 4. pp. 773–793.

GOODSON, I.F. (1982) *School Subjects And Curriculum Change*, London, Croom Helm.

GOODSON, I.F. (1983) 'The use of life histories in the study of teaching, in HAMMERSLEY M. (Ed.) *The Ethnography of Schooling*, Driffield, Nafferton.

GRACE, G. (1978) *Teachers, Ideology and Control*, London, Routledge and Kegan Paul.

HAMMERSLEY, M. (1981) 'Ideology in the staffroom?' in BARTON, L. and WALKER, S. (Eds) *Schools, Teachers and Teaching*, Lewes, Falmer Press.

HARGREAVES, D. (1980) 'The occupational culture of teachers' in WOODS, P. (Ed.) *Teacher Strategies*, London, Croom Helm.

HARGREAVES, D. (1982) *The Challenge For The Comprehensive School*, London, Routledge and Kegan Paul.

HILSUM, S. & STMART, K.P. (1974) *Promotion And Careers in Teaching*, Slough, NFER.

HOYLE, E. (1982) 'Micropolitics of educational organizations', *Educational Management and Administration*, **10**, 2, pp. 87–98.

LACEY, C. (1970) *Hightown Grammar*, Manchester, Manchester University Press.

MANKOFF, M. (1971) 'Societal reaction and career deviance', *Sociological Quarterly*, **12**, pp. 204–18.

MEASOR, L. (1984) *Critical Incidents in the Classroom*.

REYNOLDS, D. and SULLIVAN, M. (1979) 'Bringing schools back' in BARTON, L. and MEIGHAN, R. (Ed.) *Schools, Pupils and Deviance*, Driffield, Nafferton.

RISEBOROUGH, G.F. (1981) Teacher careers and comprehensive schooling, *Sociology*, **15**, 3, pp. 352–380.

SHIPMAN, M. (1973) Bias in the Sociology of Education, *Educational Review*, **25**, pp. 190–200.

SMITH, L. and KEITH, P. (1971) *Anatomy Of An Educational Innovation*, London, Wiley.

THOMAS, W.I. and ZNANIECKI, F. (1972) *The Polish Peasant In Europe and America*, New York, City Press.

TURNER, G. (1983) *Pupil Activity In A Comprehensive School*, London, Croom Helm.

WALKER, R. and ADELMAN, C. (1976) '*Strawberries*' in STUBBS, M. and DELAMONT, S. (Eds) *Explorations In Classroom Observation*, London, Wiley.

WILENSKY, H.L. and EDWARDS, H. (1959) 'The skidders' in *American Sociological Review*, **24**, pp. 215–31.

WOODS, P. (1979) *The Divided School*, London, Routledge & Kegan Paul.

WOODS, P. (1981) 'Making and breaking the teacher role' in BARTON, L. and WALKER, S. (Eds) *Schools, Teachers and Teaching*, Lewes, Falmer Press.

WOODS, P. (1983) *Sociology And The School*, London, Routledge and Kegan Paul.

Educational Innovators: A Decade and a Half Later

Louis M. Smith, Paul F. Kleine, David C. Dwyer and John J. Prunty

Editors' Note: This paper is based on the project *Innovation and Change in American Education —
Kensington Revisited: A Fifteen Year Follow-Up of an Innovative Elementary School and Its Faculty*
supported by NIE grant G78-0074. The analysis and interpretation represent official policy of
neither the National Institute of Education nor the Milford School District.

The research reported in this chapter is drawn from a much larger study of
innovation and change in American education. It began as *Kensington Revisited: A
Fifteen Year Follow-Up of an Innovative School and Its Faculty*, and ended as a six
volume report, *Innovation and Change in American Education* (Smith, Prunty, Dwyer,
and Kleine, 1984). The particular volume from which these data and ideas are taken
is, *Educational Innovators: Then and Now*, devoted to a follow-up of the faculty of the
original Kensington School.

That original study, *Anatomy of Educational Innovation* (Smith and Keith, 1971),
was a lone ethnographic account of the first year in the life of the innovative
Kensington Elementary School. By innovative, we mean it was an attempt to bring
'the new elementary education' of the 1960s to a middle class suburban elementary
school. The innovative facets included: (i) a child centered philosophy with its
concerns for internal rather than external motivation; (ii) a multi-age, continuous
progress organizational scheme with Divisions (Basic Skills, Transition, and
Independent Study) rather than grade levels; (iii) an individualized program of
curriculum and instruction; (iv) a team teaching staff organization; (v) an open space
architectural building; (vi) democratic administration; and (vii) a talented faculty
assembled from across the country.

The intent of the present study began innocently enough: We wanted to find the
original faculty of Kensington, trace their intellectual and geographical meanderings
and learn something about the nature of educational reformers and educational
innovation. We phrased the problem as follows in the original proposal:

> In regard to the follow up of the original faculty members, the first round of
> questions/foreshadowed problems would include:

1   Where did the faculty go? What have they done? What are they doing now?
2   What role did the Kensington experience play in their lives? How do they see the experience now?
3   What is their general educational perspective now? What is their point of view about educational innovation? (Proposal p. 5)

Methodological Issues

As can be inferred from our opening comments we had phrased our problem around careers and life experiences subsequent to the first year of Kensington of some twenty teachers and administrators. From the first interview, partly out of our unstructured approach, partly out of seeing old friends from years ago, and partly from a never ending and unbounded kind of curiosity, we talked of many more events. The early lives of our subjects/colleagues/friends flowed easily and naturally. We were into life histories immediately and the phrasing of our problem shaded off into broader and deeper channels.

More specifically, we undertook the development of those biographical life histories of participants based on two to seven hour taped interviews sometimes conducted by one of us, sometimes by the other but usually conducted by two of us (Smith and Kleine) present in the interview. Further, we had career resumes from some of the individuals who had recently changed jobs. Finally, a few of the faculty members had written and published on topics relevant to Kensington; we tried to gather and read a good bit of this material.

Finding the People

In our original proposal we rather blithely described our task to '. . . locate, observe, and interview the two dozen key administrators and teachers who originated the school'. By rather circuitous routes this search mission was accomplished and we smiled as we recalled Skeels' (1966, p. 28) advice concerning 'flexibility, ingenuity, and tenacity' as qualities to assist in the search. Upon reflection those are characteristics deemed useful and we would underscore tenacity as perhaps the greatest virtue.

Our search could be described as a series of post holes drilled into our social and professional networks with the pursuit of leads from each drilling until we reached a dead end. We then repeated the drilling in a new location. The first and easiest step was to locate the several people who had resided in the immediate vicinity and could be located through the telephone directory. This step was easily accomplished, but our hopes for an intricate network of Christmas card lists or other forms of address links were quickly dashed. We found, rather surprisingly, that very few links existed among the participants. In this initial foray, two couples and two individuals have remained in close contact with one another but beyond these pairs, at this time, the routes from Kensington were varied and disparate.

In addition to these individuals still in the area, another group of participants was known to us as a result of professional contacts since Kensington and hence, easily reached. This group, all male, included the former Principal, Superintendent, and Curriculum Director who have maintained professional association membership. In general, their whereabouts were known to the researchers even though only a few contacts had been maintained during the fifteen year interval. One of the teachers was located through a chance event growing out of a national conference. A former participant of Kensington noted the Washington University label on a name tag of a colleague of the senior author and inquired about him. This led to an exchange of letters and his eventual participation in the study. Again, rather surprisingly, there was practically no interchange between and among members of this group during the fifteen year period.

Our next venture led us to a graduate school which had been known to be the next stop for two of our participants. One individual was immediately located but the other eluded us because of name changes. We were struck by the impact of name changes upon professional identities. Beyond making life difficult for researchers the larger issue of women 'disappearing' due to marriage and the distinct possibility of being under represented in research pools of this nature was a challenge which we chose to meet head on. We were determined to find everyone in spite of this difficulty.

We attempted to trace individuals forward in time from their last known address after leaving Kensington but apparently too many moves had been made by our highly mobile staff to achieve results by this method. Failing in our efforts to move forward in time we went back to original records and phoned parents of participants who were listed in the cumulative folders stored in a back room of the Milford School District Central Office. This ploy yielded several current addresses and phone numbers and in addition located the one individual who had current addresses of five participants as a result of Christmas card exchanges. The 'unlocking' of this group then provided us with enough new post holes to complete our search.

Two rather isolated efforts are worthy of mention in that they might be overlooked. One individual was particularly difficult to locate until a call was made to the church in the individual's home town which had been listed in the original records. Even though no living relatives of the individual were still in the area we were pleasantly surprised to learn that the individual in question had married, returned home, and was an active member of the church. Secretaries again demonstrated their value as repositories of information. A second effort involved pursuing other listings in a small town with the same last name as the participant on the chance that an uncle or cousin might assist us in our search and this yielded our 'missing' person. Ultimately we reached all but two: one individual, a young woman, had died recently. The other individual's whereabouts remain unknown.

The Life History Vehicle

We share the concerns and trepidations expressed by White (1952) in his classic study *Lives in Progress* regarding the frail vessels in which research data must be gathered.

Each method, regardless of its position on the quantitative or qualitative, the structured or unstructured, the controlled or naturalistic continua, has its peculiar assets and liabilities. White expressed his concern as follows:

> . . . it will be clear that the study of another person is a difficult undertaking which cannot be handled in a cut-and-dried fashion. Perhaps the very first thing to consider is the other person's motivation for taking part in such a study. Unless his interest is enlisted to a rather unusual extent he is not likely to be disposed toward whole-hearted participation and candid self-disclosure. Even when cooperation is perfect, a further difficulty arises from the very nature of the material. No interviews or available tests, no existing methods of observation, can possibly be considered complete or definitive. Furthermore, all methods yield information of a sort that leaves much to be judged and interpreted by the examiners. In this way the frailties of the examiners enter the study and constitute a liability in reaching valid conclusions. It clearly behoves us to reflect a little on what is involved in trying to understand other people. (pp. 92–93)

Balanced against those cautions is the compelling power and richness of life histories for our purposes. In addition to the fascination and richness of life histories for their own sake, we were drawn to them as ideal for our purpose of exploring the experiences which occurred between the time of the original study and the current life space of our teachers and staff. In effect, we had entered the lives of twenty-one professional educators at a point in time when they were beginning an exciting venture of developing the Kensington School and then we returned fifteen years later to again collect data in an intensive one or two day interview. These two studies were similar to selecting two frames from a full length movie for inspection and making comparisons and contrasts between them. Of utmost importance for our study was the inference of processes prior to and since the original Kensington. For example, we were puzzled by the origins of educational ideology which culminated in the decision to respond to the exciting and frustrating venture of building a new and different school. What varied routes did our educators take as they were being socialized on the farms and in the hamlets of this country? Similarly, what had occurred during the fifteen year interim to influence the maintenance and/or modification of these same educational perspectives? In short, could we learn anything about the thousands of frames which made up the full reel of our participants' life movie?

Becker (1966) provided further support as he argued persuasively for the life history approach in the following words:

> We can, for instance, give people a questionnaire at two periods of their life and infer an underlying process of change from the differences in their answers. But our interpretation has significance only if our imagery of the underlying process is accurate. And this accuracy of imagery — this congruence of theoretically posited process with what we could observe if we took the necessary time and trouble — can be partially achieved by the

use of life history documents. For the life history, if it is well done, will give us the details of that process whose character we would otherwise only be able to speculate about, the process to which our data must ultimately be referred if they are to have theoretical and not just an operational and predictive significance. (p. XIV)

We would particularly stress the use of life history sketches for unraveling threads as intricate as motive structures and personal value systems. For instance, to ask participants to state reasons for undertaking the original task of building Kensington after fifteen years have passed is to invite superficial and self-serving answers. The answers themselves are current word moulds but the original castings may have long since submerged from sight or recall. However, those current moulds are more likely to be interpretable within a life history which dredges up childhood dreams and disappointments. A participant may recall joining the faculty because at that point in her life she was somewhat bored and sought a new challenge while playing down any latent zeal to foster social reform. This same participant might weave a fascinating story of a childhood spent righting wrongs, mending birds' wings and serving as a resident story teller for young children which suggests a more active motive structure than alleviation of boredom.

Our commitment to the use of life history material is clearly strong and enthusiastic and not born out of a lack of a 'better' method for data collection. It grew out of our initial yet evolving conception of our problem.

Emergent Themes

Introduction

In the complete report of this study, *Educational Innovators Then and Now: The Original Faculty of the Kensington Elementary School*, we finally settled on several broad themes to interpret our life histories. The first was 'Educational Careers: People and Positions Over Time'. This tended to be a more outside, behavioral view of what has happened to our innovators over the last fifteen years. The second theme, elaborated in the complete report, was really a further analysis and interpretation of the career theme. We have called it 'Issues in Careers' and extended the discussion with reference to 'Rethinking teaching as a woman's career', 'Reformers as administrators', and an old issue 'PhD programs: Do it and forget it'.

The third theme, 'The Natural History of Belief Systems', has had a more tumultuous time in its construal and development. It began with our early observations in 1964–5 of the staff as a group of true believers, men and women of fanatical faith in a cause. In the current analysis we had difficulty deciding whether the accent was on 'true' or on 'belief' or on 'the person', which seemed to be the, components of true believer. Two preliminary generalizations arose from our data. First, we were surprised at the religious backgrounds of the individuals in our group and we began to think and talk about 'Educational Reform as Secular Religion'.

This was doubly surprising in that we used a number of religious or quasi-religious concepts — true belief, commitment, crusader, pursuit of the Holy Grail — in our earlier account, *Anatomy of Educational Innovation*. Secondly, we were surprized by the fact that these innovative, *avant garde*, change the world types '*do* go home again.' Many, after years of wandering about the country, returned to places of origin. The issue was not even on our minds initially. Geographically, intellectually, and attitudinally they returned to their origins, reverted to more basic values in greater numbers and to a larger degree than we would have guessed even if we had thought about it at all. That suggested the possibility of very basic personality dispositions at work. These items plus other clusters of data and other low level abstractions led us gradually to formulate the broader, more abstract 'Natural History of Belief Systems'. This theme broke into (i) some introductory remarks on currents beliefs; (ii) the complexity of belief systems, (iii) the origins, development and transformation of belief systems; and (iv) the you-*do*-go-home-again them. Finally, we raised conclusions and implications about belief systems, about educational innovation, and about the relation between the two. The most fundamental of these implications became a concern for the reconstrual of the perspectives on educational innovation as summarized by House (1979).

In short, this very unusual group of educators was seen from the outside perspective of their careers or positions over time. The inside perspective accented the conception of belief systems. We tried for a look at the natural history of its structure and content. We thought that such views provided a major elaboration of current views of educational innovation.

Educational Reform as Secular Religion: The Complex Nature of Belief Systems

Throughout our methodological essays we have commented on the strange path of creativity as one does qualitative field work. Now in our life history materials the strange career of creativity recurs. Nowhere has that been more clear than our coming to the hunch, hypothesis, or theme 'Educational Reform as Secular Religion'. In a sense it should have been obvious from our original work, *Anatomy of Educational Innovation*. One of our key explanatory concepts was 'true believer', from Hoffer's (1951) work. Similarly we resonated to Klapp's (1969) concept of 'crusaders'. And we dragged in a few of our own, eg. 'pursuit of the holy grail' and 'testimonials'. In a sense, we took those concepts as 'givens', items brought to the organization by this unusual staff. In an ahistorical way we treated the items as assumptions. In retrospect, this seemed to be the stance taken by the organization, the Kensington School and the Milford District, as it started on its way to create a school. We did not make true belief problematic and we did not ask ourselves: Why did people like this come to Kensington? Nor did we ask: What makes people this way? Further, we were still working heavily from a more behaviouristic, functionalist, outside, non-interfering perspective. We tended to observe more than to interview. We were not consciously and intensively pursuing the 'inner perspective'; the world of interrelated beliefs and feelings, except for those that erupted into overt behavior and interaction. An interpretive metatheory or paradigm was, at best, implicit.

In our follow-up study of the faculty, which was mostly an intensive interview-oriented attempt to obtain life histories from an inner perspective, we found religion. Religion seemed everywhere. Beyond all the particulars of several faculty studying for the ministry, one being born again, another finding 'all the truth you need to know in this one book, the Holy Bible', and others with twenty year histories of teaching Sunday School and adult Bible classes, the hypothesis that emerged involved the conversion of religious motivation, ideals, and actions into the world of educational reform. In effect, our general claim is that 'educational reform is secularized religion'. In this section we try to look into the nooks and crannies of this hunch and capture its meaning. In a sense, this is a kind of interpretive anthropology or psychology, a thick description as Geertz (1973) might use the term.

There can be little doubt that the original staff shared a strong idealogical commitment which grew out of a rather intense religious socialization. Consider the following:

1   The Superintendent of the District and the Principal he selected to implement the school were fellow Bible Class students for several years earlier in their careers. The close church contacts led to family social exchanges and some years later the working relationship in the Milford district.

2   A staff member had been active as a youth lay minister and maintained the ministerial function in addition to his career as an educator.

3   One staff member spent his youth in various Jewish youth and athletic groups and has maintained a position of leadership in his temple.

4   One staff member, in addition to an active church life is married to an ex-seminarian with several years of theological training.

5   One faculty member was active in the preaching ministry just prior to undertaking graduate work in education which led to employment at Kensington.

6   Another staff member completed undergraduate work in theology, attended Divinity school, and served a year as an intern in the parish ministry before joining the Kensington staff.

7   Another staff member had plans after high school to become an agricultural missionary following a very active involvement in his local church.

In addition to these specific examples of religious involvement the role of religion in early socialization was obvious in most of the remaining interviews as well. Nor was the significance of the religious socialization lost on the participants themselves. The tenor and context of the missionary theme follows in a teacher's comment:

So, the religious thing, let me go back to when I was a child 'cause this did affect what I did at Kensington. I grew up in a Baptist Church, my mother was a Catholic, my father was a Protestant who never went to church and somehow we ended up going to a Baptist church, and I became very involved in the church as a child, and I grew up in the church and was active in the church through high school. I was so active and so committed that when I left high school and started college my goal was to become an agricultural missionary.

One faculty member, Tom Mack the Curriculum Coordinator, spent considerable time tracing the twisting path which led to Kensington. The early religious experience was clearly there but very quickly it became more complicated. Ethnic origins, the Depression, early exposure to racial injustice, the Second World War and a nearly fatal illness all interacted with religion to shape a belief system which held learning and the improvement of our society in high regard. Here is the religious part of his story:

Obs: And the religious experience?

T.M: Yeah, I think the thing that got me thinking about religion more than anything else was not my dad who was not a very religious man, nor my mother as far as that goes. She was a Baptist and he was a German Lutheran. And, oh, Grandad told me that during World War I when they closed the church, soldiers actually came into the German Lutheran churches, and this was in Illinois, and told them that they could not give their services in German or any of those things, and Grandpa said some of those people felt so badly about that, that they didn't think God could hear them unless they talked in German.

So, I thought, you know, that was a pitiful thing, and some of my experiences since then have been the same. I remember once I was giving Communion in a church camp, when I was down in Texas at the end of a weekend retreat, and these were all seniors in college and seniors in high school and freshmen in college and I forgot to bring the darn kit, you know, with the little cups and things in it, and so I madly looked around and found some little Pepsi Cola sample cups, and I went in and got some wine and I also got some unsalted crackers, but you know, out of twenty eight kids there were nineteen of them that refused to take the sacrament because it was not in the proper kind of container, as if that made a damn bit of difference!

And so, I guess my whole life as I read in the Bible and I studied, you know, I'm going to say something as an educator you probably can't accept, but I don't go in for a lot of this psychological gobble-de-goop that comes out. Everything that you need to know to solve your problems, if you think about it, is right there in that Holy Bible. There are no new concepts on how you cure yourself or cure others. There are new medications, but as far as the positiveness of the thought process, so on and so forth, it is, it has been there all the time. And so, knowing that that was true, or feeling that that was true, I just felt a compulsion to get it across to people whether in a secular sense or within the framework of the church.

Initially we were struck by the importance of religion in the lives of our group of innovators. This seemed beyond just the amount and kind of 'church going' among adults in general or even teachers in general. Rather it seemed that several other manifestations were afoot — a number of individuals were struggling actively with the place of religion in their lives, several had studied for the ministry, and others were unusually active in adult Sunday School teaching as well as church going.

As we reflected on the protocols of the open ended interviews we tried to piece together the 'linkages' between religious views and educational views. We do not see these as 'mechanisms' in any blind deterministic sense. Rather we took a more personality theory and social psychological position, that is, what personal and interpersonal events contributed to individual choices and decisions, actions and interactions which got them from there to here. Our synthesis or model has a patchwork quilt quality, for several reasons. First, much of it is heavily dependent on our analysis of a few individuals in our group. Second, we do cut and sew bits and pieces from a number of our staff. And third, we appeal to a bit of more general history and sociology literature, eg. Cremin (1980) and Bernbaum (1977); their accounts raise a number of issues regarding rural, small town America and teacher education sources of teacher beliefs.

The conversion of religious impulses to secular educational reform represented a complex set of events for Alec Thurman, the Kensington math teacher. Early in the interview he commented about the economic conditions of supporting a wife and two kids, beginning seminary and the difficulties in being a student pastor for two small town churches. He continued:

AT: In fact, I was — I worked at doing that and then I went to another town in Illinois that had a larger Methodist Church and continued to attend seminary and many of the pressures on the family were even greater there. The kids were getting older and we just decided to leave and really didn't know what to do because we never really considered going back to the farm. That was . . .

Obs: Were you specifically unhappy with the conditions there or was it a similar disenchantment with the ecclesiastical life, the life of the minister?

AT: Yeah, okay, yeah, we felt when we left that we would be much more active and that we would do more good religiously out of the ministry. We felt frustrated by the politics of the ministry. Ministerial groups were, you know, frustrating experience, dealing with the politics of the church, all the factions of people fighting with each other. Those were the things that were most oppressing to us and as I said, we felt we would be more active after we left but we weren't, that didn't happen at all. Now, this has been coming up for a long time. I don't even know how long because it took us a long time for me to make that change. My wife really had to push too — she was the primary push to get us out of the church. Part of that was because my family was big on, you know, when you start something, you finish it kind of thing and that was a very powerful thing in my life and it relates — I think it ties some of this together because after making that first change it was a lot easier in the future to look at alternatives. We left the church there.

As the interview continued, he reported arriving at State University with his family and a U-Haul trailer, finding a mix-up in his admission to the History Department, and entering a MAT program. From comments such as these in the interview, we reconstructed Alec Thurman's reconsideration of this early decision to shift from the ministry to teaching. We would argue it's one fragment toward a more general model underlying the interpretive theme, educational reform as secular religion.

For some, the religious aspect was a part of the process of the Kensington experience itself. When Sue Norton raised it we tried to get her to back off, feeling we might have suggested the idea:

Obs: And you didn't go, again, like Eugene for instance, or Steven or people of that sort, at that point?

Sue N.: No, I didn't — Kensington was dead.

Obs: Yeah, not long live Kensington.

SN: Right, yeah, it was gone — and part — okay, part of that, I think and I'm not sure about this, this is just top of the head, to go back to any of the individuals from the original would be like trying to make something whole with only splintered parts of it.

Obs: A disloyalty?

SN: No, not a disloyalty — it could never be the same and it would hurt more to be reminded of what could have been by having something to do with someone who had been involved in it. Very visceral reaction to Kensington, very emotional, it was a — in a way, a religious experience, yeah, and the terminology conversion — all this is — it's very much there.

Obs: Is that out of our discussions or when you think of that, you use the work religious experience, is — if somebody across the back fence, would have asked you about Kensington would you have used that kind of an expression or ...?

SN: I think I might have 'cause I think that there was always a feeling — I can remember going over there nights typing kids stories and I would be there 'til eleven or twelve o'clock at night, alone in the building and then because I — we lived a block away and walking home and almost having the feeling of, you know, the commitment of a nun to teaching, that kind of thing and feeling, boy, now — the Catholics really have it.

Obs: You understand that now?

SN: I understand that now — right.

Obs: As you walked back home sort of?

SN: Right.

Obs: So that was a feeling from fifteen years ago?

SN: Yeah, that was the feeling from fifteen years ago — again, balanced against a really wild social life, you know, which has nothing to do with being a nun at all but . . . [Laughter]

Obs: Did you talk to anybody about that kind of a feeling for instance?

SN: I'm sure I did, I don't know to whom. I did talk to anybody who'd listen.

Obs: You remember, to carry on the religious a bit, if you were in the order at that time, or were a nun, was your primary commitment to those specific children, to the kind of change of public education in America or to the abstract? Do you have any feelings as to what it was you were struggling for?

SN: Primary was to the kids, primary was to the particular kids within that group, little Suzy, the one who got written up in National Review, whatever it was — particular kids but with long range view of always in mind that maybe we can effect a permanent change in education.

Obs: So that kind of reform urge was very much a part of your . . .?

SN: Yeah, can't get away from that vocabulary can we? Yeah, it's there.

As the various faculty members presented their life histories and as their stories elaborated the various religious themes, the concept which seems to best capture much of what we were hearing was 'secularization of religious values'. Tom Mack's story, which we have presented earlier, seems a vivid account of the mix of educational and religious values. His deeply held view of the Bible and its teaching: 'Everything that you need to know to solve your problems, if you think about it, is right there in that Holy Bible' captures it vividly, potently, and succinctly. In other individuals the same tenor of intense moral commitment, true belief if you like, exists. But it has gotten converted, secularized. Alec Thurman's story seems the prototype. Ironically, the core idea was caught in a phrase that appeared and reappeared in his long, two-day interview: 'No one right way!' That was a telling comment.

The struggle with moral issues was demonstrated by this remark. Alec admitted that he frequently watched the 700 Club as an example of conservative religious television programming and he was struck with the faith and fervor of the righteous shown on television extending an index finger and shouting 'One Right Way!' In addition, Alec indicated his surprize and regret that a youth hero, Bob Dylan, had become a born again Christian. He further admitted that he listened to Dylan's recent work with the expectation that such a religious conversion would probably lead to a deterioration of musical quality. Alec concluded however, that that had not happened. Alec's reform orientation and his return to the University in the late 1960s was to involve him more dramatically in the anti-war and communal movements.

The issue of the moral component of public educators has always been a thorny thicket for educational theorists. Ironically, the only times and places when educators can clearly resolve church and state issues is when they are so intertwined that they cannot be clearly seen, let alone separated. For instance, educational communities with very homogeneous religious beliefs might agree that prayer in school is legitimate but only if it is not denominationally specific. In this case, harmony prevails. In a setting with more heterogeneous religious views, a determination is often impossible to make as to when moral education becomes religious in nature and when it is secular. Therefore it is not surprizing at one level, that our educational reformers took root in religious soil. Probably Madalyn Murray and Jerry Falwell could both accept Dewey's notion that true education must be moral education. However, what is surprizing and worthy of note is the lack of discussion in the literature regarding the intricate relationship of religious belief and educational commitment. The subject rarely comes up in discussions of motives for teaching or factors which drive innovation in education.

While research literature may avoid the topic it was clear to almost each and everyone of our participants that their own motive structure was heavily influenced by early religious experiences. They were not uncomfortable with the religious connections and readily picked up references from the original study (eg. holy grail) and described their earlier commitment as intense, fervent and yes, religious. As Sue put it, '. . . we lived a block away and walking home and almost having a feeling of you know, the commitment of a nun to teaching'. As the interviews began unfolding, a strand became visible and subsequent interviews sharpened the image until it stood out in bold relief. As we indicate in a later section on educational beliefs, for a number of the faculty, the passage of years had not dimmed the religious commitment to an educational idea. For some, the years had altered the means but not the ends; for others even the means had not been changed. There was evidence that the commitment carried both a secular component as well as the more typical examples of religiosity. Some had rekindled early religious commitment to organized religion while others had rejected rather violently the role of religion but retained a strong ethical, moral component. Finally, some had undergone rather dramatic religious conversion as 'born again' Christians. The strong belief theme, so evident in the original Kensington as a commitment to an educational ideology appears to have sprung from a much broader religious base than was earlier realized. As we pushed and probed in the interviews it appeared that religious belief and its modification was one of the most powerful melodies which we heard played out time and time again.

You Do Go Home Again

The Anomaly One of the most surprising and unanticipated anomalies in our research is caught in the phrase, 'You *do* go home again'. In the initial staffing of the

Kensington School, part of the innovation was searching the country, mostly the middle west region, for the best faculty available, a rare and unusual elementary school staffing pattern. The majority of teachers came from places other than Milford and its metropolitan area. After Kensington, many of the administrators and faculty wandered widely geographically on vocational odysseys or crusades. But many, and several in striking fashion, returned home, that is, ended up geographically close to where they had begun. Unraveling this anomaly is at the heart of the discussion in this portion of the chapter.

A related, second puzzlement lies in the mixture of a return to earlier values, attitudes, and beliefs for some and the centrality of early life experiences for others. The image we had was one of childhood influences which would not go away or which kept playing themselves out in the current or contemporary struggles regarding their belief systems, another kind of going home.

A third ingredient to the anomaly is that most, but not all, returned to positions and careers considerably higher in status — Deans, professors, administrators — than their parents, who tended to be 'poor, but hard working and proud'. It is almost as though, in their return, they had something to prove to themselves, their families, or their communities. Finally, one of the most interesting aspects of the anomaly in the natural history of belief systems arises in the contrast between two of the off hand labels each of which seemed to capture so much meaning; 'old reformers neither die nor fade away' and 'you *do* go home again'. The former captures the basic meaning that the personality systems and the belief systems within the personality system are central, pervasive, and long-standing within the individuals. Belief systems are not given up easily.

In short, our concerns began in our initial experiences from fifteen years ago, for in the original study of the Kensington School we were interested in the problem of the genesis of a faculty peer group (Smith and Keith, 1971a, p. 6). One dimension of that was the fact that the faculty had come from all over the country, mostly from the Midwest. After the first year most had left the school and the local metropolitan area. They had scattered. A few we had kept up with had 'wandered' about a good deal. For instance, we had known that Jerl Cohen, the Assistant Superintendent, had spent time in Washington, DC, California, New York, and a midwestern state. Then we found that he was now a Dean in the State University from which he had done his undergraduate teacher training in the town in which he had grown up. As we found other instances, almost as dramatic, the inference arose, in contrast to Thomas Wolfe, that you *do* go home again, that educational innovators and reformers eventually return to their places of origin. If more generally true, this seems an issue of immense proportion. Why would a group of people move to Milford, a place a long way from home for most, to teach in the innovative Kensington School? Why, too, would they wander, in some instances back and forth across the country? What would call them home? What has all this to do with the phenomenon of educational innovation? And for those who are prone to theorizing, what does this return home have to say to or for a theory of educational innovation? *The Long Way Home* Bill Kirkham, an original member of the ISD staff, is one of those who 'came home' to the town of Lafayette where he had grown up. He was teaching secondary school Social Studies in the very same classroom he had studied Social Studies as a high school student twenty years before. At the time of the interview we did not appreciate the importance of the theme.

To clarify the one form of the importance of 'going home', it is necessary to sketch the kind of odyssey individuals, such as Bill Kirkham, have been on. After his year in Milford he spent two years in a Midwest State Department of Education as a Title I supervisor, then two years as a Title III Director in a small town in a rural Midwest State. A key part of the program there was developing Bi-cultural Programs for the indigenous population and a growing urban population. This put him in contact with OEO personnel and programs for racial desegregation. Ultimately he went to Washington, DC with a National Foundation doing community desegregation work with task forces sent to communities throughout the nation. Later he lived several years in Eastern State, also working on desegregation issues for a national organization. And now, full circle, Bill is teaching Social Studies and peering out of the same window as a teacher he used to gaze through as an adolescent.

Variations on the Theme. Without going into great detail, nor adding every instance in our records, a few brief illustrations extend the meaning of the theme. The dynamics of 'going home again', as we have indicated, vary considerably. In one instance it seemed quite simple — Meg Adrian, a teacher in the Transition Division, is single, her parents have retired, and she has a brother and sister-in-law within driving distance in a nearby state. As she commented:

> My brother is here and going to be teaching after June. So we have a unique situation here. So, he's living here, has an apartment here, but he's also keeping his home in Nearby State. So when my sister-in-law comes over here to be with him, my mother and dad come to stay with me. So it's kind of a half and half thing.

Family resolutions seem important.

But others, as we have indicated returned earlier for other, perhaps similar reasons. Kay Abbot, an ISD teacher, was one of these:

> Subsequent to my leaving Kensington, I really intended to be there only one year, because at the time that I went down there the gentleman and I had an understanding that we would be married in June, 1965. So I intended at the time only to be there for one year. But I thought it was a valuable experience that, despite certain personal complications that it would be worthwhile to go down there. But in June of 1965 I came back home and was married. My husband, being involved with a family business in Hoganstown, has pretty much dictated the fact that we have stayed here subsequent to that. I did go back to the school in which I did my intern teaching, and became a staff member there in a team teaching situation.

Her situation captures a part of the motivation of several of the younger women.

'Going home' has multiple forms and each form has multiple antecedents. Sue Norton's return was to the small town in which she had grown up. Her father died the year she was at Kensington. She went to City University for an MAT degree, completing certification requirements prior to returning home:

SN: I really didn't feel I had that choice — I really felt I had to come home.

Obs: To your mother?

SN: To my mother, yeah, I really did. I don't know that she ever said, 'You must come home'. I think this was just ingrained. As my father was gone, mother needed someone strong to take care of her and that's gonna' be me which is absolutely, patently absurd. My mother is one of the strongest people around but I really perceived that she needed me to come home and in a way she did. I think, you know, she would have been fine if I had gone off somewhere else.. But, and it was also the safe choice. I was going back, I was teaching in the same building I had started elementary school in. One of the teachers I had had, my favorite teacher in elementary school, was still in that building, still teaching, we were going to be colleagues.

Obs: But you did go the first year to City University for your MAT?

SN: In between Kensington, yeah — that was a year . . .

Obs: Your father died?

SN: Right, okay, I couldn't come back here and teach so mother lived alone for a year.

Obs: Okay, so that was the stop gap part?

SN: Right, while I was at City University.

Obs: In retrospect, do you think it was more her need or your need that brought you here for the three years?

SN: I think it was both — I think it was my perception of her need plus my lack of willingness to really try something different.

As we have reported on 'You *Do* Go Home Again', the major illustrations were the vivid geographical returns of several of the faculty. In other interviews, before we realized the generality of the theme and pursued it in more detail, small, but in retrospect, important comments were made and passed over by the interviewers. After a lengthy set of comments on his estrangement from his father and the alternative kind of relationship he is developing with his own children, David Nichols, another of the ISD teachers, commented to a question:

Obs: Do your parents play a role in your children's lives now, are they dead or passed on?

DN: My mother's dead. We just had a reunion with my father and my sister at this Thanksgiving so at this point, we're going to be spending more and more time with my family.

Obs: First time in years or . . .?

DN: First time in about eight years, so there's been some healing there which has really been good and — but I had, as a child, I had a just a real strong desire to spend time with my father and to have him

Obs: Retired?

DN: And I'm forty one, yeah, and he married one of my aunts whose husband died and they're very happy together. And we had a tremendous reunion with them two weeks ago so I'm looking forward to it.

A variety of thoughts arose from his brief comment. First, there is one more manifestion of 'you *do* go home again'. In his case there's a long term estrangement and an attempt to build a relationship frustrated earlier by their problems. Secondly, immediately afterwards in the interview he made the following comments intertwining an almost fatherly view of God:

> I would say that the, my early childhood plus the experience at the University of totally turning away from anything spiritual and being totally on a mind trip where the two major causes of my immaturity. And both of those have been overcome since that time, by Grace. It's incredible, I'm so glad that God is gracious, you know, reading the Old Testament and you look at the history of the Jewish people and you know, the coming out of Egypt and forty years in the wilderness and then the Promised Land and how many times they rebelled against God's plan for their nation and were punished, judged, thousands of them were killed in the wilderness, just wiped out. You probably know the history of the Old Testament and yet God was still merciful and still loved His chosen people and still has a plan for them even today, even though they've scattered all over the world, but I'm glad that He is a merciful God because He would have given up on a guy like me a long time ago. [laughter]

> So, He always told the Jews, even though you rebel against Me and disobey, if you come back and ask for forgiveness, I'll have mercy on you and I still love you and so I know that ...

In a sense, he's gone home religiously as well.

The Gouldian Hypothesis. We were surprised that these highly innovative, change-the-world true believers seemed to return home, some after years of purposeful wandering and after being engaged in socially important activities all over the country. Although Jerl Cohen and Bill Kirkham are the prototypes, the pheno-menon was considerably broader. Every generalization such as this one kept nagging away with a why, why, why? Late in the day, long after the interviews had been conducted and the pattern noted we were 'reading around' in the recent adult developmental literature — Levinson (1978), Sheehy (1974), Vaillant (1977), Smelzer and Erikson (1980) and Neugarten (1968). We kept coming upon the name of Roger Gould, his 1972 paper and later his 1978 book, *Transformations*.

In his book, Gould (1978) does not used the concept 'belief' or 'belief system'.

His synonyms are consciousness, assumptions, rules, illusions. In his introduction he tells a story of the initial disillusionment and depression he and his wife felt in buying their dream house and the relation of that event to childhood illusions. He concludes:

> This forgotten childhood assumption, that I would live my adult life in my hometown near my family and friends, is not the same kind of assumption one thinks of in a debate or an exploratory conversation. It is more like a wish and therefore leads to unrealistic expectation — and disappointment, which in this instance was expressed by feelings of sadness. As I later discovered, my disappointment at having to give up this rather minor false assumption of my childhood is part of a process of shedding a whole network of assumptions, rules, fantasies, irrationalities and rigidities that tie us to our childhood consciousness. This network of assumptions allows us to believe, on a nonrational, emotional level, that we've never really left the safe world provided by omnipotent parents. The act of taking a step into an adult life — our moving into our new house — exposed this second, unsuspected emotional reality: a *childhood consciousness* coexisted alongside our rational, adult view of reality. (p. 11)

The specific item, 'I would live my life in my home town' and the reference to synonyms of beliefs, 'assumptions', 'protective illusions' triggered what we have come to call the Gouldian hypothesis. *If* a significant number of innovators do return home *and if* all of us, but especially them, are trying progressively to live with, escape from, cope with, or grow out of our childhood consciousness, *then* the phenomenon of educational innovation takes on significance well beyond the discussions most educationists and social scientists have made about innovation and change, e.g. House's (1979) account of models of innovation. Perhaps, too, we seem to be nudging into the roots of true belief and crusades as Hoffer (1951) and Klapp (1969) have used the terms. Briefly, we would like to explore such notions in the context of a fuller presentation of Gould's ideas and the data from our interviews. He phrases the unfinished business of childhood consciousness this way:

> To brew up an adult, it seems that some leftover childhood must be mixed in; a little unfinished business from the past periodically intrudes on our adult life, confusing our relationships and disturbing our sense of self. (p. 17)

The leftover unfinished business he speaks of as 'childhood demons'. Without raising all the details of the interlocking childhood beliefs and assumptions and the age related periods when one copes with them, our hypothesizing goes something like this:

1 Our innovative reform oriented educators internalize early and strongly, that is, much more than the population at large, such childhood demons.
2 In their twenties they are influenced by the major false assumption 'Doing things my parents way, with will power and perseverance, will bring results'. (p. 71) The true believer almost seems defined by Gould's four component assumptions within that overall one (p. 76):

(i)   Rewards will come automatically if we do what we are supposed to do.

(ii)   There is only one right way to do things.

(iii) Those in a special relationship with us can do for us what we haven't been able to do for ourself.

(iv)   Rationality, commitment and effort will always prevail over all other forces.

Those items might well have come out of our first study of Kensington, when most of the faculty were in their twenties and thirties and they were building their utopian educational world. True believers, so we argue, see the reformation in the outside world rather than in themselves. Hoffer (1951) makes this point very strongly as ridding oneself of an unwanted self or being intensely discontented.

3   The issue that seemed to be taking the largest amount of psychic time and effort, since their departure from Kensington and Milford, was Gould's major false assumption: 'Life is simple and controllable. There are no significant coexisting contradictory forces within me'. (p. 153) The component assumptions, also all false, describe some of the more particular internal battles (p. 164):

(i)   What I know intellectually, I know emotionally.

(ii)   I am not like my parents in ways I don't want to be.

(iii) I can see the reality of those close to me quite clearly.

(iv)   Threats to my security aren't real.

The accumulation of self perceptions some of which are highly contradictory, is not incongruent with our data.

4   Equally important for true believers is the false assumption of the midlife decade: 'There is no evil or death in the world. The sinister has been destroyed.' (p. 217) We would argue that the growing realization that this is false, that evil remains in the world, in spite of their crusades and attempts to destroy it becomes the ultimately difficult childhood demon with which they must deal.

Although Gould does not use nor index the concept of regression, his conception of adulthood as an active, dynamic period, his conception of directionality in growth, from childhood to adulthood, and his explicit conception of the unconscious suggest it is a derivable idea. He comments:

I concluded that my report on the 'posturing of the self' over the adult years was useful to all because it brought home the obvious fact that childhood is not a plateau; rather, it is a dynamic and changing time for all of us. As we grow and change, we take steps away from childhood and toward adulthood — steps such as marriage, work, consciously developing a talent or buying a home. With each step, the unfinished business of childhood intrudes, disturbing our emotions and requiring psychological work. With this in mind, adults may now view their disturbed feelings at particular periods as a posible sign of progress, as part of their attempted movement toward a fuller adult life. (p. 14)

One might argue, that 'going home' is a form of regression. Or perhaps, one might argue it is directly confronting and coping with the 'unfinished business of childhood'. Either of these interpretations, insofar as they have any validity, in our data and more generally, suggests the complications underlying educational innovation.

In an overly simplified form, from our point of view, Gould suggests a seven item 'inner dialogue' which each individual must go through to be free from the 'demonic past' (p. 74):

1 Recognize our tension and confusion.
2 Understand that we respond to two contradictory realities.
3 Give full intensity to the childhood reality; that is, let it be real.
4 Realize that both contradictory realities still exist. We're not sure which one is real. Confusion again, but more intense and better defined.
5 Test reality. Take a risk that discriminates one view from another.
6 Fight off the strong urge to retreat just on the edge of discovery.
7 Reach an integrated, trustworthy view of a section of reality unencumbered by the demonic past.

As we said in the beginning, *the Gouldian hypothesis*, is an hypothesis. The anomaly was the 'you *do* go home again' data and theme. For us, this was a startling end to some quite dramatic odysseys and pilgrimages. Nowhere in our report does the tired cliche 'need for future research' fit better than here. In the interim, we believe we have presented enough of the participants' view points that the careful reader can read both the manifest things the people are saying and can read between the lines for additional meaning and begin the assessment of the hypothesis.

Belief Systems: Conceptions and Conclusions

The development of the theme, 'Natural History of Belief Systems' has followed a troubled path in our work.[1] Early on, we were impressed by themes and patterns which we labeled variously: old reformers never die, educational reform as secular religion, origins of educational ideology. Finally, as we struggled, reading and rereading the interviews, reviewing our interpretive asides and summary observations and interpretations, and meeting, talking, and debating with ourselves over several years now, we came to the realization that one way to phrase what we were grappling with was 'the natural history of belief systems'. In a slightly more restricted sense it is the life history of systems of belief regarding educational innovation and reform, among a special group of educational innovators, those who staffed Kensington School and the leadership positions in the Milford Schools in 1964–5.

Our conception of belief draws heavily on Rokeach (1960; 1964; 1975), and Trueblood (1942). The most general and yet most particular set of illustrations is Trueblood's:

We have beliefs about history, beliefs about the structure of material aggregates, beliefs about God, beliefs about what is beautiful or what we ought to do. Most of these beliefs we state categorically. We say, 'Columbus landed in the West Indies', 'Water is composed of hydrogen and oxygen', Rain is falling today', 'There will be snowstorm tomorrow', 'God knows each individual', 'Greek temples are more beautiful than Egyptian temples', I ought to work rather than play tennis today'. Each of these statements, similar to thousands we make every day, is elliptical in that the preliminary statement is omitted. We might reasonably preface each of these propositions by the words, 'I believe', or 'There seems to be good evidence that'. Every proposition becomes in fact a judgment, and man is a creature greatly concerned with his own judgments. We take our judgments seriously and, foolish as we are, we are deeply interested in the correctness of our judgments. (p. 24)

In a later volume in which he builds upon Trueblood's conception, Rokeach (1968) defines belief this way:

> . . . *A belief is any simple proposition, conscious or unconscious, inferred from what a person says or does, capable of being preceded by the phrase 'I believe that . . .'* The content of a belief may describe the object of belief as true or false, correct or incorrect; evaluate it as good or bad; or advocate a certain course of action or a certain state of existence as desirable or undesirable. The first kind of belief may be called descriptive or existential belief (I believe that the sun rises in the east); the second kind of belief may be called an evaluative belief (I believe this ice cream is good); the third kind may be called a prescriptive or exhortatory belief (I believe it is desirable that children should obey their parents). (1968, p. 113)

When the totality of one's beliefs are considered in their content and structure one has a belief system: 'The belief system is conceived to represent *all the beliefs, sets, expectancies, or hypotheses, conscious and unconscious, that a person at a given time accepts as true of the world he lives in*'. (1960, p. 33)

Along the way, toward the end of our construing we began to use the phrase 'the natural history of belief systems'. That caught very well some of the early antecedents that seemed influential in the development of the belief systems of the individuals, long before they seemed to be making conscious decisions about their lives.

Another important linkage in our move toward a final outline was our original perception of the Kensington faculty as 'true believers'. In retrospect it seems a simple step in the unpacking of that term to get to 'belief systems in general' to a special form of belief system that might be called 'true belief' and to the nature of other personality dispositions involved with individuals who are true believers. Along the way, for us, as non philosophers, that was a difficult journey.

The selection of 'belief systems' as the central label vied with formal doctrine, schema, ideology, perspectives, norms, point of view, cognitions, ideas and conceptions. Beliefs seemed a more generic term regarding an individual's view of the world. For us it encompassed, straddled a number of dichotomies made popular by the positivist paradigm. For instance, we did not want to split so dramatically our conceptual and observational language, nor did we want value statements separated sharply from 'scientific' discourse. Finally, beliefs seemed at first glance less reducible to behaviouristic and biological terms. They belonged more to human beings who have grown up in a social, cultural context and who continue to act in that context.

In this essay we have chosen to accent aspects of two major sets of beliefs which are caught in our colloquial labels — 'educational reform as secular religion' and 'you *do* go home again'. The group of people who designed and implemented the Kensington innovation, in our view, were an unusual cluster of educators. They were not stamped from one simple mold. The 'new elementary education' was not a simple set of truisms originating and learned in a college principles of teaching course. They were beliefs couched in and framed by long term pervasive and core religious beliefs. Further they were woven, in ways we still do not well understand, with beliefs about 'home' — a geographic place, parents, and family.

In some very fundamental sense we believe that the debate on 'innovation and change in American education' needs to be reconstrued and recentered (Smith, Prunty, Dwyer and Kleine, in press). Much of that needs to deal with the belief systems, the personalities, and the life histories of the critical participants. In this context, our study of *Educational Innovators: Then and Now*, and especially our accent on the natural history of belief systems, is an attempt to redress the under emphasis and, in some instances, the omission of the individual person in the innovative process. This part of our inquiry accents the biography, the life history of the individuals involved. In a sense it reflects a position among the multiple theories of personality currently in debate in social science. Further, as a point of view about human personality, it also can be seen as a kind of psychological perspective. As a psychological perspective it is considerably different both methodologically and substantively from most of the psychological perspectives and efforts that have occurred within educational innovation. From our point of view such a difference is important and one of the main contributions of our effort. Our attempt has focused on a small group of teachers and administrators. Pupils, parents and patrons need the same kind of attention.

Notes

1 We treat in considerable detail that intellectual struggle in our methodological piece, *Educational Innovation: A Life History Perspective* presented at the St Hilda's Conference, September 1983, and published in Volume VI of our final report.

References

BECKER, H.S. (1966) 'Introduction', in SHAW, C. *The Jackroller*, Chicago, University of Chicago Press.

BERNBAUM, G. (1977) *Knowledge and Ideology in the Sociology of Education*, London, Macmillan Press.

CREMIN, L.A. (1980) *American Education: The National Experience 1783–1876*, New York, Harper and Row.

GEERTZ, C. (1973) *The Interpretation of Cultures*, New York, Basic Books.

GOULD, R.L. (1972) 'The Phases of adult life: a study in developmental psychology', *American Journal of Psychiatry*, **129**, pp. 521–31.

GOULD, R.L. (1978) *Transformations: Growth and Change in Adult Life*, New York, Simon and Schuster.

HOFFER, E. (1951) *The True Believer*, New York, Mentor.

HOUSE, E (1979) 'Technology vs. craft: a ten year perspective on innovation', *Journal of Curriculum Studies*, **11**, pp. 1–15.

KLAPP, O.E. (1969) *Collective Search for Identity*, New York, Holt Rinehart and Winston.

LEVINSON, D. *et al.* (1978) *The Seasons of a Man's Life*, New York, Knopf.

NEUGARTEN, B.L. (Ed.) (1965) *Middle Age and Aging*, Chicago, University of Chicago Press.

ROKEACH, M. (1960) *The Open and Closed Mind*, New York, Basic Books.

ROKEACH, M. (1964) *The Three Christs of Ypsilanti: A Psychological Study*, New York, Knopf.

ROKEACH, M. (1968) *Beliefs, Attitudes, and Values*, San Francisco, Jossey-Bass.

SHEEHY, G. (1974) *Passages: Predictable Crises of Adult Life*, New York, Dutton.

SKEELS, H.M. (1966) Adult status of children with contrasting early life experiences', *Monograph, Society for Research in Child Development*, **31**, 3, Serial #105.

SMELZER, N.J. and ERIKSON, E.H. (Eds) (1980) *Themes of Work and Love in Adulthood*, Cambridge, Mass. Harvard University Press.

SMITH, L.M. and KEITH, P. (1971) *Anatomy of Educational Innovation*, New York, Wiley.

SMITH, L.M. PRUNTY, J., DWYER, D. and KLEINE, P. (1984) *Kensington Revisited: A Fifteen Year Follow-up of an Innovative School and its Faculty* (Volumes 1–6), Washington, DC, National Institute of Education.

SMITH, L.M. PRUNTY, J., DWYER, D. and KLEINE, P. (in press) 'Reconstruing educational innovation', *Teachers College Record*.

TRUEBLOOD, D.E. (1942) *The Logic of Belief*, New York, Harper.

VAILLANT, G.E. (1977) *Adaptation to Life*, New York, Little, Brown.

WHITE, R.W. (1952) *Lives in Progress*, New York, Dryden Press.

Pupils, Teachers' Careers and Schooling: An Empirical Study

George F. Riseborough

Editors' Note: This is a long and difficult paper which explores in dramatic fashion a poorly understood aspect of teachers' work, that is the impact often painful and stressful, of pupil activity. Riseborough uses teachers' stories of their relationships with pupils to develop an analysis of teacher survival. Newcomers to sociology should not be put off and, perhaps, should read the Raw data in the first instance.

I'm a fairly young teacher from college, and know all there is to be known;
Last month I taught before Tutors, but now I'm away on my own.
I've bags of brilliant ideas, discovery methods galore;
It's a pity there's old-fashioned teachers, but their counsel I ignore.
Let's mix all the subjects together — why sort them out separately?
When they're stirred like a spotted dog pudding, they smell like a nice pot-
    pourri.
I don't like my pupils all sitting, as if they were filling a bus;
I like half of their backs towards me, and the maximum chaos and fuss.
I'd hate the children to fear me, to treat me as if I were God.
I'd hate them to respect or revere me; I'd prefer them to call me a clod.
When we're all level, I'll help them, for children and staff are the same;
And none are more equal than others, for learning's a levelling game.
Who made me? I'm asked by the ancients, as they sneer at my hair and my
    jeans.
Well, there's Cambridge, and Aston, and Darwin, and chromosomes and
    genes.

I'm a forceful old fossilized teacher, with retirement direct in his gaze,
Who taught when training and teaching were not a political craze.
I used to discipline children, and in cleanliness stood tall and proud:
I'd still do something about it, if only I were allowed.
I used to think I was with it, and now I find all I've learnt,
Like the books in Berlin, and the Reichstag, are just fuel to be gathered and
    burnt.
I know I'm outliving my use sir, and sweeping the flood with a broom,

I know that I merit abuse sir, for preaching a gospel of gloom.
Who made me? — I thought it was Reason, Ideals and a Light from the
  sky,
But now wrap me up in my pension, and God, let me crawl off and die.
Part of a poem by a now-retired teacher,
published in a school magazine whilst
in the twilight of his career.

Introduction

Books and magazines contain generalized notions and only sketch the
course of events in the world as best they can; they never let you have an
immediate, direct, animated sense of the lives of Tom, Dick and Harry. If
you're not able to understand real individuals, you can't understand what is
universal and general. (Gramsci, *Letter to Tatiana 19 November 1928*, in
Lawner, 1973, p. 136)

In spite of successive perspectival revolutions, most sociology of education has
consistently failed to grasp, analytically and empirically, the richness of everyday
school life. This is not to deny that sociologists have been very successful in
demonstrating that educational processes are *social* processes and to be understood, as
such, through the study of its summative project. However, it is to argue that much
work suffers from an over-socialized objectivism or an over-individualized subject-
ivism which often does not gell convincingly with commonsensical conceptions of
'how the world goes', uncluttered by sociologically contrived, mutually exclusive
dichotomies.

The propensity of sociologists to single out one dimension of human existence
and make it paramount to their understandings generates a species of undialectical
theorizing that gainsays the contradictions inhering in the human predicament. They
are, thereby, culpable of a distorting oversimplification which Gramsci has aptly
castigated as 'empty metaphysics' (Boggs, 1976, p. 23). People *are* subject-objects. As
such, they experience, at one and the same time, a freedom that palls on notions of
constraint; and a constraint that palls on notions of freedom. Within a radical
humanist paradigm (Burrell & Morgan, 1979), the critique that follows is not
dismissive of the substantial achievements within the sociology of education but it
will be incrementally argued that much work on schooling suffers from *hemianopia*,
that is, a paradigmatic blindness affecting half the field of vision. Consequently,
although such sociology is revelatory, the revelation is, usually, matched by a degree
of obfuscation.

Thus, the prime purpose of this chapter is to help to begin construct a *syncretic*
rather than a *synthetic* sociology of schooling which compensates for these alluded
deficiencies by coupling, rather than isolating, traditional antinomies into 'a
dialectical "unity of opposites"' (Gouldner, 1980, p. 54). This will be attempted, on
this occasion, through the medium of a consideration of teachers' careers, utilizing

materials garnered from observation of and recorded interviews with teachers and pupils in schools in cities and towns in the north of England:

Becker (1952a; 1952b) has discussed already the problematic nature of the teacher-pupil relationship and some career implications for teachers. He argued, 'The cultures of particular social-class groups may operate to produce clients who make the worker's position extremely difficult' (1952a, p. 119). This chapter develops this earlier theme by exploring, primarily, the *moral* career consequences for teachers of social class variation in the teacher-pupil relationship. The overall thesis, is that in a class society[1] the school is an internecine class-cultural battlefield not simply a bourgeoise institution. As such, pupils are also the initiators and controllers of schooling; they also occupy critical reality defining positions in school being determining mediators of teachers' identities and careers.

I have illustrated elsewhere (Riseborough, 1981), concentrating on teacher-headteacher interaction, how the school is importantly *a teacher processing organiz-ation*. This chapter develops this notion further by arguing that teachers' 'objective' and 'subjective' aspects of careers must be understood two-sidedly, that is, in relation additionally, to pupil activity. This is at the same time as children are being processed by teachers. In short, the teacher-pupil relationship has to be considered dialectically. It is not a parasitic relation but one characterized by commensalism. Teacher career movements in, around and out of schools are symbiotically related to pupils' careers in, around and out of schools. As subject-objects both parties are mutually 'determined' and 'determining'. Within a cultural Marxism, which defers to Kant's maxim that 'Concepts without perceptions are empty; perceptions without concepts are blind' it will be argued that children are central to any consideration of how teachers become what they are within the school as successive work experiences shape and reshape role and self. 'Teaching does something to those who teach.' (Waller, 1932, p. 375); and it is pupils who do *some* of the doing.

Towards a Dialectic of Teaching and Learning

> The idea of 'permanent class hegemony', or of 'permanent incorporation' must be ditched ... Capitalist production, Marx suggested, reproduces capital and labour in their ever-antagonistic forms ... Hegemony can never wholly and absolutely absorb the working-class into the dominant order. *Society may seem to be, but cannot actually ever be, in the capitalist mode of production, 'one-dimensional'* ... Class conflict never disappears. (my italics) (Clarke *et al.*, 1976, p. 41)

The paradigmatic shift inaugurated by Young (1971) marked a significant move-ment away from 'taken' educators' problems but what has followed in his wake? Interestingly, one major consequence has been that teacher activity is now pivotal to much sociological theorizing. Yet, paradoxically, in spite of this centrality, a lacuna exists when it comes to the consideration of teacher identities and careers, even though Becker (1952b) laid the seminal foundations some considerable time ago. The explanation for this lies in the intellectual trajectories sociology of education took after the call for 'new' directions.

One trajectory, via the sociology of knowledge and interactionism largely *retook* educators' problems. Researchers in this tradition moved away from the major structural functionalist question of 'Why do some children fail?' and answers sought in out-of-school determinants; to the 'new' question' ... what are the processes by which rates of educational success and failure come to be produced?' (Young, 1971, p. 25)

As such, homage must be paid to the 'new' sociologists who have achieved much in cracking open and problematizing the facile blackbox of structural functionalism; giving the kiss of life to its in-school cadaver; exposing the conservative ideology implicit in its concerns with 'the problem of order' and policy orientated 'problems'; and, thus, transforming what counts as the sociology of education. By *making* more of a sociological problem interpretive sociologists have left us with an appreciative, corrective and reflective understanding (Hargreaves, 1978, pp. 19–20), particularly of how pupil educational identities and careers are socially constructed within the process of schooling.

However, metatheoretical difficulties associated with the trajectory[2] result often in nothing more than paradigmatic 'sleight of mind' which simply supplants one set of educators' problems with another set; albeit shifting concern from extra-school factors over which educators have few controls to in-school factors over which educators exercise some considerable control. As such, 'new' membership befuddled many 'members' who ought to have known better given the phenomenological injunction to 'bracket' the world. Many relied and still rely on tacit teacher knowledge which defines research 'reality' in certain ways and, which is, remarkably, left unexplored and unexplicated. Too often, interpretive research is the product of teachers *qua* sociologists rather than sociologists *qua* teachers; is commonsensical sociology rather than sociology of commonsense; distorted occupational ideology rather than a detailing of the everyday richness of the teacher-pupil relationship. Thus, it is hardly surprising that the appellation of 'blame the teacher' (Woods, 1979, p. 12) sociology has been applied to much work by interpretive sociologists, since their critique of teacher and pupil activities is premised on a teacher-orientated problematization of *the sociological problem*. This is not to say that 'new' sociologists have not studied children; they clearly have but pupils' meanings are often taken to be the ones which are refracted through official/teacher commonsense. As Woods (1979) has argued, much work on 'the pupils' own point of view' is often 'encased within official frameworks' (p. 14) and, consequently, 'The channel such studies sail up may be a minor tributary in the pupils' scheme of things' (p. 15).

The result of this overall research orientation of the 'new' sociologists is that often children are conceived as phenomenological *reactors*; their points of view, their identities and careers, their cultures are merely contingent on teacher practices (see, for example, Woods (1977; 1979); Hargreaves (1967); Hargreaves *et al.* (1975); and seen as adaptive and accommodative, without holding out the possibility that they can be occasionally originative and creative.

The role of culture carrying actor is often denied the child in school. An over-emphasized situationalism often ignores 'People carry culture with them; when they leave one group setting for another they do not shed the cultural premises of the first setting.' (Becker and Geer, 1960, p. 57) A paradoxical phenomenological 'vacuum ideology' (Wax and Wax, 1964) becomes integral to the theorizing. To confirm and compound this criticism some of the ostensibly pupil-centric work is, usually, redolent with hidden curricular messages for teachers (see, for example, Furlong (1976; 1977); Gannaway (1976); Nash (1974); Woods (1976; 1980b).

The alternative trajectory, premised on structuralism has substituted educators' problems with *the* theoretical problem of Marxism generally, that is, with the enigmatic incubus of an apparently perpetual capitalism. Grounded in a paradigm of disappointment, schooling is to be understood primarily, in terms of effective social control and effective social reproduction. There is no way out of this vicious circle until there is a catastrophe in the economic base; for changes in the dependently variable superstructure cannot precede the long-awaited cataclysmic changes in the independently variable infrastructure. In this formulation teachers become mediating 'cultural dopes' (Garfinkel, 1967, p. 68); unthinking 'policemen without boots' successfully quiescing and dulling children with a massive inoculum of ruling ideology insinuated into their minds through the medium of certain overt and covert curricular contents wrapped up in 'corresponding' social relations of schooling (Althusser, 1971; Bourdieu, 1971a; 1971b; 1973; 1974; Bowles and Gintis, 1976; Dale *et al.* (Eds) 1976; Bourdieu and Passeron, 1977). All of which conspires to conserve capitalism.

This perspective is now increasingly considered *passé* (Nash, 1984) even amongst some of its initial committed adherents. It has failed to stand up particularly to the crushing intellectual blow to its corpus by cultural Marxists, especially the perspicacity of Willis (1977). Thus, the sociologically unimaginative license of structural Marxists is now recognized as incredible. Theorists of this ilk are guilty of a specious armchair theorizing which is incestuously developed without reference to the world which pupils and teachers inhabit and is, as such, dehumanizing. The gravamen, is that they are guilty of a hopeless, ahistorical, deterministic realism. They present a distorted caricature for human beings become societally honed square pegs that ultimately fit perfectly the square roles prescribed by the imperatives of the capitalistic economy. They trivialize and render invisible the lived agony and ecstasy of the chalkface. They convert the crude blackbox into a crude *blue box*. Teachers and pupils become mere passive ciphers ideologically subjugated by factors outside of themselves playing on and through them. The demiurgic proclivities of teachers and pupils become denied for intentionality is *un*-intended because it is *super*-intended by the dominative deep structures of capitalism (Gouldner, 1980, p. 317).

Thus, the indictment against structural Marxists now is that their immaculate conception of schooling in capitalism ignores the complexities of everyday life within capitalistic social formations which vitiates notions of the simple functional fit of humankind, underpinned by a straightforward socialization process. Teachers are erroneously conceived as automatons, reproduced reproducers simply and easily subjugating children because teachers are State functionaries, 'high priests of the ruling ideology' (Althusser, 1971, p. 246) and, as such, thoroughly pickled in it themselves. Their over-socialized conception of the pupil is equally muddled for they deny the empirical possibility that schools may be 'highly inefficient in creating a docile, deferential and subservient workforce' (Bernstein, 1977). It is one thing to argue schooling in capitalism attempts to instil conformity but facile to extrapolate that it actually succeeds.

In the monochrome of the overall structural analysis, in which *cowed* teachers are *cowing* pupils, irridescent existential variations in teacher and pupil activity are denied and of no consequence. Children and teachers are trapped, crushed and thingified. Unconvinced teachers assuaged by self-doubt as to their efficacy while they go about the daily grind in the classroom are deluded. So are Keith Joseph and Rhodes Boyson with their paranoia concerning 'incompetent' and 'red' teachers. Pupils do not know the meaning of insubordination for the reified child is 'vulnerable' (Althusser, 1971, p. 260), ideologically sanitized, laundered and mangled between 'the family-school couple' (Althusser, 1971, p. 259). Working class culture as a source of not-so-vulnerable, counter-ideologically robust children is denied (Hall and Jefferson, 1976; Willis, 1977).

Structural Marxists offer us a *cow* sociology and this, of course, is not a humanistic sociology. Licentiously extending the analogy, capitalist society becomes a pseudo-contented *herd* exploitatively *milked* by an hypostasized system; whose comprehension lies beyond total ignorance and, therefore, cannot be grasped and defied except by a few unconvincing *maverick* Marxists who alone have the anti-empiricistic understandings that allow apprehension of 'the reality' beneath 'appearances'.

Whichever of these *two* trajectories is favoured, even though premised on divergent ontologies and epistemologies, the result is the same. That is, a recurring bipartisan theme of teacher-centricity emphasizing *one-dimensionally* how the child's educational identity and career is a function of the way *it* is processed through school by teachers. Neither get far beyond the spectre of children as manipulated objects on the receiving end of schooling. On the occasions subjectivity is granted to children, it is a subjectivity of reactivity rather than of proactivity; pupil cultures are conceived contingently rather than creatively. In short, both normatively *take*, one *implicitly*, the other *explicitly*, a 'top-down' view of social reality; people at 'the top' act, people at 'the bottom' merely react. Teachers are conceived as the initiators and controllers of schooling; they occupy critical reality defining positions within the schools, being determining mediators of pupils' identities and careers.

Thus, it is small wonder that both trajectories are guilty of a myopic assumption of teacher stasis. Conceptually, teachers become the catalytic pivot around which children are processed. In consequence, it is now commonplace to talk of schools as pupil and knowledge processing organizations but it seems to have historically eluded many sociologists that the school is also importantly a teacher processing organization. The argument advanced here is that it is the 'trialectic' of these processes that must be the basis for a sociology of schooling.

By not yet *making* a fully sociological problem, a restricted conceptualization of teaching and learning is constructed which ignores that all social arenas are educative for actors within them. The categories of 'teacher' and 'taught' have yet to be treated as problematic. Thus, sociologists have yet to realize fully in their work that teachers are also learners in schools and it is important to study what, how, and from whom they learn. More importantly, it has not yet occurred to sociologists how supposedly learning pupils are teachers of their teachers and it is important to study what and how they teach. Further, they have yet to elaborate sociologically how in the contested terrain of the classroom, corridor, yard and playing field teachers teaching children, children learning from teachers, children teaching teachers and teachers learning from children has to be understood in terms of a dialectic of concatenated action. Consequently, the learning/teaching outcomes from teacher-pupil interaction are far more than those hitherto catalogued.

   Admittedly, there are huge chinks of light in the work of *some* interactionists (see, for example, Werthman, 1963; Delamont, 1976; Furlong, 1976; 1977; Rosser and Harré, 1976; Stubbs and Delamont, 1976; Woods, 1976; 1977a; 1978a; 1978b; 1979; 1980b; Beynon, 1984; Beynon and Delamont, 1983); and Marxists (Willis, 1977; and Corrigan, 1979) which attenuates some of the thrust of this overall critique. Both have incorporated into their analyses of schooling a pupil-centricity which is wholly refreshing. This paper is indeed a developmental tribute to the pupil proactivity which they acknowledge. After all, Geer (1968) wrote '. . . the largely unspoken bargain his pupils make with him *constrains the teacher's behaviour* whether he knows it or not. Pupils have effective sanctions which they use to reward and punish teachers who fail to live up to the bargain, *sanctions few teachers can withstand*' (p. 5) (my italics). However, sociologists, *generally*, have rarely delivered any substantive insights along these lines.

   Further, just as the 'new' sociology and structural Marxism generally are teacher-centric and fail to realize the *relational* nature of teaching and learning; so pupil-centric researchers from their respective perspectives fail equally to develop analytically *the reciprocity* of social relations in which pupils are enmeshed with their teachers. Pupil-centric interactionists replace freefloating 'baddie' teachers with freefloating 'baddie' pupils. Amongst Marxists, Willis (1977) alone tangently alludes to consequences of pupil activity on the selves and careers of teachers. The rich vein which these writers expose has yet to be cashed by sociologists anxious to build an authentic sociology of schooling.

   Thus, what is now required is a 'top-down' and 'bottom-up' *two-dimensional* view of reality which will allow consideration of the symbiotic mutuality (albeit, often antagonistic) of pupil and teacher identities and careers, rather than a consideration of a one-sided parasitism of pupils on their teachers. An adequate grounded theory of teaching, as controlled and controlling work, must incorporate a theory of learners as controlling as well as controlled. To assume that children are something culturally qualitatively less than total human beings misleads. It assigns an unwarranted differential world-building potentiality to adults *vis à vis* children and, as such, trivializes the processes of cultural transmission in schools. Sociologists, in their studies of how schooling happens, need to grant a far greater degree of cultural competency to children, especially, when it comes to a consideration of the social construction of their teachers' identities and careers.

THE DATA

'At one level — the horizontal — are all those ties which bind spaces and institutions to locality, neighbourhood, local culture and tradition. At another level — the vertical — are those structures which tie them to dominant institutions and cultures. The local school is a classic instance of such 'double-binding'. It is the *local* school, next to houses, streets and shops where generations of working-class children have been 'schooled', and where ties of friendship, peer-group and marriage are forged and unmade. Yet, in terms of vertical relationships the school has stood for certain kinds of learning, types of discipline and authority relations, affirmed experiences quite at variance with the local culture. Its selective mechanisms of streaming, 'tracking', eleven-plus, its knowledge boundaries, its intolerance of language and experience outside the range of formal education, link the urban working-class locality to the wider world of education and occupations in ways which are connected but also, crucially, *disconnective. It remains a classic, negotiated, or mediated class institution.* (Last sentence my italics) (Clarke *et al.*, 1976, p. 43–4)

Pupils as Overt Curriculum and Hidden Curriculum Decision Makers

Sociological analysis of the curriculum (for example, Bernstein, 1971, Bourdieu, 1973; 1974; Young, 1971; Apple, 1979) is usually premised on uni-dimensional assumptions and consequently does not get to the nub of what it is to be schooled. For example, Young's (1971, p. 28) passing discussion of Gramsci tantalizingly states 'what he called the cultural hegemony which he saw as imposed on the working classes who are thus prevented from thinking for themselves, is important for any consideration of the content of education'. Consequently, the class content of children's educational experience is seen by Young as uncontaminated by their own class culture; it is imposed from above.

But, it is also important to remember that hegemony is inconceivable from Gramsci without its twin concept, counter-hegemony. The latter is generated from peoples' everyday experience of conflictual relations of subordination and superordination within capitalism and enables people 'to think for themselves', if only fragmentarily and contradictorily. This is equally important for any consideration of the content of education. Gramsci also asserted: 'But it is not possible to conceive of any man who is not also a philosopher, who doesn't think, because thought is proper to man as such, or at least to any man who is not a pathological cretin' (Prison Notebooks, 1971, p. 347). Ideological and cultural hegemony may work to freeze out working class commonsense from formal schooling but, informally, counter-hegemony may significantly skew knowledge exchanges in the classroom. However, sociologists of the curriculum seem immune to the consideration that children are 'philosophers'.

One girl, she completely shut off. Just sat there for a year. Not hostile. Not friendly. Completely unemotional. Nothing. Cold. All day, every day. No inkling. Just sat there. Just like talking to a wall. She'd answer you. Work away at her own rate, did what she wanted. No response. I never saw her worked up about anything. Strange girl. She was only going to work at a certain rate. She wasn't going to enjoy herself at my expense. She wasn't interested in that. All she was interested in was she had to come in because if she didn't her dad would leather her. It was just to get through the day. I said, 'Do something, otherwise the day is going to pass slowly, you might even find something that interests you'. No. She passively manipulated me. I never got past her. At the end of the day she'd have two or three comprehension questions, couple of sums at maths. A bit of this, a bit of that. Not a lot. At the end of the day you'd say, 'Why are you doing nothing?', 'Boring, boring, boring'. I tried to find something relevant to her, that she might accept as being relevant. She used to smoke. I know it is bad educational practice but I started to do work on cigarette advertising. Which one do you think is best? Which ones are getting through to you? Compare prices. The wall. I never got past her eyeballs. Nothing was relevant to her. Life was something she floated through. You could never raise a spark of interest. She cut herself off. The glazed look. That's the worst of it. She won't offer up anything. I'd speak to her, she'd speak back. I said, 'Hurry up'. She won't. It's an understanding. You play your game, and I'll play my game and we'll be alright. Don't bother me and I won't bother you. I think the only thing she's learned is that when you look at the school fence outside certain shapes tessellate. I don't know. (Primary school teacher)

Thus, it is all very well to argue 'that those in positions of power will attempt to define what is to be taken as knowledge, how accessible to different groups any knowledge is, and what are the accepted relations between different knowledge areas and between those who have access to them and make them available' (Young, 1971, p. 32). But such a sociology is theoretically emasculated if the power of pupils to interpolate their countervailing 'philosophical' assumptions is not recognized; if their power to make the official curriculum redundant by converting it into a *ricochetted* curriculum due to a 'philosophical' withdrawal of learning is not recognized; and if the oft desperate reactive negotiations of teachers are not included in the analysis. The notion of the stratification of knowledge is very important but a more profound question is to ask what children do with it. If they do not neatly receive it, any theory of knowledge and control has to be a little bit more sophisticated than Young appears to accept.

This particular time, he looked up this teacher, he was on the ball and said, 'Where is Jones?' So I said, 'I think he's left the room', winking, and he said, 'Where is he?' Anyway, he was in the cupboard. I saw him climb in and he just wanted to cause a big disturbance and none of the other kids saw him climb in. I thought, 'Let's leave him in the cupboard' because, all the other kids were working. He came to me panic stricken and said to me, 'No, we can't do that'. I said, 'Leave him, because he just wants to stop the lesson and say, "Where is Abdullah"? All the kids will then laugh'. He said, 'He could suffocate. He could become unconscious'. I said, 'No, it's too well ventilated'. 'No, no', he said. 'I'll have to get him out'. And he did. And of course, the lesson stopped and all the kids left their work and were hooting with laughter and the rest of the lesson this kid sits there making funny faces. He was young and inexperienced. (Team-teacher)

He came into my room one day, it was a withdrawal group. And he had got this lighter and he adjusted the flame and I was talking and all of a sudden I saw this great flame in the corner of my eye. I looked round and said, 'What's that?' 'Nothing'. I just carried on. I knew I'd see this again shortly. I kept my eye open. It was like a flame-thrower. One to two foot long. I caught him, I said, 'You can't have that, it's dangerous. Give it me'. 'Right, Miss', he says, 'But I can have it at the end of the lesson?' 'No', I said. But he wouldn't give it me. I said, 'I'm not going to make an issue of it, I want it on my desk by the end of the lesson'. He didn't light it again but he didn't put it on the desk. I sent for the year tutor and he came. This kid, I never saw anything so fast in my life. The year tutor came. It was so quick. A flick of the wrist. I didn't see it. The year tutor didn't know what had gone on, but he turned round and grabbed the first kid he saw by his hair, and this kid said, 'It's not my lighter'. Anyway, got it off him and the year tutor said, 'I've had enough'. And this kid ends up on the far side of the room on his knees begging. He was terrified. 'Please don't hit me, don't hit me'. He was terrified, because he was beaten at home a lot. (Remedial teacher)

The official curriculum, therefore premised on the formal institutional paradigm is richochetted and further converted counter-culturally into a *differentiated* (Willis, 1977, pp. 62–63) 'counter-curriculum' manifested in the informal pupil group 'having a laff', 'mucking about', and 'doing nothing' etc. (Willis, 1977; Corrigan, 1979).

Me and Bungey found the keys to Lockyers cupboard. We used to go in at eight o'clock every morning, get his key out of a little drawer, we could get it out of the back. When I was in 4G we nicked half an hundredweight of A4. It was sound. Bungey nicked two dozen pork sausages from Coniston's and we put them under Lockyer's desk on a shelf like. He never found them, they did 'arf chuck up, by the end of term they were green and mouldy. (Pupil)

We went to the swimming pool. Everyone bet Deardrie that she wouldn't jump in. She jumped in, fully dressed, just for a bet. Pretended she slipped in and knocked her head. The teachers were right worried, were really nice, thinking she'd slipped and hurt herself, got her clothes dry and everything. They never knew about it. She got two quid for that. (Pupil)

For example, we had this lesson with Sister Mary. This window cleaner came and we were giggling and he put his ladder up and was cleaning his window. One of the girls lifted up the window and undid his fly double quick. He went dead red and nearly fell off his ladder. (Pupil)

She is a lovely gentle teacher, out of school we like her, but I don't know what it is. We have this small radio. We turn it on, very low. And she turned round and said, 'Can you hear music?' and we all said, 'No, it must be outside'. She said, 'I thought it was coming from over there'. 'No', we said. And we passed it round under the desk and the music was coming very faint all over the place. And she said, 'I'm sure I can hear music'. She never found out. It ended up in every single person's hand under the desks. She was totally blind. (Pupil)

In metalwork we were putting chuck keys in the lathes, turning it on and seeing if we could get them through the ceiling. We were making fifty-pence coins for the cig machines as well and weighing them in physics and I honestly got a few to work, you know? Getting the right size and weighing it on proper scales, filing bits off. It wasn't worth the time though, about ten hours work for 50p. (Pupil)

This coloured guy, and it was the end of the day, and there was a small oven in the room and this guy called this coloured guy something, and he just lifted the oven and threw it. It was just this one coloured guy against the rest. There were chairs and tables flying and it went through into the toilets. The fluorescent lights got smashed. It was a riot. They went spare, threatened us with the police and our parents were brought in. All this because someone had called him a black bastard. (Pupil)

I felt really sorry for the guy who did human biology, sex lessons. That fella' must have felt awful. It really was awful. I hope you never have to do it. Some of the questions people asked! We knew more than he did. We had games. It was ace. Doses and VD! Can you get it off toilet seats, sir? Can you get it off door handles? Only if you're tall enough, we told him. (Pupil)

Similarly, the hidden curriculum, the supposedly subtle inculcation of the dominant values, training in obedience and docility etc. associated with social control (Vallence, 1974) is richochetted and differentiated as pupils import subordinate values. Indeed, pupils proffer a hidden counter-curriculum to their teachers.

I had a kid, very badly disturbed. He was only eleven and a friend of mine came in and said, 'Have you seen that Jason? That gorgeous face? About three foot six? A beautiful child?'First day in school and she said, 'The Deputy Head is going absolutely berserk at him'. She said, 'Go and have a look'. And she said, 'And as I walked past I looked at him. I said, 'What a beautiful child'. And this great big Deputy Head woman was screaming at him at top note, 'Do you think you are coming to this school and doing this on your first day?' And she thought, 'Poor little thing', felt sorry for him.

And he looked at her as she passed and he winked at her. He winked at her! It was all washing over him. He wasn't taking a damn bit of notice. (Teacher)

In our school there are some kids who don't want to learn anything, who want to lead their own life, and they do this in school. There are certain places where they live it. They do this brushing down thing. It is very frustrating. If you happen to brush past them in a classroom they look at you even if your coat touches them. They start doing this (disdainful brushing gesture). Brushing your aura away. Sneering. (Teacher)

All this reaches a point where little teaching and learning, as commonsensically understood, takes place.

It was during the Falklands and all of a sudden, the school is near the city airport, and this plane went over the playground, really low. All the kids jumped over these desks, knocking them all flat to get to the window. Shouting, 'It's the Argies, It's the Argies! Get down Miss! They're coming to bomb us!' Jumping over the desks, how do you control that? They didn't feel there was anything bad in behaving like that. They destroyed the lesson. They do that sort of thing and there's nothing you can do about it. (Teacher)

We had this diesel room. This is good. It was a separate place and because of the fumes they had this big extractor fan and there is me and my mate Joey. We were never out of trouble. Sent home, back to work. Reports and everything. And there was this massive, big extractor fan and there was this massive big roll of paper to wipe your hands on. This roll was here and the fan over there. So we started pulling it out and Joe, he flicks it on and guides it. And the motor went whine and all this smoke came out. And Rupert (we always called him that because of the trousers he used to wear), he says, 'What the fucking hell is going on in here?' We said, 'Bit of an accident'. He said, 'Bit of an accident?', smoke coming out of his nose, whining just like the fan. We was reported, nearly got sacked. (Day-release, technical college student)

We used to break into this pub and swipe cider and bring 'em into school and flog 'em five-pence a bottle and we used to sit under the stairs drinking this cider. Amazing. Never caught doing it. Dickenson walked round like a ruptured duck, falling all over these bottles under the stairs and had a bit of a snapper about it. Then there was the horses when we was in the 4th form, go down to the bookies. Gambling. Sound it was. We made a fiver fiddling dinner tickets and put the money on horses. We never won nowt. It went on for two months. Never won. (Pupil)

Nine and ten-year olds. I was teaching a geography lesson and I was doing coastline formations — spits and stacks and coves and I was drawing spits on the blackboard and I turned around and the windows were full of spit.

They were all gobbing at each other. All up the walls, and they thought that was hilarious. Every time I said 'spit', they were spitting you see. They thought it hilarious. (Teacher)

We used to have to do cookery. The lads had to do it. We had to make this sponge cake-thing. I was really interested in the first place, know what I mean? They had these things that came out of the ceiling, variable food mixer-things. I like things that are noisy and flash. I switched it on and gives it number six. Whum! And all my mix went over everything and everybody. The old bag burst, you should have seen her, My mix over everything. It was nesh. (Pupil)

Thus, the lesson does not simply belong to the teacher, children can and do make it their own. They put so much on the agenda of the lesson, to a point where, they are the curriculum decision-makers. They make a major contribution to the social construction of classroom knowledge. Children actively select, organize and evaluate knowledge in schools. Further, lesson time is not solely the teacher's time, it is 'a stake and site of class struggle'.

I had one boy and he came in and I had a terrible time with him for two or three months. And he'd just come in, he'd sling his book on the floor. 'I'm not doing anything'. Luckily the others didn't bother. He did nothing, just sat there. This happened for months. I said, 'If you're going to carry on like this, I'll have to send you out to see if somebody else can cope'. He said, 'I've got to go out anyway to get my guitar'. 'So', I said, 'Do you play the guitar?' He said, 'Yes, I do. I have lessons once a week'. So I said, 'Go and get it now'. So he went off to get it, came back and he played it for us. The others thought it was great. So I said, 'Every Wednesday, don't leave your guitar, get it and we'll have ten minutes, you playing it'. I didn't have any trouble after that. He was always happy. (Teacher)

Once, he said, 'Imagine the most facinating thing you could take to people in the jungle'. I said, 'A vacuum cleaner. If you put some muck in their hut they could hoover it up'. He says, 'You're stupid boy'. So I said, 'You name something better'. He said, 'How about running water?' I said, 'They've got that already, you stupid berk. Otherwise they'd die of thirst'. He said, 'No, no, they haven't. No, no they haven't. He was absolutely blue. (Pupil)

I had to do a talk for CSE, like, so I brought my motorbike in the lesson and it dripped oil all over the carpet. She went spare. I went through it all and I got nine out of ten for this talk. I did about the documents and everything. The legal requirements. Not that I had any. I said, 'This is where the tax should be'. MOT, you have to be sixteen. She says, 'Very good, Stewart'. And I said, 'Look, look, Miss Smith, see how well it starts'. And I just got, I got carried right away, and I roared it down the corridor. I was stopped from bringing it. (Pupil)

We used to have this remedial group, me and this other teacher, Friday afternoon. And it was supposed to be drama. We got this book of plays which we read and it was bad. And then one afternoon they said, 'Can we do a play for you?' It was fantastic. We went in on Friday afternoon. They said, 'Can we do a court? because I've been to court. We've got the judge and jury, barrister'. They knew all the people we didn't know. They had it all sorted out, and it was absolutely fantastic. If you'd seen the kids' face, the kid who was the policeman, did all the things policemen say, all the cliches off pat, fantastic. We were completely out of our depth. The pair of us realized afterwards that the book of plays might have been within the writers' experience and within ours but to those kids, those plays in the book, had nothing to do with them. It was fantastic. We had no trouble. It was no effort to them. It was pure delight. We sat at the back and really enjoyed it. No discipline. They knew all the procedures, no-one laughed. We heard all these sentences we didn't understand. One was going off to some community home, they had a social worker there, it was an eyeopener. (Teacher)

There was this national quiz on theory and we got through to the area finals at Leeds and I was the team leader. I was dead chuffed. Everybody was in their shirts and ties and I had my denim jacket, dead scruffy-like. We got onto this coach and had cans at the back. We were giving it this, right. [drinking gesture] We get there, giving it this again. [drinking gesture] It was the practical first and I had to dismantle this rocker-shaft and put it back together again. And the springs went 'bong' and I was staggering around half pissed looking for it, pale as anything. Then it was the theory. Scrooge thought we did really well to get there. We didn't win. We were last. We ballsed it up something chronic. (Technical-college student)

I had this class. They had come to a standstill. So I just sat down and read this poem to them about street gangs, violence in the streets and so gave them an opportunity to talk if any were in any gangs anything like this. I said, 'Could we make a drama out of this sort of intimidation, victimization on the streets?' We made up two factions. We set up a scene in a cafe. I was unaware of some personal conflict amongst the two leaders of these two groups. I was totally unaware. They really worked well. The role-play was magnificent. But then this confrontation came out of the improvization. They started to push each other about. So I didn't know whether to intervene because it was drama. All of a sudden there was a chair crash down on this chap's back. 'Smash!' The Headmaster walked passed, here was a boy laid out with a chair on his back! It really was ugly. I intervened physically. There was some gangs in school. That really frightened me. (Teacher)

George F. Riseborough

Pupils as Moral 'Labourers'

Labelling theorists are similarly one-sided in their analysis of schooling. Teachers as *moral entrepreneurs* (Becker, 1963, pp. 147–60) may act as labellers and hegemonic agents of social control who thus might victimize underdog pupils who are more sinned against than sinning. But this ignores how 'philosophical' children might be *moral labourers* who act as counter-labellers and as counter-hegemonic agents of social control who, thus, might victimize overdog teachers who are more sinned against than sinning. It is, always, possible to have victimized victimizers and victimizing victimized; overdog underdogs and underdog overdogs in the social kaleidoscopy that is the school.

> To begin with, when I was introduced and when I chatted to one of the teachers he said one of the kids had come up to him and says it was not right he should have a Paki teaching him. That was the first reaction. I didn't have problems with my own classes. It was when I walked down corridors. They shouted out racist comments. 'Paki go home!' or things like that, basically. Or put on an accent whilst they were talking as I walked by. They'd stare me out, sly comments all the time out of the corner of their mouths.
>   I've learned that if you try and deal with it you cause more problems. Mainly at breaktimes it got worse and worse. It's not them, it's their parents. The worst incident was, I was doing some marking in the prep room. And they were coming up to the glass door, giving the 'V' and shouting, and I could have gone off chasing them. But I've learnt that if they are trying to hurt you the best thing is not show your hurt. I try to ignore it. I should have dealt with it. At one stage, I did go in, I saw them and walked into the classroom and asked them who was shouting. They just pushed their way past me, on their way.
>   I was talking to a teacher friend and saying, what do you do when you've got kids glaring at you on the corridor, trying to stare you out. Do you look away? What do you do? It becomes a tension. I used to walk down the corridors as little as possible because I was bored with the confrontations. I didn't move around when they were moving around. I felt they were threatening me. I was definitely threatened. I didn't enjoy it. I experienced fear, not of being hurt but because there was nothing I could do. If I knew what to do! What to say! It got worse because I ignored it. If I'd done something about it it would have got worse. Ignoring it, they didn't gain what they wanted from it, and so they pushed me a bit more. Gestures at first, then words. I just don't want to know, that is my way of dealing with it. (Anglo-Irani student-teacher with no intention, at present, of taking up teaching)

Commonsensically children come to know if only fragmentarily, that schooling is not neutral but underpinned by dominant assumptions and often staffed by culturally biased teachers who are in turn assigned a range of culturally offensive epithets (labels).

> I can remember when I was at school, we had a probationary teacher and for some reason everybody decided he was gay and he had a hell of a time. He left the school eventually. No-one knew if he was gay, but we decided he was. So that was it. We made his life like hell. He had a harsh time. And he gave a speech when he left and he literally had tears running down his eyes. It broke him. It was unfortunate he got this label. (Teacher)

> Oh yeah, Fuller, we used to write 'Cannon' on his jacket. We used to put it on his back with chalk. Get chalk. Walk round all day with Cannon. His belly was out here. Huge. But right short. Suede boots. (Pupil)

> He had a fight with the 'Tank' in the changing room. He got all bruised down his neck. He got his mum in. She got the 'Tank' in the middle of the basketball game. It was ace. She did 'arf slag him. (Pupil)

> Schooltrips were the best abroad. They were sound. We went to Amsterdam and we were on this boat and there were oranges in the bedrooms and we got forty of these oranges. And there were all these brand new cars waiting to be taken to dealers. Ladas, Russian and we were lugging all these oranges off the boat and it was a high boat and they landed all over these cars. It was sound. I'll tell you what, I had to walk around with Rin-Tin-Tin all the holiday. I had to hold his hand, honestly. (Pupil)

As such, some children are equally 'deviance provocative' (cf. Hargreaves *et al.*, 1975, pp. 260–66). They are integral to, not outside, 'deviance amplification spirals' in which some teachers can get locked.

> Effectively he is affecting pupil-teacher ratios but what is going on is deeper than that. He is affecting the structure of the school. He is destroying teachers. He is destroying the school. He is doing it single-handedly. The relationship between the Head and the staff is now, you know, that you are either on his side or against him.
>
> It is a case of a destructive child, an intelligent child who for reasons known to himself has taken it upon himself to be disruptive and anti-social. The teacher then, asked that the child be assessed by the local assessment service which he was. And they found that he was a perfectly normal child which he was, when they were there. Not wanting to be sent to any special education he was, he didn't want to leave the school etc., etc. and consequently he behaved perfectly and was assessed as being perfectly normal and teachable.
>
> But the teacher in charge of the lad disagreed violently and he complained to the Head saying he wished the child to be withdrawn. And the Head refused being of the opinion children with slightly less than normal tendencies are more likely to respond to a normal class situation rather than a withdrawal situation.

So the teacher took it to the Union. Perhaps, it is important to say this is a Group Nine primary, very large, Headmaster MBE for services to education, the whole bit and this sort of thing. A well established school. The school is not in a run down area or anything like that. So he went to the Union and the Union backed him and the Union then went back to the Headteacher and said 'We agree that the behaviour that is going on in the classroom is disruptive of the class, and the other thirty-odd children who are in there and it is impossible for Mr Jackson to teach'. The Head then disagreed so the Union withdrew its goodwill. Consequently they refused to cover, they refused to teach this child and they refused to take football etc., etc. all the peripheral things teachers do take part in.

At this the Head took umbrage and suspended the teacher on the grounds that he was refusing to do his job. So the Union put pressure on him, the Union therefore threatened to take bigger action unless something was done. So the Secretary of the Union was called in to see what could be done. Well he had just taken over from Johnson and he in his first days wanted to get to first base safely. So he didn't want too much hassle and so he concocted a way with the Director of Education for settling it quite amicably. And the result of this discussion was that another teacher was to be put in the classroom with the classteacher and the disruptive child to work together. Which, of course, meant that the two teachers, one not wanting to watch the other spying, suspicion between the two teachers sort of thing etc., etc. and a most unhealthy situation.

The original teacher went back to the Union and says, 'I want out. All I want is the child out, withdrawing'. Again, a refusal to withdraw the child so the Union, local branch of the Union decided they were going to meet with the General Secretary and it was going to be at Smallport in the near future. So they sent their most vociferous advocate to plead this teacher's case and they got no joy whatsoever from the General Secretary. And at the end of this harangue he produced from his pocket an knife which he waved at the General Secretary, which he demonstrated was the knife which the General Secretary was stabbing in the back of the member. And this took the General Secretary by surprize and this was followed with the production of a stick of rock which he suggested he could stick it up his arse and after that it has since developed.

It has calmed down a lot because the teacher realized he didn't want it to become a national incident 'cos he doesn't want to be painted as a Union hardliner, or anything like that. He merely wants the situation resolved amicably. But this friend of mine, where all this trouble has happened, he was saying, the kids are completely out of control now, that the school is completely out of control. The Head has lost control because half the staff are for him and half are actively against him. The pupils can see this and consequently the whole discipline of the school is caving in. You get instances of kids playing cars at the back of the class and being openly insolent to the teachers which frankly is more easily identifiable in a comprehensive school but it is not expected in a primary school where children are under the age of eleven. But the case goes on. It is incredible isn't it? It is unbelievable.

And, of course, the children see what is happening to this school which has been proud of its record over the years and all because of this kid. It is now putting up a facade to the outside and trying to paper over its own cracks. He's going to find it very difficult because of what has happened. Parents and the local press are aware of it.

(What kind of things did this disruptive child get up to?)

Well, general antisocial things, taking no part in the lessons, outrageous chattering, insolence to the teacher, refusing to cooperate. He wasn't violent. No violence involved in it. (Primary school teacher)

Thus, pupils are not neatly on the receiving end of teachers' labels. They do not neatly incorporate teachers' typifications into notions of self. For example, Hargreaves (1976, p. 292) asserts working class children ultimately are constrained to accept a deviant label, but there is a world of difference between constraint at the social level and constraint at the psychological level. Labelling theory is often premised on a dubious social psychology. Cool-Hand Luke was shot dead. Mac (Jack Nicholson) in *One Flew Over the Cuckoo's Nest* was labotomized and Gramsci died in prison but none assimilated totally, if at all, into their psyches the labels applied to them by their controllers. Equally, large numbers of children although they cannot necessarily wish away their teachers' powerful typifications do not simply accept them (cf. Bird, 1970). Further, teachers' labels are partially reactive to pupils' labels. They are not a 'freefloating' matter of will or skill (of consciousness) which can liberally be wished away (cf. Hargreaves *et al.*, 1977, pp. 257–64), for their generation is often born of bitter 'traumatic learning' (Waller, 1932, pp. 398–401) experiences of pupils.

I'm not a women's libber, if someone whisks me off my feet I wouldn't say no. I want a life without aggravation, but children hate you, despise you. Another twenty-five or thirty years like this, no chance. I'm going to try and find a rich man quickly. I couldn't do twenty-five years. I will be surprised if I am still teaching in five years, really. Getting up in the morning and saying 'I don't mind the day'. I don't have one day like that, not at all. I can feel it making me ill if I am not ill. Mentally I am not enjoying myself. I'm not enjoying my life at the moment. When I am at school I am not enjoying it and when I am at home I am not enjoying it, and when I go out I am not enjoying it. When I think to myself, I have got to this age and I am not enjoying life when I should be. That's what children are doing to me. People say, 'Are you happy?', and if I was honest I would have to turn round and say, 'No, I am not. I am not enjoying what I am doing'. And even when I am not doing it I have to recover from doing it. The weekend I spend, most of the time asleep or trying to get myself out, but I become really antisocial. I can't make the effort to go out 'cos if I do I feel ill in the morning. No-one can begin to imagine. (Teacher)

Thus, children teach their teachers and further evaluate their performances, offering remedial education.

> They were making all these paper aeroplanes. It became a standing joke. I ignored it, it didn't matter too much. I put them in the bin. It never got out of control. And during one lesson I heard them say, I was writing on the board, 'Throw it, throw it'. 'Right', I said, 'I'll catch them this time'. I walked down to the back, and this time they had made a paper dart about five foot in size, and they said, 'You're ignoring the small ones, so we thought we'd send you this one'. (Teacher)

> I said to them, 'What do you expect me to do?' They came up with a solution, to solve the problem of their misbehaviour. They said, 'Well, separate us. Next time we come in, make sure we're not sitting together'. I said, 'Fine'. Next lesson they tried to sit next to one another. I said, 'Well, do you remember what you said? Sit apart?' And this they did and the lesson went fairly well. But they told me to be more stricter because I wasn't always strict. They told me if I was prepared to be hard they would work. (Teacher)

Bourdieu (1977) may be right in asserting mediating entrepreneurial teachers exert symbolic violence over the lower classes by attempting to make legitimate only the cultural forms of the upper classes but working class pupils meet symbolic violence with their own symbolic violence.

> The best one ever I reckon. We had this woman. A new one. Miss Muffet, right? From behind she looked really fit, when she turned round she had an ingrowing chest. She used to like us in a circle. Right? She used to stare at you and I used to blow her kisses. I got this sticky 'L' plate and put it on her chair and when she sat down she sat on it. Then she started walking with the 'L' plate stuck to her arse like a learner on the game. We were killing ourselves. Eventually Joan Singer, a real creep spilled the beans. She collared me, she told me I was, what is it, in-, insub-, insubordinate and all this lot, I want you to write a two-page essay. I got home and I wrote Miss Muffet, I am of a very nervous disposition. I said I was on tablets from the doctor and all this. She came up to me next day and said, 'I'm very sorry John. I'm very sorry. I didn't know. I am sorry, I didn't mean to put you under any stress or strain.' You can really wind them up. (Pupil)

> One teacher had a high desk and a high chair and we took it away and put a little chair there. She was a really strict teacher and everybody was scared stiff of her. She went round the whole class accusing everybody. We were really scared of her, really nervous. She came to me and I said, 'I know who's done it'. I was stood out in front of the class shaking like but I said to her, 'I'm not telling you who's done it'. I never told her. (Pupil)

Pupils also meet teacher symbolic (and physical) violence with their own physical violence.

We had to rescue him a couple of times. He had a tough time in the playground. The kids went up, 'How are you today, sir?' and they would go right up to him and take his arms and squeeze him, and another would walk on the other side. It ended up with six or so all crushing around him, all around him, squeezing him. And all the other kids looking on.

He had a Beetle. And the kids were all sitting on the bonnet, on the roof, on the boot, clinging. At the end of school. And he never ... I was sitting in my car. I didn't say anything to the kids because he was coming and he must deal with it himself. I thought he would say 'Right! Off my car'. Or walk back into school until they had gone home. But he didn't. He opened the car as if they weren't there. [laughter] He opened it as if they didn't exist. He got in his car and he drove off at enormous speed and they fell off. [laughter] There could have been a terrible accident. He just reved off and they just fell off. How he could see where he was going I don't know. He just carried on driving. It's terrible isn't it? (Teacher)

He said to me, something to me, I didn't like. He used to get nasty and aerated. He used to wind up. He said, 'put your fists where your mouth is', or something. I just grabbed hold of his arms and pushed him where you put all your clothes up. He came towards me to grab me so I kneed him. I got dragged up to the Head and my old boy had to come in. (Pupil)

It all started at the beginning of the term, September, yeah. Within three weeks I had my purse pinched out of my room. These kids who were involved, I had a do with anyway. Just about discipline, 4th years, just resented it and the next minute I went into my room and my purse was gone. And luckily the kids who were having PE with me had noticed them down there. So straight away three of them came into me saying they had seen these kids around my room. Anyway I investigated and they had been seen running out of school about ten minutes after the incident. We didn't catch them, but we went out onto the estate because there is an overspill estate just next to our upper school and we found the purse empty. No money. We managed to find a cheque card and everything else. So we called the police in which is very rare in our place. Normally the police are taboo. Anyway I managed to get one of the senior teachers and he called the police in and we had it finger-printed and everything. And eventually the next day we had them in the room one by one and they all started accusing each other eventually. They all denied it at first being as hard-faced as hell. All denied it. In the end I had them all done.

But what annoyed me was they weren't picked up by the police 'til the week after and they thought they had got away with it, although they had been caught. So the day after they were brought into the police station and they came back into school and I had happened to be teaching two of them and they had been charged the night before and I walked into the room they were straight at me. Pushing me up against the wall and door, f'ing and blinding at me. Very hard these girls. The ring leader is hard as nails, harder than any lad I know. The other two followed. I got slammed up against the door, the fact that why was I taking them to court because the police had got me in it. They told the kids at the police station that they had suggested to me that I let them off with a caution but I had insisted on prosecution. Which I had, I said I wanted them prosecuted. I wanted them done, not just for the nicking but for the whole thing. They had been getting away with murder since the first year. These kids had been getting away with murder, getting away with things like assaulting staff. One of our pregnant staff got kicked in the stomach by one of them. I was determined to go through with it. I thought that this is the opportunity now to get something done. So I immediately threw them out. I couldn't teach them, I had another twenty-eight in the class. They had seen it going on and they had all heard them telling me to f-off and all the rest. So I managed to get them thrown out of the class and the next thing is dropping the netball base. Different class actually, not the same kids. The rest of the school had picked this up and all were going at me. They weren't suspended after the little bit of intimidating. They carried on in the school. School did nothing about it. Not at all. They just said 'We'll take these girls out of your class'. So it all got around. That I had been beaten up by these three girls which was an over-exaggeration. So because I had taken them to court all their mates in the school were looking for aggro.

The girls who had told me about the theft, they got beat up in the toilets. So they were taken out of school, the poor kids who had told them. It all got around. Then one day another 4th year lesson. I was just arranging the kids and just as I was turning around I saw this kid swing this base around and just let go of it. Smashed straight across my toes. I knew damn well they had done it on purpose and so did the other kids. So anyway I couldn't prove that. Once I started accusing her of doing it on purpose all her friends said, 'No she didn't, she just dropped it'. So she stayed in school as well. She became a little folk hero. Anyway I was off school then for three weeks because I had broken three of my toes. That was that incident.

A bit later I took the kids to City High. As fate would have it the girl who was involved in this incident was the cousin of that hard case that nicked my money. I didn't know this 'til afterwards. They had exchanged tales. I didn't realize they were related. Two netball teams and all the way through the game I knew there was something going on and my kids just lost and they were just not interested in playing the game. My kids were hard but they were just not interested. Apparently they were being intimidated on court and their teacher told them to stop it and immediately had been told to f-off and they just carried on and on.

We went to get changed in the changing room and it started, kicking, spitting between the two teams and the spectators. The two schools were having a gang war. The other teacher tried to lock her spectators in the toilets but that didn't work. They managed to break out of there. So anyway we were going towards the minibus and all of a sudden out of the corner of my eye I saw one of my kids being dragged by her hair. She was swung around and her head was smashed on the pavement and all these girls are in there kicking the hell out of her. So I went over to stop it and dragged this girl off by the hair and she started hitting me. She started laying into me. So I had a bag luckily, with a load of netballs and I swung them around and knocked her off her feet. All her mates were around her then and the language was just incredible. So I then piled the kids onto the minibus and the back door of the minibus swung straight round and banged me on the back of the head. That didn't please me any. Eventually I realized that this kid was related to the one that stole my money. She was not even playing. She had known that we were going to be there and she took her mates to get me. Dreadful. It was incredible.

So I had to have time off school because I had broken my toes, so at our place there is just a load of aggravation. It has died a bit with me now but it is still there generally. You can feel it. They got a conditional discharge.

It depressed me terribly. I took it personally. I really took it personally because at the time my relationships with kids were really good. It was a personal thing. It got so heated all their friends getting involved. I was quite upset. I didn't want to go into school. In a way those three toes being broken gave me a breathing space to get back together again because it happened within two days of taking them to court.

It helped. It's like this for most teachers. It's a game for most of our kids coming to school. A horrible girl is worse than any bad boy. There are a hell of a lot of hard kids flying around this place. They'd got me to the point where I thought I'd give up teaching. I began really thinking of getting out. The aggravation that generally goes on. It does want me to pack it in but there is nowhere to go though. (Teacher)

They used to say to me, 'You boy, you boy'. I grew one summer, quickly. The difference in the same teachers. Instead of 'You boy, you boy, you football, you running, you something'. Now they came to me and said, 'Right John, what would you like to do? Do you fancy cricket today?' I looked at them and said, 'Yeah, I'm bigger than you this year'. It all depends on size and weight. If you are bigger than they are they treat you as equals. It's tough if you happen to be little. I could do what I wanted once I got big. (Pupil)

The Child as a Teacher Processor

Thus, Althusser's Educational Ideological State Apparatus, his pupil mincer (Open University, 1977, p. 10) is synchronously informally converted, by moral labouring pupils richochetting and differentiating the curriculum and hidden curriculum, into an Educational Counter-Ideological Counter-State Apparatus, a teacher mincer. Consequently, it is hardly surprising that certain teachers face personal crises.

There was a group of children that were causing a big disturbance and a lot of the children had left school, fifty per cent, I would say who helped to cause the riot had left the previous term and unemployed, nothing to do. So they were larking about. It was reported to the local authority what was going on. These children were coming back to school. So all this is going on. And the Deputy Head, because the Head was off, asked the authority for help with these trouble-makers and she was told she would have to contain them within the school.

The teachers said they did not want these kids back in school, they were not prepared to teach them. The Deputy Head said that she would teach these herself in a group, every day, all day. But the staff wouldn't have that. There was a big staff meeting and one said that we are not prepared to teach whilst these kids are in the school. She had been severely threatened.

This particular day, all of a sudden, nobody quite knew how, they had felt it all week, something in the air. This particular playtime. They didn't know what happened but all of a sudden all these kids were running down corridors, banging doors and throwing bricks. They smashed all the glass in the classrooms. Bricks had been thrown in the lab and there was this teacher in the lab alone who couldn't get out and they threatened to throw bricks at her. And they literally destroyed the place. It lasted a day. They smashed the school.

The police came in on horses, that was a mistake. I don't know if the bricks were thrown before or after the police. It was the sight of the police. A lot of our kids are really, really anti-police. So when these horses came in, they started to throw things at the horses and things. I don't know what happened but it sparked something because the kids that were just watching got involved. They were all shouting and jeering.

It is hard to work out why it started. It was not just our school, there were some from others, word got around. The men teachers get the kids' back up. I don't know, women avoid trouble, the men rise up.

But there was this woman teacher. I could hear noise. I went to her room. Glass was all around. She came out crying. It didn't calm down with the police, there were little pockets all over. The kids didn't run away. We had one woman teacher who had a nervous breakdown, she just could not stop crying. I had never seen her crying before. It affected her so badly. She cried in the staffroom all the time. In the meeting, she broke down, crying, the voice broken. She said, 'I can't say what I feel. I never thought it would come to this. I've been teaching for twenty years and never had any trouble, and the next minute the kids I really like and helped and who themselves had gone out of their way to stop and do anything for me, they were the ones at the window throwing bricks at me'. It really upset her. She said, 'I don't think I can take any more'. She slowly, slowly, came to. A lot were ill with this. There are now a lot of teachers who do not want to be there. Most of the teachers did like children. They wanted the best for them. Now there is no heart. The Head of the Lower School had a breakdown. People don't care now, there is no heart there. The kids wander about saying, 'No-one cares any more'.

The staffroom is empty. No-one cares. It was appalling. The staff didn't want these children. They wanted them out. And afterwards there was a staff meeting and some of the staff said that if nothing is done, we resign from teaching, but not before we've told all the newspapers and all the world what it's really like in this school, if you don't do something. And they have suspended some. And it's going to be reorganized. (Teacher)

He came in. He was very strange in the staffroom. He'd sit in the staffroom, never spoke to us, not to anybody, he just looked at you. Just stared at you. Never said anything. Barely answered you.

He went into his classroom, he evidently prepared his work well, did maths. And on this particular day, I was looking out of the window. I saw arms coming out, two arms and a head. Another kid pushed the legs out. They were all falling out into the playground. You could see someone starting to come out and evidently being pulled back in. Evidently the teacher was trying to pull them back in. As he was pulling one side, they were falling out the other.

On another occasion, an English teacher was in the room next door, said that he had a free and went to mark in the empty classroom. And between the two classrooms was a stockroom and evidently in this room he taught in was a manhole of some sort. And the kids managed to kick it to one side and as he was turning around and writing on the board one was quickly pushing another into the loft. And he never noticed! And the English teacher in the other room said that he could hear a noise above and said, 'That's a big bird!' and he said, all of a sudden this kid dropped out into his room. Saw him and had a fit. He said, 'Not a sound'. A few minutes another little kid arrived, and he ended up with six! He said, 'I could not believe that the other teacher didn't realize six kids had disappeared out of his room'. He didn't. Every time he turned round, they sat up dead straight and up they went across the top. (Teacher)

Some teachers resolve these crises by 'a withdrawal of knowledge' (Willis, 1979, p. 77). They resign their teaching without resigning their jobs.

He was obviously on drugs of some sort because he had dilated pupils. He had large pupils. He was weird. He was always dressed in black. He taught his subject, art and craft. There was this terrible noise, so I just looked over the top of the door. I could hear this noise. They weren't fantastically noisy but there was this noise.

And you could see these paper aeroplanes going all over the room. They were going out to the front to this wad of paper, and helping themselves. And he was sitting there reading *The Guardian*, with his feet on the top of the desk, crossed. Completely ignoring them, and I went in and

said, 'I hope you don't mind me saying but do you know what's going on?'
I said, 'I've just looked behind that cupboard' and literally it was full to the
very top. It sounds daft but in one hour all that paper. They were seeing
how many they could get behind the back of this ten-foot high cupboard.
He just looked up and said, 'I am paid to teach, not look after this lot, and
you can't teach this lot'. So he just read. I complained but was told to cool
it. Let's cool it. He left eventually. (Senior teacher)

Occasionally, 'the withdrawal of teaching' is manifested not merely by a psychological but also by a physical withdrawal from the classroom.

She was notorious, absolutely notorious. You could find her anywhere but
in her classroom. Anywhere. She couldn't stay in the same room a minute
with them. I'm sure she was an alchi. (Teacher)

We were all girls and we had this teacher, quite young and he couldn't cope
with us. We weren't particularly naughty. He just couldn't cope with thirty
girls sat in front of him. He was terrible. He used to leave the room. We did
nothing. A lot of girls like Dawn, my friend, just talked. (Pupil)

Thus, some teachers, the naively assumed 'highpriests of the ruling ideology',
find it difficult to hang onto 'a viable, sacred self' (Goffman, 1956, p. 497). As such,
some suffer from school phobia.

There are a few teachers who are school phobics. God yes. There are three
women who don't even look the part — thin, small, quiet. Now out of
them two of their husbands are redundant. The only money going into
their house is coming from these women and they've got young kids. Two
are leaving teaching without having another job. They have just said, 'I
have just had enough'. Mortgages and everything. 'It's my health and it's
not worth it'. So they are just packing it in completely without another job
to go to. All the others that are off are getting school phobia, I thought I
was. It was funny. I had a bad cold and felt dreadful. I had one day off. A
Friday. And I went in on Monday and the secretary said to me, 'Good
morning, SP', 'Pardon?' 'Good morning, SP'. I said, 'What does SP stand
for?' She said, 'I just thought you were getting a bit of school phobia'. Since
then I have been called SP. I said, 'I haven't got school phobia!' So if I am
dying now I have to drag myself in. This is it. They are all on pills, things
like that and they come in looking like death. I mean there are about three
women, there is one actually who has decided she can't face the end of term
and she was flashing these pills around on Friday, apparently valium and
saying the doctor thinks I ought to have valium. She was making everyone
aware that she wasn't going to be in for at least three days and sure enough
Monday morning Pat's away. She's got a sore throat! They are all chucking
these valium tablets around. (Teacher)

If stress, anxiety, depression, nervous breakdown and mental illness generally
are understood sociologically then it is hardly surprizing teachers suffer from them.

For children can present teachers with profound crises of self, can render teachers dramaturgically incompetent by not allowing them to play their official paradigmatic role. The teacher's ability to control and protect 'a viable, sacred self' is suddenly taken away in classroom degradation ceremonies and collusive pupil conspiracies.

I don't know why he had a breakdown. It was awful. It affected him so much. But as soon as he had this breakdown he couldn't face the kids. His wife said he never went out of the house. Just stopped in, week after week, after week. She said we never had a holiday since the breakdown. He was a gentle man and all of a sudden he just couldn't cope. It was though he couldn't cope with children. He was brilliant at his subject. He has never said. It's sad. He never discussed it with his wife. He just came home one night and said, 'I'm not going back'. She could see he was getting a bit depressed and aggravated at home, but he just came in and said, 'I'm not going back'. He never went back. Pensioned off about fifty-five. He reached a point where he could not cope with kids. I suppose he was rigid and couldn't bend a little. (Teacher/friend)

The Head had a nervous breakdown, I don't know why. I never knew what it was. I loved this class and loved to teach them. They were fantastic. But he had a breakdown. I don't know why. He taught the top class. He taught them in the room next door and one day he walked into my room and never said anything to me, excuse me or anything. He walked around and took six exercise books off the kids and tore them to shreds and threw them in the air and walked back out again. I don't know why he did it. The kids just looked but because it was a very strange thing it didn't register.

He sent this girl to me, a lovely girl, I don't know why she had to be caned. He never told me. But he would not cane her himself. I got on really well with this girl. He came in, strange like and said to me, 'You've got to cane her', and he gave me the cane. I just didn't know what to do. I didn't know what she'd done or anything. I don't think she had done anything. I had to cane and it was awful, and he stood there while I did it. I lifted it, I remember, and closed my eyes. I couldn't look. She came to me at 4 o'clock and she said, 'Don't let it worry you because when I looked at your face it didn't hurt because I could see you didn't want to'. But I had to. He went away not long after and was in a nursing home for three months. He came back for six weeks and then retired. (Teacher)

In our school now there are four teachers who have had nervous breakdowns since September. Our Head of English has been two months having this nervous breakdown and there are other people that are taking time off. At the moment because of the kids, we have at Lower School alone, first and second years, we have got four supply teachers in for people who are having long-term medical time off. And that makes it worse. Because they see all these supply people coming in, in and out like and they like chalk it up as another one they have got rid of, another member of staff.

It is as bad as that. One class in particular in the second year, their whole, they have admitted this to various people, their whole meaning for coming into school is to play the teachers up and have a damn good time and get them to lose their temper and they never learn anything. They come in, have a damn good laugh at the teachers' expense by getting them aggravated. And it's 'God, I've got 2Z next'. They just love it these kids. That's the feeling in the staffroom. A lot of antagonism. Your image of Roman Catholic schools is 'God's on your side', sort of thing. It's a myth, it really is. We had four muggings in one night. I don't know what the answer is. Why has it gone so bad?

We are going to be reorganized soon, but we are going to be the same. Nobody will apply for our school at all, because they know, it goes down the grapevine. Most teachers will be trying to move sideways out. (Teacher)

Becker (1952b, p. 76) has already related the importance of working class children to teacher horizontal career movements to schools where 'problems are least aggravated and most susceptible of solution'.

It certainly taught me what comprehensive schools were like. I realized if I was going to teach in a comp I would have to be a little harder. It didn't disillusion me from teaching, but I wouldn't go back to a comprehensive school, or if I did I would have to go to a good school. I was basically surprized, I never realized how much time you spent disciplining and hassling. It did not put me off but I did not want to teach there. I had times when, times when I said, 'What am I doing here? All this work, you try to prepare, and you're not doing anything.' One thing I quickly found was with classes like this that at least you didn't have to prepare anything because you knew you were not going to get through much.

The first shock I had is I was told by my head of department, he told me this is where he keeps the books and he collects the books in every lesson. But I said, 'How do they do their homework?' He said, 'Don't worry about that, if they take the books home they'll lose them, they'll be wrecked, ripped by the parents'. That was amazing. I said, 'How are they going to learn?' He said, 'Don't worry about that, about learning at home. If they take the books home we'll never see them again'. Exercise and texts books, they'd be damaged and lost and they weren't going to do any homework.

I expected to teach, that people would listen and respect you and I quickly came to terms with the fact that they don't. These kids don't want to learn and they're not going to conform. There is no point in trying to teach them, especially low ability ones.

This was the time I realized I didn't want to teach in comprehensive schools. I wanted to go in and teach my subject. You have to have people who want and are interested in the subject and these children weren't. I lost the enthusiasm I had, due to the kids. I realized that there was a problem with my relationship with the children and I wasn't treating them in the way they should be, like a bastard. I thought, I can't treat them the way I want to treat them so I'm out. But they wouldn't cooperate with me. I have to be angry to shout and I wasn't angry. I couldn't get worked up about it. I couldn't lose my temper which is the only way I could become authoritarian. I wanted to treat them like adults but they rejected that. All the teachers were bastards. They said, 'If you're going to stay here, you've got to be a bastard'. I could see myself becoming like that. How many times have they got to kick you? You've got to become a bastard or resign, just give up. I didn't want that. I enjoyed the children one bit but there was something I didn't understand about them. (Grammar school teacher)

Another solution to the problems generated by children is teacher absenteeism and 'walking out' of the school altogether, an *instantaneous* movement out of teaching.

It was pretty obvious he was unhappy with kids, he wanted to get to another school. One of the ways he relieved his stress was to have days off, high absent rates, days off, you know there are certain members of staff you suspect of not genuine absence and it is a coping action. He was quite obviously one of those. He didn't want to be in the school. At Christmas he went, our Advisor is a washout and kept a job open for him elsewhere. I said, 'If you can find me a replacement who is reasonable, that's OK because he's doing no good here'. I said, 'I'd rather he went out'. In fact, he left the other school half way through the next term anyway. Just walked out. Never saw him again. He had a PhD. and thought he could get a job anyway. If you can't stand the pressure and stress, you just walk out. If you're unstable, this situation here exposes these things, if you have abnormalities in your character if you like, are unstable. If you can't stand the stress you do something about it, just walk out. (Head of Department)

Thus, children are often central to teacher decisions to terminate their careers.

Young teachers, they try to look smart in their Windsor jackets and flannel trousers, cowboy shoes and ties. They're trying to be like you but they're not. They don't behave like other teachers. No. We had one, chemistry. We found his first name out and we used to call him, 'Steven, could you please come over here and help?' That was him who cracked up. It was really sound.

I had this baseball bat, and he took it off me. So I got his pencil case and fed it to the gerbils. That's how it all started. I said, 'Steven, Steven, give my baseball bat back', and he wouldn't. Baxter took the gaspipe and fed it into the goldfish bowl and gassed all the goldfish. He walked around saying, 'I'll light your bunsen burners', and everybody had lit their own. It was sound.

He bottled out. He cracked up. We'd get syringes and squirt them at the blackboard, the chalk wouldn't stick. He used to walk out and get other teachers to control us. Heathcliffe had to come in. Other teachers came in to protect him and we had to do some work then. He really was clueless. We used to get detentions off him and not go. By the end of term we should have been there the whole holiday.

He broke. We did this thing on static electricity and somebody did something to it and he got a right belt off it, a right belt he got off it. He walked off right at the end. We got sent to Jackson, but it wasn't really a punishment. He married that ox-basher in PE and he was a right dipstick. If you've got a real bunch of lads it doesn't matter who it is, they haven't got a chance. If they went in with a pair of docs and a flicknife they'd probably still have trouble. (Pupil)

Teachers' Careers

The Plunger

Goffman (1959) was led to observe that mental patients' careers fell into three distinct phases: pre-patient, in-patient and post-patient. In discussing teachers' moral careers *vis-à-vis* children it would be a mistake to suggest they are neatly patterned and phased. However, for many teachers there is a career sequence. The *plunger* (cf. Lacey, 1977, p. 128) is typical of the tiro or a new, but experienced, member of the school staff who is morally 'treading water'. Caught up in 'a theatre of struggle of opposite forces', these teachers morally and physically exhaust themselves keeping afloat, earnestly trying to square a contradictory circle.

They weren't working toward anything. No satisfaction. They didn't want to be there. They'd opted for science but because they were badly behaved, they burnt through a table with a bunsen burner and burnt someone's hair, because the science teachers didn't want them in their lessons then they had drama.

In the third year, I only had them one period a week. They were lower ability but they could come up with some good results because they hadn't got any inhibitions. They are quite willing to loosen up, they were always loose! They wandered amongst each other, making silly comments, pushing each other off chairs, they used to have these clicky badges and make silly noises, kick each other, hold conversations, they were really interested. The girls would brush each others' hair, make up, talk about the youth club, try each others' clothes on, but the boys were the most badly behaved, but one period a week, to be honest, I didn't care what they did and I went along with them.

By the fourth year, I came across this new method of approach where you sit down and decide what the drama is to be. They decide what they want to do. It's like improvization but it rolls. Anything can happen, they don't know what is going to happen. So you work through experience.

They thought it was quite good at first, because it was new. I'm not saying they were revolutionary. But it was a wonderful vehicle for the boys to go absolutely over the top. All they wanted to do was entertain and make a fool of themselves. They came out with good results, they tried very hard to be stupid. So things improved, but they had a very low concentration level, their span of attention is minimal. Mucking about still but not as badly.

They got into this bad habit of working in small groups, I think it's a bad habit because if I suggested another group, just to give them some variation, try split these disruptive pupils, they wouldn't break and even if they did, nothing would be done because of the disruption. The damage had already been done, they dictated how I should group them. They had these friendship cliques and stayed in them. And that was the only way you could get them to work. I did try, obviously, but there was confrontation and they just refused. I did have them in different groups one session, nothing was done by the whole class because the disruptive pupils were all clinging about the hall, talking to each other and breaking up the whole group. So they had won, you know and I resigned myself to that because if I was going to do anything constructive then I had to, you know.

These boys fascinated me. They did have something to offer but my head of department who is the most patient man I've met, couldn't get them to do anything. They'd come to a standstill with him. I couldn't get them to do anything but he had no solution. It was a failure. Very often they were absent from lessons, they just wouldn't turn up.

Very often there was chaos because there was a stage, so that was an interesting distraction, pulling the curtains, getting into the prop cupboard and coming dressed up in all sorts. The boys would climb up the walls because they had these ropes, window-ropes hanging, and they would hang by their necks from these window-ropes which they thought was highly amusing. I was spare. All the time they were bored and just fed up.

I wanted to, my whole aim was to integrate, to work as a whole class because I felt they were getting nowhere. In the boys' friendship cliques it was just one competition for who could be the biggest fool, who could make the most trouble for the teacher. So they were so influential in the class that you had to play along with them.

One day the girls went off and they were alright, this group of boys decided they would do something on smuggling. We talked about it, all the sort of thing you could do. I asked them for suggestions for things people could smuggle. We asked for suggestions. There was one boy who was really interested in drama. And every suggestion he made, they just took the piss out of him. The rest made him look a fool, the only one who was suggesting anything constructive, They all wanted to do telly stuff, copying The Minders, the Professionals, Kojak and I didn't feel it was of any worth. Drama is about problem solving, making decisions.

So they changed their minds, they would have an old-fashioned

Spanish galleon. So they set this up. The only idea was to get into the prop cupboard, dress up, hide behind these ridiculous outfits, get the handcuffs out, whips and set up a boat. This one boy, they made him dress up as a harem girl, she was tied up in the galleon. It was quite kinky actually and this other lad got his big whip, whipping the slaves. The personalities fitted, it was just amazing. You could see the born leaders. The captain of the ship had a camera and he turned out to be a spy. All these fantasy things they did. All of a sudden it just disintegrated into a raucous activity. I wasn't amused. They were enjoying it but there was nothing educational, no value.

So I sat down with them and said, 'We haven't got anywhere have we?' They said, 'It's boring, we don't want to do it'. I said, 'Why don't you stop fighting me?' I got some on my side, they liked me as a teacher.

One day I thought it worked, we got on with it and we made a pact. I thought it was going to be a turning point, I thought at last it had worked. I got a lot out of it and they did. So we made a pact, this agreement at the end of the lesson, that we were all going to work the next lesson. We all sat down and had this pact.

The very next week they had forgotten the pact. The following week inside I thought, 'Oh, my God'. I hated them. I felt like strangling them because the whole lesson went so badly. They would not admit making this pact. It wasn't cool, it wasn't the done thing.

The girls went off and worked on their own and tried to work with the boys but they were just fooling around. They didn't want to know. They didn't do anything all lesson. I was really fed up because previously I had thought, finally, I didn't think I had an answer to the problem but I thought they had some kind of respect for me.

And then the week after they'd watched *Boys from the Blackstuff*, so they wanted to do a play, a complete takeoff which didn't please me in the slightest but the mere fact they were dedicated to it. They actually wanted to do it. I couldn't stop them because if I did they would . . . they worked, they were brilliant, there wasn't any silliness, constructive. The fact that this was on tv and obviously being passed as good, then they probably found some safety in it. They were so serious about it. They thought it was real life, their parents were in the same situation. It was real. I was pleased for them that they had got something out of it. But I didn't want them just to imitate what was on telly, so we had a discussion on authority which was a wonderful opportunity for them. They said that you need someone in authority. I said, 'What about teacher authority and they said, 'Well that's different. It's a laugh isn't it?'. The whole intention was to make the teacher's life a misery.

I thought I found a solution, but I was so disheartened. They were interested in the dole and drinking. They enjoyed the drinking scene.

From then on it was as bad as ever. I was depressed for they just totally rejected me and failed to stick to their words. Going back to this pact, I took it personally because I'd given them my word and I don't go back on my promises, but the thing is they just don't have the same sorts of values as I have. If I give my word I stick to it and expect people to do the same. And if I am prepared to give my all I don't expect to get kicked in the face, and that is what they did. I took it personally and I thought they had won, hadn't they? I hadn't lost totally but I was feeling pretty fed up. And I was feeling personally that I'd been kicked in the teeth and they were back to their old routine. They loved the idea that they are being told off and they couldn't tolerate anything different. I never imagined I would come across people like that. They were so two-faced. You're bound to feel disheartened, aren't you? Human nature doesn't allow you to go on, knocking your head against a brick wall, because it hurts. And like if your teaching is not getting any results, or negative results, you're going to feel like that, aren't you?

Pupils have a far greater hold on teachers than they will admit to. I admit that if the kids are not going to do anything, then they have got me by the short and curlies, haven't they? They have got you even more by the short and curlies when the head walks past the door. So it's hardly surprising that control becomes more important than any content.

Every day colleagues say, 'I don't know why you bother doing all this work, because they don't bloody-well deserve it, this shower. They want putting in a cage and poking'. Half of them don't give a damn about the kids. They don't care about the real welfare of the kids. They're not interested in the kids' education. Why do teachers become like this? Possibly because they don't get the results they want from the kids. Because they don't resign themselves to teachers, they have to be written off. Even the remedial teachers say, 'I don't know what to do with them', and end up doing nothing with them. They didn't know the solution. I mean, what do you think they could have done? They experienced rejection, are constantly problematic, constantly refusing to come to any agreement or compromize.

One chap, and this is true, has a great stick, he is a woodwork teacher and he says things like, 'If you don't bloody well shut up I'll bloody well come round and bloody well snap your head off', things like that. (Does it work?) Yes, oh yes, but they absolutely loathe him, they hate him, they detest him and they all . . . he loves it, this is part of the aura he carries, you can tell he is a mean man. He is a real ex-army type. But most don't cope, but he contains them.

At the other end, there's the Deputy Head who teaches history, this is true. He honestly has them swinging from the rafters in his classroom, literally from the rafters. They have these metal strips down the classroom, on the ceiling with a ledge on each side, and during his lessons they are swinging. It's part of the folklore of the staffroom.

And that seems the choice available to me. I'm getting more and more exhausted, chasing my tail. I must be doing it all wrong. It's quite obvious I can't teach. It must be me, me. I don't know how much more I can take, I feel as though I've failed as a person. I think I'm a nice enough woman. I'm bright enough, why don't they react to me in some positive way? I'm a big baby. If someone says to me, long enough, 'You're an ugly bitch' well, I'd lock myself away and not come out. Same with children. If they're going to say to me, 'You're crap, Miss', then I will be crap, and resign myself to it.

In the long run I don't know if I can hang on in. At this moment in time I'm probably at a low ebb, you know, apprehension with the job. I'm worried. I don't want to get like the teachers that are in my school now. So many of them say, they went in with high ideals and then . . . They make your life hell. And they can make you feel absolute shit all the time, can't they? And I'm frightened of slowly getting sucked into it. (Teacher in second year)

The Sinker

The *sinker* is a failed teacher who has morally gone under or is in imminent danger of doing so. The pressing practical problem for 'high priest' teachers is to ensure they do not take up a *defrocked* career which is very difficult when met with very competent 'anticlerical' moral career gatekeepers on the chalkface. Teacher moral careers are pupil constructions and destructions; and pupil moral careers are teacher constructions and destructions; and it can be a holy war! It is small wonder some teachers embrace callous fanaticism in order to cope with the 'heathen'; and the heathen embrace callous fanaticism in order to cope with the 'high priest'.

When I moved over to Blackheath the children in the first class I took, it was a demolition job on me, it was very, very difficult for me to take. Well, I was moving from a school with a very middle class academic type background to a school in a very rundown working class area. Very tough kids. It was open plan which I had never been in before and I was taking over and this was a challenge one does. Obviously in my first year as a deputy you want to make some kind of name for yourself and to be demolished in public. (How did they demolish you?) Oh, it was hell, there was this caucus, a group of lads and some girls. They were ten to eleven, fourth year primary.

The leader of the whole hotchpotch was a boy, Carl. Did you see *Made in Britain*, last Sunday? (No) Trevor, you missed a treat, a skinhead. He was that boy minus six years. He was that boy at the age of eleven, a bright boy, a good looking boy. Well built lad. Good at sports. You know, everything going for him except his home where his father was in jail for various things, usually involving violence.

His family were the local mafiosa. When there was any trouble they would go to that family for the strong arm, rather than the police. They would come and sort it out for you, for a price. And there were five brothers, four uncles and a mother who was, you know, loose in her morals, if you like, but then her husband was away all the time. She used to tell the children he was away decorating one of the Queen's castles, because he was invariably in Lancaster jail. So when you asked him he would say his dad was decorating one of the Queen's castles.

He used to manipulate me by constantly chattering, talk at the top of his voice all the time, all the time. Incessantly. Deliberately. He went on and on and on. So you could get nothing done. It was a special job on me. He was naturally garrulous but at the same time it was a special job on me to see what he could do. The idea behind it was to wind me up, basically because he would. He was the one kid in the class who got the attendance prize at the end of the year. He never missed a day. He was always in and always messing.

He was a very violent boy. He had a terrible temper and that temper used to manifest itself in real acts of violence. He would flare up in the classroom. A girl on one occasion had said something to him and he was out in the playground and he wasn't going to come in the school in the afternoon. He sat in the playground and would not come in. So I went out. I said, 'Carl, I don't want you out here. I want you in here'. I didn't actually want him anywhere! But he was safer in than out there. He came in and fortunately, [laughter] on that day we had an HMI in and he started running around the classroom chasing this girl. He shouted, 'I'm going to fucking well kill you, Brownie'. He pursued her round the class. I had to manoeuvre into a position where I could get hold of the girl and say 'Go to the Head' and at the same time head him off which is difficult in open plan and so in this cowboy routine it was going on. But it wasn't something I could ignore because if it was allowed to continue then he would disrupt the rest of this class and school. Anyway, that was calmed down.

We had a thirteen year old who thought he was the cock of the local comprehensive who came down one afternoon because he had learned of this boy, his reputation extended far and wide. And they finished up having a bottle fight in the yard which I had to go out and split up and the pair of them got milk bottles, smashed them against the wall and they were going against each other, sort of thing.

But he's come in the next day and be as nice as pie. Be grateful. Until he got fed up again. And then the incessant chat, chat, chat that started. And he was surrounded with three of them, just three of them. He was the catalyst that set them going. Then he'd start to do something, pinch a pencil here, put on ink on somebody's work for no reason that was apparent. The reason was to be disruptive but the motive for doing it was probably pure boredom. Because I was coming out of a situation where I'd given children things to do and they'd done them, to a situation where I'd got children who were in fact there because if they didn't go their parents would beat them. It was a day nursery, it was a daily child-minding service in which some of the children didn't want to be in.

On one occasion I was walking around marking some of the work with the kids and he was doing maths and he had done a couple of sums in an hour and I said, 'This is not enough, you've got to get on with it', his work. He looked up and said, 'Fuck this, and fuck you and all, Jones'. He closed his book, went out of the classroom into the yard, climbed a ten foot railing and sat on the top of it. He didn't do anything at all. He just sat there. I was looking at him. He was doing nothing. He was just sitting there. I thought the only way to get him down is to do something he wants to do, so I took the children out for rounders. Anyway, he slowly came down and sat at the bottom of the fence and he ambled across the grass and he sat on the grass for a couple of minutes and then came onto the pitch. He said, 'I'm sorry, Mr Jones, I do some daft things'. So I thought, 'What do I do here? I'm not going to beat him. I'm going to join him'. I said, 'Get out on the field and get fielding', and for the rest of the day he was fine. You know, he'd won. He'd done what he wanted to do. I think for the whole twelve month period I never worked out how to get him to do what I wanted him to do. He knew damn well how to get me to do what he wanted to do. He was that sort of child.

He tried to, at one stage, in a fit of rage, to take a swing at me and I pinned him by his throat to the wall. And his face was puce and his fists were out and I just said, 'If you do that then you are going to get one back, Carl'. I was by this time at the end of my tether.

I'd gone through ten years in my other school without a single day off, and all through this year I was suffering from migraine, from all sorts of things. I wasn't making them up, making excuses for staying off. I had them. They were obviously psychosomatic but they were real headaches. They were not imagined. They were real migraines. I'd want to go home from school with them and on a couple of occasions they just came on top of me and I just went over.

It affected my health. I'd never before had any discipline problems, I've never since that had discipline problems. I expected it to undermine my authority in the school for ever, but it didn't because this boy was accepted as being the main man. The kids looked up to him being the main man. When he got to the top of the primary school, when there were no other fourth years to control him, well, he was the controlling influence. In a way he didn't control the school because I managed to keep him confined to my area, so I soaked up the punishment, to try and keep him away from everybody else. He was a very violent boy.

I tried to get him down to the city youth theatre, because he was dramatically very good, he practiced all day! He was very good [laughter] but they didn't take him, because he was a skinhead. They didn't want that sort, they could see he was a problem. But that sort of thing might have brought him out, but they didn't want to know. And he in a way, he resented that. He resented me for putting him in a position where he wasn't going to succeed. I took him down and when he was refused he turned on me because I had led him into a situation where he had felt he had been made a fool. So that worked against me.

We tried all sorts of ways to control this boy, I'd send him to the Head to sit on his own, and that worked. It was the only thing that would work. In fact, when he was put away from others, put away on his own he was OK. No audience. No-one to play to, no-one to play up. But you could not do that all day. No. Not all day, every day of the year. So that only came as a last sanction.

You didn't bother using the strap because the strap was just a laugh. The strap wouldn't hurt him at all. No value whatsoever. Where with some children you can wave the strap in front of them which tends to calm them down. With him, he would stick out his hand out, and enjoy the ... He said to me on one occasion, I gave him the slipper for something. He said afterwards. He said, 'It's quite nice and warm afterwards. Isn't it?' [laughter] I'd just tried to punish him! [laughter] I can laugh about it now, but at the time I was at my tether. (I have to deal in stereotypes but you're a six-foot rugby player, a big bloke) Yeah, but he demolished me. He demolished me in a year, singlehanded. Until at the end of it I did in fact go home on several occasions crying. I could just not see a way through.

I like the boy. This was what was so strange, that I liked him and I wanted to get through to him, and I wanted him to do well. But he didn't want to. This was three years ago and since he has been in court for stealing lead, breaking into the school stores, all the petty juvenile things, but which start building up to something more major. We said in the staff room at the time that he was going to kill somebody. It wouldn't surprize me if sometime in the near future his temper doesn't blaze away and he kills somebody.

The other staff had not had the same problem. He set his cap at me because I was his class teacher in the fourth year. In his second year this class had had three teachers. In the third year they were supposed to have the old Deputy Head, but he left and they got a female teacher in and she survived. She had more trouble with the girls than with Carl. So in the fourth year he got me and then he was more than the cock of the school, he was the Godfather. If you wanted anything you went to him. He sorted all out. It was as simple as that. The girls loved him but in the sort of way of a 'beat me, beat me' relationship, you know, the whole macho bit. Girls would have laid down in his path to be trodden on. (It is incredible for an eleven year old, isn't it?) I have never seen anything like it before or since. I've never met anybody like him, never. I've met strong kids. I've met big kids. I've met brutal kids but no-one like him. I've not met anybody who has channelled all their intelligence into working a teacher. I don't think he was out to make me ill, that was just a sideline to him doing what he wanted to do. And knowing that the sanctions available to me would have no effect on him at all.

His father was in jail, his mother was interested but she didn't know what to do as well. He was interested in boxing so I'd ply him with boxing books, projects on boxing, his maths was how many punches would so and so . . . get in a minute, and all this sort of thing. [laughter] Flog boxing to death. Just to keep him interested. But his mother would say, 'I don't know what to do, I've tried everything, when he's bad. I've beaten him black and blue and sent him upstairs. I've tried every sanction I know and it has not worked'. We tried every sanction we knew and it had not worked.

He'd found a way to buck the system by just not conforming in anything. He would take out our formal punishments and just laugh because they had no effect on him. You could give an essay at dinner time, keep him in. He'd do a marvellous essay and he'd give it you and then walk out and take his break. He'd take his dinner time. You'd say, 'Where are you going?' He'd say, 'You've had your dinner time, I'm having mine'. And he'd go out in the yard. Sit in the yard, you'd punish and he'd write a beautiful essay, and then he'd say, 'I'll have my break now'. And that was it.

I was literally in tears of frustration. I'd tried everything I knew to get this lad round. If it'd gone on any longer, another two or three months I would have brutalized him. There were times when I had to turn away. I had to turn around and walk away. Because I knew once I started on him, I wasn't going to stop. I wasn't going to finish 'til I saw blood. [laughter] But I mean that. (I believe you) He's educated me. Everything now is roses. Because I hope to God, I hope I never see a kid like that again. I was beaten. I had him for one year.

But he had this group of girls who he could tee-up and set them going and it was like a chain reaction. You know, he'd start, then they would seize their chance. Once he'd run out on one occasion. [laughter] He'd run out and on this occasion he ran into the hall while the infants were having PE and just sat there. He wasn't going to move, he was quite happy watching the infants doing PE. So I went in and got hold of him and said, 'You cannot sit there. If you are going to sit anywhere, go and sit in the loo'. I flung him towards the toilets. Anyway whilst I was sorting this out, two of the girls had gone to the toilet. I've got hold of Carl and I hear this shout from the girls' toilet, 'Me periods have started!' shouts of joy. This could be heard all round the school [laughter] She was just playing on the situation. She was trying to embarrass. But I found that easy to handle, you could demolish them with sarcasm which I didn't particularly like using, it was an unfair weapon. But you could calm them down.

It was funny really because I wanted him to take part in everything. When we went away on school camp, the Head didn't want him. But I said that I'd take responsibility. We'll take him. We had an instance when we went to Derbyshire. One of the boys on the Wednesday became violently homesick, weeping, crying and wanting his mother. And the person who sorted it out was Carl. He went to him and he was absolutely marvellous with him. He was wonderful. He brought Peter right round.

We had a situation where there was a pack of dogs in the playground and the nursery children had to come across a gap of fifteen feet and all these dogs are yapping and snarling in the yard and Carl takes it upon himself and to bring the nursery children across and kick these dogs away. He was almost schizophrenic in a way. There was this softness and humanity in him with young children. But when it came to anything that smacked of discipline or doing something, didn't want to know, that was it. No way was he going to do it.

I never thought of leaving but I did wonder what the hell I had done. After that one year it was it. Baptism by fire and blood! [laughter] It really was and that was the sort of child he was. That was the sort of reaction he got from me. I tried everything I knew to get him round and there was no way in which he was going to respond. He did as he pleased. Nothing I could do.

It was affecting everything. My home life. It was affecting my relationship with my wife and my own kids. I carried it all home. I tried to drop it at the gate. I did all sorts of things. I took to doing a crossword on the train going home, to forget. I took up getting off the train and going for a drink at the pub to try and get it all away. But the wife complained that I was more out than in. You know, so you are getting pressures from home to be the normal husband and father and yet you've got the pressure inside that is all the time trying to work out how to deal with tomorrow's situation. So at home I was surly, morose and depressed. Yeah. With my own children. I was getting pissed a lot more. I was drinking. People joke about drinking to forget. But it is quite true. I even went to the stage of taking drugs, something I had done at college. You know, smoking. Anything to get rid of it. It was horrifying. There is no escape. You know that at nine o'clock the next morning he was going to be there. None of those things worked for me because I knew no matter what the next morning he was going to be there, whether it was on the other side of a headache or not, he was still going to be there. The little bastard got his attendance prize at the end of the year.

It's still real. It's the feeling that no matter what tomorrow you're back at the front. It's like shell shock and you know you are going to get sent back to the front. You're a quivering mass of humanity but you've got to go and I went.

It's had a value for what it was worth. Teaching's like that. You've got to take the rough with the smooth. It's an up and down profession, high points and low points. I get a bit manic. It doesn't surprise me looking back I suffered with migraine, knowing myself. I went to the doctor. He knew what it was, he knew what was needed and he provided it. He knew the problem was psychosomatic. I knew the problem was psychosomatic. But knowing it and curing it are two different things.

I'm laughing now but then I was crying. I was trapped with that lad five days a week for thirty weeks and that's what did it. The feeling that there being no escape. Knowing exactly what was going on but being powerless to stop it. It is that feeling basically when you think about it, of that feeling of impotence, of failure.

You're promoted to Deputy Head and no matter how you try, you know to be very humble, inside you feel that warm glow of success. That you're OK and that you're confident. I had been at my previous school for seven years, I'd been taking the top class for three years. I'd been successful and popular with the kids, parents I think. That was destroyed in a year, in a fortnight. [laughter] The great god was debased in a fortnight. It was a good experience. It got me away from having inflated opinions of myself.

But I have had to spend the time since then in reclaiming my position with the staff who had seen me demolished. Some were very happy about that because they didn't get the deputy headship. I got the rough end of that. I wasn't getting any support from the staff. The staff withdrew from it, laughing behind their hands and sometimes quite openly. But you see, the efforts I was making to me were quite valid. Trying to get him to go places, taking him places, giving him things to do. To them it appeared stupid because they knew his behaviour. But I couldn't accept that without trying to . . . consequently I was failing in public where they said I would fail, and I wanted to try it and it undermined my position.

This is three years ago. I still haven't got the confidence of them. That boy next to one other bloke I know has had the greatest influence on me in my teaching career. In, I don't know, teaching there is always someone somewhere who is going to get the better of me. I don't think he is on his own. Coming up through the third year is another lot.

They try, they are in the process of demolishing a supply teacher and they have done quite well. She is now on tranquilizers and all sorts of things. Because everyday she has to face this lot of boys who are just dopes or seeming to be. They are competent dopes. They are bright, not academically bright but very street-wise. And they have demolished her. She's on valium. She's going.

Last night I was trying to umpire a rounders match and she stood by me giving me the tale of woe. You can't walk anywhere without her walking up to you and I've got three or four of her kids sat in my room all the time. She needs to get it off her chest all the time. She's crying all the time. She's an experienced teacher in her forties. Here again, it's the effects of the children on the school, inasmuch as they're in my class because all the time I've got these three or four in my class because she can't cope and they've been sent to me for a variety of pifling reasons which have suddenly become major issues with the teacher. I'm running out of punishments. It's been going on all year.

I don't feel now after that year with Carl that anything can scratch me. Because I know, I've seen the worst, I think. I've certainly seen the best! I've been through the spectrum. From the sublime to the ridiculous. He did for that year influence me, he had an influence on my family, and he had an influence on the school. That influence is for life, bigger than my tutors at college. Not bigger than my first Headmaster, he had the greatest single influence on my philosophy but the greatest single influence on the practical application has been Carl. It's this kid. Some accomplishment!

The boy is brilliant. He is not brilliant at the things we want him to be brilliant at. In a situation where we are expected to put over certain mores, certain traditions, certain blocks of knowledge and be able to teach in certain way, when someone like him comes along that is going to blow the whole system, I was going to say it is very dangerous. I don't know. Perhaps we are too inflexible but there is no way we could have presented him with anything that could have settled him down.

I still see him. He is as nice as pie in the street. He comes up to me and shakes my hand. It's over. It's like, he's got another teacher now. He's at Sockem Comprehensive now, they demolish them by the dozen there. But it's like a teacher chastizing a child. Afterwards it's over, it's finished, you've done wrong, I've found out, you've been punished. Incident closed. My year of him is over, he's had his fun out of me, incident closed. It's all over. It's 'Hello, Mr Jones'. He really is as nice as pie. Skinhead haircut, still got his earring, botherboots, jeans up to his shin. The whole bother bit but he's polite, he'll always come and say hello, always shakes the hand, as nice as pie. But someone else is copping for it. Someone somewhere is getting it at the moment. [laughter] My heart goes out to whoever it is.

I'm glad I met. Yeah. I feel any situation that crops up now regarding a child, I've seen something worse. Perhaps, I can handle it a little better but I certainly don't know how to solve the problem. If another Carl came up I'd probably have the same problem but I've learned how to handle it better personally.

The feeling of relief on that last day, utter relief, it was orgasmic. [laughter] It really was. I sat in the staff room and they had been talking the previous couple of days, 'We'll egg him. On the last day we'll egg 'im'. They come with eggs and they break eggs on each other and I heard the whisper they were going to egg me. I was terrified of going out of that gate in case they were lurking, every corner, every back alley. Paranoid, not half. That I'd be destroyed by this egging. And I sat down in that staff room and breathed a sigh of relief that must have been audible over the whole city. They didn't egg me, but it was over.

It was like an awakening. It was a physical thing. It had a physical effect. I never thought of suicide. I get depressed anyway but that went beyond getting depressed. It was a feeling of intruding into something that I shouldn't actually be in but which I wanted to be in but that would not accept me in it. I wanted to do something for him but he didn't want anything doing for him. He didn't want it. He was quite happy. You've got to keep grinding away in hope that something gets through.

He affected the rest of the class, for twelve months they had a substandard education. Really when you look back all my efforts were going into him, all my efforts into crowd control, not education. Consequently, the rest of the class suffered. I knew it. They knew it. Their parents knew it. They all saw it was happening. It was public.

I'm quite prepared to stay in a school like this because I think too many people are moving away from them. There are schools in Liverchester, in the centre which are decimated. I would say that I want to stay in a school like this, I like the children. I come from that kind of background myself.

We had a bout of graffiti in the school. Really obscene, really bad stuff and I've seen bad stuff. And Carl came in, in the morning and said, 'Mr Jones, have you seen it?' He said, 'There's dicks and cunts all over the nursery'. I said, I had. And he says, 'Can I clean if off?' And he took a scrubbing brush and a tin of Chemico and scrubbed the walls clean. Incredible kid. People say, how could you like him and I say because there is some good in him.

But it wasn't going to come out because he wasn't going to let it out. He was the macho man and he was going to be macho if it killed him. He had to be seen to be on the top of every situation and he was. You feel envious of these sorts of people who have that degree of control and that sort of power. Because it was power. I read somewhere, I agree with it, that you teach by consensus and if they don't want to be taught you've had it, if they don't want to accept you as the teacher. I could not coerce this kid, couldn't frighten him. I could've used physical punishment, that would have meant something to him but it would have had to have been horrendously violent, really violent. I only ever frightened him once and that was after that incident he raised his fists to me and was going to hit me but I told him, 'If I start on you, I won't finish. There will be limbs all round the room'. It would have been a dreadfully wrong thing to do. I know if I had started there would have been the frustrations of the year and I would have beaten him and that would have been illegal and immoral and wrong in every sense. It would have been an explosion of frustration.

The feeling of impotence, that was the biggest one. The feeling that someone was pulling your strings. It is difficult to accept the fact that children do pull the strings and the feeling that it is they who are manipulating you is something that is difficult to swallow. I think what I have tried to do is try and rather than squash that, to try and turn it around and use it for their own good. For my ends although it appears that they are doing the manipulating.

It doesn't worry me now, you know, whereas it did. And I think in certain types of school it still does. I don't think our school is exceptional. You'll find thousands like it, I think. I don't know, to this day, what his motive was, whether it was to enjoy himself at school without any work, or what. In Liverchester schools they have these guys by the million. I'm no nearer knowing the answer to handling that sort of kid now than I was three years ago. I know what it feels like now, and I can handle the tension better. But that's it. I know what would help me, But I still don't know what would help them. (Deputy Headteacher)

The Swimmer

For survivors the typical teacher career moves from liberal, 'thinskinned', 'paedophile' to reactionary, callous misopaedist; from innervated, optimistic role-embracer to enervated, pessimistic role-distancer; and from an initial career race to find 'cleanwork' to pride that they have the skills and stomach to do 'dirtywork'. These adaptations and adjustments are not mere 'phantoms of the mind'. Newcomers to the school are prey to occupational culture because it works. It is an experientially worked out solution to *real* not *imaginary* pressing practical problems. Teachers' commonsensical professional knowledge cannot be separated from the social processes which produce it; it is a legitimate and rational response to their oft traumatic experiences of children. Ultimately, dignity comes to be found in 'dirt'; to have the moral qualities to be able to handle the 'dirtywork' respectable society wants handling. By so doing teachers become *pachydermized*; battlehardening experiences help develop a monocoque professionality (cf. Hargreaves, 1972; Woods, 1979). Further, teacher consciousness has no will to radically change for this would be suicidal of self and flies in the face of commonsense.

> You go in. A whole hour. You sit there. You go in, get your books out and he says, 'We'll carry on from last lesson'. And you just write down the whole lesson from the blackboard or dictation, week after week. Nothing was said. He never talked to us. We never take it in. We write off the blackboard. We haven't a clue. They try and catch us out and write, 'spaghetti hoops' or something in the middle. Nobody says 'What have you wrote "spaghetti hoops" for'. We just write. Most of the time I don't even bother writing. Teachers are liars. They always said I was good and they tell my parents I was good but I never do anything. (Pupil)

> That woman, Ethelberta, she grabbed hold of me by my ears and lifted me. A real snapper, ox-basher. We had a lesson on the Third Reich and everybody was going 'Seig Heil' behind her back. The one time I said it, she saw me. She grabbed hold of my ears and dragged me out to the front. It was really bad and you couldn't really hit a woman. She was vicious. She stuck all her nails into the side of my head. (Pupil)

> I went to community studies and this teacher is a real old school ma'am. They were absolutely silent. It was amazing. I couldn't believe it. They just got on with the work. She didn't even talk to them, they just sat down, possibly because they were just copying from books. I'm not sure. They just sat and drew pretty little pictures and copied from books. And that lesson the Head came in to see this teacher and their faces, I just couldn't believe it. They didn't even look up. They had some sense of decorum. She

had them behind desks. She had this command in her voice. I don't know if they were frightened of her, intimidated by her. There wasn't a murmur. She had them quiet. They were working through this textbook of comprehension and all year they had been working through it. She didn't even ask them what they read. The could have written anything. They walked in, books were out, they were like robots, tuned-in to this writing down. No teacher–pupil interaction whatsoever. She didn't have to reprimand them. She just sat at her desk. No-one walked up to her. No. No. They just handed them in at the end of the lesson. She was just not involved. Perhaps the answer is to be totally detached, outside of what is happening. (Student-teacher on observation)

He was my best mate, you know what I mean? He thought he was really tough and unfortunately he was. I forgot my kit. It was a mixed lesson on the trampolene. Each week I'd forgotten my kit. I used to have athlete's foot, anything, piles or anything. And he says to me, 'Where's your kit boy?' and I said, 'I was christened'. He says, 'Where's your kit Jones?' He said, 'I'll fit you up with some kit boy'. He brought a pair of shorts that were that [gesture] wide. The kecks were like kites and a piece of pyjama cord to hold them up and I was put on the trampolene. Mixed group. It was really humiliating, 'Saddle jump, boy'. (Pupil)

He used to chuck the board rubber at all the girls or chalk or something and he sat me and my two friends in front of him, in front of his desk. We never did any work. We sat there talking about his contact lenses. We never did any work. He picked up one lad out of his chair by his ears, stood him in the wastebin, put a white dot on the blackboard and he had to put his nose on it. And he was stood there the rest of the lesson. (Pupil)

I used to skive PE in the fifth year. I used to fire my bike up and go home on Fridays. One day he lifted the back wheel off the ground. I put the clutch on to go and nothing happened. I turned round and there's Mighty Mouse giving it this. He said, 'Where are you going Smith? Get off that bike boy and get in that shower' and it was the middle of winter and he gave you cold showers. So cold your balls hit your head and he's sneering saying, 'Is that warm enough for you boy?' (Pupil)

He was our year tutor. He didn't know who I was. I walked into my form and he said, 'What are you doing in here?' and I said, 'Pardon?' and he said, 'Pardon, Sir'. He said, 'You should be in your own form'. 'But', I said, 'This is my form, Sir'. He said, 'It is not. This is the fourth year'. I said, 'I am a fourth year'. He had no idea who I was, and this was at the end of the year. This was the year tutor. It was stupid. (Pupil)

My friend couldn't afford PE kit. She didn't have any. She came in and didn't do it. They had no kit to do it. She was standing at the edge. Mr White (Senior Master) who had nothing to do with the girl, he says, 'What are you doing standing here?' She says, 'I've got no PE kit'. He took her outside, picked her up, and shook her, awful with her, shouting. We all heard him, shouting, at the top of his voice. (Pupil)

We have this member of staff, still there and we went to a retirement party of someone else at the end of term and he says, 'They didn't have a party for me when I retired', smirking. We all know what he meant. He's still there. (Teacher)

The pachydermized professional is the *swimmer* who is a 'successful' ex-plunger or ex-sinker who is now deftly morally on 'the top'. Usually they resolve their problem with a 'domination mode of adaptation to children' (Hargreaves, 1967, p. 104) or 'a tactical withdrawl for strategic containment' (Willis, 1977, p. 81) premised on a trucial abdication of futile attempts to win hearts and minds in favour of the control of pupils' bodies. Swimmers commonsensically know that schooling in their society is not about 'ideological incorporation' but 'institutional incorporation' (Corrigan and Frith, 1976).

Becker (1952b) has already discussed the *swimmer* by elaborating how certain teachers develop careers 'characterized by a permanent adjustment to the "slum" school situation'. This chapter develops Becker's considerations morally. The teacher career denouement is a move from plunging idealism to swimming cynicism. Such teachers invert dominant vertical and horizontal career assumptions and celebrate morally their professional ability to do dirty work and despise those who career race into cleanwork. They are the experts *par excellence* in 'teaching for survival' (Woods, 1977b) 'Official' horizontal and vertical career 'failure' becomes moral 'success'; 'official' horizontal and vertical career 'success' becomes moral 'failure'. They may be losers in the promotional, selective recruitment process but winners in the process of *'natural selection'*, the 'fittest survivors'. This is the basis of a major segmental polarization within the teaching profession between clean workers and dirty workers, each with distinctive pedagogical and ideological styles generated out of the dialectical relations with either 'ideal', 'clean' or 'non-ideal', 'dirty' clients. Teachers of the 'ideal' and 'clean' can ideologically hang on to idealism and optimism, with 'non-ideal' and 'dirty' pupils teachers cannot.

Thus, teachers become 'policemen without boots' out of their dialectic experience of pupils. Teachers are not simply pre-socialized and selectively recruited agents of repression imposed on children from above by an arbitrary State power; they become what they are culturally through negotiation on the chalkface. It is hardly surprising teachers contradict themselves as they move from the educationalist context (that is, the educational paradigm) to the teacher context (that is, a class paradigm) (Keddie, 1971). It is a symptom of a teacher's lived experience of a wider societal contradiction mediated on the chalkface. As such, children are central to any consideration of retrogressive practices by putative progressive teachers (cf. Sharp and Green, 1975; Keddie, 1971). In a class society teachers become *proactive* reactionaries because they are reagents of children.

The ways you have to adjust are first of all, my method of teaching science was along heuristic lines. That was the time when Nuffield and so on were beginning to come in and I was a convinced sort of discovery-method teacher and I still am really but that meant in a lab you would have around a great deal of apparatus and so on because you had to be ready for all sorts of different things. You didn't know what kids were going to do, very practical, you had to have stuff available pretty easily all the time. I found out when I came to Manpool that you have to be very careful about the apparatus. All the apparatus had to be checked out and checked in, otherwise it would tend to disappear, or get damaged or interfered with, or someone else's experiment would be ruined. That situation meant it was so much more difficult to teach the science in the way I was used to and I had to reorganize the way I set out the lab very carefully. I had to remanage the labs. That is one of the biggest drawbacks to teaching at Manpool. The practical work had to be modified a great deal and you could not have the same free-wheeling development. You had to plan in advance what you were going to do which is the antithesis of the heuristic method. Now you have to say, 'Well, we're going to do this particular work today' and one of the problems is making sure they do it properly without smashing it up. That was an adjustment I had to make.

The other one I found, and this is true of every other teacher in the school, is I had to modify my language. You have to realize that the vocabulary you normally use is not going to be understood by many of the classes you take, they have never ever come across the words. You have to to be very careful how you give out instructions, otherwise they don't understand, they're not listening. For example, you might say, 'Today we are going to investigate the problem of burning', if I was talking to a grammar school class, but here they don't know what they're going to do. They don't understand the word 'investigate'. They don't understand what is meant by the problem of burning. I have to modify the concepts. You have to turn that and say, 'Today we are going to try and find out what happens when something burns'. Sometimes it is more extreme than that. If you have kids with IQs in their 80s you've got to use even simpler language. This is the biggest problem.

I have a new member of my department and he had problems because he hasn't adjusted to the language. He can't help using language which they don't understand, they simply miss what he means. That is a big adjustment.

They are also pretty ill-motivated in the sense that in an academic field like science, science was generated by people who wanted to know things for its own sake. Why something was happening. They had curiosity. Most of the kids I teach have not got that curiosity to find things, certainly about science and worse still don't understand anybody who does. It makes no sense. I don't think in essence, you get round the problem. The way you get round them to do things, I think, is to get them to do it for you, if you like, rather than the sake of the subject. But this personal appeal doesn't necessarily come through being nice to them. You have to be hard with them sometimes. You've got to be. But that doesn't seem to make you unpopular. The most unpopular teachers are the ones who don't control them. If you don't lead what they are doing in a strict way, they don't do it, or get anything out of it. You've got to make them listen. You have to be strict on keeping their attention and repeat things several times and say suddenly to a kid, 'What did I say then?' You've got to be on top of them all the time. Otherwise off they go, and they won't learn. I still don't think I've got all the skills to handle them. All I can say is I have got a few years experience of handling these kids that would show up against somebody who is new. It's very difficult to pinpoint.

Going back to this new chap, who's just arrived. He's got these problems. He's older than I am. He's intelligent, interesting as an adult, but when he gets into a group of kids he doesn't fit. He is, in their eyes, very naive. He's no idea what kids like that can get up to. He's never come across them before. They can sense his naivity, they can sense he's a beginner. They can smell he's a beginner even though he is mature. They can tell he's not done the job before. If I was to ask them how they knew, then they wouldn't be able to tell you. And I am not sure I could tell you.

They do things in his classrooms that I would never anticipate because they would never do them in mine. For example, they had magnets and it was a hot day and I went into the class, for some reason and discovered that they had, in fact, been throwing them out of the window and a few hand lenses were missing. Behaving in a ridiculous way which they would not with me. I don't think he even saw it. I don't know why because they would never throw them out of the window with me. I know I would have had to count the things in at the end because I know kids like magnets and hand lenses.

This new chap once said, 'These kids are very keen. When I get to the door they say "Are we going to do an experiment, Sir"?' and he says, 'Yes', and then he says, 'I discovered when I went in that they didn't want to accompany me on a voyage of exploration, all they wanted to do was light the bunsen burners, and generally bugger around with bits of apparatus'. That is what an experiment is for them and I could have told him that, an opportunity to lark about.

Another example: I saw him once get into the body of the class because if a kid had a problem he went to him. By doing that you put yourself at a disadvantage because there's kids behind you, you can't see. Where possible I always remain away from the bulk of the class so I can keep surveillance. In many schools this wouldn't be a problem, not so in our place.

This new bloke is mysterious to them. They've never met a bloke like it before, because of the way he speaks; of his caring attitude; his enthusiasm for the subject; and he is very polite and courteous in his manner and to them he is a rather odd sort of figure, and they see this, not as something to be respected or admired, but something to be taken advantage of. He will learn from experience not to do certain things, to do other things, and what to look for.

They tried it on with me years ago and I had problems, not unlike the ones he's facing. They are more alert as to what I am likely to do. Because of this I suggested he takes them out of the lab altogether and give them written work instead. To show them we can go back to the board and the writing if they want. It is what we use with varying degrees of success because a lot of the time kids are not bothered about doing practical work. To solve a problem is something they don't like doing particularly and one of the things you get is that after two or three minutes a child will say 'I don't want to do this', and push it away. You have to push it back but you have to ask yourself if it is really beyond him. You've got to learn how to pitch it. But kids will back away, because that is what a lot of them are like. I've learned that the idea that if you only followed a child's inclination that would solve a lot of these problems but this is not so with our kids. If you followed these kids' inclinations you'll end up doing nothing at all. Sitting around, football, anything. You have to make them face up to a task and you have to fall back on analogies. So in Manpool, for example you use football a lot, say, Dalgleish wasn't born able to head that ball, the only reason he can do it so well now is that he practiced at it for week after week after week, and that is how he got his skills. Often it was boring and often he must have said, 'God, I'm fed up. I'll never do this', and the trainers made him do it, but the problem is, they don't see the need to acquire these skills. The vast majority are going to get a poor crop of CSEs or not even that. They don't like doing a proper job of it. 'Go and make it right', they don't like that. It's nothing to do with the unemployment situation. The kids have always been like that. When I started teaching twenty four years ago I was in a secondary modern in Bradleeds and they displayed the exact characteristic even though they were all then heading for a job. Overall I always feel the need to improve what I am doing, but I don't feel I've got the answers to teaching children of this low ability, IQs below 90s. I don't think I've got the answers to it. That is frustrating. Nowhere to turn to for assistance, advisors, inspectors. They don't know how to do it. It's a great temptation to stop looking for answers. Everybody does that. There are days when you say, 'I'm not up to doing this' so you take the easy way out, do something with them which minimizes the hassle. It is quite wrong to do it but you can't live at the level all the time. The real aim of the lesson often gets lost in the practical problem they overshadow the real aim. The idea of teaching them some chemistry gets lost in the problem of control.

On days when the practical problems get out of hand I set them some written work to do which is connected with the topic. That is an easy situation to handle. It is easy with kids in desks with blackboards than in a lab. I can't get these kids to become academically and intellectually interested in the science. I can't do that. It is impossible.

Why don't I blow my brains out? It sometimes worries me that I could do better but I don't know how to do better. The other problem is the sheer work load. You can spend your whole life giving work. You can go on for ever. Obviously you don't do that because you say there is a limit to what I am going to do. Otherwise, towards the end of term you'd feel flat, fatigued. You need feedback and when you're not getting that and most of the time you're not, then when you find it difficult, you begrudge the work you do. Why the hell should I spend all night typing these bloody worksheets when all these buggers are interested in is football?

I often resort to the writing on the blackboard syndrome because these kids wherever they are, if they get you get it on the board and they have paper in front of them, they will copy it. It is an amazing thing. They get absolutely nothing from it. It doesn't matter what you put up, they will copy it. The content of it doesn't matter. You could write a passage from the bible or a section from the Communist Manifesto, and they would copy it down and think nothing of it. It's amazing. So when you want a quiet life you use it.

One of the things I've realized, and a lot of teachers haven't, is that when you go into a class whatever it may be, they come in, and they are yelling and bawling, doing this and doing that, then it is not against you. I used to think this was so once, they are doing this because of me, but I have learned since then that it is nothing to do with me. It wouldn't matter who the hell was in the room, this is the way these kids are, you know. If you realize that it is a big step forward, that helps. And when you've quietened them down it is not a personal thing. It is not a personal antagonism.

It is frustrating when you look at the generality of it, if you say, step back and ask, 'Have I achieved anything over the years with these kids?'. You say, 'Very little'. But teaching is made up on a series of highpoints because the kid who has not been doing very much might suddenly one day come out with a beautiful drawing he has slaved over, or he might suddenly cottoned on to something you've been hammering at him for weeks on end, you know. It is these little things that keep you going. That is another thing, you have to understand, that is, it is a series of highpoints but a lot of the time there are low points, there are low points when nobody's learning anything. At Manpool this is how most teachers experience it. There are very few starry-eyed idealists who think they are achieving wonderful things with the kids. There are many who don't think about their teaching anymore, who do carry on in their old ways and don't adapt.

I would like to do some academic work as well but now I would not like to eliminate absolutely the teaching of the bottom streams. There is a reward. There is an inverted status, if you like, as well. You know, people in our school say about teachers in the leafy suburbs 'Bloody hell, that is a nice cushy number, you want to come down here and do a real job'. It's an inverted thing that because you are teaching in a school like ours you really are teaching, not just getting children through examinations. In Manpool, teachers are proud they work in the inner-city part, because they know when you say that, that they say 'God, he must be good to survive that', and so on. So people do say they work in these places with a certain amount of pride. I have attempted to get out but only for promotion, not to get to the middle-class leafy suburbs. I would apply for jobs in Salford, Oldham, anywhere except Skelmersdale, because I know somebody who worked there.

At times you get cynical. At times you say, this is ridiculous. You get more cynical when people outside start telling you what you should be doing and how you should be doing it. (Sociologists must really get up your nose!) (laughter) Not really, it's people who are in education who give you different advice like bloody useless advisors and inspectors.

There is even your own feeling that you're not doing enough, that is always present now, that you could do more. There's no point. You've got to put your job in perspective. In holidays I don't think about it a great deal. I see it as time for gathering strength. You just relax. You develop certain personality traits in teaching. You spend most of your working life in a room with kids, many of whom are not very bright and you have a certain relationship with them which is not like relationships with other adults or even other kids outside. There is a danger you carry this into your private life. I am always pleased when people outside don't recognize I'm a teacher, that I've covered it up.

Sometimes you feel drained at the end of the day and you just want to sit for a while. People don't understand how it really is. Trying to extract a little something from kids who are not willing to do it.

You always as a teacher have the feeling you're sitting on a volcano. You never know what's going to happen next. You can never predict the behaviour of some of the kids and you do have kids who are time-bombs, if you like, who sit there and one day they will explode, can do anything at all. There are all these kids with psychological problems. Living on the edge of a volcano is the nearest description I can get to it. Suddenly the whole thing might blow up. I'm always worried about accidents in the lab.

They are always grabbing your attention. You can be marking a book, then it's 'Sir, Sir, Sir'. That's draining. Instant attention.

What is always depressing is when you see others being destroyed. Some kids can get under the skin of teachers and some teachers invite it. We had a Miss Smith and in the short time she was here the kids did to her what they would not do to any other member of staff, for whatever reason. For some reason she invited it. Somehow the kids got their teeth into her, let her tyres down, hid her clothes. It was terrible.

There is a natural selection process working in schools like ours and those who can't cope leave. Those who are left are mostly able to cope but now people can't get out. In fairness, though our school is not the worst, no ethnic or religious problems. We have developed ways of approaching these kids. It is the easiest thing in the world to reach a massive conflict situation, very, very easy and part of the art and the skill is knowing how and when to avoid it. You've got to be on good firm ground, you've got to be sure that you've got them for something they can see is not the right thing to do. Take earrings, you could easily get into a situation with that and you don't. But take something like getting out of school with a forged note, you've got them there. They know they've done wrong. You've got to work within a framework of justice they recognize. Don't mess around with trivia. Leave it at that. You can so easily get into a lather. I try to avoid corporal punishment but I believe it should be there as a last resort. I don't like to use it much. There are plenty of other ways. I'm not keen. These kids have a level beyond which they will not go. If you implement every school rule you'd run yourself ragged and create an awful lot of hostility. You've got to use them realistically. (Head of Department)

Children as 'Double' Career Gatekeepers

Clearly it has been shown that the objective aspects of teachers' careers are related to the subjective moral aspects which children *directly* gatekeep. Further, superordinate teacher career gatekeepers' major commonsensical criteria for selective recruitment, promotion and deployment is, *inter alia*, the ability to appear to control pupils and the ability to appear to teach. Thus, children, inasmuch as they deny control of themselves and withdraw their learning are important *indirect* horizontal and vertical career gatekeepers. In this sense children are *double* gatekeepers for they are additionally *significant turnkeys* of the gates that superordinates keep. Consequently, there is a simultaneous controlling imperative operating on teacher careers; 'successful survival' in the classroom with children results in career pachydermization and this is also essential for 'successful' career development mediated by superordinates.

Anyway when I finally arrived at the school, I was given a three and four junior mixed kids which I was told later, well it was described to me as the 'dustbin class' by one of the blokes who had just completed his probationary year. He said that the general run of things was, if you manage to get to the end of your probationary year and stayed on you were given the choice of a class you wanted next year. So there were three probationers starting the same year as me. The other two were in the infant department. I was the only new junior teacher at that time and I got the 'dustbin class'.

They turned out, actually, to be a very nice class I think probably 'cos you have that sort of, something there in your first year of teaching that you never experience quite the same again. It is the first class of your own and they were a nice bunch of kids. I mean a lot of them had problems but we got on alright and I got through the year. And at the end of the year the Headmistress said to me, that when I had first come for interview she didn't think I would last more than six weeks and in fact the other two probationers who started at the same time as me, one left after three weeks and the other left at the end of the first term and during the year several other people left for various reasons. People were coming in and more often than not lasting a matter of weeks. Entirely because of the kids, actually.

I had problems with the Headmistress later on but in that first year she was reasonable towards me probably because she was pleased that things were going very well with this class. Anyway, she told me she had not expected me to last but because I had she was going to give me a good class. I was very pleased because it did look like a very good class. But what had happened was the bloke who had had this class was one of nature's great teachers. He really was one of the best teachers I had ever seen and of course he had whipped this class into a very smooth running entity. So it all looked very nice for me.

But I went in the first day of the second year of my time there with this class and even on my probationary year it was a week before the kids let themselves go, so I was expecting on the first day that they were going to be quiet and knuckle down. That it was going to be just a question of building up a relationship. But I remember that ten minutes after we got into the room from assembly I got them all sitting down. We started some work. And this girl stood up, stood up on the desk and was looking out of the window and I tried to get her to sit down and what have you and she wouldn't. She was totally oblivious to virtually everything I said. Obviously didn't give a bugger and as soon as it came evident to the rest of the class that I was not able to manage her, that of course had an effect on them. And although they were reasonable this kid was such hard work that I was spending all my time just trying to get her to sit down, let alone shut up or whatever.

From that first day the conflicts got worse and worse, particularly with her but with a lot of the others as well. There was quite, a very strong group of girls in that class. They were third year juniors, ten years old on average but there was one girl in this group who was very intelligent, a very good mimic, very witty in a razor-blade kind of way and she orchestrated the piss-takes, you know and this other one just concentrated on the nutty behaviour.

Every lesson, let alone every day, became a minor battle. I tried all sorts of things. I tried keeping her in. I remember one day in particular when she had been particularly obnoxious. And I said, 'Right, everyone can go except Shirley'. So it was all pouting and stamping and she, after the other kids had filed out, she picked up a chair and threw it at the window. It didn't break, it bounced off. I did my best to try and pretend that I was disciplining her and I thought, 'Sod it, Get rid of the little bugger'. So I said, 'You can go now', pointing at the door and she ignored the door. Went to the firedoor and slammed it so hard the wall was going like that. [gesture]

So I went tearing out. Completely lost my temper which I something I had managed not to do. It takes a lot. I really went berserk. Haring out and got hold of her by the wrists, did not hit her or any thing. Got hold of her by the wrists and said, 'Don't you ever slam a door like that in my room', or something and she just, she just sank her teeth into my hand and she had a beautiful set of pearly-white teeth, you know, and as these sank into the muscles in my thumb. I thought, 'Jesus, what do I do now?' 'Cos I just couldn't get her off. It was like iguanas where you can't get rid of the bastards. So I just dragged her, well I say I dragged her, I moved to the headmistress' room with this child attached to my hand and said, 'Excuse me, could you do something with this girl?' [Laughter]

Anyway, I mention that but it was a fairly typical event with this particular child. I went to the bloke who had had this class, the good teacher, because I got a lot of tips from him. I respected him as a good teacher. Genuinely helpful. ·And it was becoming a matter of surprize amongst the rest of the staff that having got through the probationary year with the 'dustbin class' alright, that I was having problems with Tom's brilliant class, you know. I began to feel that the other teachers thought there was something wrong with me. That I couldn't manage these kids when they'd been so beautiful with Tom. I said to Tom, 'What is the secret with this girl?' and he said, 'Well, she wants affection really, she wants to be liked'. I thought, 'God, how can I like her, this kid?' By this time I hated her, you know. Euthanasia, anything, I would've gone along with it. So I thought, 'Right, I'll go in and be nice to her', you know and I mean, I tried gentle persuasion anyway, but it was, 'Hello luv, how are you this morning?' and tried to jolly her along and everything. She smiled sweetly and did look a bit flattered at first but after twenty seconds she went nutty again, you know and started throwing books around.

Anyway, after a few weeks the rest of the class, particularly this group of girls, were developing quite considerable expertise in manipulating me and whipping me into an hysterical state and I think they actually really, really enjoyed it. I think they enjoyed coming into school because they were getting a lot of attention from the teacher which may have been very negative attention but it was a bit of a laugh for them. It was really beginning to get me down.

I think probably about half way through the year, no, no, it was sooner than that, towards the end of the first term, the headmistress was calling me in saying, 'Look, you know, I gave you this wonderful class and what are you doing wrong?' She said she wanted to come in and see me teach which got me wound up really. And she came in and was fairly disgusted by what she saw. Then the next day she gave me a demonstration lesson where she walked in, and of course all the kids sat down, arms folded, didn't say a word and she did this pretty boring lesson. But because she had this power over them it all went smoothly and she took me aside later in the day and said, 'That's how it's done and if I can do it, you can do it'. But that had no effect at all except it probably clued up the kids even more that there were problems for me. So they began to play me up even more.

And then she began, the Headmistress this is, she, I was getting personally very dispirited, despondent and everything and she ran the school on very strong principles. She thought the most important things in education was courtesy and cleanliness. In fact she got up at a meeting and said, you know, they were all talking educational theory and she said, 'Why are we not talking about cleanliness?' This was the kind of woman she was and she, the Headmistress, called me into the room again one night and said, she started off about the state of my discipline and what was happening to this class and things got quite heated and she asked me in the end, 'Are you trying to subvert everything this school stands for?' She said, 'You are like an infiltrator who is trying to undo all the good work that the rest of us are trying to build up'. And I got into quite a slanging match with her. Because at the same time as this was happening a new teacher had come into the school on a Scale 3 and I was only on a Scale 1 and this new Scale 3 was having much more worse problems than I was. The boys used to lie on the floor and sort of stare up her skirt, things like that and she just couldn't control any of them, let alone the difficult ones. And the deputy head was also having problems with her class but she got half the week off for what was called 'administration'. And I was saying, 'Listen, you know, I am in my second year teaching here and I am having a bloody hard time teaching with these kids but you are not calling in the deputy head and saying "Why are you only teaching half the week and why have you got problems?", you're not saying to the Scale 3 "Why can't you control these kids?"'. I said, 'What are you picking on me for?' you know. She launched into this, you know, thing about me being like an agent provocateur or something, urban guerilla. Anyway, she just wore me down and I came out of that little interview and I went into the bogs and cried. It really, it really pissed me off.

And that coincided with the worst time I had with these girls. I mean it was obvious there was just nothing I could do by this time that was going to win these kids over, Although when I say that it was only this nutty one who obviously disliked me. The little clique, actually we got on very, very well outside of lessons because they had such a sharp sense of humour. I used to really enjoy teaching, no, talking to them, but not teaching them.

By that time I was convinced that I was a loser, a hopeless teacher. And one of the interviews with the head I was really looking for encouragement. I wanted her to say, 'Look, you did very well last year, you know, just buck up and I'll give you all the help I can'. If she said that I would've been alright. I remember saying to her, I said, and as I said it I was thinking when I say this I want her to say 'Oh no' and what I said was, 'I think perhaps I'm in the wrong profession'. And I wanted her to say, 'No, you've got the makings of a great teacher, look what you did last year'. And she said, 'Yes, Mr Charles, you are'. So I thought, you know, 'Up yours', sort of thing.

Anyway, I could have just about got through the year with these kids if the Headmistress had given me a bit of support and if I thought I was doing alright with the kids and the Headmistress was getting at me I could've handled it but because I was getting it from both sides I just thought, 'Jesus, I just don't want to do this anymore'. And I went to the doctor's and I was in a fairly emaciated condition by then. I was losing weight. I felt rough all the time. The Headmistress said that I looked awful when I came into the school. I obviously didn't conform to her ideas of cleanliness. I looked like the infiltrator she thought I was.

Anyway, I was in a bad way. The kids had really got me down, virtually destroyed me, this girl in particular. Partly because I was thinking 'If Tom could do it, even though he was a good teacher, anybody ought to be able to do it, really', just by following his model. But I tried it, I tried everything. I tried threats, cajoling. The works, you know. The full repertoire. Nothing worked. So I went to the doctor, told him all about it. He said, did I want him to write a letter to the Headmistress, and I said, 'No, because I think she will just make things worse'. But in fact he did write a letter to her. Anyway he gave me six weeks off school, towards the end of the spring term. The sick note said, 'Anxiety state'. I think because that was on the sicknote she probably contacted the doctor to find out what it was. Anyway, for whatever reason he wrote her a letter. He probably didn't say to her what I said to him, he probably didn't say, 'This bloke is bloody sick of you jumping down his throat all the time'. She probably thought it was, I don't know, he must have said it was the kids. I said to him, it was the kids and the head. I couldn't handle them both.

Anyway when I came back she gave me another class. Now the nice way of looking at that was she identified the problem as being the class and therefore 'We'll give him another class'. But she gave me a class which, although they were younger, there were some really bloody nutcases in this class. I think she just thought 'I'll get rid of this bugger by the end of the year', and she gave me the worst class she could come up with.

I had never taught kids this young before, seven and eight these kids. But there was a very volatile group of kids amongst them. Quite severely maladjusted I thought at the time. Looking back on it, some of them were and others were very lively and this was just like a magnification of the other class. Instead of just having one girl who whipped up everything, it seemed that the whole bloody class were lunatics.

And there was one lovely, lovely girl called Joan Mills, West Indian, very pretty, plaits and summery dresses all the time. She was really sweet and I thought I'll try and get through the best I can, with these good kids, with these nutty lads. I'll try and get something out of it with the nice kids in the class. There were some nice kids but they began to suffer in the end because I spent all my time ranting and raving at the troublemakers, whatever you want to call them.

And I remember one boy who just refused, refused on principle to do anything I said. If I said, 'Sit down', he stood up. Whatever I said to him, he did the opposite, always with a grin on his face. I just wanted to walk up to him and smack him in the teeth. He really wound me up. Sometimes I really lost my temper. A couple of times I hit people, to my eternal shame.

But, you know, I used to stand in that room sometimes looking at the sea of faces, some of whom were bored, some of whom were frightened because there were a few very introverted types in there. The majority of the nutters running around screaming, what have you. And I used to look at them with a mixture of loathing and terror and everything. Then I used to try and look over the heads and look out at the window. And I'd see women going shopping and window cleaners on the way to work and I used to think to myself, why aren't I a window cleaner? Why can't I be a bus conductor and just go out and do a bloody job and go home forgetting it? You are in there on your own and through the windows you see these normal people going about ordinary jobs. They look like the real world and even though you are in that world there is nothing real about it. It is real but when it is all going against you it is a bloody nightmare. It is a nightmare.

What was happening to me was when I went home I was thinking about these kids. I was dreaming about these kids. I saw them everywhere. I went out for a drink with my oldest friends. They went out for a goodtime drink and I started talking about the kids which is about one of the worst things about teachers. Talking about school. And I burst into tears in a crowded pub, telling them about these kids.

You know, it was having a drastic effect on my homelife and everything. My wife was really fed up. My son had just been born. I was awake most nights. I used to wake up two and three times in the night. Changing nappies and what have you. And then getting up, groggy-eyed, going into school, getting stick from the Headmistress and the kids crapping on me from a great height, and I was just, er, probably, I mean at one point in every day I used to look at them and try detach myself and think, what would a normal, because by this time I was convinced I wasn't normal, what would a normal person do in this situation? And the answer always came back, 'Get your bloody coat on and walk out'. So many times I came close to just walking out. The only thing that stopped me was the fact that if I did then my wife and child would be in a mess financially. So I had to keep doing it for the money. By that time, I was, in my probationary year I had a sort of love affair with the kids. I really loved kids, that bunch of kids in particular. A year later I was hating kids, you know. I just wanted to get away from them as much as possible.

An interview came up. It was the Headmistress' practice to bring all the teachers around the school, and she was going to do this first thing in the afternoon. And she always came to my room last. But she must have realized if she had brought these teachers late in the day the kids were just going to be crawling up the walls, the chairs would be flying and everything. So she decided to bring them to me but she hadn't told me that. So I thought, well, I'm not going to keep these kids buttoned down all afternoon. So I'll save my fireworks for later in the day. I'll throw a few chairs myself about two o'clock and get them knuckled under. And I remember writing some work on the board, half past one, the class had just come in, and I knew behind me two of the kids were kicking holes out of each other on the floor, and the rest were wandering about chucking books or whatever. And the door opened and I looked to my left and there was the Headmistress with a face like thunder and six people behind her whose jaws had hit the floor. They just couldn't believe what they were seeing in this room, you know. And I turned and there were these bloody kids hanging from the lampshades and everything.

And I thought, right, you know, that wasn't the, the, occasion when I said, I've got to get out of here, but I'd just had it with kids really and I thought the first cushy sounding job that comes up I'm going for it and early in the summer term a job came up at the Open Air School which was described as a school for delicate kids and I thought, that's for me, wilting lilies who can barely pick up a pencil, you know, sitting there saying, 'Excuse me, Sir, could you please help me write my name?' And I thought, that will do me, you know. Shorter hours, the works. So I applied for it and was lucky enough to get it. And although it didn't work out quite how, you know, rosy as I expected it was a piece of cake compared to what I'd been through. So I was there for years.

That anxiety has hung over me since because, because of the nature of the school I had been at, the second school, I feel in a way, for nine or ten years or whatever it is, I had been in a fairly cushy environment that I had been able to handle. And there is still within me the memories of those terrible times and the failure, the failure of that second class. That one of my fears of moving into a new school is that all that is going to happen again. I can't go to a school now without a sense of panic. I have had to visit seven or eight schools recently and I was sweating, shaking, inside. I am still like that when I walk into a school now. I do feel deep down inside that I can't teach. I have been at a school where I could teach where it all worked for me but it is closing now, has died the death. Doesn't exist any more. And I have got particular strengths with kids at an interpersonal level but they seem to be denied me now, so, you know, I do ultimately want to get out of teaching.

It is the sort of thing that never ever gets mentioned in the staffroom. To be fair, at that primary school I couldn't admit in front of everybody that the Headmistress made me cry and the kids made me cry. There were a couple of people who knew who I wouldn't have bothered hiding it from but although I saw regularly teacher after teacher disappear after a matter of a few weeks. By the time I left that school I was the second or third longest serving member of staff and yet I should have felt some sort of achievement but all I felt was a sense of failure. Teachers don't like to hear about other teachers' problems because they've got enough of their own. It is a very, very lonely sort of thing. I can distance myself now and say, at least I managed to last the course, you know, by hook or by crook. But it does take something away from you. (Special school teacher)

Thus, the 'lowerarchy' and hierarchy conjointly maintain a socially controlling 'pincer hold' upon the teacher. Indeed, pachydermized superordinates can occasionally implicitly and cynically collude with children in 'the cooling out' of certain teachers.

You've got to be careful but it is easy if you're careful. Now our Head did it, but he got caught and the Union was brought in. But if you're clever you can get the message across easy enough. Just give him the right classes, that usually sees them off! [laughter] It's fair enough don't you think? There's no use in keeping dead-legs. (Deputy Headmaster)

Teachers' Careers: Linear or Cyclical?

Although there might be a broad sequence to teachers' careers from plungers to swimmers, there is nothing developmentally inevitable about the process. Teachers can be plungers or sinkers throughout their careers! However, if the generality of teachers did not develop their careers in these ways there would be a societal crisis of hegemony. Even so, these moral career dimensions can be experienced cyclically in the biography of individual teachers. As we have seen, a swimmer can become a sinker, a sinker can become a plunger or a swimmer etc. With each new class or timetable a teacher becomes a plunger. Some teachers in certain schools with certain timetables can be all three at one and the same time. Indeed some teachers can be all three in the cut and thrust of a single lesson. Teachers' careers are not simplistically unilinear. To mix metaphors, on 'the edge of a volcano' it is always possible for children to get under the densest of moral armour plating. Experienced swimming teachers know this; having an omnipresent fear that they will morally sink sometime in the future, despite their present apparent invulnerability. Invulnerability always has to be struggled for and won, it cannot be taken for granted. This explains the offensiveness of many teachers for moral career transforming 'critical incidents' (Measor, 1985) can occur at any time in one's career.

It's the kids. They're giving people hell. Colleagues are getting up in the morning and just saying, 'Hell, God, I've got to go to school'. I'm like that myself about tomorrow morning. I think God, no kids want to do it, they all want to mess about. It is just horrible to think of. Dreadful. I think I can cope but it is a lot of hassle to cope and there is the fear at the back of your mind that you won't be able to cope, eventually and I think that's what gets me the worst. If I have a bad lesson where a kid is flaunting my authority. That depresses me all day. I think to myself, God I am losing my touch. Can I cope? Are these kids getting the better of me at last? And the time you say yes they are getting the better of me is to pack up. But at the moment there are a lot of teachers at our place who are going under and they can't cope. And if a kid tells them to f-off they just say nothing, tears, weeping, all sorts etc.

What happens now is we have to have a hit squad walking around the school who will go in if there is hell going on or whatever. They will go in and double-up. They have no timetable, senior management and pastoral year tutors with a lightened timetable so they can be around. It's happening all the time. People need help all the time. You know when kids have gone berserk and thrown a chair out of the window. You have to have someone to go in there and pull him out, or make sure there is order.

But you see there is a fear in the back of your mind that you can't cope and what will happen when you can't? Nobody admits they can't cope, it is a sad admission to make. That's what happens in lessons these days. I mean, normally I am quite calculated in what I do and how I approach the kids but I am finding myself more and more just acting on the spur of the moment and losing my rag.

The only good part is I am on a Scale 3 and people are going through what I am going through on a Scale I, and if you are going to be mercenary about it and at least I have the joy at the end of the month knowing I have more money in the bank.

I can't see myself there in five years, at all. I fear the kids will win in the end. I think eventually I'm going to turn around and break. I don't want to fail. If I did fail after nine years of teaching it would be a real personal defeat. I've seen what it does to others. I don't want them to beat me. I'm determined it's not going to happen to me. I And yet there is still that doubt in my mind. I worry what it is doing to me all the time. It hardens you and makes you bitter, cynical about the kids. I really am. I mean I'm getting cynical about it. It is turning me against kids, I am very hard, I'm embittered by what the kids can do. When I started teaching I would give them everything I had. Prepared to give up the time. Prepared to give them what they needed. But now really, I am not . If any kid wants me to do anything after school I think, why the bloody hell should I? Because what do they give me all day, but hassle. So really I'm not giving as much as I could be. It has made me far less willing to give time. I think it's a shame. You start hating yourself.

You start hating yourself. They wear you down during the day. And you go home and you think about it and you think and you think. Even if you go out drinking you are still thinking about what has happened. You can't switch off. No, never. I've started dreaming about it. No. Even when I am asleep I can't get away from it. I wake up feeling really angry and aggressive.

When I get to school I sit in the staff room. I feel myself getting more and more angry and aggressive. If I have a nice lesson it's a bonus. Having a nice lesson these days is a bonus. You go in now with a preconceived idea of what's going to happen and if it doesn't happen — great. But you prepare yourself in your mind to have a load of aggro. And I think that is dreadful. Kids who want to talk to me now, I am not interested in talking to them. Because they are a nuisance, they are a pain and you have got other things to do and there is somebody kicking the hell out of someone over there. So you can't speak to the kids who want to talk to you. I used to spend a lot of time speaking to kids. But all I want to do now is get the bell and it's dreadful. I am always prepared to see the worst in them now, whereas before I was prepared to see the good and be convinced otherwise. But now I see them as being naughty, nasty, aggressive, wanting to wind you up.

I get aggressive. You either do one thing or the other. Go into yourself and cry and moan and say you can't cope or say, what I do which is unfortunately get aggressive. I just can't turn it off. A lot of people do though, burst into tears in front of the kids. I would never ever give those kids the satisfaction, no matter what happened. No way.

Your reputation is enhanced by being aggressive. It works. It is a matter of being hard. If you're hard, that makes sense to them. If you are hard then they don't like you but at least they respect you. If you are soft they can't bear you, they really can't. They hate soft teachers. Even the kids who have a rough time with the hard ones will tell you they prefer the hard ones every time. You get pushed along the route of agression and cynicism. It's a shame. If you lapse into talking to them in our place, they start becoming familiar. You have to keep them at arms length I'm afraid. It's not very good. I don't like it.

My mother reckons I'm having a nervous breakdown. Every time she sees me which isn't very often because she lives in South Wales, she'll say, 'You're looking dreadful these days. You're not the girl I used to know'. I say, 'Why not, mother?' She says, 'You always look so pale and you are very aggressive these days. I remember when you used to be really calm. I can tell there is aggression there'. She is of the opinion I am going on my way to a nervous breakdown, but I am the last sort of person to have one of those. I am not the type. (Teacher)

Conclusion

'But when one affirms that a reality would exist even if man did not, one is either speaking metaphorically or one is falling into a form of mysticism.' (Gramsci's *Prison Notebooks*, 19, p. 446)

This chapter empirically fills out Clarke *et al*'s (1976, pp. 43–4) assertion that the school is a 'classic, negotiated or mediated class institution'. It has been shown that the 'top-down', 'vertical' 'imposition of a cultural arbitrariness by an arbitrary power' (Bourdieu and Passeron, 1970, p. 19) is met by the 'bottom-up', 'horizontal' imposition of a counter-cultural arbitrariness by an arbitrary counter-power. Bourdieu suffers from a monocular cultural imperialism, unable to perceive the possibility that working class children can and do counter-culturally invade the school and, informally, make it their own by 'warrening it from within' (Clarke *et al.*, 1976, p. 12)

Given that officially there is a cultural discontinuity between home (parent subordinate culture) and school (dominant culture) the child powerfully, informally, artfully and unofficially constructs a cultural continuity. It is difficult to concede, on the basis of this chapter, that in many schools 'What the education system both hands on and demands is an aristocratic culture, and above all an aristocratic relationship to it' (Bourdieu, 1900 p. 9). Indeed, given pupil cultural subversion and insurgency; and the consequent space teachers have to surrender in the their negotiations, the school as 'a stake and site of class struggle' legitimates working class children's own cultural forms. It can, thus be argued contrary to the cultural homogenizing intentions of the powerful controllers that what the education system informally hands on and demands is a working class culture and above all a working class relationship to it.

Teacher careers are a biographical unfolding of these contradictions for the individual teacher is caught on a 'horizontal' and 'vertical' *cross*. Teachers expect, at least initially, and are expected to instil 'the collective cultural heritage' but are forced to negotiate that in order to physically and psychologically survive in the face of pupil importation of a 'counter-habitas' and a 'cultural counter-capital'. Their latent class culture (Becker and Geer, 1960, p. 56–60) is made manifest in a hostile and antipathetic disposition to the dominant values of schooling. Further, this imported 'counter-habitas' and 'cultural counter-capital' frictionally *appreciates* as pupils' experiences of schooling penetrate a system which *depreciates* their cultural currency.

Children's and teachers' parent cultures inure them to and activate them for the conflict they encounter in the schools; and the social relations of schooling inure pupils and teachers to and activate them for the conflictual social relations they encounter elsewhere. Schooling cannot be conceptually snapped off from the social totality. The school is a conflictual web of inter-relationships and this is part and parcel of the conflictual web characterizing the ensemble of social relations within capitalism.

This chapter, like Willis (1977), exposes the antagonistically sapped nature of schooling in capitalism. 'The Lads' classically warren the school from within. This chapter elaborates a corollary of this, how teachers at the psychological level are warrened by pupils from without. The 'vertical' educational paradigm resides in the person of the teacher and chalkfacial penetration by a class logic of this educational paradigm by pupils is penetration of the teacher as a moral being. 'By penetrating the contradictions at the heart of the working class school the counter-school culture' (Willis, 1977, p. 130) strikes at 'the heart' (the sacred self) of the teacher as a person in such schools. Such penetration pivots on a pupil-inverted equivalent of 'the class insult' (Willis, 1977, p. 77), a symbolic and occasional physical violence on the teacher. Teacher moral careers are an unfolding of such pupil penetrations and, as has been seen, there is a repertoire of teacher responses from mortification of self to pachydermized, monocoque professionality.

As such, this chapter argues the importance of the pupil *qua* 'critical reality definer' as the teacher career gatekeeper who constructs and sustains, through interaction, the identities and careers of teachers. The social construction of 'good' and 'bad' teachers in schools and the social distribution of their competencies is related to the ideological and cultural hegemony exercised by their superiors and *counter-hegemony exercised by their inferiors*. Thus, it has been argued that a teacher's framework of imagery for judging him/herself and his/her pupils is to be understood partially in terms of the activity of pupils. Equally the pupil's framework of imagery for judging him/herself and his/her teachers is to be understood partially in terms of the activity of teachers.

This overall thesis of children as 'critical reality definers' who have consequences for teachers' careers extends our understanding of the school as a rate-producing agency. As has been argued, the dominant sociological concern has been with how children have been processed through schools by teachers. This teacher-centricity results in schools being conceived as *teacher* rate-producing agencies. For example, Reynold's (1976) delinquent school is largely the product of teachers; pupil rates of deviance being contingent on their activity. Pupils are denied a share in the social construction of their delinquent schooling; teacher activity being implicitly conceived as independent and in no way contingent on pupils.

This chapter argues the importance of pupils also as rate-producers. Their commonsense assumptions and activities are instrumental in the generation of differential rates of teacher 'achievement', vertical and horizontal promotion, 'satisfaction', absenteeism, nervous breakdown, 'deviance', resignation, turnover, physical and psychological illness, physical attack, suicide, knowledge withdrawal etc. Any conception of schooling must build into it children as world (school) builders, whose activities have implications for teachers' careers and identities. Of course, it goes without saying that pupil-produced rates and teacher-produced rates have to be conceived dialectically. *The critical question then is 'how are rates of pupil career and teacher career "success" and "failure" reciprocally produced?'* Further, the study of this synergy reveals 'the nature and "working constitution" of a society' (Hughes, 1937, p. 413), a conflictual capitalist one in historic process.

In conclusion, children in capitalism, especially depressing in the 'new barbarism' (Horkheimer, 1972, p. 227) of Thatcherism, are co-constructors of their schooling and society. The paradox is the more efficiently they mince teachers, the more they ultimately ensure the efficacy of the pupil mincer. The 'praxical' problem for Marxists is can injustice be done to a constructing and consenting party, and if the oppressed willingly aid their oppression how can they be encouraged to wilfully begin to de-construct it? The question for would-be liberal and radical tiros is how is it possible to hang on to one's liberalism or radicalism? The question for the minority of teachers interested is how is it possible in a class society to ensure pupils and teachers conjointly construct an emancipatory *education* which critically but non-oppressively denies pupils' propensity to participate in the construction of their own *schooling.* How are working class children to be humanely prevented from operating a mincer which exhausts and cynicalizes their teachers? How can pupils be humanely prevented from socially constructing the kinds of teachers they 'deserve'? For Hall (1974, p. 54) rightly asks, '. . . can the deprived classes ever win power in the system if they are educationally unprepared and unequipped for the struggle?' and 'Until the educational millennium comes, what indeed is to become of the majority working class school and who is to teach its children?'[3]

Notes

1 I am not using class in a crude, structural sense. See E.P. THOMPSON (1965) who offers a critique of sociologists' use of the concept. This includes the aphorism '. . . class is not *a thing*, it is *a happening*'. (p. 357, my italics)
2 I allude there to the incipient idealism with a consequent superficial treatment of consciousness; naive possibilitarianism; solipsistic relativism and cultural pluralism; and extreme idiographic antitheoretical empiricism with resultant macro-blindness etc. associated with the interpretive perspective.
3 I would like to thank Bob Burgess, Mike Garfield, Phil Lyon, Andy Pickard and Margaret Riseborough for their critical reading of early drafts. I would like to record the immense intellectual and moral debt I owe Andy Pickard and Margaret Riseborough. Thanks also to Stephen Ball for his very patient, editorial support; sufferance of my residual 'Carl-like' qualities; and his correction of some of my ignorant excesses. All errors and omissions are now my own. Finally, *but not least*, I must thank all the subjects of the study for their time, trust and confidence.

References

ALTHUSSER, L. (1971) 'Ideology and ideological state apparatuses', in COSIN B.R. (Ed.) *Education: Structure and Society*, Harmondsworth, Penguin.

APPLE, M. (1979) *Ideology and the Curriculum*, London, Routledge and Kegan Paul.

BECKER, H.S. (1952a). 'Social-class variations in the teacher-pupil relationship', in COSIN, B. *et al.* (Eds) *School and Society: A Sociological Reader*, London, Routledge and Kegan Paul.

BECKER, H.S. (1952b) 'The career of the Chicago public schoolteacher', in HAMMERSLEY, M. and WOODS, P. (Eds) *The Process of Schooling*, London, Routledge and Kegan Paul.

BECKER, H.S. (1963) *Outsiders*, New York, Free Press.

BECKER, H.S..and GEER, B. (1960) 'Latent culture: a note on the theory of latent social roles', in COSIN, B.R. *et al.* (Eds) *School and Society: A Sociological Reader*, London, Routledge and Kegan Paul.

BERNSTEIN, B. (1971). 'On the classification and framing of educational knowledge', in YOUNG M.F.D. (Ed.) *Knowledge and Control*, London, Macmillam.

BERNSTEIN, B. (1977) *Class, Codes and Control*, Volume 3, London, Routledge and Kegan Paul.

BEYNON, J. (1984). 'Sussing out teachers: pupils as data gatherers', in HAMMERSLEY, M. and WOODS, P. (Eds) *Life in School: The Sociology of Pupil Culture*, Milton Keynes, Open Univerity Press.

BEYNON, J. and DELAMONT, S. (1983) 'The sound and the fury: Pupil perceptions of school violence', in GAULT, H. and FRUDE, N. (Eds) *Children's Aggression at School*, London, Wiley.

BIRD, C. (1980). 'Deviant labelling in school: The pupils' perspective', in WOODS, P. (Ed.) *Pupil Strategies*, London, Croom Helm.

BOGGS, C. (1976) *Gramsci's Marxism*, London, Pluto Press.

BOURDIEU, P. (1971a). 'Systems of education and systems of thought', in YOUNG, M.F.D. (Ed.) *Knowledge and Control*, London, Macmillan.

BOURDIEU, P. (1971b) 'Intellectual field and creative project', in YOUNG, M.F.D. (Ed.) *Knowledge and Control*, London, Collier-Macmillan.

BOURDIEU, P. (1973). 'Cultural reproduction and social reproduction', in BROWN, R. (Ed.) *Knowledge, Education and Social Change*, London, Tavistock.

BOURDIEU, P. (1974) 'The school as a conservative force', in DALE, R. *et al.* (Eds) *Schooling and Capitalism*, London, Routledge and Kegan Paul.

BOURDIEU, P. and PASSERON, J. (1977) *Reproduction in Education, Society and Culture*, London, Sage.

BOWLES, S. and GINTIS, H. (1976) *Schooling in Capitalist America*, London, Routledge and Kegan Paul.

BURRELL, G. and MORGAN, G. (1979) *Sociological Paradigms and Organisational Analysis*, London, Heinemann.

CLARKE, J. *et al.* (1976) 'Subcultures, cultures and class', in HALL, S. and JEFFERSON, T. (Eds) *Resistance Through Rituals*, London, Hutchinson.

CORRIGAN, P. (1979) *Schooling the Smash Street Kids*, London, Macmillan.

CORRIGAN, P. and FRITH, S. (1976) 'The politics of youth culture', in HALL, S. and JEFFERSON, T. (Eds) *Resistance Through Rituals*, London; Hutchinson.

DALE, R. *et al.* (1976) *Schooling and Capitalism: A sociological Reader*, London, Routledge and Kegan Paul.

DELAMONT, S. (1976) *Interaction in the Classroom*, London, Methuen.

FURLONG, V. (1976) 'Interaction sets in the classroom: Towards a study of pupil knowledge', in STUBBS, M. and DELAMONT, S. *Explorations in Classroom Observation*, London, Wiley.

FURLONG, V. (1977) 'Anancy goes to school: a case study of pupils' knowledge of their teachers', in WOODS, P. and HAMMERSLEY, M. (Eds), *School Experience*, London, Croom Helm.

GANNAWAY, H. (1976) 'Making sense of school', in STUBBS, M. and DELAMONT, S. (Eds) *Explorations in Classroom Observation*, London, Wiley.

GARFINKEL, H. (1967) *Studies in Ethnomethodology*, Englewood Cliffs, New Jersey, Prentice Hall.

GEER, B. (1968). 'Teaching' in COSIN, B.R. *et al.* (Eds) *School and Society*, London, Routledge and Kegan Paul.

GOFFMAN, E. (1956) 'The nature of deference and demeanor', *American Anthropologist*, **58**, p. 485–93.

GOFFMAN, E. (1968) *Asylums*, Harmondsworth, Penguin.

GOULDNER, A.W. (1980) *The Two Marxisms* London, Macmillan.

HALL, S. (1974) 'Education and the crisis of the urban school', in Open University, *Issues in Urban Education*, Milton Keynes, Open Univensity Press.

HALL, S. and JEFFERSON, T. (Eds) (1976) *Resistance through Rituals*, London, Hutchinson.

HAMMERSLEY, M. and WOODS, P. (Eds.) (1976) *The Process of Schooling*, London, Routledge and Kegan Paul.

HARGREAVES, D.H. (1967) *Social Relations in a Secondary School*, London, Routledge and Kegan Paul.

HARGREAVES, D.H. (1972) *Interpersonal Relations and Education*, London, Routledge and Kegan Paul.

HARGREAVES, D.H. (1976) 'Reactions to labelling', in HAMMERSLEY, M. and WOODS, P. (Eds) *The Process of Schooling*, London, Routledge and Kegan Paul.

HARGREAVES, D.H. (1978). 'Whatever happened to symbolic interactionism?', in BARTON, L. and MEIGHAN, R. (Eds) *Sociological Interpretations of Schooling and Classroms: A Reappraisal*, Driffield, Nafferton Books.

HARGREAVES, D.H. *et al.* (1975) *Deviance in Classrooms*, London, Routledge and Kegan Paul.

HOARE, Q. and NOWELL-SMITH, G. (Eds) (1971) *Selections from the Prison Notebooks of Antonio*

Gramsci, London, Lawrence and Wishart.

HORKHEIMER, M. (1972) *Critical Theory*, New York, Herder and Herder.

HUGHES, E.C. (1937) 'Institutional office and the person', in HUGHES, E.C. *Men and their Work*, Glencoe, Illinois, Free Press.

KEDDIE, N. (1971) 'Classroom knowledge', in YOUNG, M.F.D. (Ed.) *Knowledge and Control*, London, Collier-Macmillan.

LACEY, C. (1977) *The Socialization of Teachers*, London, Methuen.

LAWNER, L. (Ed.) (1973) *Letters from Prison by Antonio Gramsci*, New York, Harper and Row.

MEASOR, L. (1984) 'Critical incidents' (in this volume).

NASH, R. (1974) 'Pupils' expectations for their teachers', *Research in Education*, **12**, November, p. 46 – 71.

NASH, R. (1984) 'On two critiques of the Marxist sociology of education', *British Journal of sociology of Education*, **5**, 1.

OPEN UNIVERSITY (1977) E202 *Schooling and Society*, Block III *Knowledge, Ideology and the Curriculum*, Unit 16, Culture, Class and the Curriculum, Milton Keynes; Open Unversity Press.

REYNOLDS, D. (1976) 'The delinquent school', in HAMMERSLEY, M. and WOODS, P. (Eds) *The Process of Schooling*, London, Routledge and Kegan Paul.

RISEBÒROUGH, G.F. (1981) 'Teacher careers and comprehensive schooling', *Sociology*, **15**, 3.

ROSSER, E. and HARRE, R. (1976) 'The meaning of "trouble"', in HAMMERSLEY, M. and WOODS, P. (Eds) *The Process of Schooling*, London, Routledge and Kegan Paul.

SHARP, R. and GREEN, A. (1975) *Education and Social Control*, London, Routledge and Kegan Paul.

STUBBS, M. and DELAMONT, S. (Eds) (1976) *Explorations in Classroom Observations*, London, Wiley.

THOMPSON, E.P. (1965) *The Making of the English Working Classes*, Harmondsworth, Penguin.

VALLENCE, E. (1974). 'Hiding the hidden curriculum', *Curriculum Theory Network*, **4**, 1.

WALLER, W. (1932) *The Sociology of Teaching*, London, Wiley.

WAX, M.L. and WAX, R.H. (1964) 'Cultural deprivation as an educational ideology', in LEACOCK, E.B. (Ed.) *The Culture of Poverty: A Critique*, New York, Simon and Schuster.

WERTHMAN, C. (1963) 'Delinquents in school: A test for the legitimacy of authority', in COSIN, B. *et al.* (Eds) *School and Society*, London, Routledge and Kegan Paul.

WILLIS, P. (1977) *Learning to Labour*, Farnborough, Saxon House.

WOODS, P. (1976) 'Pupils' views of school', *Educational Review*, **28**, 2.

WOODS, P. (1977a) *The Pupil's Experience*, Milton Keynes, Open University Press.

WOODS, P. (1977b) 'Teaching for survival', in WOODS, P. and HAMMERSLEY, M. (Eds) *School Experience*, London, Croom Helm.

WOODS, P. (1978a) 'Negotiating the demands of schoolwork', *Journal of Curriculum Studies*, **10**, 4.

WOODS, P. (1978b) 'Relating to schoolwork: Some pupil perceptions', *Educational Review*, **30**, 2.

WOODS, P. (1979) *The Divided School*, London, Routledge and Kegan Paul.

WOODS, P. (Ed.) (1980a) *Teacher Strategies*, London, Croom Helm.

WOODS, P. (Ed.) (1980b) *Pupil Strategies*, London, Croom Helm.

YOUNG, M.F.D. (1971), *Knowledge and Control*, London, Collier-Macmillan.

Notes on Contributors

Stephen Ball is now Director of Research in the Education Area of the University of Sussex, several years into an academic career. He previously began and rejected careers in Trust administration, librarianship and social work. His own educational experiences at school provided the major impetus for later research and study. He found his own school and home life as a pupil reflected in Jackson and Marsden's *Education and the Working Class* and Lacey's *Hightown Grammar*, and these studies provided a model for research and engagement in educational issues which he has attempted to pursue in his own work.

Carey Bennet studied for her degree in Art and Education at at the Froebel Institute, Roehampton. She was involved in a variety of projects in community arts, education and conservation, before taking a PGCE at Manchester Polytechnic. She is currently conducting DPhil research at Oxford University Department of Educational Studies, and intends to move next into secondary art and design teaching.

John Beynon regards himself as a product of the 1944 Education Act and received a typical grammar school education in South West Wales in the 1950s and 60s. After University and a PGCE at the London Institute he taught in a number of schools, amongst which was a grammar busily preparing itself to become a comprehensive, and then a comprehensive which had recently emerged out of a grammar school. The short and long term effects of these metamorphses have continued to interest him, along with the subsequent careers of those trained, like him, in the midst of heady 1960s, progressivism. His dual interest in fieldwork and documentary writing has led him to write a book on pupils 'sussing' teachers (Falmer Press, 1985).

John Burke has a wide experience of teaching including primary, prep, middle, comprehensive, sixth form college, vocational training and postgraduate courses at university. His experience as a student ranges over ten years in a seminary, college of education and two universities. In 1981 he obtained an MA in Curriculum Development at the University of Sussex and in the same year he was awarded a full time SSRC studentship for research. He is currently Visiting Research Fellow in Education at the University of Sussex.

Martin Cole is senior lecturer in Teaching Studies at Newman College, Birmingham. He describes himself as the product of an unusually literate working class home in the home counties. After grammar school he took an honours degree in Social Theory and Institutions (at Reading) and, after a late decision to enter teaching, a Postgraduate Diploma in Education. He subsequently taught English for three years in a large comprehensive school in a South Yorkshire mining village, where he also taught 'O' level sociology to adult evening classes. For the next five years he was Head of Sociology at a Midlands comprehensive school before taking up his present post in 1975. In 1980–81 he was seconded to research the sociology of teaching at Keele University for the MA degree.

Ivor Goodson is Director of the Schools Unit at the University of Sussex. His work in a sense reflects the birthright concerns and hopes of his family and culture. His father Frederick was the youngest and only son in a family of thirteen; his elder sisters all worked in domestic service and he worked in the same job for fifty one years as a gas fitter. He left school weeks before his fourteenth birthday. His mother Lily also left school at fourteen. She had in fact 'passed' to Central School but had to leave to 'support her family'. Both his parents saw the 1944 Act as a central avenue to the opportunities they did not have. Ivor studied economics at University College and LSE before going to teach at Countesthorpe and Stantonbury Campus. He moved to Sussex in 1975.

Lynda Measor is a Research Fellow in the Faculty of Education at the Open University. She attended a single-sex grammar school in the North of England, and then did undergraduate and postgraduate work at the University of Sussex. She taught for eight years in a variety of institutions and countries and in 1979 began research into education at the Open University together with Peter Woods. The first research project dealt with pupils transfer from primary to secondary school, and the second with a life history approach to teachers' careers.

Jennifer Nias is tutor at the Cambridge Institute of Education. She has taught, at various times and in different parts of the world, children from three to fifteen and adults from eighteen to fifty-six. Before moving to Cambridge in 1977 she was tutor to the primary PGCE course at the University of Liverpool. Her present job involves participation in in-service education of many sorts of primary and middle school teachers.

George F. Riseborough was born in 1943 in Manchester. He was reared on a massive post-war council-housing estate. He was of five children; the only one to pass the eleven-plus and obtain any educational credentials. No great success at school, ultimately achieving 'a poor crop' of O and A-levels. At eighteen failed to get into a teacher training college and became a temporary, unqualified teacher. Eventually went to a finishing school for working class lads. Here, far from being the ideal student, he just achieved qualified teacher status. He left college in 1965 with spouse and hit the hippie trail to India. He came back and entered teaching in the east of was quickly promoted to a head of department in a comprehensive school. Studied part-time in the evening for a London external degree in sociology. Then did a full-time MA (Sociology) at Essex whilst teaching part-time. Became a lecturer in education at Manchester Polytechnic in 1972. Now, acutely depressed by the prevailing 'new barbarism'. Pessimistically, feels things could get worse. Optimistically, sees teaching and learning as just one way of trying to ensure they do not.

Pat Sikes regards herself as fortunate in having gone to school in Leicestershire during the 1960s and early 1970s, and in having known and worked with Lawrence Stenhouse. She trained as a drama teacher but after leaving college with a BEd went to work at the Centre for Applied Research in Education where her job was to produce materials for training teachers to teach about race relations. Her interest in teacher careers began with post-graduate research, at Leeds University, into how teachers were perceiving and experiencing reduced promotional opportunities. She then went to work with Peter Woods at the Open University on a project investigating teachers' careers using life history method. Pat has also worked, for brief periods, as an archivist, a bibliographer, a supply teacher, an artist's model and a night school tutor of vegetarian cookery.

Louis M. Smith is Professor of Education at the University of Washington, St. Louis, and joint author of the original Kensington School Study. He began in academia as an educational psychologist, and is joint author of a best-selling textbook, but in recent years he has 'converted' to ethnographic research methods. The research team for the *Kensington Revisited Project* were Paul F. Kleine, Professor of Education at the University of Oklahoma, David C. Dwyer, now project director at the Far West Laboratory for Educational Research and Development in San Francisco, and John J. Prunty, now with the Maritz Communication Corporation of St. Louis.

Rodman B. Webb is Associate Professor of Education in the Department of Foundations of Education at the University of Florida in Gainesville. He recently spent a term at the University of East Anglia as an exchange lecturer. His current research is concerned with teacher effficacy. He is author of several books on education including *The Presence of the Past?* an examination of the work of Alfred Schutz and John Dewey.

Author Index

Subject Index

'A' levels, 138–40, 141, 143, 144, 147, 149, 150
Abbot, K., 193
accountability, 4, 5, 8
Adrian, M., 193
age
    see also ageing
    and occupation, 28–9
age distribution
    of teachers, 39–40
age status asynchronization, 29
Age Thirty Transition phase, 44–7
ageing, 14, 27–60
amalgamation
    of schools
    see comprehensivization
Anatomy of Educational Innovation, 180, 185
Arnold, 139
art
    and teaching, 131–1
    see also art teachers
art teachers
    and adaptation, 16
    attitudes to career development of, 129–30
    attitudes to careers of, 120–37
    and concurrent careers, 131–2
    and critical incidents, 62–76
    and identity, 19, 22, 62–76, life cycles of, 27–58
    and opportunities in higher education, 128–9
    and promotion, 123–8
    see also teachers
Artists in Schools schemes, 133
authority

see teachers, and authority

Beachside [Comprehensive School], 149–50
belief systems
    natural history of, 198–200
biographies
    of teachers, 61–77
    see also life history method
Bishop McGregor [School], 159
Board of Education, 6
Black Papers, 3, 4
Boys from the Blackstuff, 232
Bristol, University of, 10
bureaucratization
    see teachers, and bureaucratization

Callaghan, [Prime Minister] James, 4
career continuance, 20–2
career development, 202–63
career histories
    see life history method
career 'maps', 21, 22
career path
    phases of, 29–58
career phases, 62, 76
career sequence, 230–51
career structure
    for art teachers, 12203
careers, passim
    as cyclical, 258–60
    as linear, 258–60
    as 'objective', 11–18, 121, 204–63
    as 'subjective', 11–18, 121, 204–63
Casterbridge [school], 162
central government
    and curriculum, 5–6, 10

274